Public Private Partnerships in Transport

T0358867

Over the last 30 years Public Private Partnerships (PPPs) have been used to deliver transport capital projects and services. PPPs are complex arrangements that require a multi-disciplinary approach in order to assure their success. However, research on the subject has been fragmented. This book fills the gap in existing literature by providing insight into these complex arrangements at their various stages of development.

Public Private Partnerships in Transport is structured to follow the life-cycle of a PPP project and strikes a balance between theory and practice. Divided into four parts, each section highlights major concerns and offers an array of views and policy recommendations. Parts consider the context for national implementation, decision models, performance measures and efficiency.

This book includes an extended discussion on the findings presented, discussed and analysed at the closing event of the COST Action TU1001 network on the topic of PPP in transport and is of interest to the academic community, policy makers and practitioners.

Athena Roumboutsos is an Associate Professor at the Department of Shipping, Trade and Transport, University of the Aegean, Greece.

Routledge Studies in Transport Analysis

Public Private Partnerships in Transport

Trends and theory

Edited by Athena Roumboutsos

LONDON AND NEW YORK

EUROPEAN COOPERATION
IN SCIENCE AND TECHNOLOGY

COST is
supported by the
EU Framework
Programme
Horizon 2020

First published 2016
by Routledge

2 Park Square, Milton Park, Abingdon, Oxfordshire OX14 4RN

52 Vanderbilt Avenue, New York, NY 10017

Routledge is an imprint of the Taylor & Francis Group, an informa business.

First issued in paperback 2020

British Library Cataloguing in Publication Data
A catalogue record for this book is available from the British Library.

Library of Congress Cataloging in Publication Data
Roumboutsos, Athena.
Public private partnerships in transport : trends and theory / Athena Roumboutsos.
Includes bibliographical references and index.
1. Transportation–European Union countries. 2. Transportation and state–European Union countries. 3. Public-private sector cooperation–European Union countries. I. Title.
HE242.A2R677 2015
388'.049–dc23
2015003889

ISBN: 978-1-138-89816-5 (hbk)
ISBN: 978-0-367-59857-0 (pbk)

Typeset in Times New Roman
by Cenveo Publisher Services

Contents

Figures

Tables

Contributors

Robert Ågren, University of Lund, Sweden.

Nunzia Carbonara, Polytechnic University of Bari, Italy

Joana Costa, Instituto Superior Técnico, Universidade de Lisboa, Portugal.

Nicola Costantino, Politecnico di Bari, Italy

Rui Couchinho, Instituto Superior Técnico, Universidade de Lisboa, Portugal

Geert Dewulf, University of Twente, Netherlands

Sergio Domingues, University of Antwerp, Belgium

Colin Duffield, University of Melbourne, Australia

Sheila Farrell, Imperial College, UK

Michael J. Garvin, Virginia Tech, USA

Louis Gunnigan, Dublin Institute of Technology, Ireland

Veiko Lember, Tallinn University of Technology, Estonia

Pekka Leviäkangas, University of Oulu, Finland

Champika Liyanage, University of Central Lancashire, UK

Agnieszka Łukasiewicz, Road and Bridge Research Institute, Poland

Rosário Macário, Instituto Superior Técnico, Universidade de Lisboa, Portugal

Stanley Njuangang, University of Central Lancashire, UK

Matheus Oliveira, Instituto Superior Técnico, Universidade de Lisboa, Portugal

Aristeidis Pantelias, University College London, UK

Roberta Pellegrino, Polytechnic of Bari, Italy

Ole Helby Petersen, Roskilde University, Denmark

Joana Ribeiro, Instituto Superior Técnico, Universidade de Lisboa, Portugal

Athena Roumboutsos, University of the Aegean, Greece

Walter Scherrer, Salzburg University, Austria

Emmanouil Sfakianakis, Maastricht University, Netherlands

Murwantara Soecipto, University of Antwerp, Belgium

Ancor Suárez-Alemán, University of Las Palmas de Gran Canaria, Spain

Theodore Syriopoulos, University of the Aegean, Greece

Alenka Temeljotov-Salaj, European Faculty of Law, Slovenia

Martijn van den Hurk, University of Antwerp, Belgium

Thierry Vanelslander, University of Antwerp, Belgium

Koen Verhoest, University of Antwerp, Belgium

Felix Villalba-Romero, Universidad Autónoma de Madrid, Spain

Johannes T. Voordijk, University of Twente, Netherlands

Tom Willems, University of Antwerp, Belgium

Petr Witz, Charles University in Prague, Czech Republic

Foreword

COST (European Cooperation in Science and Technology) is a pan-European intergovernmental organisation allowing scientists, engineers and scholars to jointly develop their ideas and initiatives across all scientific disciplines. It does so by funding science and technology networks called COST Actions, which give impetus to research, careers and innovation.

Overall, COST Actions help coordinate nationally funded research activities throughout Europe. COST ensures that less research-intensive countries gain better access to European knowledge hubs, which also allows for their integration in the European Research Area.

By promoting trans-disciplinary, original approaches and topics, addressing societal questions, COST enables breakthrough scientific and technological developments leading to new concepts and products. It thereby contributes to strengthening Europe's research and innovation capacities.

COST is implemented through the COST Association, an international not-for-profit association under Belgian law, whose members are the COST Member Countries.

www.cost.eu

Preface

Over the last 30 years Public Private Partnerships (PPPs) have been used in many countries to deliver transport capital projects and services. Research has been descriptive and fragmented, focusing on specific transport modes or country developments. However, PPPs are complex arrangements extending over time and they require a multi-disciplinary approach to address the fundamental issues relating to their potential success in achieving anticipated outcomes.

COST Action TU1001: Public Private Partnerships in Transport: Trends and Theory was initiated in January 2011 with the scope to contribute to the theoretical development of the PPP model focusing on: (i) the decision-making process for selection, implementation and operation of PPP transport projects; (ii) identification of critical success factors, test criteria and knowledge bases for improved PPP performance; (iii) efficiency implications of the arrangement. The national perspective is also addressed.

Research does not have closure. The present edited book includes research on the topic at various stages of development, elaborated in connection with policy makers' and practitioners' views as presented, discussed and analysed within the Action. While it is, in principle, geared to the transport sector, it is of equal interest to other sectors of PPP implementation.

The book is written assuming that the reader already has a fundamental understanding of the PPP infrastructure delivery model and it is designed to address policy makers, practitioners and the academic community.

Acknowledgements

The research presented in this book has been made possible through the funding of the COST Programme to COST Action TU1001 and the commitment and dedication of the Action's members and friends.

Introduction

Athena Roumboutsos

Transport is fundamental to our economy and society. Mobility is vital for growth and job creation. Investments in infrastructure are crucial to sustain competitiveness and provide state-of-the-art services endorsing efficiency through innovation and adjusting to new trends both in passenger travel behaviour and supply chains. However, public budgets are overstretched and the need to mobilise private finance is apparent.

Over the last 30 years, different means of transport infrastructure financing have been exploited including private financing under the umbrella term Public Private Partnerships (PPPs). They have been adopted by governments 'as a means to launch investment programmes, which would not have been possible within the available public-sector budget, within reasonable time'[1]. Between 1990 and 2013 more than 1,600 PPP contracts were signed within the EU, representing a capital value of more than EUR 300 billion (see Chapter 19). While impressive, this figure only represents a fraction of the overall investments in infrastructure (transport and other sectors) during this period and pales with respect to the estimated cost of EUR 1.5 trillion for EU infrastructure development needed to match the demand for transport investments between 2010-2030[2]. The need to tap further into private sources of finance is ever greater, but setbacks and less than favourable outcomes increase concerns about PPPs.

Not suprisingly, over the decades there has been substantial institutional, archival and popular literature and debate concerning the political, social and economic acceptance of the scheme. The latter has been generally focused in varying forms around the issue of value for money (VfM), loosely defined as the optimum combination of life cycle costs and quality to meet user requirements (cfr. Grimsey and Lewis 2004 and Akintoye *et al.* 2003). However, the key issue when addressing the topic of PPPs in transport, as well as in other sectors, has been the fragmented nature of generated research and practice reports.

Research within COST Action TU1001 was aimed at filling this gap by pooling multidisciplinary resources from 29 countries to provide added value. Evidently what is produced is a form of standardisation of reported research conducted within the Action.

Structure and organisation

The present edited book is structured so that it follows the life-cycle flow of a PPP project, including the national implementation context, the decision process and performance, and then the book discusses efficiency through the lens of standardisation versus contextualisation. More specifically, the book is organised in four parts that include chapters contributing to the respective topic or offering alternative views. Each part is introduced with a short chapter highlighting the major issues addressed and concluded by stating major findings and their inter-relations, proposals for future research and policy recommendations. Contributions throughout strike a balance between theory and practice by exploiting case data collected within the framework of COST Action TU1001. The description of this data may be found in the introduction of Part 1 and in the Appendix.

Part 1: National implementation context

During the previous century infrastructure projects were, in principal, financed by governments and paid for by the taxpayer. Over the past few decades, policies, regulations and supporting institutions have spread out across the globe to promote the uptake of Public Private Partnerships (PPPs). However, countries vary with respect to adopting PPP approaches. The basic questions addressed in this Part are as follows. Which nationally driven elements are vital to the (non-) development of PPPs in practice? Which contextual factors provide a conducive or stimulating climate for PPPs, and which tend to be rather inhibiting? How are countries classified with respect to the adoption of PPP support policies and insti-tutions (see Chapter 2)? Is there a maturity process and how are countries grouped in this respect (see Chapter 3)? Can we actually make groupings of countries that, macroscopically, seem similar (Chapter 4)?

Part 2: Decision models

PPPs comprise numerous decisions. Decision-making in PPPs is a complex process as it aims to secure efficiencies and benefits in order to justify the PPP delivery model choice and the multifarious, and sometimes conflicting, interests of the different stakeholders involved. Usually the emphasis has been placed on initiating the process (assessment, tendering, contracting) and less so on the imple-mentation. This is to be expected considering the need to assess the viability of the PPP option and to reduce the transaction costs involved in awarding the contract. What is usually overlooked is the fact that decisions influencing the outcome are made over the entire life-cycle of a PPP. Chapter 7 reports a PPP Decision System (DS) framework in a tree structure indicating the phase of the PPP life-cycle in which the decision should be taken (When), the area of decision (What), the issues to deal with in order to take the decision (Which), the instruments/processes to be used to take the decision (How), and the actors involved in the decision (Who). This decision tree may be populated with models (as the ones described in

Chapter 8 and referenced in Chapter 10), alternative instruments (see Chapter 9) or other available decision models reported in literature or applied in practice.

Part 3: Performance

The definition of 'performance' can be viewed from various perspectives. The stakeholder view is important when measuring the success of projects. This is even more important for a PPP project, as it is a long-term partnership between the public and private sector, and users. In this Part, a stakeholder point of view was taken as the main basis for the measurement of performance. Stakeholders are grouped into three categories: public sector, private sector and users. Using the same sample basis (the COST Action TU1001 case studies), four alternative approaches are presented and discussed with respect to assessing critical success factors and key performance indicators. As expected, optimal risk allocation was identified across all studies. 'Trust' was also considered crucial, as well as the need to use performance indicators to monitor performance.

Part 4: Efficiency

Part 4 of this book focuses on topics of efficiency through the concepts of standardisation and contextualisation. 'While standardisation is necessary in order to improve market efficiency, reduce transaction costs and increase transparency and accountability, contextualisation is what makes PPP projects relevant to their end users and caters to their inherently individual characteristics', as noted in Chapter 17. The two concepts describe a natural tension and mapping their efficiency areas is a challenge. The three contributions in this Part describe efficiency from different aspects. Efficiency can ultimately be achieved by combining the three and harvesting their complementarities. Moreover, while standardisation is a transparency driver, transparency is a prerequisite of contextualisation.

Discussion

The notion of standardisation is the underlying thread in all four Parts of the book: classifying countries based on the existence of a number of indicators defined as supporting PPP implementation; organising a Decision System Framework overarching all phases of the PPP life-cycle; defining sets of performance indicators and methodologies; describing efficiency and effectiveness on the basis of standardisation.

Standardisation, as noted by Dewulf, Garvin and Duffield in Chapter 18, drives accountability, norms and generality upward, while it reduces transaction costs and enhances transparency. The same notions are important in research, as standardisation and typologies are important in the organisation of the 'universe' to be studied.

Organising knowledge is also important for the actors in the PPP environment. Verhoest *et al.* (Chapter 5) suggest the benefit of benchmarking between countries and public authorities with respect to PPP-enhancing institutions and note the importance this may have for investors. Organised knowledge is supportive of knowledge transfer and competence building. Carbonara *et al.*, in Chapter 7, propose a standard process of decisions. The authors describe how it may support the public sector where it lags behind in respective experience and expertise. Carbonara (Chapter 10), however, highlights its use as a tool rather than an objective and presents research in support of managerial flexibility and win-win scenarios between the public and private counterparts. Organised knowledge is important in order to understand what to monitor, when and how in order to secure stakeholder objectives. Liyanage (Chapter 16) proposes that performance indicators should be typically included in all PPP contracts. Their scope, however, should not be to penalise underperformance but to 'motivate', leading to overall performance improvement. In addition, shifting away from the notion of standardisation, Liyanage names, as a common finding in Part 3 based on case study analysis, 'trust' as a critical success factor. Notably, 'trust' allows for contextualisation leading to improved outcomes. In contrast to Part 1 and the promotion of further standardisation, Part 4 takes a more critical view. A more challenging perspective is offered by Roumboutsos, Pantelias and Sfakianakis (Chapter 20). Credit ratings are a standardisation that opens the infrastructure debt market to a wide range of potential investors and instruments (for example, see Syriopoulos in Chapter 9). However, PPP projects are not directly comparable to one another due to their inherently unique characteristics. The authors highlight the need to supplement existing standard assessment methodologies with the consideration of project contextual issues. Exploiting standardisation and contextualising on transport business models has been the vehicle for PPP transport strategic investors to achieve market share and create a more concentrated market, raising questions with respect to competition (Suarez-Aleman, Roumboutsos and Carbonara, Chapter 19). Obviously, standardisation may be harvested in many ways.

Hence, ideas move through the book from standardisation to contexualisation, requiring more activities to be adaptive and flexible in order to produce value for stakeholders. Dewulf, Garvin and Duffield (Chapter 18) compare the process in their respective countries of professional activity. Standardisation trends from high to low as we look from the Netherlands to Australia to the US. Is it because of the number of PPPs to be considered, in which case the overall transaction costs are low? Is it about competence? Is it about the social context of 'trust' between stakeholders?

While too many topics of further research remain open, as proposed in the respective concluding chapters of each Part, the topic of standardisation versus contextualisation in its various expressions threads through all considerations.

Policy recommendations

The same notion threads through policy recommendations, as expressed in the conclusions of each Part. More specifically, Verhoest *et al.* (Chapter 5) recommend further standardisation with respect to institutions, legal framework and assessment (*ex-ante* and *ex-post*). The underlining theme is transparency and social accountability, which will also lead to the availability of data. Along the same lines and noting that performance data are frequently unavailable, especially with respect to user satisfaction, Liyanage (Chapter 16) proposes the frequent and regular monitoring of implementation.

Stepping further away, Carbonara, concluding Chapter 10, places emphasis on developing the competence of public authorities, which will allow actors to endorse flexibility in PPP contracts and to successfully address contractual incompleteness leading to win-win scenarios of PPP implementation. Finally, Pantelias and Roumboutsos (Chapter 21) recommend a critical review of efficiency through the balance of standardisation and contextualisation to be addressed by policy and decision makers, and set transparency and contextualisation as the basis of achieving efficiency.

Notes

1 EIB (2005) *Evaluation of PPP Projects* financed by the EIB, EIB Publications, available at www.eib.org/projects/publications/evaluation-of-ppp-projects-financed-by-theeib.htm
2 CEF Regulation: Regulation (EU) No 1316/2013 of the European Parliament and of the Council of 11 December 2013 establishing the Connecting Europe Facility, amending Regulation (EU) No 913/2010 and repealing Regulations (EC) No 680/2007 and (EC) No 67/2010.

References

Akintoye, A., Hardcastle, C., Beck, M., Chinyio, E. and Asenova, D. (2003) 'Achieving best value in private finance initiative project procurement.' *Construction Management and Economics*, 21(5), pp. 461–470
Grimsey, D. and Lewis, M. K. (2004) *Public Private Partnerships*. Cheltenham: Edward Elgar

Part 1

National context

1 Introducing the national context for PPPs – elements and dimensions

Koen Verhoest, Martijn van den Hurk,
Nunzia Carbonara, Veiko Lember,
Ole Helby Petersen, Walter Scherrer
and Murwantara Soecipto

Introduction[1]

Over the past few decades, policies and institutions to promote the uptake of Public Private Partnerships (PPPs) have spread across the globe (Hodge *et al.* 2010; Klijn and Teisman 2003). Many countries have shown an extensive development of PPP programmes, whereas many others tend to remain rather sceptical (McQuaid and Scherrer 2010; Petersen 2011). A wide divergence in national PPP approaches can be noticed, and this provides food for thought on the relationship between the national context for PPP policy-making on the one hand and the implementation of PPP policy on the other: which nationally driven elements are vital to the (non-) development of PPPs in practice? Which contextual factors provide a conducive or stimulating climate for PPPs and which tend to be rather inhibiting?

In this first Part, we discuss some of the alleged crucial elements of the national context for PPP development, drawing from a cross-country data collection that was conducted in the framework of the COST Action TU1001 'PPPs in Transport: Trends and Theory'. Within this Action, a template was developed by members of the Working Group on National Context, which is presented in the next section of this chapter. Subsequently, country teams collected descriptive country profiles for 22 European countries for the dimensions of governmental support – PPP policies, PPP regulations and PPP-supporting institutions, as described later in this introduction (see Verhoest *et al.* 2013; Roumboutsos *et al.* 2014). In this Part, three chapters are presented that use this descriptive country-specific data to develop typologies and classifications of national contexts for PPPs and to compare national context in general, and elements of governmental support for PPPs in particular, between and within groups of countries.

In the remainder of this introductory chapter we first discuss our concept of PPP context as comprised of different levels. Then we explain in more depth the different dimensions of government support for PPPs that were at the core of the comparative data collection. We end with an outline of the structure of this Part by briefly introducing the three chapters.

Before we continue the discussion on this issue, our definition of PPP requires attention. Definitions of what might be understood as PPP differ from country to country. Here, we utilise the definition provided by the OECD:

> An agreement between the government and one or more private partners (which may include the operators and the financers) according to which the private partners deliver the service in such a manner that the service delivery objectives of the government are aligned with the profit objectives of the private partners and where the effectiveness of the alignment depends on a sufficient transfer of risk to the private partners.
>
> (OECD 2008)

Within the aforementioned relationship, the government specifies the quality and quantity of the service it requires from the private partner. The private partner may be tasked with the design, construction, financing, operation and management of a capital asset and service delivery to the government or the public using that asset. The private partner will receive either payment fees from the government, or user charges levied directly on the end users, or a combination of both. If the government is responsible for paying the private partner for service delivery, the fees usually depend on the availability of the service and/or asset. Principal to the definition we use is the transfer of risks from the government to the private partner (Grimsey and Lewis 2002; Lienhard 2006). Various types of risks are identified, priced and either retained by the public sector or transferred to the private partner through an appropriate payment mechanism and specific contract terms. The transfer of risks is based on the principle that each risk should be allocated to the partner where it can be best managed. In addition to the OECD definition, the European PPP Expertise Centre (EPEC) states that PPP usually includes a long-term contract which takes account of life cycle implications for the project (EPEC 2011).

Different analytical levels of national context

The national context for PPPs should be analysed by taking into account different levels of institutions. The context for PPPs in a country is an interplay of pressures and constraints situated at different levels of government. Therefore, although national context is highly important to PPP development, the role of institutions at higher (supranational) or lower (subnational) levels needs to be taken into account as well. For countries in the European Union (EU), PPP research has illustrated that institutions like the European Commission, Eurostat and the EIB are important policy-makers and/or regulatory players (Petersen 2010). Moreover, and also relevant for countries outside the EU, international bodies such as the OECD, IMF and the World Bank have important roles as agenda setters and promoters of new governance models in general and PPPs in particular (see, for example, OECD 2008). Consequently, the institutional context of PPP development in a country can only be analysed fully if one applies a multi-level approach. In accordance with Pollitt and Bouckaert (2004) and Verhoest *et al.* (2010) we distinguish between four levels of governance (as shown in Figure 1.1). The first three levels are to be considered as jointly creating the national context for PPP development.

First, there are international-supranational pressures for countries, which stimulate them to launch PPPs. These factors include regulatory, normative and economic pressures for isomorphism. Examples of this type of pressure are: meta-regulation by the EU, for example on procurement, public debt and national budget; the propagation of PPPs by international organizations, based on the New Public Management (NPM) discourse or related neoliberal doctrines; globalization of the economy.

Second, there are pressures and constraints that can be situated at national level, and we make a distinction between macro-institutional dimensions as well as PPP-oriented governmental policies and actions. Macro-institutional variables encompass five national dimensions, which set the scene for all government policies and actions, and not only policies and actions regarding PPP development.

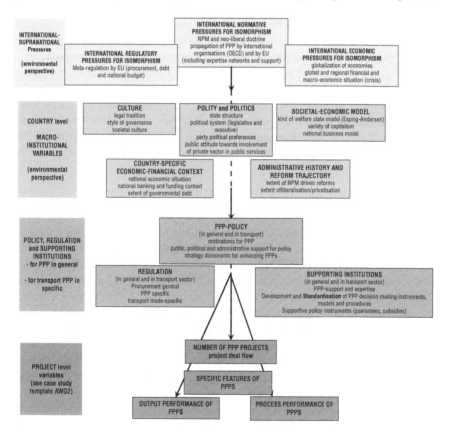

Figure 1.1 Four different institutional levels influencing the development of PPP policies and projects (based on Pollitt and Bouckaert, 2004; Verhoest, *et al.* 2010).

The first dimension is the administrative history and reform trajectory of a country, which includes the realisation of NPM-based reforms and measures of liberalisation and privatisation (Osborne and Gaebler 1992; Painter and Pierre 2005). Second, a country's socio-economic model or structure is, *inter alia*, formed by its welfare regime (Esping-Andersen 1999) and varieties of capitalism (Nölke and Vliegenthart 2009). The third dimension, polity and politics, includes state structure and political system (Hague and Harrop 2007; Lijphart 1999). Culture, then, refers to both legal and societal aspects of culture (Hofstede and Hofstede 2005; House *et al.* 2004). Finally, the financial–economic dimension addresses a country's macro-economic conditions, level of public debt and budgetary equilibrium, access to capital and credit markets, and the level of investment needs in infrastructure (European Commission 2012; WEF 2012; World Bank 2012).

The third level of analysis focuses on the specific policies and actions governments pursue in order to stimulate PPP take-up in their country, in which policy and political commitment, regulation and the legal framework, as well as supporting institutions, are crucial. This was the core focus of the data collection and analysis that was undertaken within COST Action TU1001. In the next section we will outline in more depth these different aspects of governmental support. The chapter by Soecipto *et al.* in this volume as well as Verhoest *et al.* (2015) both go a long way in grounding this conceptualisation of governmental support in literature.

Finally, the fourth level of analysis in Figure 1.1 refers to the outcome of this institutional context in the form of PPP projects, emphasising issues such as the diffusion of PPP practice, features of specific PPPs, processes of PPP implementation, and evaluations of their performance (Verhoest *et al.* 2012). This level was tackled by the Working Group on Performance, which developed a template for the description of PPP projects in different countries (Roumboutsos *et al.* 2013).

Policy, regulation and supporting institutions as core elements of PPP governmental support

To enable the descriptive analysis of the third level in Figure 1.1, which focuses on the government support for PPPs, a guiding framework was developed within the respective Working Group of COST Action TU1001. A significant part of this framework derives from practitioner-oriented literature (see, for an elaboration, Soecipto *et al.* in this volume as well as Verhoest *et al.* 2015). Table 1.1 shows the different elements that were gathered across countries concerning the political commitment to PPP and PPP policies. Emphasis is put on a country's policy framework for PPPs, its experience with PPPs, its political stability, the direct effects of the financial crisis on PPPs in general and in transport, and the respective policy changes. PPP policy is often used as a means to stimulate the growth and development of a pipeline of PPP projects. For example, while not having strictly legal status, government bodies may issue a specific policy in relation to the rules of tendering and the terms of contract. Moreover, PPP policies serve to define PPPs in comparison with other infrastructure service procurement options, and they serve to describe the reasons and goals for adopting PPP schemes.

Table 1.1 Variables and indicators for the dimension *political commitment to PPP and PPP policies*

Variables	Indicators
PPP policy framework	Separate strategic policy document that outlines an explicit policy strategy on PPP.
	PPP as an element in sectorial policy framework documents.
	Clear PPP programme with a significant pipeline and timetable of viable projects that government is committed to procure.
	Main political motivations for PPP.
Previous and current PPP experience	Number of PPP projects, in general and in transport.
	Lending volume via PPP projects, in general and in transport.
	Percentage of infrastructure investment through PPP over time, in general and in transport.
Political stability	Major changes in political landscape that have affected political will and/or support regarding PPP.
Effects of financial crisis on PPPs	Obtaining and securing financing for PPP projects.
	Number of planned and closed PPP projects.
	Duration time of PPP contracts.
	Difficulties in project operation phase.
	Financial issues.
	International financing of PPP projects.
	Transfer of risks to private sector.
	Contract renegotiations.
	Scale/size of PPP projects.
PPP policy changes due to financial crisis	Government funding of PPP projects.
	Emphasis on traditional procurement.
	Emphasis on smaller/larger scale contracts.
	Government guarantees for funding/financing.
	Government involvement in Special Purpose Vehicles (SPVs).
	Project bonds.

Finally, PPP policies can encourage good relationships by directing and coordinating cooperation between interested sectors and institutions of government (cf. OECD 2006). All in all, a country's political commitment to PPP and the form and strength of its PPP policy are vital to the PPP-development of a country (Verhoest *et al.* 2015).

Concerning the dimension of *legal and regulatory framework for PPP*, Table 1.2 presents the elements that were assessed across countries. More specifically, they discuss the presence (and content) or absence of a legal framework for PPP and relevant elements in PPP-related and public procurement legislation (European Bank for Reconstruction and Development 2012).

The third and final dimension of the guidance for the descriptive analysis is that of *PPP-supporting institutions*. The implementation of PPP policies and the development of PPP projects are likely to be affected by either the presence or absence of these institutions, such as PPP units or agencies, fixed procedures for PPP project appraisal and prioritisation, and standardised PPP contracts (EIB 2004; Farrugia *et al.* 2008; OECD 2010; World Bank and PPIAF 2006).

Table 1.2 Variables and indicators for the dimension *legal and regulatory framework for PPP*

Variables	Indicators
Legal PPP framework	Explicit general PPP or concession law.
	Transport-specific law on PPPs or concessions.
	Public procurement law.
	Accordance with EU guidelines.
Scope and boundaries of specific PPP law	PPP definition.
	Sectors and types of infrastructure/services concerned.
	Competent contracting authorities.
	Eligible private party.
Elements provided in legal framework	Procedures regarding:
	(1) Selection of private partner through competitive procedures;
	(2) Non-competitive procedure in exceptional circumstances;
	(3) Procedures for unsolicited proposals;
	(4) Review procedures.
	Accounts on:
	(1) Contract termination events;
	(2) Compensation provisions;
	(3) Provisions for collection of fees or payments by government.
	Provisions regarding:
	(1) Public authorities to support and provide guarantees;
	(2) Step-in rights for lenders or substitution by a new private partner.

Source: compiled from European Bank for Reconstruction and Development 2012; European Investment Bank 2011

Table 1.3 lists the variables and indicators that were assessed in the cross-country data gathering within COST Action TU1001.

The structure of part 1: National context

The above mentioned elements of governmental support (see Tables 1.1 to 1.3) were gathered for 22 European countries by the involved country teams and checked for consistency (see Verhoest *et al.* 2013; Roumboutsos *et al.* 2014). These include:

Western Europe:	Austria; Belgium–Flanders; France; Germany; Netherlands; Switzerland; United Kingdom.
South Europe:	Cyprus; Greece; Italy; Portugal; Spain.
Northern Europe:	Denmark; Finland; Sweden.
Central and Eastern Europe:	Albania; Czech Republic; Estonia; Hungary; Poland; Serbia; Slovakia.

In this Part on national context, three chapters are presented that process these country data in order to make cross-country comparisons. Chapter 2, 'Diverging or converging PPP policies, regulations and supporting institutions? A comparative analysis of twenty European countries' by Soecipto, Verhoest, Scherrer and

Table 1.3 Variables and indicators for the dimension *PPP-supporting institutions*

Variables	Indicators
Acting public institutions	PPP unit.
	Statute of PPP unit.
	Tasks/responsibilities of PPP unit.
	Size of PPP unit.
Procedures for project appraisal, role allocation	Use of standardised *ex ante* evaluation instruments.
	Third party approval of PPP projects:
	(1) Prior to tendering procedure;
	(2) Before final contract is signed.
	Roles and responsibilities of public agents in project cycle.
Standardised processes and documents	Use of standardised contracts.
	Use of standardised project models.
	Use of standardised tendering procedures.

Petersen, comparatively examines governmental support of PPPs across 20 European countries and covers various PPP experiences and geographical locations. Drawing on academic- and practitioner-oriented literature the authors argue for the three above-mentioned dimensions in governments' support for PPPs: policy and political commitment, regulatory frameworks and institutionalised PPP support units. They then carry out a comparative cluster analysis of governmental PPP support in the 20 countries and identify three clusters of countries characterised by significant differences in governmental PPP support. They conclude by discussing and pointing out possibilities for future research that can take the comparative PPP literature a step further.

In the following chapter 'Finding an institutional evolutionary maturity concept: an exploratory analysis for European experience in PPPs' by Oliveira, Costa, Ribeiro and Macário, the authors develop an evolutionary concept of institutional maturity for the implementation of PPPs, and apply it to a sample of European countries, grouping them according to their position in the evolutionary model. This chapter reports results of an exploratory stage of this research, obtained using multiple correspondence analysis on 17 European countries.

In Chapter 4 'Transport PPPs east of Elbe: destined to succeed or doomed to fail?' Witz, Leviäkangas and Łukasiewicz discuss the pressures and constraints in the national context for PPPs in eight European countries including the Czech Republic, Estonia, Finland, Hungary, Latvia, Poland, Serbia and Slovakia. These are countries with different levels of wealth, more or less varying cultural backgrounds, traditions, technological advancement and political structures. Moreover, Finland may be seen as a sort of outlier but serves as a benchmark in many respects. The authors believe there are sufficient historic, geopolitical and socio-economic commonalities to justify its inclusion in the sample alongside the core Central and Eastern European (CEE) countries. The variety of approaches to PPP the authors find in this group of countries disproves the idea of a uniform Central European type of public administration or a standardised CEE type of PPP. Each country in the region seems to have its own autonomous and specific PPP policy and proce-dures for PPP implementation influenced by deeply rooted patterns of governance. But there are also commonalities.

Part 1 ends with some overarching conclusions drawn from the three preceding chapters and some policy recommendations that arise from the comparative work of the COST Action TU1001 Working Group on national context presented by Verhoest, Petersen, Scherrer, Soecipto, van den Hurk, Lember, Leviäkangas, Willems, Witz and Ågren.

Note

1 Authors were active as members in the Auxiliary Working Group 1 on Country Context of the Cost Action TU 1001 'Private Public Partnerships in Transport: Trends and Theory'. This chapter draws on the introduction of Verhoest *et al.* (2013) *COST Action TU1001 Public Private Partnerships in Transport: Trends and Theory P3T3, 2013 Discussion Papers Part I Country Profiles.* ISBN: 978-88-97781-60-8, COST Office, Brussels. Available at www.ppptransport.eu

References

EIB – European Investment Bank (2004) *The EIB's Role in Public-Private Partnerships (PPPs).* Luxembourg: European Investment Bank

EPEC – European PPP Expertise Centre (2011) *The Guide to Guidance: How to Prepare, Procure and Deliver PPP Projects.* Luxembourg: European PPP Expertise Centre

European Bank for Reconstruction and Development – EBRD (2012) *Concession/PPP Laws Assessment 2011.* London: EBRD

European Commission – EC (2012) *EU Transport in Figures: Statistical Pocketbook 2012.* Brussels: European Union

European Investment Bank – EIB (2011) *Study on PPP Legal and Financial Frameworks in the Mediterranean Partner Countries, Volume 3 Best Practices and Lessons Learned: Selected Experiences from Other Countries.* Luxembourg: EIB

Esping-Andersen, G. (1999) *Social Foundations of Postindustrial Economies.* Oxford: Oxford University Press

Farrugia, C., Reynolds, T. and Orr, R. J. (2008) *Public-Private Partnership Agencies: A Global Perspective.* Stanford, CA: Collaboratory for Research on Global Projects

Grimsey, D. and Lewis, M. K. (2002) 'Evaluating the risks of Public Private Partnerships for infrastructure projects'. *International Journal of Project Management, 20*(2), pp. 107–118

Hague, R. and Harrop, M. (2007) *Comparative Government and Politics: An Introduction.* Basingstoke: Palgrave Macmillan

Hodge, G. A., Greve, C. and Boardman, A. E. (Eds) (2010) *International Handbook on Public-Private Partnerships.* Cheltenham: Edward Elgar

Hofstede, G. and Hofstede, G. J. (2005) *Cultures and Organizations: Software of the Mind.* New York: McGraw-Hill

House, R. J., Hanges, P. J., Javidan, M., Dorfman, P. W. and Gupta, V. (Eds) (2004) *Culture, Leadership, and Organizations: The GLOBE Study of 62 Societies.* London: Sage

International Monetary Fund (2004) *Public-Private Partnerships.* Washington, DC: IMF

Klijn, E.-H. and Teisman, G. R. (2003) 'Institutional and strategic barriers to Public-Private Partnership: an analysis of Dutch cases'. *Public Money and Management, 23*(3), pp. 137–145

Lienhard, A. (2006) 'Public Private Partnerships (PPPs) in Switzerland: experiences – risks – potentials'. *International Review of Administrative Sciences, 72*(4), pp. 547–563

Lijphart, A. (1999) *Patterns of Democracy: Government Forms and Performance in Thirty-Six Countries*. New Haven/London: Yale University Press

McQuaid, R. W. and Scherrer, W. (2010) 'Changing reasons for Public-Private Partnerships (PPPs)'. *Public Money and Management, 30*(1), pp. 27–34

Nölke, A. and Vliegenthart, A. (2009) 'Enlarging the varieties of capitalism: the emergence of dependent market economies in East Central Europe'. *World Politics, 61*(4), pp. 670–702

OECD – Organization for Economic Co-operation and Development (2006) *Review of the National Policy, Legislative and Institutional Environment Necessary for the Development of Municipal Public Private Partnerships (PPPs) for Public Service Delivery and Local Development in the Europe and CIS Region*. Paris: Organisation for Economic Co-operation and Development

OECD – Organization for Economic Co-operation and Development (2008) *Public-Private Partnerships: In Pursuit of Risk Sharing and Value for Money*. Paris: Organisation for Economic Co-operation and Development

OECD – Organization for Economic Co-operation and Development (2010) *Dedicated Public-Private Partnership Units: A Survey of Institutional and Governance Structures*. Paris: Organisation for Economic Co-operation and Development

Osborne, D. and Gaebler, T. (1992) *Reinventing Government: How the Entrepeneurial Spirit is Transforming the Public Sector*. New York: Addison-Wesley

Painter, M. and Pierre, J. (Eds) (2005) *Challenges to State Policy Capacity: Global Trends and Comparative Perspectives*. Basingstoke/New York: Palgrave Macmillan

Petersen, O. H. (2010) 'Emerging meta-governance as a regulation framework for Public-Private Partnerships: an examination of the European Union's approach'. *International Public Management Review, 11*(3), pp. 1–23

Petersen, O. H. (2011) 'Public-Private Partnerships as converging or diverging trends in public management? A comparative analysis of PPP policy and regulation in Denmark and Ireland'. *International Public Management Review, 12*(2), pp. 1–37

Pollitt, C. and Bouckaert, G. (2004) *Public Management Reform: A Comparative Analysis*. Oxford: Oxford University Press

Roumboutsos, A., Farrell, S., Liyanage, C. L. and Macário, R. (Eds) (2013) *COST Action TU1001 Public Private Partnerships in Transport: Trends and Theory P3T3, 2013 Discussion Papers Part II Case Studies*, ISBN 978-88-97781-61-5. Available at www.ppptransport.eu

Roumboutsos, A., Farrel, S. and Verhoest, K. (Eds) (2014) *COST Action TU1001 – Public Private Partnerships in Transport: Trends and Theory [P3T3]: 2014 Discussion Papers: Country Profiles and Case Studies*. Brussels: COST Office. Available at: www.ppptransport.eu

Verhoest, K., Roness, P. G., Verschuere, B., Rubecksen, K. and MacCarthaig, M. (2010) *Autonomy and Control of State Agencies: Comparing States and Agencies*. Basingstoke: Palgrave Macmillan

Verhoest, K., Voets, J. and Van Gestel, K. (2012) 'A theory-driven approach to PPP: the dynamics of complexity and control' in C. Greve and G. Hodge (2013) *Rethinking*

Public-Private Partnerships: Strategic Approaches for Turbulent Times. Abingdon, UK: Routledge

Verhoest, K., Carbonara, N., Lember, V., Petersen, O. H., Scherrer, W. and van den Hurk, M. (Eds) (2013) *COST Action TU1001 Public Private Partnerships in Transport: Trends and Theory [P3T3], 2013 Discussion Papers Part I Country Profiles.* Brussels: COST Office. Available at www.ppptransport.eu

Verhoest, K., Petersen, O. H., Scherrer, W. and Soecipto, R. M. (2015) 'How do governments support the development of Public Private Partnerships? Measuring and comparing governmental PPP support in 20 European countries'. *Transport Reviews*, 35(2), 118–139

WEF (2012) *The Global Competitiveness Report 2012–2013.* Geneva: World Economic Forum

World Bank (2012) *Connecting to Compete 2012: Trade Logistics in the Global Economy.* Retrieved 17 September 2012 from http://siteresources.worldbank.org/TRADE/Resources/2390701336654966193/LPI_2012_final.pdf

World Bank and PPIAF (2006) *Public-Private Partnership Units: Lessons for their Design and Use in Infrastructure.* Washington, DC: World Bank and Public-Private Infrastructure Advisory Facility

2 Diverging or converging PPP policies, regulations and supporting arrangements?

A comparative analysis of 20 European countries

Murwantara Soecipto, Koen Verhoest, Walter Scherrer and Ole Helby Petersen

Introduction

Public Private Partnerships (PPPs) have been launched in most countries in the Western world as a means of developing large-scale infrastructure projects (Grimsey and Lewis 2002; Hodge and Greve 2007; Jooste *et al.* 2011). The introduction of new partnership forms has been seen as part of a broader trend towards network forms of governance and multi-actor collaboration based on shared risks, competencies and benefits between governments and private companies (Klijn and Teisman 2003; Osborne 2010). The notion of PPP has been subject to global interest and has been characterised as 'a very-fashionable concept' (Wettenhal 2003: 77) and a model that enjoys 'international acceptance' (Johnston and Gudergan 2007: 570). However, recent comparative research also indicates that the initiatives that governments have launched to promote PPP differ considerably across countries with the result that significant differences in PPP supportive institutional frameworks now exist (Petersen 2011; van den Hurk *et al.* 2015). Within the global trend of convergence in positive PPP rhetoric there are thus clear indications of widespread divergence in governments' policies, and regulatory and institutional support arrangements for PPPs across otherwise largely similar countries in the Western world (Hammerschmid and Angerer 2005; Verhoest *et al.* 2015).

In this chapter we comparatively examine some of these differences in countries' PPP support by comparing the extent to which national governments have launched policies, regulations and dedicated support institutions to support the development of infrastructure PPPs. The objective is to examine differences and similarities in governmental support of PPPs and to cluster countries according to the ways in which they support PPP through the launch of policies, regulations and institutional units dedicated to supporting the development of PPPs. We build upon standardised data gathered by the country teams involved in the COST Action TU 1001 'PPPs in Transport: Trends and Theory' which covers 20 European countries. We address the following descriptive-comparative research questions. How do different European countries compare in terms of their governmental support for PPP? With which other European countries do they cluster with regard to the development of policies and political support of PPP, legal and regulatory frameworks and supporting arrangements for PPPs? These research questions are central to this chapter, in which we report the results of a comparative mapping of PPP policies, regulations and supporting arrangements in 20 European countries.

The remainder of the chapter is structured as follows. First, we outline and discuss the elements of governmental PPP support as defined by policy, regulatory and institutional support. Next, we present the methods used to classify and index the countries and consider strengths and weaknesses of differing clustering methods. Then, we present the results of the cluster analysis and outline some of the main characteristics of the four clusters of countries. In the penultimate section, we provide a more in-depth discussion of differences and similarities between countries in their PPP policies, regulations and supporting arrangements. Finally, we provide a conclusion to the chapter and provide some suggestions for further comparative PPP research.

How governments can support PPP: A framework and methodology

Academic literature (see, for example, Delhi *et al.* 2010; Meunier and Quinet 2010; Galilea and Medda 2010; Jooste *et al.* 2011; Mu *et al.* 2010; Matos-Castaño *et al.* 2014) suggests that the national institutional and political contexts are important determinants of the use of PPP as a mode of infrastructure delivery. Practitioner-oriented literature in the field of PPP (see, for example, Deloitte 2007; EIB 2011; The *Economist* 2011; European Bank for Reconstruction and Development 2012; EPEC 2011; OECD 2008; UNESCAP 2005; World Bank and PPIAF 2006) elaborates on this by defining the relevant components of such contexts. In this chapter we focus on three main dimensions of government support of PPP, which are considered by both academic and practitioner literature as being important formal institutions that may be supportive for creating a PPP enabling field (Jooste *et al.* 2011): policy design and expression of political commitment; legal and regulatory framework; and the existence and effectiveness of supporting arrangements.

Guidelines for governments for establishing such a PPP-enabling field have been specified in practitioner-oriented literature produced by international organisations and consultancy firms. We found four measurement methods and corresponding indices on 'PPP-readiness' (UNESCAP 2005; The *Economist* 2011), 'PPP maturity level' (Deloitte 2007) and 'quality of PPP legislation' (European Bank for Reconstruction and Development 2012). These four indices, on the one hand, combine qualitatively different aspects but none of them provide an index that covers all aspects of governmental support regarding PPPs, being policy commitment, regulatory measures and PPP supporting arrangements. On the other hand, these four indices also include aspects that are not, or only very indirectly, under the control of governments like macroeconomic conditions and the general investment climate.

Therefore, we built a framework that captures governmental support for infrastructure PPPs, which solely focuses on PPP-specific factors and on the role of government actions to enable and stimulate PPP. We deliberately did not include macro-financial or macro-economic factors in this framework because this would conflate the actual role of government. These other factors, of course, should be taken into account when explaining and contextualising government support actions and they will be examined in future research.

Table 2.1 gives an overview of the operationalisation of the three dimensions of government support for PPP. Each dimension of government support is captured by two or three indicators, which in turn comprise up to four sub-indicators. Explicit PPP policies and long-term political commitment are crucial to create legitimacy for PPP to become an accepted instrument of public investment policy (Matos-Castaño *et al.* 2014). This first dimension is captured with the following indicators: existence of relevant strategy documents and programmes; and an adequate level of legal and regulatory framework for PPP – both 'hard' and 'soft' regulations are relevant (see Mörth 2007; Petersen 2010; Bovis 2013) – can facilitate the uptake of PPPs. The second dimension is captured by two indicators: existence and contents of a specific PPP law; and adequacy of the general legal framework for the uptake of PPP. Finally, PPP-supporting arrangements that can exert a major influence on shaping a PPP-enabling field (Jooste *et al.* 2011; Mahalingam *et al.* 2011) are captured by three indicators and the respective sub-indicators: the existence and characteristics of PPP supporting units; the existence, use, and type of procedures for project appraisal and prioritisation; and the use of standardised processes and documents for PPPs in transport. Most (sub-) indicators are of a static nature and reflect the situation at a given point in time (timeframe of data collection Spring 2013), although a few (sub-) indicators such as policy political support and indicators concerning PPP-units capture evolutions over time.

We applied the framework for governmental support for PPPs to a sample of 20 European countries (see next section), which are characterised by a considerable variety of experience with PPP and by different politico-administrative traditions and regimes including Nordic, Continental, Napoleonic-Latin, Central and East European countries, and the UK as an Anglo-American country (see Painter and Peters 2010). Eighteen of these countries are member states of the European Union, one country is closely affiliated to the EU (Switzerland), and one country has a legal framework that is consistent with EU regulations in the field of PPP (Serbia); therefore a harmonising effect on the legal and regulatory framework can be expected.

Country data were collected within the COST Action TU1001 on PPP in transport, which also provided the organisational frame for developing the indicators. For reasons of data availability, data, generally, refer to the central government level, with the exception of Belgium where Flanders is taken as a proxy because in Belgium there is nearly no PPP activity outside Flanders.

Table 2.1 A framework for measuring governmental support for PPP

Dimension	Indicators	Sub-indicators	Scores			
			4	3	2	1
Policy and political commitment	Existence of a strategy document of PPP policy (Pol_1).		Yes, published before 2006 and updated afterwards.	Yes, published before 2006, but not updated.	Yes, recently published and not updated.	Non-existent.
	Existence of a general PPP programme (Pol_2).		Yes, incl. transport-specific programme, clear time schedule.	Yes, incl. transport-specific programme, but no clear time schedule.	Yes, but only general PPP programme, no clear schedule.	Non-existent.
	Political support (Pol_1).		Rather strong, stable or increasing.	Rather strong, decreasing.	Rather low, increasing.	Rather low, stable or decreasing.
Legal and regulatory framework	Specific PPP or concession law: existence (Legal_1).	(1) General PPP or concession law; (2) PPP law in transport; (3) procurement law; (4) in-line with EU.	All four criteria are met.	Three criteria are met.	Two criteria are met.	One or no criterion is met.
	Specific PPP or concession law: (b) scope regarding definitions of four items (Legal_2).	Definition of (1) PPP; (2) eligible sectors and types of infrastructures/services; (3) contracting authorities; (4) eligible private party.	All four criteria are met.	Three criteria are met.	Two criteria are met.	One or no criterion is met.
	Elements provided in the general legal framework (including public procurement law) (Legal_3).	Four sub-indicators covering procedures and recommendations, 5 sub-indicators about mandatory provisions in PPP contract.[1]	8 to 9 sub-indicators are met.	6 to 7 sub-indicators are met.	4 to 5 sub-indicators are met.	0 to 3 sub-indicators are met.

PPP-supporting arrangements					
Acting public institutions/PPP-supporting units (Arr_1).	Existence of a PPP support unit.	Yes, since before 2006.	Yes, since 2006 or later.	No, not anymore.	No, never existed.
	Legal and organisational basis of PPP support unit.	Private legal body with private sector participation.	Private legal body without private sector participation.	Public (law) body under ministry.	Non-existent.
	General functions PPP Support unit.	Dissemination, policy function and green lighting.	Dissemination and policy guidance or green lighting.	Dissemination only.	Non-existent.
	Staff size of unit.	20 or more.	5 to 20.	< 5.	Never existed.
Procedures for project appraisal and prioritisation, role of main sectors in project stages (Arr_2).	Existence of standard *ex ante* evaluation instruments.	Mandatory for all projects.	Mandatory beyond threshold.	Existing, but not mandatory.	Non-existent.
	Use of standard *ex ante* evaluation in PPP projects.	Used in all projects.	Used in majority of projects.	Used in minority of projects.	Not used.
	Existence of a third party scrutinising and approving PPP projects before project on tender.	Yes.	Yes, beyond certain threshold.	No, not anymore.	Not at all.
	Existence of a third party scrutinising and approving PPP projects before final contract signed.	Yes.	Yes, beyond certain threshold.	No, not anymore.	Not at all.
Standardised processes and documents for PPPs in transport (Arr_3).	Use of standardised contracts for PPP in transport.	Used in majority of projects.	Used in minority of projects.	Existent but not used.	Non-existent.
	Use of standardised PPP model in transport.	Used in majority of projects.	Used in minority of projects.	Existent but not used.	Non-existent.

Source: Verhoest *et al.* 2015

[1] Does the prevailing legislation include provisions and procedures regarding the following elements: selection of private partner through competitive procedures; non-competitive procedure in exceptional circumstances; procedures for unsolicited proposals; review procedures; contract termination events; compensation provisions; provisions for collection of fees or payments by government; public authorities to support and provide guarantees and step-in rights for lenders or substitution by a new private partner?

In order to warrant validity and reliability, data were collected by country experts with in-depth contextual knowledge about national institutions and practices. Based on selected interviews and the analysis of legislation and other documents, country teams delivered a narrative country profile (see Verhoest *et al.* 2013a) and a set of data in accordance with the dimensions and indicators listed in Table 2.1. Members of country teams were integrated into the process of developing the set of indicators and were provided with detailed guidelines explaining all items in order to reduce the risk of variation in data collection and misreporting. In a feedback loop with the authors of this paper completeness and consistency of data delivered by country teams was checked. In order to avoid a potential bias due to interpersonal differences in interpretation, data coding was done independently by three persons and subsequently discussed among the authors. This demanding process yielded indicators for 20 countries. However, due to limitations in availability of country teams in specific countries, we were not able to include a few important PPP countries like Ireland, Spain and Poland.

Data will be exploited in two ways: first, a PPP-Government Support Index (PPP-GSI) will be presented as it was developed in Verhoest *et al.* (2015). Item scores of the PPP-GSI are measured on an ordinal scale between 1 and 4 (see Table 2.1, second column) with 4 representing strongest and 1 representing weakest or no government support for PPP. The PPP-GSI can be conceived as consisting of three sub-indexes that each cover one of the three dimensions: a sub-index on policy and political support; a sub-index on the legal and regulatory framework; and a sub-index on PPP-supporting arrangements. The value of the overall PPP-GSI therefore is equal to the mean of its sub-indexes. Dimensions, indicators within each dimension, and sub-indicators within each indicator are given equal weights because neither theoretical considerations nor measurement problems support the allocation of different weights to the different dimensions, indicators and sub-indicators of governmental support for PPP. The method of simple weighting and calculating averages might, however, have properties which may cause some misrepresentations of actual government support profiles of countries and the resulting ranking of countries with regard to PPP government support.

In order to avoid these misrepresentations, we will apply a second approach for exploiting the dataset collected with the framework presented in Table 2.1, based on cluster analysis (CA). Cluster analysis enables us to check for the robustness of the country ranking resulting from the calculation of the PPP-GSI values and to test the meaningfulness of these results for further analyses. It will be used to explore the country data set in order to assess whether countries can be grouped meaningfully in terms of a relatively small number of groups or 'clusters' of countries that resemble each other and that differ in some respects from countries in other clusters (Everitt *et al.* 2011). We apply hierarchical clustering with agglomerative methods to specify such clusters among the 20 countries including using the Statistical Package for Social Sciences (SPSS). Agglomerative methods are widely used hierarchical methods yielding a pattern of distinct clusters and successively merging clusters together until a stopping criterion is satisfied (Everitt *et al.* 2011; Abonyi and Feil 2007). The result of such an analysis is a two-dimensional diagram (dendrogram), which represents the fusions or divisions made at each stage of the analysis.

Six variants of agglomerative cluster analysis methods are available for finding similarities and dissimilarities among countries: single linkage, complete linkage, average linkage, centroid, median and Ward's method. Single linkage was introduced by Florek *et al.* (1951), Sneath (1957) and Johnson (1967) and considers the distance between groups defined as that of the closest pair of countries, where only pairs consisting of one country from each group are considered. The complete linkage method (also called furthest neighbour method) defines distance between groups as that of the most distant pair of countries. The average linkage method defines distance between two clusters as the average of distance between all pairs of countries from each group. The centroid clustering method uses the data matrix rather than a proximity matrix and involves merging clusters with the most similar mean vector. The median linkage method is similar, but the centroids of the constituent country clusters are weighted equally to produce the new centroid of the merged cluster. Finally, Ward (1963) introduced a method in which the fusion of two clusters is based on the size of an error sum of squares criterion (Everitt *et al.* 2011).

However, it has to be recognised that different hierarchical clustering methods may give very different results on the same data, and empirical studies are rarely conclusive. No method can, in general, be considered superior to the other methods and, as Gordon (1998) points out, hierarchical methods are in any case only stepwise optimal (Everitt *et al.* 2011).

As we emphasise the extent to which countries within clusters are similar we look for compact clusters. Complete linkage is the logical opposite of single linkage clustering in that the linkage rule states that any candidate for inclusion into an existing cluster must be within a certain level of similarity to all members of that cluster (Sokal and Michener 1958). Being more rigorous in clustering than single linkage, complete linkage has a tendency to find relatively compact, hyperspherical clusters composed of highly similar cases (Aldendefer and Blashfield 1984). Studies that focus on the stability of clustering in the presence of outliers or noise include that by Hubert (1974), who found that complete linkage is less sensitive to observational errors than single linkage. Ward (1963) introduced a method in which the fusion of two clusters is based on the size of an error sum-of-squares criterion. The objective at each stage is to minimise the increase in the total within-cluster error sum of squares (Everitt *et al.* 2011). Ward's Method is also known as the within-groups sum of squares or the error sum of squares (ESS). The method works by joining those groups or cases that result in the minimum increase in the ESS. The method tends to find (or create) clusters of relatively equal sizes and shapes as hyperspheres (Aldendefer and Blashfield 1984). Ward's method performed very well when the data contained clusters with approximately the same number of points, but poorly when the clusters were of different sizes. Cunningham and Ogilvie (1972) and Blashfield (1976) also concluded that for clusters with equal numbers of points Ward's method is successful, otherwise complete linkage is preferable.

Below, we first discuss the clustering of countries when considering all three dimensions of governmental support while, in the final section, we scrutinise more closely how countries cluster when looking at each of the three dimensions separately.

Classifying countries regarding governmental support by indexation – problems and solutions

In Verhoest *et al.* (2015) we rank the 20 countries under review with respect to their PPP governmental support by creating a simple composed index based on the simple summation of the different (sub) indicators. The score of this PPP Governmental Support Index (PPP GSI) ranges between 1.0 (minimum) to 4.0 (maximum). Table 2.2 reveals that the highest score of PPP-GSI is achieved by the United Kingdom (3.0) and, on the other extreme of the range, Estonia is to be found with the lowest score of 1.2. Table 2.2 presents the detailed values of this index and the sub-indices for the different countries under review.

In Verhoest *et al.* (2015) in the analysis of country ranking and how it relates to PPP take-up across countries, we identify four groups of countries based on their PPP-GSI values, by dividing the range in to four equal parts:

Table 2.2 PPP-GSI for 20 European countries (Verhoest *et al.* 2015)

Country		PPP-GSI dimensions			Overall PPP-GSI score
		Policy and political commitment	Legal and regulatory framework	PPP supporting institutions	
AT	Austria	1.0	1.8	1.5	1.4
BE	Belgium–Flanders	3.0	1.8	2.8	2.5
CH	Switzerland	2.3	1.8	1.8	2.0
CZ	Czech Republic	1.7	2.3	2.1	2.0
DK	Denmark	2.3	1.0	1.8	1.7
EE	Estonia	1.0	1.3	1.3	1.2
FR	France	1.3	2.8	3.1	2.4
GR	Greece	2.3	2.8	2.3	2.5
IT	Italy	2.0	2.3	2.3	2.2
NL	Netherlands	3.7	1.8	3.3	2.9
PT	Portugal	2.0	2.8	2.8	2.5
RS	Serbia	1.3	2.5	2.0	1.9
SI	Slovenia	1.3	2.3	2.2	1.9
SE	Sweden	1.0	1.8	1.2	1.3
UK	United Kingdom	3.7	1.8	3.6	3.0
CY	Cyprus	1.7	2.3	1.8	1.9
FL	Finland	1.3	1.8	1.3	1.5
SL	Slovak Republic	2.0	1.8	1.9	1.9
DE	Germany	3.7	1.8	3.4	2.9
HU	Hungary	1.7	1.8	2.2	1.9

1. Countries with a PPP-GSI value of at least 3.0: The United Kingdom is the only country in this category.
2. Countries with a PPP-GSI value between 2.5 and less than 3.0: there are five countries in this cluster, listed here in order of decreasing PPP GSI value: Netherlands, Germany (both 2.9), Belgium–Flanders, Greece, Portugal (all 2.5). It should be noted that Flanders is used in this study as a proxy of Belgium[1].
3. Countries with a PPP-GSI value between 2.0 and less than 2.5: France (2.4), Italy (2.2), Switzerland and the Czech Republic (2.0) are included in this group.
4. Countries with a PPP-GSI value less than 2.0: in this group we find a large group of countries, being Serbia, Slovenia, Cyprus, Slovak Republic and Hungary (all value 1.9), Denmark (1.7), Finland (1.5), Austria (1.4), Sweden (1.3) and Estonia (1.2).

However, one might find this clustering based on the PPP-GSI scores debatable, as there are at least three methodological properties of the method to be discussed. First, the delineation of the four clusters defined above, based on PPP-GSI scores, seems very arbitrary and redefining the boundary values of the clusters would deliver different groupings.

Second, the scaling of the indicators and sub-indicators that the PPP-GSI is composed of might distort results. While the (sub-) indicators are measured on an ordinal scale (1 to 4), calculating the arithmetic mean for each country might be considered as transforming the values from an ordinal scale to a nominal one.

Third, the PPP GSI is based on the calculation of simple averages of the indicators representing the different dimensions, which in turn are calculated based on simple summation of the sub-indicators without any weighting applied. This method of calculation may obscure substantial differences in government support profiles between countries, because countries that score very high on one dimension might have the same overall score as countries that have moderate scores on all three dimensions. Therefore a correlation analysis between (sub-) indicators of the PPP-GSI using Spearman correlation[2] was conducted. Table 2.3 shows the correlation between nine indicators of the PPP-GSI: three indicators representing the dimension 'policy and political commitment'[3], three representing the dimension 'legal and regulatory framework'[4]; and three representing the dimension 'PPP supporting arrangements'[5].

Policy and political commitment indicators are significantly related with indicators representing the PPP supporting arrangements dimension (p value < 0.05), with political support for PPP (Pol_3) correlating simultaneously with all sub-indicators of PPP supporting arrangements (Arr_1, Arr_2 and Arr_3). While there is no significant correlation with political commitment indicators, some legal and regulatory framework indicators correlate with the PPP supporting arrangements dimension, particularly between Acting PPP Units (Arr_1) and existing PPP Laws (Legal_1) and Scope of PPP Laws (Legal_2). As correlation exists only between some pairs of indicators, a relatively high score on the overall

Table 2.3 Correlation of indicators of governmental support (Spearman Correlation)

		Pol_1	Pol_2	Pol_3	Legal_1	Legal_2	Legal_3	Arr_1	Arr_2	Arr_3
Pol_1	Correlation	1.000	0.394	0.321	-0.373	-0.365	-0.154	0.301	0.038	0.545*
	Sig. (2-tailed)		0.086	0.167	0.106	0.114	0.518	0.197	0.872	0.013
Pol_2	Correlation	0.394	1.000	0.250	-0.089	-0.006	-0.128	0.420	0.270	0.505*
	Sig. (2-tailed)	0.086		0.288	0.710	0.980	0.590	0.065	0.249	0.023
Pol_3	Correlation	0.321	0.250	1.000	0.165	0.196	0.000	0.655**	0.514*	0.593**
	Sig. (2-tailed)	0.167	0.288		0.486	0.408	1.000	0.002	0.020	0.006
Legal_1	Correlation	-0.373	-0.089	0.165	1.000	0.925**	-0.038	0.452*	0.406	0.133
	Sig. (2-tailed)	0.106	0.710	0.486		0.000	0.875	0.045	0.076	0.577
Legal_2	Correlation	-0.365	-0.006	0.196	0.925**	1.000	-0.156	0.484*	0.417	0.015
	Sig. (2-tailed)	0.114	0.980	0.408	0.000		0.510	0.031	0.067	0.951
Legal_3	Correlation	-0.154	-0.128	0.000	-0.038	-0.156	1.000	0.056	0.258	-0.198
	Sig. (2-tailed)	0.518	0.590	1.000	0.875	0.510		0.815	0.273	0.403
Arr_1	Correlation	0.301	0.420	0.655**	0.452*	0.484*	0.056	1.000	0.640**	0.621**
	Sig. (2-tailed)	0.197	0.065	0.002	0.045	0.031	0.815		0.002	0.003
Arr_2	Correlation	0.038	0.270	0.514*	0.406	0.417	0.258	0.640**	1.000	0.342
	Sig. (2-tailed)	0.872	0.249	0.020	0.076	0.067	0.273	0.002		0.140
Arr_3	Correlation	0.545*	0.505*	0.593**	0.133	0.015	-0.198	0.621**	0.342	1.000
	Sig. (2-tailed)	0.013	0.023	0.006	0.577	0.951	0.403	0.003	0.140	

*correlation is significant at the 0.05 level (2-tailed)
**correlation is significant at the 0.01 level (2-tailed)

index might go together with low scores on specific indicators and dimensions. Thus, clustering by indexation might group together countries that are very different in the way and the extent to which they support PPP by policies, regulations and supporting arrangements. For example, the United Kingdom (which scores highest on the PPP-GSI) has a less extensively elaborated legal and regulatory framework, while France (which also scores high on the PPP-GSI) tends to concentrate its supporting effectors more on building an extensive legal and regulatory framework rather than on framing clear PPP strategy documents and programmes.

With respect to correlation between indicators that represent the same dimension we found significant correlations only between two pairs of indicators within the supporting arrangements dimension and one pair of indicators within the legal and regulatory dimension. There is no significant correlation among the three indicators that represent the policy and political support dimension. Little correlation between indicators that represent the same dimension suggests that these indicators, by and large, capture different aspects of PPP supportiveness within each dimension independently.

In order to analyse possible implications of the three methodological concerns a cluster analysis is conducted in the next section that groups countries with similar profiles regarding governmental support towards PPP. This allows us to reconsider the clustering based on the PPP-GSI and to examine whether different techniques of analysis render fundamentally different clusters.

Classifying governmental PPP support by cluster analysis

In order to be able to group countries with similar governmental PPP support profiles, i.e. the composition and level of government support, and to distinguish them from the other countries with dissimilar profiles, we applied hierarchical clustering with agglomerative methods to specify such clusters among the 20 European countries included in our study. We conducted the clustering by examining nine indicators: three indicators related to policy and political commitment, three indicators regarding legal and regulatory framework and three indicators referring to PPP supporting arrangements. We applied clustering analysis resulting in three, four and five groups (being different levels of single solution), but the analyses with four groups of countries set as single solution yielded the clearest results in terms of grouping.

In this study we conducted the cluster analysis with all six algorithm methods (see Table 2.A.1 in annex). However, complete linkage and Ward's method provide the most balanced and most internally coherent clusters. In the remainder of this chapter we use the complete linkage method because it is superior both with regard to the internal coherence of clusters and lower standard deviations and coefficients of variance within clusters. Results of both methods are very similar (see Table 2.A.1 in the annex). When comparing both methods the position of only three countries is a matter for discussion, being Italy (IT), Serbia (RS) and Slovenia (SI). When using complete linkage these countries are categorised into two different clusters: Italy is agglomerated in the cluster with Switzerland, Czech Republic, Denmark and Slovak Republic, and Serbia as well as Slovenia are grouped into the largest group of eight countries. Using the Ward's Method, these three countries are grouped together in the group of France, Greece and Portugal. However, this re-clustering renders the cluster 1 somewhat more similar in terms of legal framework and the cluster 3 more homogeneous in terms of policy and political commitment, but increases the dissimilarities between the countries in group 4 to a large extent on multiple dimensions. Therefore we decided to follow the clustering provided by the analyses based on complete linkage.

The results of hierarchical agglomerative clustering using complete linkage (see Figure 2.A.1 in the annex) frame the 20 countries into four clusters:

- Cluster 1 includes The United Kingdom, The Netherlands, Germany and Belgium-Flanders.
- Cluster 2 includes France, Greece and Portugal.
- Cluster 3 includes the Czech Republic, Denmark, Slovakia, Switzerland and Italy.
- Cluster 4 encompasses the most countries: Austria, Estonia, Serbia, Slovenia, Sweden, Cyprus, Finland and Hungary.

Figure 2.1 shows the four clusters schematically. We will now discuss the clusters, their basic government support profiles and features, as well as the extent to which some countries deviate from that profile on specific dimensions.

Countries in cluster 1 provide strong support on two dimensions of government support for PPPs and may be considered as strong supporters of PPP through

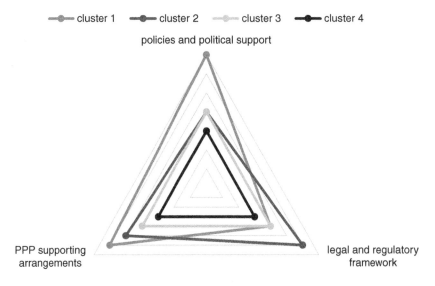

Figure 2.1 Schematic representation of the clusters.

well-developed policies, political commitment and supporting arrangements. These countries have highly developed PPP policies with clear and updated strategy documents and PPP programmes. Political support for PPP in these countries has been strong and has also remained, in most cases, stable in the recent period. PPP supporting arrangements in these countries are quite sophisticated with PPP units being present and rather well-developed with long, moderately developed procedures for project appraisal and prioritisation and the use of standardised processes and documents. However, these countries have, overall, less extensively developed legal and regulatory frameworks compared with countries in cluster 2, with the emphasis being on defining elements in the general procurement law rather than issuing general PPP laws. In the group of 20 countries under review, the UK, The Netherlands, Germany and, to a lesser extent, Belgium–Flanders belong to this cluster.

The United Kingdom has a history of government support for PPP of more than 20 years. The Private Finance Initiative (PFI) was established by the Conservative Government in 1992. Then, the new Labour Government continued with PFI in 1997 and provided the resources within the Treasury and government departments to set priorities, improve the basis of project selection, and develop both the process and a standard contract (PPP Forum 2014). Standardised PPP contracts are used in several sectors. When it comes to the legal and regulatory underpinning of PPP, the UK focuses on sound and encompassing procurement laws rather than issuing specific PPP laws. The UK has regulated public procurement in the 'Public Contract Regulation 2006'.

In the Netherlands, PPP were first mentioned in official government documents in 1986, while being introduced in the coalition agreement of the Kok II Cabinet (the second coalition of the Social Democrat Party and the Liberal-Conservative Party) in 1989 (Klijn 2009). There is no PPP law in the Netherlands. However, public procurement is regulated by the Public Procurement (Tendering Rules) Decree (Bao) (the 'Procurement Decree') and the Tendering (Special Sectors) Decree (Bass) (the 'Special Sectors Decree'). The Decrees have implemented the Directive 2004/18/EC (CMS Legal Service EEIG 2010). The PPP Knowledge Centre was established within the Dutch Ministry of Finance in 1999, developing supporting instruments such as public sector comparator, checklists for the different contract types, standard tender documents and guidelines for project procurement and contract management (OECD 2010).

Germany first introduced PPP under Chancellor Gerhard Schröder in 2001. There is no specific PPP law that encompasses all legal requirements relating to PPP projects. The German Government has taken a positive approach to PPP. For instance, several laws regarding PPP were amended through the PPP Acceleration Act of 2005. The PPP Acceleration Act partly transposed Directive 2004/18/EC on procurement law into German national law. The aim of this Act was to remove obstacles and barriers to PPP identified by the government in a Federal Report on PPP (CMS Legal Service EEIG 2010). The Federal Ministry of Finance and *Partnerschaften Deutschland-ÖPP Deutschland AG* (Partnerships Germany) share responsibility for PPP at the federal level. Partnerships Germany itself was established in 2009 as a central unit to provide advisory services to public sector clients (for example the federal government, the federal states, the municipalities) (OECD 2010).

Belgium–Flanders has a somewhat unique position in this group as it deviates in some aspects from the other countries. The policy document for PPP was first introduced in the Coalition Agreement of the Flemish Government in 1999, but its PPP programmes were less explicit in terms of planned projects and time schedules. The Flemish Government established the Flemish PPP Knowledge Centre in mid-2002, in which it has four main functions: field developer, knowledge broker, process guide and added value monitor. As to the legal and regulatory framework, The Flemish Parliament passed the Flemish Parliament Act on Public Private Partnership in July 2003, with the act covering PPP-related concepts, role of PPP Knowledge Centre and legal facilities (Vlaams Kenniscentrum PPS 2014). The public body under the auspices of the Ministry of the Interior called the PPP Knowledge Centre was established in 2002 and it has developed standardised processes and contract documents, although procedures for project appraisal and prioritisation are less well developed (van den Hurk and Verhoest 2013). The Flemish Government accepted a general PPP Decree in 2003, aimed at supporting public–private initiatives in Flanders, besides provisions in the general procurement law in line with EC directives.

Countries in cluster 2, encompassing Greece, Portugal and France, are strong legal and regulatory supporters of PPPs, as government support of PPP focuses on articulating an appropriate legal and regulatory framework. These countries also have strong PPP supporting arrangements, although policy and political commitment towards PPP is rather modest. There are some differences between the countries to be noted.

First, unlike France and Portugal, Greece has designed a PPP programme with a clear pipeline and timetable and which is regularly updated. Greece set up PPP laws (Law 3389/2005), in which the law defines the procuring authority to be the public entity with competence in the relevant sector and includes local governmental authorities, legal entities under public law and *sociétés anonymes* (with share capital subscribed by the mentioned public entities). In addition, in order to formulate policies, an Inter-Ministerial Committee for Public and Private Partnerships (IM PPP Committee) was established in 2006 (OECD 2010).

Secondly, Portugal expressed rather strong political support for PPP, which is still said to be increasing. Portugal has a long history of public service concessions that started in the 1970s, initially in the transport and water sectors. The high development of PPP activity was signified by the Vasco de Gama bridge concession contract in the mid-1990s. The Budgetary Framework Law 91/2001 was the first legislation issued by the government. Later, the government published the PPP Decree-Law 86/2003 (amended in 2006 by Decree-Law 141/2006), which provided general, largely procedural, guidance on PPP and allowed for the establishment of sector specific regulation (EPEC 2014). A PPP unit (*Parpública SA*) was established in 2003 as a private limited company owned completely by the Treasury, having as main functions policy guidance and technical assistance to ministries regarding PPP procurement processes (OECD 2010).

France has not issued a clear PPP strategy document as well as PPP programmes, although PPP in France has been introduced in the form of concession arrangements since the beginning of the second half of the twentieth century. France introduced the first form of government-paid PPP contract (*bail emphytéotique administrative*) in 1988. New legislation, creating the *contrat de partenariat* (partnership contract), was introduced in 2004, and the PPP unit (*the Mission d'appui aux partenariats public-privé or 'MAPPP'*) was also created (EPEC 2012). In contrast to the other countries in this cluster, France has developed standardised documents and processes to a substantial level, while the others have not done as much.

Countries in cluster 3 have developed most elements of government support of PPP but at a limited or moderate scale compared with the countries in cluster 1; they are considered moderate supporters of PPPs. The five countries included in this cluster are Italy, Switzerland, Czech Republic, Slovak Republic and Denmark. Political support in most of these countries is low, only in Italy has political support for PPP been relatively high and increasing. In most countries a PPP strategy document has been published early, but it has not been updated, and most countries do not issue PPP programmes with planned projects. Almost all countries have a procurement law that is in line with the EU procurement directives; only Denmark has no national procurement law and implements the EU procurement directives directly (Petersen 2013). In Italy, public procurement is regulated by the Code, which implemented EU Directives 2004/17 and 2004/18 (CMS Legal Service EEIG 2010). In the Czech Republic all PPP would be procured according to general law after the update of the national public procurement law in 2012. PPP units in most countries are developed only to a limited degree, the same holds for the definition of procedures for project appraisal, project prioritisation and the role of main sectors in PPP projects stages.

Finally, cluster 4 consists of eight countries (Austria, Estonia, Sweden, Finland, Serbia, Slovenia, Cyprus and Hungary), which are the least articulated providers of government support for PPPs. Political commitment to PPP tends to be rather limited in general and, except Hungary, no country in this cluster has developed a clear PPP programme. On the legal side all countries focus on national procurement law; only Slovenia has drafted a general PPP law. All laws are in line with the EU procurement directives. In most countries a PPP unit either does not exist or had existed only for a very short period like in Austria (Scherrer 2013), or such a unit is only developed to a rather limited degree (Serbia is an exception here). In most countries procedures for project appraisal, project prioritisation and a definition of the role of main sectors in project stages of PPP projects do not exist. There is no standardisation of processes or documents for PPPs in transport in any of these countries.

How does, finally, the pattern of country clustering compare with the country ranking obtained through the PPP-GSI method? Figure 2.2 compares the 20 countries according to their scores and rank in terms of PPP-GSI on the one hand and the country clusters resulting from the cluster analysis on the other hand. The results of the PPP-GSI are largely confirmed by the cluster analysis as

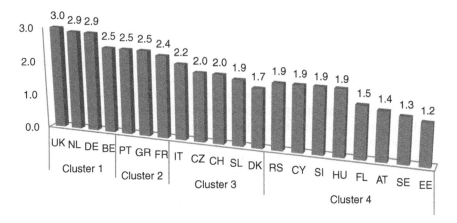

Figure 2.2 Comparison of country groupings: PPP-GSI *vs.* cluster analysis.

the composition of the clusters follows (with one exception) the ranking of the PPP-GSI. Cluster 1 resulting from the cluster analysis (the strong supporters of PPP on all three dimensions) includes the three countries with the highest PPP-GSI. Cluster 1 also includes one country that scores markedly lower (Belgium) on the PPP-GSI and which has a similar PPP-GSI score as two other countries included in cluster 2 (strong legal and regulatory supporters). Cluster 3 (moderate supporters of PPP) continues to follow the rank order of PPP-GSI scores with the exception of Denmark. Again with this exception, cluster 4 (the least articulated providers of government support for PPP) is congruent with the group of countries with the lowest PPP-GSI scores.

In conclusion, the clustering of countries by cluster analysis suggests that the PPP-GSI's methodological properties have no major distorting effect on the resulting ranking of scorings. The cluster analysis showed, however, that grouping countries along predefined threshold values of the PPP-GSI might lead to what are, indeed, somewhat arbitrary results. Finally, it is obvious that an index that comprises several different dimensions and calculating index scores based on averages may entail rankings that have countries that are characterised by dissimilarities along one or more dimensions ranked as neighbours, and this cannot be ruled out in the case of PPP-GSI. This topic will be analysed in the next section.

Digging deeper: Differences and similarities between countries in PPP policies, regulations and supporting arrangements

The analysis of the PPP-GSI and its sub-indexes showed that in no country in this sample is government support for PPP high on all three dimensions (see Table 2.3). In this section therefore we group the 20 countries according to their degree of governmental support for PPPs for each of the three dimensions separately. Within each dimension we group countries into four clusters using cluster analysis again (see Table 2.4).

On the dimension 'PPP policy and political commitment', the first cluster consisting of three countries (the Netherlands, the United Kingdom and Germany) form the group of 'strong policy and political supporters'. In all three countries a PPP strategy document was published early, and in two countries it has been updated. All three countries have a PPP programme with a clear pipeline and time schedule and, again, in two countries the programmes have been updated. Political support is rather strong in all three countries, in two of them political support tends to increase or is stable while in one country it tends to decrease.

The second cluster consisting of three countries, again, (Belgium–Flanders, Portugal and Italy) is characterised by strong and increasing political support ('strong political supporters'). In this group only one country has a clear PPP strategy document (but not updated) and only one country has a PPP programme (although without a clear pipeline and time schedule).

In the third cluster ('strategy developers providing modest political support'), which comprises four countries (Switzerland, Czech Republic, Denmark and Slovakia), a PPP strategy document has been published early; in one country it was updated. Two countries have a PPP programme but no clear pipeline and

Table 2.4 Country clusters along the dimensions of government support for PPP

Dimensions of government support for PPP		
Policy and political commitment	*Legal and regulatory framework*	*PPP supporting arrangements*
Cluster 1: '*Strong policy and political supporters*' 3 countries: NL, UK, DE	Cluster 1: '*Providers of comprehensive legal and regulatory support*' 3 countries: FR, GR, PT	Cluster 1: '*Providers of comprehensive PPP supporting arrangements*' 5 countries: FR, BE, NL, DE, UK
Cluster 2: '*Strong political supporters*' 3 countries: BE, PT, IT	Cluster 2: '*Providers of an intermediate level of legal and regulatory support*' 3 countries BE, RS, SI	Cluster 2: '*Strong providers of PPP supporting arrangements*' 1 country: PT
Cluster 3: '*Strategy developers providing modest political support*' 4 countries: CH, CZ, DK, SL	Cluster 3: '*Providers of legal and regulatory support with a clear focus on national procurement law*' 12 countries: DE, HU, AT, FL, SL, SE, UK, NL, IT, CY, CZ, CH	Cluster 3: '*Intermediate level providers of PPP supporting arrangements*' 10 countries: CH, CZ, DK, GR, IT, RS, SI, CY, SL, HU
Cluster 4: '*Modest policy and political supporters*' 10 countries: AT, EE, FR, GR, RS, SI, SE, CY, FL, HU	Cluster 4: '*Providers of limited legal and regulatory support*' 2 countries: DK, EE	Cluster 4: '*Providers of no or limited PPP supporting arrangements*' 4 countries: AT, EE, FL, SE

time schedule, while two countries have no PPP programme at all. Political support of PPP in general is low within this group; in two countries political support tends to increase.

The fourth cluster includes ten countries: Austria, Estonia, France, Greece, Serbia, Slovenia, Sweden, Cyprus, Finland and Hungary. It is the largest one and contains the 'modest policy and political supporters'. None of these countries has a clear PPP strategy document, and the majority of countries have no PPP programme. Political support in general is rather limited, in the majority of countries political support is stable at this level or even further decreasing.

On the dimension 'Legal and regulatory framework', three countries (France, Greece and Portugal) form the first cluster of 'providers of comprehensive legal and regulatory support'. In this group countries have published general PPP laws with a clear scope and boundaries.

A second cluster consists of three countries (Belgium, Serbia and Slovenia), which may be considered 'providers of an intermediate level of legal and regulatory support'. Two countries have general PPP laws, which are moderately developed in scope and boundaries. In two countries the general legal framework provides regulations that are specific for PPPs. The 12 countries in the third cluster (the United Kingdom, Germany, the Netherlands, Hungary, Austria, Finland, Slovak Republic, Sweden, Italy, Cyprus, Switzerland and Czech Republic) are 'providers of legal and regulatory support with a clear focus on national procurement law'. There is no PPP law and no PPP-specific regulations in general law but the procurement law is considered sufficient in providing a legal frame for PPPs.

The fourth cluster which includes two countries (Denmark and Estonia) can be characterised as 'providers of limited legal and regulatory support'. One of these countries applies European Union law directly as there exists no national public procurement law.

On the dimension 'PPP supporting arrangements', five countries (France, Belgium–Flanders, the Netherlands, Germany and the United Kingdom) form the first cluster of 'providers of comprehensive PPP supporting arrangements'. All countries have (at least) one dedicated PPP unit; in one country the unit can be considered as being highly developed. Three countries have moderately developed procedures for project appraisal, for prioritisation of projects and for the roles of main actors in project stages; in two countries these procedures are not quite as highly developed. All countries have developed standardised processes and documents for use in the PPP procurement process; in four countries the degree of standardisation can be considered high.

The second country cluster is formed by only one country (Portugal), which is considered a 'strong provider of PPP supporting arrangements'. Portugal has a moderately developed PPP unit and highly developed procedures for project appraisal, project prioritisation and the roles of main actors in project stages, but there are no standardised processes and documents.

The third cluster consists of 10 countries (Switzerland, Czech Republic, Denmark, Greece, Italy, Serbia, Slovenia, Cyprus, Slovak Republic and Hungary) in which PPP supporting arrangements are less well developed ('intermediate level providers of PPP supporting arrangements'). All countries in this cluster have a PPP unit and developed procedures for project appraisal and project prioritisation. In the majority of countries these units and procedures are less well developed than in the first and second country groups. No country has standardised processes and documents for procuring PPP projects.

Finally, the fourth cluster includes four countries (Austria, Estonia, Finland and Sweden) which are 'providers of no or limited PPP supporting arrangements'. These countries neither have a dedicated PPP unit (one country briefly had such a unit but abandoned it) nor have standardised processes and documents for procuring PPP projects. Only one country has developed clear procedures for project appraisal and prioritisation.

Conclusion: Relevance of clustering, limitations and future research

The starting point of the chapter was the observation that PPP are enjoying an upsurge of global interest and are often considered a converging policy phenomenon both in academic publications and practitioner reports. Yet our analysis reveals significant and enduring divergences in governmental PPP policies, regulations and institutional support mechanisms across countries. The chapter compares governmental PPP support activities across a sample of 20 European countries and, thus, provides a firm foundation for comparing and evaluating convergence and divergence in governmental PPP support across countries from all parts of Europe with different levels of PPP activity. Based on previous work (Verhoest *et al.* 2015) and a review of comparative PPP literature, we focus on policy, regulation and support organisations as indicators of governmental PPP support. We conduct cluster analysis with the aim of examining similarities and differences between countries and grouping countries with (more or less) similar governmental PPP support profile.

The 20 countries are grouped into four clusters. Cluster 1 includes the UK, Netherlands, Germany and Belgium–Flanders, which are countries with well-developed policies, political commitment and supporting arrangements. Countries in cluster 2, encompassing Greece, Portugal and France are strong legal and regulatory supporters of PPPs as their government support emphasises the articulation of an appropriate legal and regulatory framework. Countries in cluster 3, encompassing the Czech Republic, Denmark, Slovakia, Switzerland and Italy, have developed most elements of government support of PPPs but at a more limited or moderate scale; they are considered moderate supporters of PPPs. Lastly, cluster 4 consists of eight countries (Austria, Estonia, Sweden, Finland, Serbia, Slovenia, Cyprus and Hungary), which are the least articulated providers of government support for PPPs.

Comparing the four clusters along three different dimensions reveals considerable variation. Only the United Kingdom, the Netherlands and Germany are always positioned in the same cluster with regard to all dimensions, as they deliver strong policy and political commitment, provide comprehensive PPP supporting arrangements, and provide regulatory support with a clear focus on national procurement law. The rest of the countries shift clusters in terms of policies, regulations and arrangements for PPP. We are thus witnessing divergence in practice despite the convergence in rhetoric. This means that we are witnessing convergence in the global PPP policy rhetoric but widespread and enduring divergence in the actual policies, regulations and supporting arrangements enacted by governments to support (or hinder) the uptake of PPPs across countries.

Our study is subject to limitations, however. First, our concept of government support for PPPs deliberately comprises exclusively elements that can be influenced by government more or less directly. In addition to government support for PPP, other elements also contribute to PPP market maturity like macroeconomic variables and the investment climate. Moreover, we cannot take account of political actors who may adopt reforms to legitimise themselves, but 'decouple' these reforms from their actual decision-making behaviour (Meyer and Rowan 1977; DiMaggio and Powell 1983). Second, most of our (sub-) indicators are of a static nature while, ideally, government support should be measured in a dynamic way in order to observe the change of policies and political commitment, regulations and PPP supporting arrangements over time more precisely.

Further comparative PPP research could explore the possible link between the macro-economic and fiscal conditions in a country and its governmental PPP support based on the results of the PPP-GSI and the clusters analysis. This, in turn, could be linked to PPP activity in the respective countries. PPP research should also pay attention to and explore the possible link between less formal institutional aspects such as administrative culture and PPP activity. A widened research agenda on governance of PPPs would also benefit from investigating the multi-level governance aspect of PPPs more closely. This could include studies on the link and possible interdependencies between institutionalised PPP support at supra-national and national levels of government. Future comparative PPP research should address these and related issues.

Notes

1 In Belgium only limited PPP activity takes place outside Flanders. Flanders exports its expertise and regulatory frameworks to the federal level and other regions, which is different from other federal countries like Germany and Austria, where national government still takes the lead. Data for Flanders will be used as a proxy for Belgium because most mobility policies are exclusive competences of the regional governments and autonomy and financial independence of regional governments is particularly strong.

2 In this case, Spearman correlation is applied because it does not generally require normality.

3 This variables included: PPP strategic documents (Pol_1), PPP programme (Pol_2) and Political support (Pol_3).

4 Variable legal and regulatory framework embraces: existing PPP Laws (Legal_1), Scope PPP Laws (Legal_2) and Element PPP Laws (Legal_3).

5 This covers: Acting PPP Units (Arr_1), Procedures of project appraisal (Arr_2) and Standardized processes and documents (Arr_3).

References

Abonyi, J. and Feil, B. (2007) *Cluster Analysis for Data Mining and System Identification.* Basel: Birkhauser Verlag AG Basel

Aldenderfer, M. S. and Blashfield, R. K., (1984) *Cluster Analysis: Series Quantitative Application in Social Sciences.* Iowa: Sage Publications Inc.

Blashfield, R. K. (1976) 'Mixture model tests of cluster analysis. Accuracy of four agglomerative hierarchical methods'. *Psychological Bulletin*, 83, pp. 377–385

Bovis C. (2013) *Public Private Partnerships.* Oxon: Routledge (pp. 467)

CMS Legal Service EEIG (2010) *PPP in Europe.* Frankfurt: CMS

Cunningham, K. M. and Ogilvie, L. C. (1972) 'Evaluation of hierarchical grouping techniques: a preliminary study'. *Computer Journal*, 15, pp. 209–213

Dehli, V. S. K., Palukuri, S., and Mahalingam, A. (2010) *Governance Issues in Public Private Partnerships in Infrastructure Projects in India.* Paper presented at the Engineering Project Organizations Conference, South Lake Tahoe, CA

Deloitte (2007). *Closing America's Infrastructure Gap: The Role of Public Private Partnership.* A Deloitte Research Study

DiMaggio, P. J. and Powell, W. W. (1983) 'The iron cage revisited: institutional isomorphism & collective rationality in organizational fields'. *American Sociological Review*, 48, pp. 147–160

EPEC – European PPP Expertise Centre (2011) *The Guide to Guidance: How to Prepare, Procure and Deliver PPP Projects.* Luxembourg: European PPP Expertise Centre

EPEC – European PPP Expertise Centre (2012) *France-PPP Units and Related Institutional Framework.* Luxembourg: European Investment Bank

EPEC – European PPP Expertise Centre (2014) *Portugal-PPP Units and Related Institutional Framework.* Luxembourg: European Investment Bank

European Bank for Reconstruction and Development – EBRD (2012) *Concession/PPP Laws Assessment 2011.* London: EBRD

European Investment Bank – EIB (2011) *Study on PPP Legal and Financial Frameworks in the Mediterranean Partner Countries. Volume 3: Best Practices and Lessons Learned: Selected Experiences from Other Countries.* Luxembourg: EIB

Everitt, B. S., Landau, S., Leese, M. and Stahl, D. (2011) *Cluster Analysis* (5th Ed.). Chichester, UK: John Wiley and Sons

Florek, K., Lukaszewiez, L., Perkal, L., Steinhaus, H. and Zortchi, S. (1951) '*Sur la liaison et la division des points d'un ensemble fini*'. *Colloquium Mathematicum*, 2, pp. 282–285

Galilea, P. and Medda, F. (2010) 'Does the political and economic context influence the success of a transport project? An analysis of transport Public-Private Partnerships'. *Research in Transportation Economics*, 30, pp. 102–109

Grimsey, D. and Lewis, M. K. (2002) 'Evaluating the risks of Public Private Partnerships for infrastructure projects'. *International Journal of Project Management*, 20(2), pp. 107–118

Gordon, A. D. (1998) 'Cluster validation' in C. Hayashi, N. Ohsumi, K. Yajima, Y. Tanaka, H. H. Bock and Y. Baba (Eds) *Data Science, Classification and Related Methods* (pp. 22–39). Tokyo: Springer-Verlag

Hammerschmid, G. and Angerer, D. J. (2005) 'Public-Private Partnership between euphoria and disillusionment. Recent experiences from Austria and implications for countries in transformation'. *The Romanian Journal of Political Sciences*, 01, pp. 129–159

Hodge, G. A. and Greve, C. (2007) 'Public–Private Partnerships: an international performance review'. *Public Administration Review*, 67(3), pp. 545–558

Hubert, L. (1974) 'Approximate evaluation techniques for the single-link and complete-link hierarchical clustering procedures'. *Journal of the American Statistical Association*, 69, pp. 698–704

Jain, A. K., Murty, M. N. and Flynn, P. J. (1999) 'Data clustering: a review'. *ACM Computing Surveys* Vol. 31 No. 3, pp. 264–323

Johnson, S. C. (1967) 'Hierarchical clustering schemes'. *Psichometrika*, 32, pp. 241–254

Johnston, J. and Gudergan, S. (2007) 'Governance of Public-Private Partnership: lessons learnt from an Australian case?' *Journal Review of Administrative Sciences*, 73, 4, pp. 569–582

Jooste, S. F., Levitt, R. and Scott, D. (2011) 'Beyond "one size fits all": how local conditions shape PPP-enabling field development'. *The Engineering Project Organization Journal*, *1*(1), pp. 11–25

Klijn, E. H. (2009) 'Public Private Partnerships in The Netherlands: policy, projects and lessons'. *Economic Affairs*, March 2009, pp. 26–32

Klijn, E. H. and Teisman, G. R. (2003) 'Institutional and strategic barriers to Public—Private Partnership: An analysis of Dutch cases'. *Public Money and Management*, *23*(3), pp. 137–146

Mahalingam, A., Devkar, G. A. and Kalidindi, S. N. (2011) 'A comparative analysis of Public-Private Partnership (PPP) coordination agencies in India: what works and what doesn't'. *Public Works Management and Policy*, 16(4), pp. 341–372

Matos-Castaño, J., Mahalingam, A. and Dewulf, G. (2014) 'Unpacking the path-dependent process of institutional change for PPP'. *Australian Journal of Public Administration*, 73(1), pp. 47–66

Meunier, D. and Quinet, E. (2010) 'Tips and pitfalls in PPP design'. *Research in Transportation Economics*, 30, pp. 126–138

Meyer, J. W. and Rowan, B. (1977) 'Institutionalized organizations: formal structure as myth and ceremony'. *American Journal of Sociology*, 83(2), pp. 340–363

Mörth, U. (2007) 'Public and Private Partnerships as dilemmas between efficiency and democratic accountability: the case of Galileo'. *Journal of European Integration*, 29(5), pp. 601–617

Mu, R., de Jong, M. and Heuvelhof, E. T. (2010) 'Public-Private Partnerships for expressways in China: an agency theory approach'. *European Journal of Transport and Infrastructure Research*, 10(1), pp. 42–62

OECD – Organisation for Economic Co-operation and Development (2008) *Public-Private Partnerships: In Pursuit of Risk Sharing and Value for Money*. Paris: Organisation for Economic Co-operation and Development

OECD – Organisation for Economic Co-operation and Development (2010) *Dedicated Public Private Partnership Unit: A Survey of Institutional and Governance Structures*. Paris: Organisation for Economic Co-operation and Development

Osborne, S. P. (Ed.) (2010) *The New Public Governance? Emerging Perspectives on the Theory and Practice of Public Governance*. Abingdon, UK: Routledge

Painter, M. and Peters, B. G. (2010) *Tradition and public administration*. Basingstoke: Palgrave Macmillan

Petersen, O. H. (2010) 'Emerging meta-governance as a regulation framework for Public-Private Partnerships: an examination of the European Union's approach'. *International Public Management Review*, *11*(3), pp. 1–23

Petersen, O. H. (2011) 'Public-Private Partnerships as converging or diverging trends in public management? A comparative analysis of PPP policy and regulation in Denmark and Ireland'. *International Public Management Review*, *12*(2), pp. 1–37

Petersen, O. H. (2013) 'Denmark' in K. Verhoest, N. Carbonara, V. Lember, O. H. Petersen, W. Scherrer and M. van den Hurk (Eds) *COST Action TU1001 Public Private Partnerships in Transport: Trends and Theory P3T3, 2013 Discussion Papers Part I Country Profiles*. ISBN: 978-88-97781-60-8, COST Office, Brussels. Available at www.ppptransport.eu

PPP Forum (2014) Retrieved 28 November 2014 from pppforum.com

Roumboutsos, A., Farrell, S., Liyanage, C. L. and Macário, R. (2013) *COST Action TU1001 Public Private Partnerships in Transport: Trends and Theory P3T3, 2013 Discussion Papers Part II Case Studies*, ISBN 978-88-97781-61-5. Available at www. ppptransport.eu

Scherrer, W. (2013) 'Austria' in K. Verhoest, N. Carbonara, V. Lember, O. H. Petersen, W. Scherrer and M. van den Hurk (Eds) *COST Action TU1001 Public Private Partnerships in Transport: Trends and Theory P3T3, 2013 Discussion Papers Part I Country Profiles*. ISBN: 978-88-97781-60-8, COST Office, Brussels. Available at www.ppptransport.eu

Sneath, P. H. A. (1957) 'The application of computers to taxonomy'. *Journal of General Microbiology*, 17, pp. 201–226

Sokal, R. R. and Michener, C. D. (1958) 'A statistical method for evaluating systematic relationships'. *University of Kansas Scientific Bulletin* 38: pp. 1409–1438

The *Economist* (2011) *Evaluating the Environment for Public Private Partnerships in Asia-Pacific. The 2011 Infrascope: Findings and Methodology*. Economist Intelligence Units-ADB

UNESCAP (2005). *PPP Readiness Self-Assessment*. Transport and Tourism Division: UNESCAP

van den Hurk, M., Brogaard, L., Lember, V., Petersen, O. H. and Witz, P. (forthcoming 2015). National varieties of Public-Private Partnerships (PPP): A comparative policy analysis of PPP-supporting units in 19 European countries. *Journal of Comparative Policy Analysis*.

van den Hurk, M. and Verhoest, K. (2013) 'Flanders, Belgium' in K. Verhoest, N. Carbonara, V. Lember, O. H. Petersen, W. Scherrer and M. van den Hurk (Eds) *COST Action TU1001 Public Private Partnerships in Transport: Trends and Theory P3T3, 2013 Discussion Papers Part I Country Profiles*. ISBN: 978-88-97781-60-8, COST Office, Brussels. Available at www.ppptransport.eu

Verhoest, K., Carbonara, N., Lember, V., Petersen, O. H., Scherrer, W. and van den Hurk, M. (Eds) (2013a) *COST Action TU1001 Public Private Partnerships in Transport: Trends and Theory P3T3, 2013 Discussion Papers Part I Country Profiles*. ISBN: 978-88-97781-60-8, COST Office, Brussels. Available at www.ppptransport.eu

Verhoest, K., Petersen, O. H., Scherrer, W., Akintoye, A. and Soecipto, R. M. (2013b) *Indexing and Comparing the PPP-enhancing Institutional Framework across Countries*. Paper presented at the International Conference 'Global Challenges in PPP: cross-sectoral, and cross-disciplinary solutions?' University of Antwerp, 6-7 November 2013

Verhoest, K., Petersen, O. H., Scherrer, W. and Soecipto, R. M. (2015) 'How do governments support the development of Public Private Partnerships? Measuring and comparing PPP governmental support in 20 European countries'. *Transport Reviews*, 35(2), 118–139

Vining, A. R. and Boardman, A. E. (2008) 'Public-Private Partnership: Eight Rules for Governments'. *Public Works Management and Policy* Vol. 13, No. 2, pp. 149–161

Ward, J. H. (1963) 'Hierarchical groupings to optimize an objective function'. *Journal of the American Statistical Association*, 58, pp. 236–244

Wettenhall, R. (2003) 'The rhetoric and reality of Public-Private Partnership'. *Public Organization Review*, 3, pp. 77–107

World Bank and Public Private Infrastructure Advisory Facility (2006) *Public-Private Partnership Units: Lessons for their Design and Use in Infrastructure*. Washington, DC: World Bank and PPIAF

Annex

Table 2.A.1 Comparison of the results of six different clustering methods

Clusters	Clustering Methods					
	Nearest	*Furthest*	*Average*	*Centroid*	*Median*	*Ward's*
1	15 countries	8 countries	10 countries	13 countries	13 countries	6 countries
	AT, CH, CZ, DK, EE, FR, GR, IT, RS, SI, SE, CY, FL, SL, HU	AT, EE, RS, SI, SE, CY, FL, HU	AT, CH, CZ, DK, EE, SE, CY, FL, SL, HU	AT, CH, CZ, DK, EE, IT, RS, SI, SE, CY, FL, SL, HU	AT, CH, CZ, DK, EE, IT, RS, SI, SE, CY, FL, SL, HU	AT, EE, SE, CY, FL, HU
2	1 country	4 countries	4 countries	4 countries	4 countries	4 countries
	BE	BE, NL, UK, DE	BE, NL, UK, DE	BE, NL, UK, DE	BE, NL, UK, DE	BE, NL, UK, DE
3	3 countries	5 countries	5 countries	2 countries	2 countries	4 countries
	NL, UK, DE	CH, CZ, DK, IT, SL	FR, GR, PT, RS, SI	FR, PT	FR, PT	CH, CZ, DK, SL
4	1 country	3 countries	1 country	1 country	1 country	6 countries
	PT	FR, GR, PT	IT	GR	GR	FR, GR, PT, IT, RS, SI

Rescaled Distance Cluster Combine

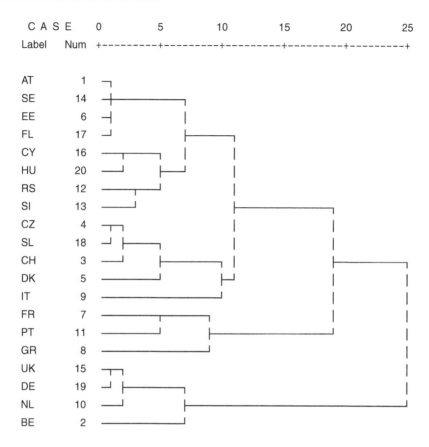

Figure 2.A.1 Dendrogram hierarchical clustering PPP-GSI.

3 Finding an institutional evolutionary maturity concept

An exploratory analysis for European experience in PPPs

*Matheus Oliveira, Joana Costa,
Joana Ribeiro and Rosário Macário*

Introduction

Public Private Partnerships (PPPs) have been broadly used in the past two decades to deliver infrastructure and services around the world. PPPs are arrangements between public institutions and private companies where authority, responsibility and risk are shared among partners in the delivery of an infrastructure or service, usually for a lengthy period of time, with a financing structure normally assured at least in part by the private sector (European Commission 2004: 3).

Governments have adopted PPPs in order to expand their investment capacity by diversifying resources, joining initiatives and delegating risks and responsibilities. By this principle, all PPPs projects have been designed with a view to producing more value for money than through traditionally procuring projects. Additional value for money is generated by the private sector's ability and incentive to innovate, from considering life-cycle costs, and adequately sharing risk, while specifying outputs and performance, and providing appropriate incentives (Grimsey and Lewis 2005: 347; Roumboutsos and Saussier 2014).

Different countries operate within different contexts when they start to use PPPs, and they also approach PPPs in different ways. Some countries create policies, regulations and institutional structures to support and encourage the use of PPPs in several sectors. It is expected that, as more and more PPPs are implemented, these structures will become more refined and better adjusted to the purpose of creating a PPP-supporting environment. What is the institutional environment like for implementing PPPs in European countries? How can we define the relevant features of this environment? How sophisticated and refined is the institutional context that supports PPP implementation? Also, in which ways are European countries similar and dissimilar in this respect?

Regarding these questions, the purpose of this research is to develop an evolutionary concept of institutional maturity for the implementation of PPPs, and apply it to a sample of European countries, grouping them according to their position in the evolutionary model.

The present chapter reports the results of an exploratory stage of this research, obtained using multiple correspondence analysis on 17 European countries, members of the COST action TU1001 – Public Private Partnerships in Transport: Trends and Theory (P3T3). It is composed of this introduction, followed by a literature review section that attempts to justify the evolutionary maturity concept by reviewing available literature on innovation and maturity on one hand, and PPP institutional context factors on the other. The third section describes the methodology, including case selection, variable definition and data collection. The fourth section presents results in terms of factors, variables and cases, and an attempt at grouping cases and variables into groups is made. The final section draws conclusions, reflects on limitations and suggests future research.

Literature review

Finding a maturity concept

According to the principles described in institutional theory (Williamson 2000), the performance of every economic environment is determined by its institutions. A broad definition of these institutions comprises policy centres, governments, legal frameworks and any other elements responsible for guiding the relationships between stakeholders. Under this assumption, the development theory proposed by the institutional school depends on the reproduction of the capability required by the sector, in this case PPPs. This deficiency is caused by the dynamics of the institutional framework and demands the outline of a different approach. In other words, the development of a maturity-oriented roadmap is based on an approach that respects the natural evolutionary property of the institutional system. According to Nelson and Winter (1982), this misconception exists because the inherent temporal property of every economic system hinders the researcher's observation of future technologies, processes and institutions. Considering this request, the comparison between objects in an evolutionary scenario must create a performance scale among them, which can point to the elements responsible for that performance, but also takes into account the fact that this scenario does not evolve in a closed system and therefore can be shifted by other elements that are not always apparent.

To overcome this methodological restriction, Nelson and Winter (1982) propose the analysis of the evolutionary scenario according to two dynamic components: copy and innovation. These components are derived from Schumpeter's development theory. According to Schumpeter (1934), economic development is a consequence of the innovative profits generated by the exclusive production knowledge about a certain good. Thus, based on market laws, these profits are negatively correlated to knowledge transmission. This scenario creates two trends in economic development: innovation and knowledge appropriation. Both elements contain principles for the proposed analysis about the maturity concept. In short, according to Nelson and Winter (1982), the innovation principle addresses the clarification of the structural tendencies of the sector, whereas the knowledge appropriation principle is associated with the dissemination of best practices by copy.

In the appropriation of evolutionary principles according to institutional economy, the orientation of economic development initiatives must be towards two goals: institutional innovation and institutional routine replication. Each one is associated with different movements in the comparative scenario construction. Innovation is associated with structural tendencies of the institutional scenario. This element represents the validation of the comparison by referencing a situational success case, or the pioneer (Schumpeter 1934). Put differently, the innovative component determines that the case with better institutions is the best performer in the current scenario. Nevertheless, it is important to keep in mind that these elements are also responsible for guaranteeing the evolutionary property in terms of the structure of the performance scales.

Within the current scenario, the institutional routine replication is the base for the construction of an institutional performance scale. According to Schumpeter's (1934) theory, other countries tend to copy the pioneer's routines in order to reduce the technological dependence. In the institutional scenario, this copying process aims to produce the same output as the pioneer in a certain sector. It means that, once the reference of success in the comparative scenario is defined, the institutional maturity scale among the countries is defined by the number of institutions of the success case that each country has replicated in its own institutional scenario. It is thus a transferability process associated with a learning curve.

This chapter assumes that the institutional framework relating to PPPs can be understood as an evolutionary framework. Historically developed by the introduction of new tools to the traditional procurement system, the PPP sector internalises the property of the innovative effect by being born out of a paradigm shift in the concession framework. Moreover, the conception of the dynamic between the necessary tasks required within the PPP framework and the way they are developed in each country requires a methodology capable of providing situational robustness and temporal perspective to the model.

The methodological path to this maturity scale design being thus reasoned out, the chosen method now requires an extensive literature review about the composition of the institutional design necessary for the best implementation of the PPP policy. This research was conducted as a literature review analysing published papers on PPP critical success factors as well as the discussion papers of institutional guidelines specifically related to PPP context. It is described in the following section.

Institutional setting

Any conceptual approach oriented towards the representation of institutional scenarios is destined to examine an extremely complex object. Its dimension, dynamic and essence will never be reduced to a limited conceptual model. The institutional research on PPPs is no exception to that rule. In this way, even the most comprehensive representation of the endless elements, routines, variables and dimensions of this framework cannot help but be a limited description of the greater environment. In this case, the present research contributes to other efforts already made in this area towards defining more clearly the most favourable PPPs environment. The stepping stones to achieving these objectives are the delimitation of the scope of the project and the selection of the analytical variables. Verhoest *et al.* (2013: xvii), based on Pollit and Bouckaert (2004) and Verhoest *et al.* (2010), describe four institutional levels influencing the development of PPPs: (1) the supra-national level; (2) the country level macro-institutional variables; (3) the policy, regulation and supporting institutions; and (4) the project level variables. This research focuses on the third level, which relates to the State's motivations for PPP, public, political and administrative support for the PPP policy, strategy documents, procurement regulation, PPP and transport regulation, PPP support and expertise, standardisation of models and procedures, and supportive policy instruments.

Concerning this level, authors and practitioners mostly consider it as a role to be played by the government. According to this research objective, the responsibility of setting up and sustaining the institutional framework that serves as a supporting environment for the successful implementation of PPPs must be mainly pursued by the public body (see, for example, Kwak *et al.* 2009: 57 and Economic Consultants Associates 2010).

However, specific research about how the institutional setting determines PPP success is limited and not conclusive. The main bulk of reported research examines critical success factors for PPP so as to understand these routines. In general, it proposes lists of success factors through literature review, case studies and interviews, drawing lessons learned from about two decades of experience of use of this model of project delivery. Several authors include institutional context aspects as critical success factors for PPP (Aziz 2007; Koch and Buser 2007; Kumaraswamy and Zhang 2001 and Pongsin 2002, cited by Kwak *et al.* 2009: 60), which can be grouped into four areas, namely legal and policy framework, capacity building, procurement and finance:

- legal and policy framework: to establish a broad and comprehensive PPP legal framework, well-defined but not overregulated; to provide a stable political environment;
- capacity building: to create a central PPP unit for policy development and/ or implementation and monitoring and to provide counselling; to standardise procedures and contracts, and to develop guidelines and tools; to investigate potential sectors for PPP and run a set of pilot projects; to continuously assess project progress and performance;
- procurement: to conduct and/or subsidise feasibility studies; to assess value-for-money when selecting a delivery system; to ensure a fair and competitive procurement procedure, to maintain transparency in the selection process, and to select the most adequate service provider and contractual regime;
- finance: to provide adequate government assistance and guarantees; to develop the domestic capital market; to support the interest of the international capital market.

From a different perspective, a great part of the literature on the institutional contexts determining PPP success is practitioner-oriented. Several guidebooks published by governments and multilateral organisations draw on experience to provide guidance for the successful implementation of PPPs. They cover most of the levels of the analysis mentioned by Verhoest *et al.* (2013). However, the major focus is usually on project-specific aspects, such as how to carry out an appropriate allocation of risks (see, for example, EPEC 2011). Mainly presented in guidebooks, this approach includes recommendations on creating a favourable institutional setting (see, for example, ADB 2008; World Bank 2012; UN-ESCAP 2011; UNECE 2008) which mostly falls under the categories described in the research literature, with slight differences associated with diverse approaches (for example, the UNECE guidebook's approach is to provide governance principles and includes recommendations on environmental protection and public participation). In the end both streams run towards the same direction in which the most important research goal may be resumed in a deeper analysis of the four topics described earlier.

In the literature much attention has been paid to providing a clear definition of a PPP policy programme and a clear attribution of roles and responsibilities to the agencies to be involved in the PPP process, including those of oversight and financial management. Adequate and compatible legislation with regard to PPPs, be it procurement law, public financial management law, tax rules, or labour laws, is also a key subject for these guidebooks. Additional focus is given to the country's policy and regulation for the specific sectors where PPPs are to be considered, in the form of the examination of dedicated regulation on infrastructure or services, on technical specifications, as well as on whether tariffs can be charged and how. Capacity building is also very relevant in the available guidance. PPP units, central and regional, are seen as key organisational arrangements to support PPPs, with functions ranging from think tank to operational unit carrying out decision-making and contract monitoring. The use of hired consultants is discussed, as well as strategies to improve the capacity of the public sector through learning structures that may or may not be centred in the PPP unit.

Not only at the project level, but also at the institutional context level, procurement has to be examined/included in the analysis of the institutional scenario. Guidebooks present recommendations based on transparency, neutrality and non-discriminating selection of bidders, and the majority indicate several-step procedures with negotiation and competitive negotiation. In parallel with empirical research (see, for example, Grimsey and Lewis 2005), guidebooks mention assessing the value for money of a proposed PPP, usually through the use of a public sector comparator (PSC). The public sector comparator will compare the financial or economic cost to the government incurred by the project when delivered through PPP with the cost of delivering it through traditional procurement, focusing on costs and the pricing of infrastructure provision and on the way incentives can be formulated to stimulate expected behaviour from economic agents (Macário 2010).

The topic of finance is usually approached at the project level as finance strategies and best practices. However, there are also certain recommendations for governments at the policy level, some of which bear a particular emphasis on the development of control tools against financial exposure to PPPs. Another aspect of this field is the existence of a mature financial market, which turns out to be more supportive of the use of PPPs, and PPPs will also contribute to the development of a country's financial market (ADB 2008: 9). Regulatory transparency and stability are also mentioned as fundamental elements within the context of finance, to make PPPs more creditworthy or attractive to financial investors both domestic and global. Finally, the option of government financial involvement is mentioned, where the government is referred to as the provider of debt, equity, or guarantees, directly or through State financial institutions such as development banks and pension funds.

Eggers and Dovey (2007: 9) present a maturity framework for the implementation of PPP and place several countries in one of the three evolutionary stages defined with the help of institutional and organisational context factors. Approving legal and policy frameworks, starting a central PPP unit, and developing deal structures and a public sector comparator are typical of stage one countries. Stage two countries establish dedicated PPP units in agencies, develop hybrid delivery models, leverage new sources of funds from capital markets, use PPPs to drive service innovation, and demonstrate activity in several sectors. Countries in stage three are more creative in the application of PPPs, use sophisticated risk models, with greater focus on total project lifecycle, and their public sector has undergone changes to support the greater role of PPPs. The authors derived the existence of these stages from their consulting experience, according to which countries tend to go through those stages before their national PPP programmes become fully operational. According to their model, countries move up the maturity curve as they develop the required institutions, the capital markets, and the know-how and expertise that enables them to take on more sophisticated projects and financial arrangements (UNECE 2008: 9).

Methodology

In order to explore the concept of evolutionary stages in the application of PPPs the applied methodology covered three analytical steps. In the first, 10 institutional context variables were defined to characterise countries. Then, those variables were populated with data from selected sources. Finally, similarity and dissimilarity between them were analysed using multiple correspondence analysis (MCA).

The cases were chosen according to the availability criterion – those with country profiles available from the COST action TU1001 database (Verhoest *et al.* 2013) were selected, as this source of information had been treated to be coherent across countries and focused on institutional context. Because the authors are based in Portugal and are at the cutting edge of institutional and organisational developments, updates in the context variables for this country were included. The full list of countries analysed in this research comprises: Austria, Cyprus, Czech Republic, Denmark, Estonia, Finland, Belgium–Flanders, France, Greece, Italy, Portugal, Serbia, Slovakia, Sweden, Switzerland, The Netherlands and the United Kingdom (UK).

The variables were chosen in accordance with the results of the literature review that was carried out earlier in the research (see Table 3.1), which were grouped into four main categories (see Figure 3.1).

All variables were populated with data from the COST TU1001 database, namely country profiles (Verhoest *et al.* 2013 and Roumboutsos *et al.* 2014), and project case studies (Roumboutsos *et al.* 2013 and Roumboutsos *et al.* 2014). These sources present data in the form of narratives and in the form of nominal variables.

Nevertheless, the simple collection and comparison of textual information could only produce segmented qualitative data which, in turn, cannot be systematically compared with the MCA method. To solve this problem a three-stage coding was carried out over the sources to populate the variables with systematic data. First, a case-coding phase was applied in order to group the whole information presented in different sources and formats (i.e. country profiles and case studies) under country categories. After the first round of coding, a thematic coding assigned the qualitative information to the variables they referred to. In the third stage, the information in each variable group was assigned according to statement valence categories (see Table 3.2). Designed to be mutually exclusive, each valence scale has been created to connect the situations observed in the study of the source material with the literature review. They reflect growing degrees of sophistication in each variable of the institutional context. Initially, statement valences coding was designed according to nominal categories but, in order to facilitate the application of the MCA method further on, the nominal variables were then transformed into binary (0 or 1). In some cases this adjustment required the addition of auxiliary variables to avoid false exclusion problems between complementary variables (see Table 3.2).

In the following section, the role of supplementary variables in the validation of the MCA results is explained. In theory, these variables aim to test the MCA factors against an exogenous element. In order to perform this comparison task, five supplementary (one quantitative and four qualitative) variables were selected according to the results of the analysis, without influencing the algorithms. The total gross fixed capital formation from 2000 to 2010 (GFCF, data from the World Bank) was considered a proxy for testing the institutional framework against the general investment. Considering that the PPP institutional framework is associated with greater investments, this variable is expected to validate the good performance elements. The other four qualitative variables were also populated through coding of the source materials. In this case, statement valences all referred to the presence of creativity, and classified it according to areas: financial, operational, technological and tendering creativity. A binary version of these variables was also developed, supported by those categories. Regarding the theoretical framework, those variables were considered in the model in order to

Table 3.1 Variables

Variable code	Variable	Description
V01	PPP law	Indicates whether or not the country has approved specific PPP legislation in the form of a PPP framework law.
V02	Central PPP unit	Indicates whether or not the country has a central PPP unit and, if it does, if it is functioning as a think tank only, or carrying out operational responsibilities within the PPP pipeline.
V03	Specific PPP policy	Indicates whether or not the country has approved a PPP programme or any national strategy documents endorsing PPPs and defining a specific policy.
V04	Experience with PPPs	Indicates whether the country has been using PPPs since 2000, or earlier than this.
V05	*Ex-ante* value-for-money assessment	Indicates whether or not the country has mandatory *ex-ante* value-for-money assessment of PPP projects (such as the PSC tool) and, if it does, whether it is implemented in practice.
V06	Learning structure	Indicates whether or not the country's public sector has some sort of structure for learning and knowledge transfer and, if it does, whether it is a formal PPP knowledge centre or, rather, a generic public sector learning structure.
V07	Sectorial PPP unit	Indicates whether or not the country has PPP units specific to the sectors where PPPs are implemented.
V08	Cross-sector bundling	Indicates whether the cases described for each country include cross-sector or cross-mode bundling such as a PPP contract for operating trains bundled with managing a car park.
V09	Mature financial capital	Indicates whether the cases described for each country are financed through loans, private equity and/or public finance alone or, rather, they include other sources of finance such as bonds.
V10	PPPs in several sectors	Indicates whether the country has implemented PPPs in 4 or less sectors or, rather, in 5 or more sectors.

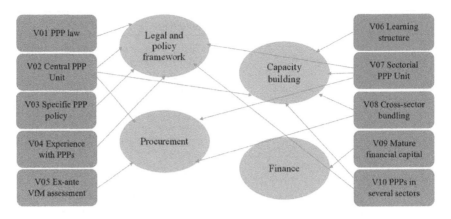

Figure 3.1 Variables and the main literature topics.

Table 3.2 Variables and classifications

Variable code	Variable	Possible classifications
V01	PPP law	0 – Non-existent 1 – Existent
V02	Central PPP unit	0 – Non-existent 1 – Existent
V02.1	Operational responsibilities	0 – Existent, in the form of a think tank only 1 – Existent, with operational responsibilities
V03	Specific PPP policy	0 – Non-existent 1 – Existent
V04	Experience with PPPs	0 – Not significant – using PPPs only after 2000 1 – Significant – using PPPs since earlier than 2005
V05	*Ex-ante* value-for-money assessment	0 – Non-existent 1 – Existent
V05.1	Implemented	0 – Existent, but not implemented 1 – Existent, and implemented
V06	Learning structure	0 – Non-existent 1 – Existent
V06.1	Formal	0 – Existent, as a generic learning reference only 1 – Existent, as a formal knowledge centre
V07	Sectorial PPP unit	0 – Non-existent 1 – Existent
V08	Cross-sector bundling	0 – Non-existent 1 – Existent
V09	Mature financial capital	0 – PPPs financed through loans, private equity or public finance only 1 – PPPs financed through loans, private equity, public finance, and other finance sources
V10	PPPs in several sectors	0 – PPPs in 4 or less than 4 sectors 1 – PPPs in more than 4 sectors

validate the association between creativity performance and technological development. The resulting database of cases x variables was the basis for a multiple correspondence analysis.

Analytical method: Multiple correspondence analysis

Mainly marked by qualitative data, analytical procedures for institutional interpretation usually require different techniques under statistical principles. As described in the second section, the analysis proposed in this chapter depends on the construction of an evolutionary framework based on the comparison between variables not easily convertible to quantitative data. For those cases, specific analytical techniques have been considered, in methodological terms, as more suitable to ensure robustness and accuracy in the model than the traditional linear models.

Nevertheless, along with the database composition, the methodological approach has to be identified as the most important component in the identification of the analytical technique. In the present case, the definition of a comparative framework based on the distribution of institutional characteristics among the cases of the sample requires the development of a relative scale among the variables based on their frequency and correlation. Thus, in order to fulfil both requirements and simultaneously present the results visually, this research was conducted according to a Multiple Correspondence Analysis (MCA) method.

Developed from the expansion of Correspondence Analysis (CA), MCA is a technique used to assess a comparative pattern and scale for several categorical dependent variables. Similar to the Factor Analysis method, the CA algorithm is based on the estimation of orthogonal components and, for each item in a table of cases x variables, a set of scores (Abdi and Valentin 2007). In MCA, the CA algorithm is applied to an individuals x variables indicator matrix by calculating the chi-square distance between different categories of the variables and between the individuals (or respondents). The components and scores are grouped in two orthogonal factors based on their covariance and weight. Subsequently, these associations are then represented graphically as 'maps', a method that facilitates the interpretation of the structures in the data (Roux and Rouanet 2004).

The output of the MCA process is mainly interpreted by the proximity between elements in the low-dimensional map. According to Abdi and Valentin (2007), in MCA, cases presented closely in the map tend to select the same level of nominal variables, whereas the proximity between levels of different nominal variables means that these levels tend to appear together in the observations. However, Abdi and Valentin (2007) recommend caution in the construction of proximity links between variables and observations. In some cases, assumptions constructed by this kind of analysis may be biased by the influence of other cases in the construction of the factors. These mistakes occur because all the characteristics have been translated to orthogonal components and different combinations of variables can compose the same nominal factor level.

This brief review of MCA justifies the selection of the method by the analysis/ examination of its characteristics that have been considered as suitable for the project. Qualitative data acceptability, graphical presentation and comparative capability can be numbered among the procedural requirements of the analysis but, finally, the exploratory capacity of the MCA has to be pointed out as the cornerstone of the connection between the method and the analysis.

Since the MCA method is almost exclusively supported by the relative distance among the observed data, it dismisses the fulfilment of greater statistical assumptions. The provision of those analytical degrees of freedom is important in the conduction of research marked by the exploratory component. More complex statistical tools seem to endanger our purpose since the statistical space of the institutional maturity scenario for the PPP framework is not outlined with statistical robustness. Under an exploratory approach, the avoidance of bigger statistical commitment is a choice that implies sacrificing deeper inference goals to achieve greater conceptual sharpness. This trade-off becomes evident in the next section of the chapter where the results are presented.

Results

This section presents the results of the proposed methodology. In the context of a three-level analysis the main findings about the factors, variables and cases are presented. The interpretations, which are mainly based on a graphical proximity procedure, also implement the contingency method to overcome the limitations described in the previous section.

Factors composition

The present approach begins with the analysis of the factor compositions. Assuming the same perspective of the factor analysis, the association between K variables is estimated by the chi-square distance between different categories of the variables and between the countries (rows x columns). From the estimated column and row matrices of scores, K factors were calculated and plotted respecting a baricenter. By the maximisation of the variance of the squared cosine between the score in the matrix row and the score in the matrix column in two factors, these scores are summarised in a two-dimensional factor analysis.

According to this principle, innumerous factors could be estimated with different explanatory loads of the variables. In this case, the principle of the selection of the two factors was guided by the cumulative explanatory capacity of the two dimensions. Figure 3.2 presents four factors estimated for this analysis.

F1 and F2 were selected with a combined explanatory power of 78.47 per cent of the variance of the variables scores. Moreover, Figure 3.2 highlights the model's dependency on F1. In some cases, a more balanced composition would be desirable. However, in MCA this composition may depend on the composition of the covariance between variables and with the non-observed institutional similarities among cases (i.e. historical roots). Due to those limitations, the analysed variables appear to be deeply distinguished in one dimension (F1) and only superficially in the second one (F2).

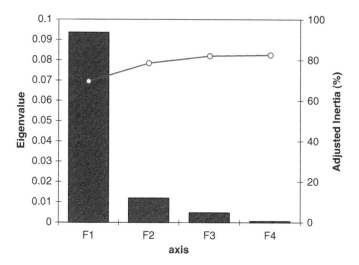

Figure 3.2 Eigenvalue and Adjusted Explanatory Capacity of the four most important factors.

The composition of Factor 1 assumes almost 89 per cent of the explanatory capacity of the model. The factor presents significant scores (at 5 per cent) for all variables except specific policy on PPP, cross-sector bundling, mature financial capital, *ex-ante* value-for-money assessment and the assessment implementation. Among those variables, specific policy on PPPs and *ex-ante* value-for-money assessment are significantly estimated by F2. Moreover, Factor 2 also explains the variance of the variables of the Central PPP unit with operational responsibility and the *ex-ante* value-for-money assessment.

Individually, the factors can hardly provide the dimensions of the big picture of this analysis. Nevertheless, at the present point, two general characteristics shall be highlighted. First, in F1 all variables stating presence of institutional characteristics are defined with negative values. This general trend supports a tendency of PPP institutional interest, more so if it is considered that some of them switch value signal in F2. Secondly, the orthogonality of the variables of mature financial capital and the Implemented *ex-ante* value-for-money assessment could be a clue for the institutional complexity differentiation.

Variables

MCA models are able to consider variables in two different ways: analytical and supplementary. The analytical variables are the ones directly considered in the development of the model by the construction of the factors. In the present case, the analytical institutional variables are described in Table 2.1. These variables are the only ones that are going to be actively considered in the classification of the framework and cases.

On the other hand, the supplementary variables are used as a passive tool for the validation of the model. In MCA, supplementary variables are removed from the estimation of the factors phase but plotted according to the estimated vectors. The supplementary data can be segmented in two groups according to the data format, qualitative or quantitative. In the present analysis, the group of creativity variables was introduced as the qualitative supplementary data, whereas the gross fixed capital formation (GFCF) investment mean within 2000-10 is a quantitative one. Assuming a positive correlation between total investment and PPP investment, the GFCF variable was introduced as a proxy for PPP investment. This simplification was forced by the absence of specific data about the investment in PPPs. As control variables, either the creativity or the GFCF are expected to be positively associated with PPP institutional variables.

In the case of the GFCF, the expected positive relation would indicate that PPP institutional development is associated with the expansion of the investment capacity of the countries. The creativity questions are associated with the innovative/pioneering characteristic of the institutional framework. Thus, the creativity questions are expected to appear connected with the variables and cases in the higher level of institutional maturity.

Back to the results, the analysis proceeds from what has been discussed about the factors' composition. Figure 3.3 presents the two-dimensional plot of the MCA results for the variables. Illustrating what is described in the factor composition analysis, all the presence variables are plotted on the left side of the graph. Besides the 'interest in PPP' dimension proposed in the previous section, the

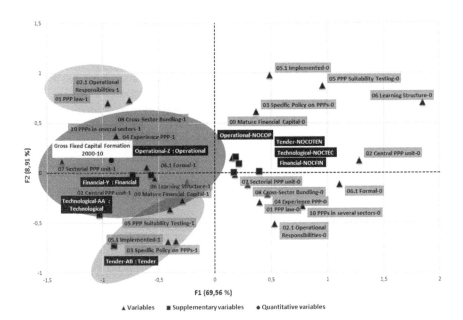

Figure 3.3 MCA variables plot.

approximation of the presence variables in the F1 axis supports the evolutionary hypothesis by the demonstration of cumulative tendency among the variables.

Nevertheless, not all the presence variables are close in the plot. The opposition of signals observed in part of the F1 coefficients in its correspondent coordinates in F2, which were understood as complexity variations according to the factor analysis, might be pointing to structural differences. In other words, the complexity at elemental variables would be originating incompatibility patterns or the development of parallel PPP institutional dynamics.

Following the methodology presented in the second section, the selection of the variables was meant to cover as widely as possible the institutional framework of PPP. By this principle, all the variables were conceived so as to be synchronised with a certain routine that should be developed by every country. According to this perspective, the general trend of the presented graph was expected to follow a linear path with minor deviations derived from institutional gaps in the countries or observation flaws. Those flaws principally occur due to limitations imposed by the coding routine for different variables, which may produce similar capabilities. For those cases, the same routine might be coded differently according to the chosen variable. This may be the case for PPP law, which was considered a basic variable in terms of a maturity concept. However, in mature countries like the Netherlands or the UK, the variable did not provide insight on the evolution of the PPP legal framework hidden in the contractual review process (for example, the UK's legal system follows a case law structure).

Despite the fact that this analytical bias was already considered as an eventual methodological restriction of the present research, it was not expected to open the doors for the emergence of the hypothesis of a segmented framework. As it was observed in the low dimensional gap, the expected linear trend does not appear. Instead, the graph breaks into two parallel groups of variables. This break was exposed by the presentation of some complementary variables at opposite quadrants.

In the analysis, the present variables can be grouped into two groups: the first is mainly marked by two variables plotted on the upper side of the graphs and the other marked by three on the lower. The space between those core variables is marked by many other variables which appear in both groups regarding what was expected in the general trend. Group 1 (G1) is defined by two variables plotted in the upper left-hand extreme corner: PPP law and Operational responsibilities. On the lower Group 2 (G2) formed around the variables of *ex-ante* value-for-money assessment, Specific policy on PPP and Mature financial capital. However, the association of the latter variable to this group may be considered an eventual mismatch caused by the natural accessibility of the components of this group to the most complex financial markets.

In an *ex-ante* analysis, it was expected that the variable of PPP law would be connected to the elaboration of a PPP policy, but the opposition of those variables in the plot, supported by the association between PPP unit and operational responsibilities variables, might present a new hypothesis about the tasks carried out by the Law and Policy institutions in each group. In short, the results may indicate that the PPP policy and the PPP law could be playing the same roles in different institutional frameworks. More implications may be expected by the addition of inference on the characteristics of the cases related to those groups. Looking at France, Portugal, Greece and Italy, it is possible to infer the correlation of an organisational scenario with the G1 variables. On the other hand, the presence of countries governed by a regulatory-based framework on the lower side of the plot supports their association with regulatory practices (specific PPP policy and Learning structures not structured in a formal knowledge centre). Nevertheless, at the present moment these hypotheses are only exploratory findings and cannot be supported by the research presented in this paper. In order to obtain a deeper understanding of this subject, further research is required.

Back to the analysis of the variables, some conclusions may be drawn on the supplementary variables. The GFCF variable positioned on the left side of the F1 axis meets the expectations about the positive relation between total investment and interest in PPP. In other words, countries under investment pressure tend to diversify their financial scope to a wider range of investment contracts like PPP. The creativity variables appear to be associated with the other variables in the lower left-hand corner, which could indicate that the cases in this quadrant are pushing the technological boundaries of the PPP framework. In the following section, the analytical perspective changes its focus to the cases. In contrast to the present section, the case analysis is oriented to the construction of proximity clusters among the cases.

Cases

The results from the analysis of the cases are presented in the last group as part of the conclusions of the present research. In alignment with the findings presented in the previous section the effort in this section is oriented towards the illustration of the findings of the chapter.

For this purpose, the section is structured following the construction of clusters of the cases. During the practical research phase, an attempt was made at clustering but it was abandoned when the mismatches between the scope of the database and the proposed methodology were made apparent. Hence, the analysis shifted from the contingency method to the justification of the proximity clustering procedure.

As to the results, in accordance with the previous presentation of all the sections with their perspectives, the principal point to be illustrated is the classification of the data according to their institutional levels which, in turn, may represent different levels of interest and usage regarding PPP. One can observe that the most mature countries regarding PPP are those on the left side of the graph (see Figure 3.4), while the countries to be found on the right side of the graph do not use PPP much, either because they have not much interest in them or because they had not the time to develop their interest or, ultimately, because they have abandoned the procedure (see Figure 3.4).

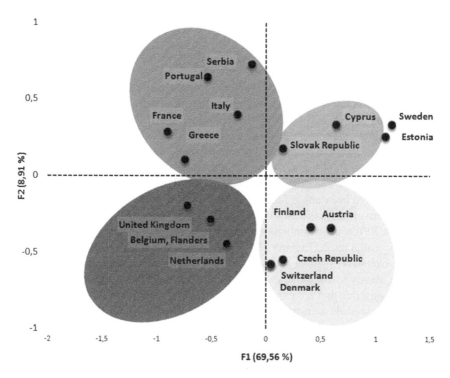

Figure 3.4 MCA cases plot.

From the left side of the graph, the two clusters of countries C1 and C2 including Serbia, Portugal, Italy, Greece, France, Belgium (Flanders), United Kingdom (UK) and Netherlands have a central PPP unit (V02) and a formal knowledge centre (V06.1) either in the form of a PPP Unit or of a centre of excellence of knowledge. Moreover, all countries of C1 and C2 employ PPPs in more than four sectors (V10), a fact that suggests not only a good level of maturity but also a wider PPP employment. The main difference between these two clusters is the mature financial capital (V09). While Serbia, Portugal, Italy and Greece resort only to loans, private equity or public finance, other financial sources are employed in Belgium, UK and the Netherlands. France also uses other sources of finance, but is grouped with Serbia, Portugal, Italy and Greece because all these countries have a similar dependence on organisational institutional setting (PPP law, PPP unit with operational responsibilities). UK, Belgium and the Netherlands on the other hand have a more regulatory approach (specific PPP policy).

Considering the number of failures in the history of PPP projects in Serbia, its presence in the C2 might be considered a late membership. Contrasting with Portugal, Italy or Greece, the Serbian institutional framework has historically blocked the development of the PPP policy at the national level. However, Serbia has recently enacted a PPP law and the implementation of PPPs, especially at a local level, gained momentum after mid-2012 when the governing party changed (Mladenovic and Vajdic 2013).

On the right side of the graph, the other two groups of countries C3 and C4 include Cyprus, Slovakia, Austria, Finland, Denmark, Switzerland and the Czech Republic.

Here, Sweden and Estonia, both northern European countries, were considered outliers. Both countries have shown very little interest in PPPs with no specific PPP policies (Agren and Olander 2013; Lember 2013). Estonia has been rather sceptical about adopting PPPs in general, with the exception of interest for the port of Tallin. This can be justified because Estonia has had access to alternative financial sources (V09), mainly the EU Structural Funds. In addition, the prevalent political stance has been in conflict with the idea of PPP. In Estonia, governing parties have been either hesitant or straightforwardly opposed to the idea of PPPs. Moreover, there is a lack of clear PPP policy and support structures, which has left the PPP concept ambiguous and underdeveloped for most PPP stakeholders and potential users (Lember 2013).

While Denmark, Estonia and Sweden have a similar institutional background, Denmark seems to be moving out of the PPP-sceptic category into a broader group of countries that are experimenting with PPPs for the initiation of various types of large-scale construction and infrastructure projects (Petersen 2013). With the exception of Slovakia, no C3 and C4 country has a PPP law (V01) or a central PPP unit (V02). In Slovakia, a central PPP-dedicated department supported by five employees was established within the Ministry of Finance back in 2007, only to be abolished four years later. The short existence of this unit was extremely important for the PPP institutional context in the country. During those years, the government supported the development of 'the three PPP package'. Unfortunately only one came to be implemented (Szekeres 2013).

Only the Czech Republic, Denmark and Slovakia display a specific policy on PPP (V03). However, regarding Slovakia, the introduction of this policy has been blocked by the negative political orientation of the current government to PPPs (Szekeres 2013).

Back to the clusters analysis, it is surprising to notice that the countries least interested in PPP, which formed the C4 cluster, have all implemented an *ex-ante* value-for-money assessment (V05.1) contrary to C3 (Cyprus and Slovakia). In addition, all countries of C3 and C4 have a learning structure (V05), but only Denmark, Switzerland and the Slovak Republic have a formal one (V05.1).

As expected, none of these countries displays a sectorial PPP unit (V07) or PPPs in several sectors (V10). Furthermore, in all countries, funds are raised through debt bank loans, private equity or public finance, with the exception of Finland, demonstrating the low maturity level of financial capital (V09).

Slovakia and Cyprus – the C3 cluster – feature cases of cross-sector bundling (V08) showing that they are more mature than countries in the cluster C4. In fact, both countries have taken significant steps towards the construction of a PPP institutional framework. The major barriers to their transition are, according to the literature, the general political or investment context. According to Christodoulou and Efstathiades (2013), PPP initiatives in Cyprus have been historically blocked by its financial isolation from the European continent, whereas Szekeres (2013) pointed to the political environment in Slovakia as a systematic barrier to the development of PPP projects.

Neither Austria nor Finland have been forerunners of PPPs. The major motivation for PPP in Austria was to relieve public budgets of the financial burden the PPPs eventually assumed and, in the aftermath of the financial crisis, a more sceptical view of PPPs emerged at the federal level. Moreover, a dedicated PPP unit in the Austrian public sector did not survive longer than two years; it was abandoned in 2008 and it had little impact. In addition, Austria does not dispose of a standard *ex-ante* evaluation instrument, specific to PPP projects (Scherrer 2013).

Differences between C3 and C4 are hard to observe but it is possible to identify some points. The distance between them seems to be in the level of scepticism. However, while Estonia and Sweden have shown no interest in PPPs accompanied with specific PPP policies, Austria and Finland have shown interest at a low level, which has been diminishing over time.

Conclusions, limitations and future research

It is not unusual for exploratory analysis to conclude with further questions rather than with final results and this research cannot be an exception to the rule. The inability to meet methodological requirements for the use of more complex statistical methods may justify the use of this exploratory approach but it also limits the depth of the analysis. For the moment, the reader should keep in mind that, the present sample being limited to the countries participating in the COST TU1001 action, it has significant representation but does not have an equitable enough distribution of all context factors to grant universality to our conclusions. In this sense, the conclusions presented in this final section are structured according to two categories: insights about the validation of the methodology and specific conclusions for the analysed context.

Regarding the general insights about the validation of the methodology, the robustness of the evolutionary approach may be considered the main successful conclusion of the present study. The comprehension of the innovative and relativity components made the configuration of the scenario based on two streams of institutional development possible. The conclusion in question has been strongly supported by the applicability of the Multiple Correspondence Analysis method in the construction of the PPP institutional maturity concept. It is expected that this methodology may be even more fruitful when replicated using larger samples.

Regarding the specific conclusions, the outline of the evolutionary PPP context begins with the observation of the existence of two general structures for the institutional framework – organisational and regulatory. This layout is supported by results analysed in the previous section, which have presented the hypothesis that PPP policy and PPP law seem to be performing similar functions in different institutional contexts. In addition, the existence of a PPP-specific law was not considered a feature of the group of most advanced institutional frameworks. According to the results, these countries have been approving several regulations, guidance and standards along their history of PPP use, but not necessarily a formal PPP framework law. In contrast, countries that appear enthusiastic with the PPP delivery model and which approve PPP laws may be doing this to accelerate the evolution process and catch up with other, more mature countries. This might be the case of Serbia or Flanders, which only recently adopted PPP institutional designs and already have their own PPP law, whereas the UK, a well-known player, has never designed a specific legal framework for PPP. This evidence calls for the potential relation of coherence between the PPP law and policy, which may well become a main recommendation for newcomers into the use of PPP. In fact, in terms of policy design, the design of the law is a key instrument, representing an element of coherence between the strategic level of decision (policy-making) and the tactical level of planning (design of law instrument).

In the findings of this chapter, the variables employed mapped the sample of PPP-enthusiastic countries onto two categories: more organisational and more regulatory countries. In the first group were placed the countries marked by a PPP institutional model dependent on public organisation, while the second group was populated by countries in which PPP routines are mostly supported by regulatory bodies.

Instead of clarifying the general institutional concept, the definition of the evolutionary paths in two ways raises some additional questions. Is the impact of the regulatory and that of the organisational frameworks in the PPP policy the same? Does this lead to a different performance in the use of PPP? Is there a structure that is better suited for certain objectives than for others? The answer to these questions is not far from being found. Experience and performance in PPPs were considered as essential factors in the analysis, and further elaborating the issue, as well as increasing its importance in the analysis, will improve this research further. For this paper, experience with PPPs has already been characterised by quantitative variables like the number of implemented PPPs and the amount of investment in PPP projects. However, such data not being readily available, they could not be included in the analysis.

In the same context, the identification of the performance variable was even harder to achieve. In addition to the problem of specific data availability, the analysis did not point to an indicator of this element. Both variables need to be considered in future studies, considering in particular the results from auditing processes carried out in some of the selected countries. It should however be noted that performance analysis requires an additional dimension of complexity, since performance must be assessed in the perspective of the different stakeholders engaged in a PPP process, eventually leading to conflicting results. These additional variables are expected to add more explanatory capacity to this model.

References

Abdi, H. and Valentin, D. (2007) 'Multiple correspondence analysis' in N. J. Salkind (Ed.) (2007) *Encyclopedia of Measurement and Statistics*. Thousand Oaks, CA: Sage Publications, pp. 651–657

Agren, R. and Olander, St. (2013) 'Sweden' in K. Verhoest, N. Carbonara, V. Lember, O. H. Petersen, W. Scherrer and M. van den Hurk (Eds) (2013) *COST Action TU1001 Public Private Partnerships in Transport: Trends and Theory P3T3, 2013 Discussion Papers Part I Country Profiles*. ISBN: 978-88-97781-60-8, COST Office, Brussels. Available online at: www.ppptransport.eu

Asian Development Bank (ADB) (2008) *Public-Private Partnership Handbook*. ADB

Christodoulou, Ch. A. and Efstathiades, Ch. O. (2013) 'Cyprus' in K. Verhoest, N. Carbonara, V. Lember, O. H. Petersen, W. Scherrer and M. van den Hurk (Eds) (2013) *COST Action TU1001 Public Private Partnerships in Transport: Trends and Theory P3T3, 2013 Discussion Papers Part I Country Profiles*. ISBN: 978-88-97781-60-8, COST Office, Brussels. Available online at: www.ppptransport.eu

European Commission (2004) *Green Paper on Public-Private Partnerships and Community Law on Public Contracts and Concessions* (No. COM (2004) 327 final). Brussels: EC

Economic Consultants Associates (2010) *PPP Toolkit for Improving PPP Decision-Making Processes* website. Dept of Economic Affairs, Ministry of Finance, Government of India: ECA. Available online at: http://toolkit.pppinindia.com/start-toolkits.php?sector_id=4

Eggers, W.D. and Dovey, T. (2007) 'Closing America's Infrastructure Gap: The Role of Public-Private Partnerships'. Deloitte Research

European PPP Expertise Centre (EPEC) (2011) *The Guide to Guidance – How to Prepare, Procure and Deliver PPP Projects*. EPEC. Available online at: www.eib.org/epec/resources/guide-to-guidance-en.pdf

Grimsey, D. and Lewis, M. K. (2005) 'Are Public Private Partnerships value for money? Evaluating alternative approaches and comparing academic and practitioner views'. *Accounting Forum, 29* (4 December 2005), pp. 345–378

Kwak, Y. H., Chih, Y. and Ibbs, C. H. (2009) 'Towards a comprehensive understanding of Public Private Partnerships for infrastructure development'. *California Management Review, 51* 2 (Winter 2009), pp. 51–78

Le Roux, B. and Rouanet, H. (2004) *Geometric Data Analysis: From Correspondence Analysis to Structured Data Analysis*. Dordrecht: Kluwer (p. 180)

Lember, V. (2013) 'Estonia' in K. Verhoest, N. Carbonara, V. Lember, O. H. Petersen, W. Scherrer and M. van den Hurk (Eds) (2013) *COST Action TU1001 Public Private Partnerships in Transport: Trends and Theory P3T3, 2013 Discussion Papers Part I Country Profiles*. ISBN: 978-88-97781-60-8, COST Office, Brussels. Available at: www.ppptransport.eu

Macário, R. (2010) 'Future challenges for transport infrastructure pricing in PPP arrangements'. *Research in Transportation Economics*, Vol. 30, no. 1, pp. 145–154

Mladenovic, G. and Vajdic, N. (2013) 'Serbia' in K. Verhoest, N. Carbonara, V. Lember, O. H. Petersen, W. Scherrer and M. van den Hurk (Eds) (2013) *COST Action TU1001 Public Private Partnerships in Transport: Trends and Theory P3T3, 2013 Discussion Papers Part I Country Profiles*. ISBN: 978-88-97781-60-8, COST Office, Brussels. Available at: www.ppptransport.eu

Nelson, R. R. and Winter, S. G. (1982) *An Evolutionary Theory of Economic Change*. Cambridge, MA: Harvard University Press

Petersen, O. H. (2013) 'Denmark' in K. Verhoest, N. Carbonara, V. Lember, O. H. Petersen, W. Scherrer and M. van den Hurk (Eds) (2013) *COST Action TU1001 Public Private Partnerships in Transport: Trends and Theory P3T3, 2013 Discussion Papers Part I Country Profiles*. ISBN: 978-88-97781-60-8, COST Office, Brussels. Available at: www.ppptransport.eu

Pollitt, C. and Bouckaert, G. (2004) *Public Management Reform: A Comparative Analysis*. Oxford: Oxford University Press

Roumboutsos, A., Farrell, S., Liyanage, C. L. and Macário, R. (2013) *COST Action TU1001 Public Private Partnerships in Transport: Trends and Theory P3T3, 2013 Discussion Papers Part II Case Studies*. ISBN 978-88-97781-61-5 Available online at: www.ppptransport.eu

Roumboutsos, A., Farrel, S. and Verhoest, K. (Eds) (2014) *COST Action TU1001 – Public Private Partnerships in Transport: Trends and Theory: 2014 Discussion Series: Country Profiles and Case Studies*. ISBN 978-88-6922-009-8, COST Office, Brussels. Available online at: www.ppptransport.eu

Roumboutsos A. and Saussier, St. (2014) 'Public-Private Partnerships and investments in innovation: the influence of the contractual arrangement'. *Construction Management and Economics*, 32:4, pp. 349–361

Scherrer, W. (2013) 'Austria' in K. Verhoest, N. Carbonara, V. Lember, O. H. Petersen, W. Scherrer and M. van den Hurk (Eds) (2013) *COST Action TU1001 Public Private Partnerships in Transport: Trends and Theory P3T3, 2013 Discussion Papers Part I Country Profiles*. ISBN: 978-88-97781-60-8, COST Office, Brussels. Available online at: www.ppptransport.eu

Schumpeter, J. A. (1934) *The Theory of Economic Development*. Cambridge, MA: Harvard University Press

Szekeres, K. (2013) 'Slovak Republic' in K. Verhoest, N. Carbonara, V. Lember, O. H. Petersen, W. Scherrer and M. van den Hurk (Eds) (2013) *COST Action TU1001 Public Private Partnerships in Transport: Trends and Theory P3T3, 2013 Discussion Papers Part I Country Profiles*. ISBN: 978-88-97781-60-8, COST Office, Brussels. Available online at: www.ppptransport.eu

United Nations Economic Commission for Europe (UNECE) (2008) *Guidebook on Promoting Good Governance in Public-Private Partnerships*. New York and Geneva: UNECE

United Nations Economic and Social Commission for Asia and the Pacific (UN-ESCAP) (2011) *A Guidebook on Public-Private Partnership in Infrastructure*. Bangkok: UN-ESCAP

Verhoest, K., Carbonara, N., Lember, V., Petersen, O. H., Scherrer, W. and van den Hurk, M. (Eds) (2013) *COST Action TU1001 Public Private Partnerships in Transport: Trends and Theory P3T3, 2013 Discussion Papers Part I Country Profiles*. ISBN: 978-88-97781-60-8, COST Office, Brussels. Available online at: www.ppptransport.eu

Verhoest, K., Roness, P.G., Verschuere, B., Rubecksen, K. and MacCarthaig, M. (2010) *Autonomy and Control of State Agencies: Comparing States and Agencies*. Basingstoke: Palgrave Macmillan

Williamson, O. E. (2000) 'The new institutional economics: taking stock, looking ahead'. *Journal of Economic Literature* Vol. 38, No. 3 (Sep., 2000), pp. 595–613, American Economic Association

World Bank (2012) *Public-Private Partnership Reference Guide 1.0*. The World Bank Institute, Public-Private Infrastructure Advisory Facility (PPIAF)

4 Transport PPP east of the Elbe

Destined to succeed or doomed to fail?

*Petr Witz, Pekka Leviäkangas and
Agnieszka Łukasiewicz*

Introduction

In the course of the previous century transport infrastructure projects were, principally, financed by governments and paid for by the taxpayer. During recent decades project finance (and other forms under the umbrella term Public Private Partnerships (PPPs)) has been used in many countries to deliver crucial infrastructure capital projects. Privately financed projects have emerged in response to the ever-growing need for infrastructure capacity deployment, the availability of private finance and the need to bring forward infrastructure development schedules that would not have been possible within the public budget. The effective management of public funds is at the heart of political and social acceptance of these schemes (Grimsey and Lewis 2005; Akintoye *et al.* 2003; Debande 2002), especially when the latter are compared to traditional forms of publicly procured works and services. Countries that firmly champion the social value of the public provision of critical infrastructure (such as transport) may resist the adoption of procurement and delivery schemes based on private involvement and financing.

A fair amount of analytical work deals with the implementation of Public Private Partnerships in traditional and highly developed PPP markets in Anglo-Saxon and other mainly West-European countries. Researchers have, to a lesser extent, turned their attention towards PPP in countries undergoing a complex transformative change or in highly developed welfare states. Only recently has the research community focused on the respective relative experiences of countries of Central and Eastern Europe (CEE) and the European North. A broader comparative analysis of the PPP phenomenon in this part of Europe has been largely missing. Indeed, no single distinctive study has attempted to explain the specific factors that differentiate the implementation of transport PPP in new EU member states from that of the rest of Europe.

This chapter covers eight European countries including the Czech Republic, Estonia, Finland, Hungary, Latvia, Poland, Serbia and Slovakia. In the present work we compare the transition economies to Finland – a country with a well-rooted sense of public/social provision – on the basis of the PPP implementation context, which includes political commitment, legal and institutional frameworks. We aim first to establish to what extent PPPs have been endorsed by the aforementioned countries, which are characterised by less experienced markets and democratic architectures, as well as the reasons behind the difference between levels of PPP uptake in the transport sector. Secondly, we identify common denominators as well as differences in the process of PPP implementation within the sample. In particular, we will compare PPP activity with the actual output. Subsequently, we contrast PPP failure rates in the sample countries and try to explain common factors associated with the success or failure of PPP implementation. Special attention is paid to the role of political and external pressures, institutional solidity and legal framing of PPP as key factors determining PPP performance. Finally, we try to determine to what extent PPP has been a working solution for the post-communist countries and under what preconditions partnerships between private and public sector in infrastructure projects can work in the future.

Theoretical background

Considering PPP developments in CEE countries one needs to take into account the political, cultural, economic and administrative specificities of the region – as well as of the individual countries – that determine the way 'imported' models like PPP are accepted and implemented. With the exception of Finland, being a part of the former Eastern Bloc over a long period and the subsequent transition towards modern market economy that resulted in joining the European Union are definitely among the main common features of CEE countries. Therefore, one can deduce that the challenges faced by these countries in the years of transition would be similar. The legacy of recent history is probably the most frequently cited reason for the slow changes and failed reforms.

It is generally agreed that patterns and habits of totalitarianism slow the promotion of key reforms (Nunberg 1999; Verheijen 2001), including the reform of public administration. Dimitrov *et al.* (2006) highlight the discrepancy between the official rules and laws and the observed governance, hence the practices in public administration. This is a common feature of post-communist regime countries as is the excessive interference of political parties in matters of state administration and administrative processes (Goetz and Wollmann 2001, Meyer-Sahling 2008). As noted by Sajó (1998), the existing formal decision-making procedures in post-communist countries have been largely replaced by backstage agreements within unofficially operating power networks.

There are many opinions, initiatives and groupings that tend to suggest that the transition countries of Central and Eastern Europe can indeed be classified under one group in terms of both administrative tradition and public policy-making procedures. One even refers to a 'Central European type of public administration' where the burden of the communist past represents an important element. Whether this element can still be considered as the decisive factor determining the reality of governance and public administration in all post-communist countries of Central and Eastern Europe is another question. Agreeing with this definition would imply that the implementation of NPM-inspired policies like PPP suffers from the same type of problems and leads to similar outcomes in the aforementioned countries.

A number of scholars have been rather sceptical about the dominance of communist legacy in CEE pointing out the existence of non-negligible differences. This opinion is expressed by Meyer-Sahling (2009), who states that the pre-and post-totalitarian traditions are equally responsible for the current state of governance in the region. Before the emergence of the Soviet bloc, countries of Central and Eastern Europe often belonged to different cultural and political spheres and their administrative systems were subject to other influences. This is, after all, reflected in the nature of communist regimes in these countries that, on a closer inspection, had been to a large extent distinct. Thus, after the restoration of democratic order, all states in the region embarked on a process of transformation, often looking back for patterns in the functioning of the inter-war institutions or ones established even earlier, and each of them has actually followed a somewhat different approach in the development of their governance. This may have been at the origin of different approaches to a range of issues including privatisation and PPP.

Research approach

The authors have employed a comparative research design (Antal *et al.* 1987), comparing the experience of eight countries with PPP. The selection of cases was made with the intention of getting a sample of countries with, on the one hand, a traditionally strong role of state in the provision of transport infrastructure but, on the other, with different overall qualities of public institutions. That is to say we use Finland as a case to be contrasted with the CEE countries but, at the same time, we try to identify and explain the differences among CEE countries themselves. As for the sources, for basic information we draw from a substantial database collected by the members of the COST Action TU1001 between 2012 and 2014. The observations concerning the case countries' PPP policies are mostly based on published official documents, such as public procurement and PPP laws, government strategies, programmes and plans and other materials obtained upon request under the Freedom of Information acts. The official statistical data and reports by the independent international organisations are referred to in certain parts of the paper to support the main arguments.

A new indicator for comparing the performances of individual PPP programmes in both the developed and transition countries is proposed in this paper. PPP failure rate is meant to distinguish countries with a sound evaluation and decision-making system from those with a weaker institutional base. PPP failure rate of the national-level transport projects is nevertheless difficult to capture. Failures occur at different stages and the understanding of what constitutes a failure may differ from one case to another. In the context of this chapter, we define failure as a project that was abandoned, although a substantial amount of money and energy had already been invested in its preparation or realisation.

PPP in the sample countries

Introducing the PPP model in the case countries

Obviously, the sample in question cannot be considered homogeneous. These are countries with different levels of wealth, more or less varying cultural backgrounds, traditions, technological advancement, political structures, etc. In addition Finland, despite the fact that it serves as benchmark in many respects, may be seen as a sort of outlier. However, the authors believe that there are sufficient historic, geopolitical and socio-economic commonalities to justify its inclusion in the sample alongside the core CEE countries.

Among the common features, an exceptionally long history of absorbing and balancing influences from both the west and the east of the continent presents a strong common denominator. The countries' role as a buffer between mightier powers has shaped their political and economic systems for centuries. Also, the eight countries under examination did not take part in the initial phases of the European integration process, while the wave of intensive privatisation and neoliberal reforms before 1990 was echoed in Finland only. While the Central European countries were able to re-introduce free market principles after the dissolution of the former Eastern Bloc in early 1990s, Finland, enjoying a much higher degree of independence, opted to develop a market economy based on social democracy, the so-called Nordic model, soon after the end of the Second World War. Despite these differences, the role of the state in the provision of public infrastructure and services has recently been introduced rather strongly in all selected countries.

Nevertheless, after a swift probe into the history of infrastructure development in the region of Central and South-Eastern Europe, it becomes evident that PPP cannot be simply seen as a new concept only recently imported from the West. There are many examples of private companies raising funds for, and then constructing and operating, key infrastructure projects dating back to the late eighteenth and early nineteenth century just like in Western countries. They were the first concession projects that laid the ground for the railway networks connecting far ends of old empires or that enabled construction of landmark structures like bridges across Danube or Vltava rivers. Seemingly, the initial experience with private involvement in the provision of public infrastructure was in many ways similar to that of West-European countries with all its negative and positive points (Juhasz and Scharle 2014). It is hardly surprising that the first concessions suffered from very similar problems to the ones faced by today's schemes.

Yet, the tradition of private involvement was discontinued and for several decades replaced by the completely opposite type of paradigm in the countries of the former Eastern Bloc. Shortly after the fall of the communist states, privatisation of state industry was at the top of governments' agendas, followed by considerations about how to reform the public sector to make it compatible with the needs and conditions of the economy and civic society. Various reform conceptions emerged, mostly based on Western schools of thought, including the New Public Management (NPM) that placed a special emphasis on the implementation of private sector principles or private sector direct participation to the execution of tasks so far reserved to the various levels of government or government agencies (Ferlie *et al.* 1996).

At the same time, the infrastructure deficit was perceived as one of the main hindrances to a successful transformation towards modern market economy and sustained economic growth in the CEE countries. In a situation where the lack of public funding made itself manifest throughout the public sector and inhibited development, it seemed only logical to dust off the idea of private involvement in the provision of public services and infrastructure, embodied by the various types of Public Private Partnership applied in the West.

However, the experience from the first wave of PPP all around the world has shown how demanding this kind of contractual arrangement is, in terms of institutional settings and the amount of skills needed by both private and public parties. As a result the risk of a PPP project failure appears to be higher than in the case of traditional procurement methods. Yet, most countries with less mature market economies have suffered from a relative weakness of their institutional framework and the lack of skills in the civil service. Then inevitably, the question arises as to what degree the CEE countries are able to deal with the challenges posed by PPP implementation processes and, *vice versa*, whether PPP is what is needed to bridge the governance capacity gap.

PPP may arise in reaction to an economic downfall or when under-investment in public infrastructure becomes an important issue hindering its development or, indeed, as a purely innovative solution aimed at increasing the effectiveness of public spending. The common tendency to finance projects off-balance sheet lost its bearings after the Eurostat revised its rules for national accounts. All three reasons played a role to a certain extent in the selected countries' PPP implementation. PPP found its way to Finland almost a decade earlier than in other countries in the sample, which were undergoing the transition in the 1990s.

In the turbulent decade after 1989, Central Europe witnessed the initial phases of political and economic transformation. This transformation came packed with abrupt and radical changes in not only the legislation or regulatory frameworks but also, perhaps more importantly, in the structure of asset ownership and society as a whole. Such a volatile environment did not provide opportunities for the implementation of Public Private Partnerships. Reluctance towards such radical changes included not only those pertaining to public procurement but also to the overall philosophy of the public sector development. The general public had held the belief that it is the state that should take care of the transport infrastructure that would, in turn, be available to all and free of charge. Despite this fact, several proto-PPP (for example, street lighting projects) were implemented by local authorities in the Czech Republic. Several projects with PPP characteristics were also carried out in Poland.

In contrast, Finland has enjoyed a relatively stable political environment with clearly defined rules and ingrained procedures. Sound public institutions backed by a well-defined regulatory framework that had been evolving for decades are matched by one of the most efficient and most ethical business sectors in the world (World Economic Forum 2013). Nevertheless, similarly to Central Europe, the state dominance in provision of transport infrastructure had been a norm in the modern history of Finland until the serious economic crisis of the early 1990s. As noted in Leviäkangas (2013), the origins of PPP in Finland are closely connected with the increasing capital investment gap caused by rising maintenance costs that had been consuming an ever-increasing share of the state infrastructure budget. Under these circumstances, a short-term relief for the public purse in the form of the PPP method for new infrastructure investments was viewed as a viable option by the government and was supported by the private sector. The Finnish government launched the first PPP project in 1996. A few other projects followed, but no substantial PPP programme or a pipeline of projects has evolved as consecutive governments have maintained a pragmatic approach according to which no procurement method is favoured and every project has to undergo a strict and rigorous assessment and a cost/benefit analysis (Leviäkangas 2013).

In Central Europe, PPPs were introduced as the political system and economies became stable after the year 2000. Capital investment gaps became more pressing as the demand for an increased capacity and quality of infrastructure rose along with the wealth and living standards of the population. The EU funds represented a popular source of investment capital for infrastructure projects and private (co-) financing in the form of PPP was supported by large international construction and consultancy companies. The speed of growth of PPP programmes in these countries varies with a few common factors that are explained further in the next sections of this chapter.

Firstly, there is an important difference between PPP activity defined as an 'intentional and targeted line of action taken by private and public entities in favour of PPP', and the number of realised PPP projects (see Table 4.1). The obvious observations are that Poland and Hungary, both putting significant

Table 4.1 PPP activity/PPP output and PPP failure rate

	CZE	EST	FIN	HUN	LAT	POL	SVK	SER
No of transp. PPPs on the national level (realised/planned)	0/2	1/0	5/1	10/0	0/2	4/several	2/2	0/0
No of transp. PPPs on the national level (initiated/scrapped)	3/3	1/0	7/2	10/5	1/1	7/3	4/2	2/2

efforts into PPP implementation at the time, have managed to implement several PPPs on the national level (Centrum PPP 2013) while Slovakia, Serbia and the Czech Republic have lagged behind. The latter carried out some clearly identifiable PPP activity but with overall limited results. Significant amounts of money and efforts, both from the private and public sector, have yielded limited results in these countries (Szekeres 2013; Witz 2013b).

Since the early 2000s, both private and public parties in the Czech Republic and Slovakia have been heavily engaged in the preparation of several packages of PPP projects under the influence and guidance of international actors. However, most of the projects were eventually abandoned. The PPP activity in Serbia has been largely formal, with PPP institutions being in place but no PPP project brought to a successful conclusion. In contrast to that, the existing five projects in Finland were realised without any specific PPP activity or bias registered and in Estonia the zero score (with the specific exception of the Port of Tallin) corresponds to the absence of any significant pro-PPP activity in the transport sector and in general. Although Estonia has been considered a champion in introducing market principles and NPM-inspired reforms into the public sector, it has registered almost no external or internal pressures to implement PPP (Lember 2013). Finally, in Latvia, despite a relatively high level of PPP activity, no national-level transport projects have been procured so far although at least two projects have been discussed (Ministry of Finance of Latvia 2014).

The number of successful projects in itself does not provide a sufficient performance indicator of a particular PPP programme. We also need to look at the proportion of projects and at the failed or abandoned attempts that involved the loss of considerable transaction costs. There are significant differences among the case countries in this respect. Finland has so far cancelled two planned PPP projects. Both were railway projects and did not even reach the tendering phase. At the same time, two of the four transport PPP projects in Slovakia were cancelled after the contracts were signed according to the Slovak Ministry of Finance (2013). The total amount of contractual penalties and other compensations that had to be paid has not been disclosed, but a figure of about 140 million euros has been reported (Szekeres 2013). Similarly, all three transport PPP in the Czech Republic have been cancelled, one of them at an advanced stage of preparation and another after the contract was signed. These projects incurred penalty payments of more than 19.5 million euros and the loss of at least 5 million euros already invested in the projects' preparation (Czech Ministry of Finance 2013; Transparency International 2009). In comparison, early-stage PPP failures in Serbia had somewhat milder impact.

Meanwhile, of the seven motorway PPP projects in Poland, four sections have been carried out as concessions, but all with significant time overruns (Herbst *et al.* 2012). Among the three unsuccessful projects, in two cases no concessionaire was selected (neither at the tender preparation stage nor at the tender). Considering the third case, the project failed a year after the contract signing due to the lack of private financing, most probably owing to the financial crisis. The concessionaire claimed the costs of design works performed at that time. The concessionaire calculated the sum of compensation at 36 million euros (Majszyk 2013). The issue has not been resolved to date.

The exact costs of an expensive bailout of Hungarian PPP are not in the public domain. Nevertheless, the financial losses incurred by PPP failure were so substantial that the whole concept was practically abandoned after an extensive review in 2010 (Juhasz and Sharle 2014). The M1/M15 project is an exemplary case of overestimated traffic forecasts that have so far brought about dozens of PPP failures around the world and that have cast doubt over the suitability of real toll arrangements.

Although no comparable projects can be found in the Baltic countries, there are indications from other sectors in Latvia, where PPP has been applied, that a high PPP failure rate is a common problem in the countries east of the Elbe (Zabko 2013).

The data show that the transition countries register a substantially higher proportion of PPP projects abandoned at various stages, most notably during the post-procurement phase with significant costs incurred to governments. Factors behind the high PPP failure rate and possible ways of remedy will be explored in the following sections.

Political commitment to PPP

When considering the political commitment to PPP, a distinction should always be made between mere rhetoric and manifested political support. As mentioned above, active and overarching government support is critical for the successful implementation of PPP in any country. When assessing the case countries, various attitudes of political representations can be identified.

Finnish governments and the main political parties have for a long time viewed PPP as a neutral alternative infrastructure delivery method to be adopted when proven to make sense both in economic and social impact terms. In principle, the Finnish governments have simply 'tried to keep all options open' (Leviäkangas 2013; The Government Office 2011). At the same time, once a PPP project gets the final approval, the project enters 'a routine pipeline' towards its realisation. The continuity is, among other things, supported through the endorsement of all major projects by the national parliament. This makes the scheme reliable enough in the eyes of private investors who can rely on conditions agreed by all parties at the beginning. At the same time, it must be noted that the same type of measure did not prevent the Hungarian PPP from failing.

In Finland, there are examples where the PPP-option was not utilised because the result of their feasibility analysis dictated it so. For the two rail projects, the calls for tenders never reached the stage of actual tendering, as the feasibility of PPP became questionable. The public explanation for cancelling the PPP-option was extremely brief, but both projects were carried out via public funding and the projects remained a high priority in the Finnish national investment programmes.

In contrast to the Finnish case, almost half of the PPP tenders in Poland have failed so far (Lukasiewicz 2013). This cannot entirely be put down to insufficient political support. Nevertheless, the Law and Justice Party, when in power, threatened to abolish PPP signed by the previous government and only commitments connected with hosting the 2012 European Football Championship kept the projects on track.

In Hungary, the pro-PPP political representation was replaced by PPP sceptics in 2010. This fact, combined with the unsatisfactory and, in certain cases, unsustainable performance of PPP in the pipeline, brought about the end of the PPP policy.

Similarly, PPP as a procurement method was abandoned by the right-wing coalition shortly after the construction of the first and quite controversial Slovak PPP motorway, a project that was initiated by the Social Democrats. The existing government obligations were honoured, but strong ideological tensions between the left and right wings of the political spectrum have increased the likelihood of a sudden and radical political change, an occurrence which may impact even the already signed PPP contracts.

The Czech Republic also has a poor record. Judging from the public declarations of the main political parties, there should be a clear consensus in favour of PPP implementation. In contrast to most other nations, political risks were perceived as being significant by the Czech PPP professionals in the survey carried out by Roumboutsos *et al.* (2013). Their concerns were grounded on the experience of a number of PPP projects that were cancelled at various stages of development by political decisions, in two cases even after the contract was signed. As indicated above, these political interventions have caused financial losses of several hundred million crowns (Witz 2013a).

As noted by Mladenovic and Vajdic (2013), the government changes of 2012 have weakened the political support for PPP, leading to a rather bizarre situation where all formal PPP institutions instituted by previous governments are in place, but no PPP on the national level are considered.

Similarly, in Estonia, there appear to be relatively weak links and a deeply rooted mistrust between the state and the market, effectively inhibiting any attempts at creating a stable partnership. There has been a heavy political emphasis on the long term macroeconomic and fiscal stability that has constrained the use of PPP (Lember 2013).

In contrast, the PPP model in Latvia has enjoyed considerably larger and broader political support and much attention has been paid to ensuring that political changes have no effect on the implementation of already approved PPP (Zabko 2013). However, the serious damage suffered by the Latvian economy since 2008 has interrupted any further development of PPP for several years.

On the whole, a certain degree of scepticism and mistrust is present in each country (see Table 4.2). Countries like Poland managed to overcome this hurdle

Table 4.2 Political commitment

Country	Political commitment
Czech Republic	Extremely unstable
Estonia	No commitment
Finland	Stable/selective
Hungary	Unstable
Latvia	Rather stable with deviations
Poland	Rather stable with deviations
Serbia	Unstable
Slovakia	Unstable

by reaching some sort of political consensus and by being strongly motivated to use PPP. On the other hand, governments in Finland or Estonia have shown much less enthusiasm, embracing a more reserved and pragmatic approach. Finally, there are countries with fluctuating policies, namely the Czech Republic, Slovakia and Hungary. The changes in policy direction in the transition countries often have to do with radical personnel shake-ups in the key posts in the civil service after the government reshuffles and regular or not elections which, compared with more stable democracies, are not uncommon. The fluctuation can produce an expensive PPP framework that is not used or it can lead to even more expensive cancellations of already confirmed and commenced projects.

Legal framework

The resilience of the legal system is best recognised by its ability to deal with unusual situations and new impulses without a need for radical corrections or amendments. Usually the process of improving and fine-tuning the whole framework in order to make it work properly does not take years but decades. This is particularly true for the public procurement rules because there is a need for numerous institutions as well as a large number of private entities to adapt to them and to build an environment of mutual trust. Some countries have been granted more time to experiment and find the right equilibrium when compared with others. As a result, while changes to the Finnish procurement rules are rare nowadays, the procurement rules in the transition countries are in an almost constant flux (see Table 4.3). There have been 38 updates of the public procurement law in Poland since it was first issued in 2004 (Sejm 2013). Similarly, the law on public procurement has changed a number of times in the Czech Republic, Slovakia, Serbia and Latvia. The brand new Czech Public Procurement Act No. 55/2012, which replaced the original act of 2006, was almost immediately considered in need of revision by the very people who participated in designing the original law (Helikarová 2012).

Due to its specificity, PPP as a procurement method is often found to require special legal arrangements. However, among the selected countries, it was just Poland, Latvia and Serbia that adopted a dedicated PPP act. Poland did so for the

Table 4.3 Legal framework

Country	Stability	Special PPP law
Czech Republic	Unstable	No
Estonia	Unstable	No
Finland	Stable	No
Hungary	Unstable	No
Latvia	Unstable	Yes
Poland	Unstable	Yes (first one had to be replaced)
Serbia	Unstable	Yes (unused)
Slovakia	Unstable	No

first time in 2005 and again with a completely new act in 2008. Unfortunately, the first PPP Act was considered to be so confusing that it effectively prevented PPP from being used (Panasiuk 2009). There has been a boom of PPP in Poland since the adoption of the new law, which can be partly attributed to the fact that it makes the definitions, procedures and relationships between individual actors in the process much clearer (Lukasiewicz 2013). The experience with the Latvian law of 2009 has been similarly positive due to the fact that it resulted from a long and intensive discussion with all interested parties. As Zabko (2013) notes, it is believed that the final version of the law strikes a balance between the interests of the public and the private partner with improved normative regulations. The regulations in question have dealt with one of the primary obstacles to the development of PPP in Latvia. The Serbian act, drafted in 2011, has not been used so far because of the present lack of interest in PPP at the national level.

The Czech Republic, Estonia, Hungary, Finland and Slovakia never passed any specific laws on PPP, even though in the case of the Czech Republic a special PPP act appeared in the consecutive coalition governments' programmes.

In contrast, the Finnish governments have never really felt a need for a special PPP act. There was a wide consensus that the existing legislative framework was compatible with any kind of procurement. There have been some minor adjustments, but they have been mainly of technical nature in order to facilitate PPPs and make them a level-playing field alternative for both investors and procuring bodies (Leviäkangas 2013: 225). In line with the principles of the rational PPP approach, an independent government think-tank (the Government Institute for Economic Research) suggested that rather than engaging government entities in complex contract arrangements with PPP investors, the government should remove those inefficiencies of its own actions that could prohibit PPP from working efficiently and allow them to act as a natural alternative to traditional public procurement. In other words, the procurement system should be developed so that no specific legislation would be necessary (Mälkönen 2006).

On the other hand, both private and public managers in countries with a weaker institutional framework that relies on several parallel laws for the procurement of PPP may encounter confusion, which favours uncertainty as to respective responsibilities and roles. The result has often rested on their ability to improvise. Yet, certainty is the key precondition when it comes to PPP implementation. The absence of concrete and binding requirements and a clear division of responsibilities may have contributed to the failure of PPP projects in countries like the Czech Republic, Slovakia or Hungary.

Institutional setting

From a purely institutional point of view, PPP-supporting structures in the selected countries represent interesting and, at least in three cases, quite unique models (see Table 4.4).

Unsurprisingly, Finnish governments have decided to rely for the management and delivery of PPP on institutions and procedures that had already been in place for quite some time (Leviäkangas 2013). In this sense, Finland is probably one of the few examples of a country that has procured PPP without a dedicated PPP unit, PPP guidelines or any kind of a standardised PPP contract. The results of this experiment seem to be rather mixed, as certain projects did not generate explicit value for many years after their inception. However, the initial socio-economic project appraisal has classified these projects as among those generating benefits. Nevertheless, the absence of pro- and con-PPP bias enables public managers to look at the whole range of procurement methods and choose the one that suits them best in the given context.

Although the traditional procurement procedures are rigorous enough and responsible public sector managers usually have years of experience in dealing with public procurement, almost every PPP demands specific knowledge of legal, financial and/or technical features that is simply not available in standard public administration. Private consultants are often the easiest option when it comes to filling a gap in the public sector management competences. However, overreliance on private expertise has proved to be particularly costly in some countries (Witz 2012). Poland, on the other hand, represents the other extreme – there are substantial PPP units within several ministries, state agencies and even local authorities. Employees of most central government units are available to all levels of public administration and to all potential contracting authorities, thus potentially pushing the procurement costs down. As of the end of 2013 the Polish

Table 4.4 PPP-supporting institutions

Country	Supporting institutions
Czech Republic	Deconstructed
Estonia	No never /general procurement unit only
Finland	No never/general procurement unit only
Hungary	Deconstructed
Latvia	Functional/lack of skills
Poland	Functional/multiple/oversized/lack of skills
Serbia	Dormant
Slovakia	Deconstructed

PPP units were within the Ministry of Economy (five persons), Ministry of Regional Economy (17 persons), General Directorate for national Roads and Motorways (26 persons) and the Polish Agency for Enterprise (two persons) (Lukasiewicz 2013).

The history of the Czech and Slovak PPP institutions illustrates another type of approach that is characterised by the creation of an apparently relatively strong PPP-supporting framework and its gradual erosion to the current somewhat improvised state of matters. In Slovakia, a central PPP-dedicated department employing five persons was established within the Ministry of Finance back in 2007, but it was abolished four years later (Szekeres 2013).

A similar department existed at the Czech Ministry of Finance, but the original number of employees was cut to two and, in fact, the department ceased to exist as an independent unit as the remaining staff were entrusted with a different agenda. The Czech PPP Centrum – a joint stock company owned by the Ministry of Finance – was founded in 2005 and it quickly grew to the position of a top-class centre of expertise staffed by professionals with international experience. The combination of low demand (due to government policies) and external pressures such as the competition from private consultancies brought about its end in 2011 (Witz 2013a). The new guidelines for the procurement of PPP were composed in a close cooperation with consultants after the disbandment of the PPP Centrum (Witz 2013b).

When the Slovak government started considering the construction of two PPP motorways in 2014, it realised that it lacked appropriate in-house capacity and expertise. Most of the institutional knowledge and experience was lost. Consequently the government was forced to announce a tender for external advisors who would protect the public interest in the upcoming procurement process and negotiations with constructors (Krajanová 2014).

Serbia features a unique platform for technical assistance, evaluation and approval of PPP projects – a committee consisting of representatives of various ministries and regions. A similar body used to exist in Hungary until its dissolution in 2009. It should be noted that no member of either the Serbian or the Hungarian interdepartmental PPP committees was a full-time PPP expert independent from the government.

The Latvian 'PPP advisory council' was very similar to its Serbian and Hungarian counterparts. It is an interdepartmental advisory and coordinating body dealing with issues related to PPP. In addition to the Council, there is a Central Finance and Contracting Agency within the Ministry of Finance that collects all the important competences and knowledge. Latvia is thus the only country in our sample representing a standard type of PPP supporting framework.

Finally, the Estonian Ministry of Finance has no PPP unit. When considering PPP, it is the main responsibility of the procuring authority to make sure the public interest is protected. Nevertheless, the Ministry of Finance, the Cabinet and the Estonian parliament all need to approve any project that creates long-term liabilities.

Discussion and conclusions

The picture of PPP implementation process in the countries 'east of the Elbe' is far from homogeneous. The scale ranges from the financial and political failure (Hungary) to a relatively thriving PPP market in Poland that, despite a few setbacks, seems to be gradually expanding. Then, there is a substantial group of countries the approach of which to PPP can be described as intermediate based on the number of implemented projects. This group can be further broken down into countries with a consistent approach to PPP over time, represented by Finland, Latvia or Estonia, and countries with a rather unstable PPP policy and unsettled PPP environment represented by the Czech Republic, Slovakia and Serbia.

The variety of approaches to PPP presented in this paper and demonstrated in Table 4.1 disproves the idea of a uniform Central European type of public administration or a standardised CEE type of PPP. It seems that each country in the region has its autonomous and specific PPP policy and that its procedures for PPP implementation are influenced by deeply rooted patterns of governance. However, there are still common features. Many similarities can be observed at the level of the countries' legislative and institutional frameworks as well as at that of political commitment to PPP. The expectation that the countries with certain historical reservations to the diffusion of market mechanisms in the public sector will reject PPP as incompatible with their development strategies seems to be reliably refuted. Even Estonia, the country with the lowest PPP activity in the sample, has a certain experience with this type of procurement, despite the fact that it decided not to engage in it on a large scale. At the same time, we have seen that PPPs are a challenge some countries are unable to cope with. Concerns that transition countries may face greater problems implementing PPP than the ones with long-established institutions were proven to be largely justified. Certain transition countries, burdened with the legacy of public mismanagement under previous regimes, still struggle not just with PPP but with principles of good governance in general. This fact was confirmed by the discrepancy between the intensity of PPP activity and the real PPP output in the case countries, as well as by the PPP failure rate, which is proportionate to the projects initiated but never completed and this despite their having reached various stages of the pre-procurement process and incurred public costs.

The PPP failure rate is not the same for all countries. Apparently, there are differences caused by the overall quality of each country's institutions and political stability. If we look closely at Table 4.5, we may note that the countries' PPP failure rate corresponds to the strength of their institutions as evaluated by the World Economic Forum. In Finland this rate seems to be the lowest, as all initiated projects have been implemented, and the ones which were not were cancelled at the very outset. This indicates the strength of the Finnish model where unviable projects are eliminated at early stages thanks to advanced institutions and established procedures. All projects once approved by the Finnish parliament have been carried out.

Table 4.5 Overview of PPP implementation in the case countries

	Czech Republic	Finland	Poland	Slovakia	Hungary	Estonia	Serbia	Latvia
Quality of institutions. Place in the WEF[1] rankings (score) 2014	86th (3.6)	1st (6.1)	62nd (4.0)	119st (3.3)	84th (3.7)	27th (4.9)	126th (3.2)	57th (4.1)
No of transp. PPP on the national level (signed/planned)	0/2	5/1	4/several	1/2	10/0	1/0[2]	0/0	0/2
PPP in long-term plans	lower priority	marginal	first priority /important (in combination with the EU funds)	lower priority	marginal	marginal	marginal	lower priority
PPP law	No	No	Yes	No	No	No	Yes	Yes
PPP unit	No	No	Yes	No	No	No	Yes	Yes
PPP transparency – contracts and info. on projects' performance	low	low	low	low	low	low	low	low
PPP experience/public perception	rather negative	neutral	rather positive or neutral	rather negative	extreme negative	rather negative	neutral	neutral
Problems with implementation	many serious	few minor	some, but not serious	some serious	many serious	-	some serious	some serious

[1]World Economic Forum: *Global Competitiveness Report 2013-2014*
[2]The Port of Tallin can be considered a specific case of PPP involving a range of commercial partnership deals between the state-owned company and private operators.

At the same time, Poland has demonstrated some positive efforts to formalise PPP and systematically develop a pipeline of projects. However, its complicated PPP supporting structure seems to have been unable so far to prevent the deviations of a significant part of projects and tenders, which led them to non-existence. The same applies to Hungary, the Czech and Slovak Republics. Their common high failure rate is probably not a coincidence as all three countries disbanded their PPP units at a certain point in the past. The three countries also suffer from the vulnerability of their PPP programmes, a disadvantage associated with destabilising political interventions.

In Finland, the institutional and regulatory framework was identified as a strong PPP enabler, whereas in the transition countries the young and fragile institutional architecture, and all the shortcomings associated with it, are creating obstacles to the smooth running of PPPs. Different approaches to the development of a PPP institutional framework can be detected in the countries of the sample according to their various historical and cultural backgrounds. Poland seems to tend towards the creation of numerous formal institutions as well as regulations related directly or indirectly to PPP, whereas Finland does not perceive a need for incremental PPP-related institutions and regulations. Apparently, a dichotomous approach can be observed between the two models of PPP regulatory and institutional framework building. The one that Finland represents takes the PPP management more in the direction of running PPP as part of routine societal decision-making processes, and the other, represented by Poland, has a high level of dedicated institutionalisation and additional, perhaps somewhat excessive, governance. The number of employees at the central government level is significant and raises concerns over the coordination between different units and the efficiency of the entire PPP institutional structure, especially given the actual total number of projects procured by the government so far. Compared with that, the Latvian PPP-supporting framework is more straightforward, with one central coordinating body within the Ministry of Finance providing assistance to all procuring authorities. The Czech Republic, Hungary and Slovakia seem to have underestimated the complexities of PPP deals, to have therefore abandoned or significantly reduced PPP-supporting units and to be reluctant to adopt PPP specific regulations.

Transition countries with less-developed institutions may need to define very clearly the roles and responsibilities of actors and procedures in order to facilitate PPP – as Latvia or Poland did, the latter with its second PPP act. There have been signs that transition countries with specific PPP acts that are clear and concise enough perform better. A dedicated law sets out the rules for all actors concerned and prevents misunderstandings and uncertainty. At the very least, it clarifies the terminology.

The country observations seem to imply that more systematic organisational and procedural measures should be taken by any government considering PPP. These procedural measures should start with a heightened transparency, and an improved public reflection on what went wrong in the past and why. Such a learning process is crucial for developing appropriate knowledge, skills and capacities within both the private and public sectors. PPP units seem to work in transition countries. If staffed with qualified and competent professionals and freed from a pro-PPP bias, they have the ability to identify the best procurement method available in the given context and drive the procurement costs down. Furthermore, they facilitate concentration and transfer of knowledge and skills. At the same time, too many units and overlapping competences potentially cause confusion and inefficiencies as seen in the case of Poland.

In countries with traditionally sound procurement capacities and procedures, once a PPP gets the go-ahead, political changes usually do not affect the project's completion. In contrast to that, PPPs in several transition countries suffer from negative political interference – PPPs are cancelled at a late stage in the procurement process due to various changes in government. Moreover, politics in transition countries may cause selection of unviable projects that can result in both the loss of procurement costs and penalty fees and the completion of ineffective and suboptimal projects. Therefore, it is advisable to shield PPP implementation from changing political interests and interest networks. This can be achieved by, among other things, having national-level PPPs endorsed and decided by the parliaments. There is a need to depoliticise and objectivise selection of projects and procurement process. If that is achieved, PPPs in Central Europe have a chance to do more good in the form of benefits, than harm.

Acknowledgements

The authors would like to express their gratitude to the COST Action TU1001 for facilitating networking and cooperation among the members of the authors' team. Participation of Petr Witz in the team was enabled in the frame of the research project SVV of the Faculty of Social Sciences, Charles University.

References

Akintoye, A., Beck, M. and Hardcastle, C. (2003) *Public Private Partnerships: Managing Risks and Opportunities*. Oxford: Wiley-Blackwell

Antal, A. B., Dierkes, M. and Weiler, H. N. (1987) 'Cross-national policy research: traditions, achievements and challenge' in: M. Dierkes, H. Weiler and A. Antal *Comparative Policy Research: Learning from Experience*. Gower. ISBN 978-0-566-05196-8

Centrum PPP (2013) *Baza Projektów PPP*. Available online at: http://pppbaza.pl/

Czech Ministry of Finance (2013) a response to the official request under the Freedom of Information act from the 10 November 2013

Debande, O. (2002) 'Private Financing of Transport Infrastructure: An Assessment of the UK Experience'. *Journal of Transport Economics and Policy*, 2002, vol. 36, issue 3, pp. 355–387

Dimitrov, V., Goetz, K. and Wollmann, H. (2006) *Governing After Communism*. Boulder, CO: Rowman and Littlefield

Ferlie, E., Ashburner, L., Fitzgerald, L. and Pettigrew, A. (1996) *New Public Management in Action*. Oxford: Oxford University Press

Goetz, K. H. and Wollmann, H. (2001) 'Governmentalizing central executives in post-communist Europe: a four-country comparison'. *Journal of European Public Policy* 8(6): pp. 864–87

Grimsey, D. and Lewis M. K. (2005) 'Are Public Private Partnerships value for money? Evaluating alternative approaches and comparing academic and practitioner views'. *Accounting Forum* 29, pp. 345–348

Helikarová, K. (2012) 'Financování infrastruktury vs. PPP z pohledu Ministerstva financí ČR'. Czech Infrastructure & PPP Forum 2012 – conference proceedings.

Hausner, J. (Ed.) (2013) 'Raport o partnerstwie publiczno-prywatnym w Polsce'. Warszawa: Fundacja Centrum Partnerstwa Publiczno Prywatnego

Herbst, I., Jadach-Sepioło, A. and Marczeska, E. (2012) 'Analiza potencjału podmiotów publicznych i przedsiębiorstw do realizacji projektów partnerstwa publiczno-prywatnego w Polsce'. Warszawa: Polska Agencja Rozwoju Przedsiębiorczości

Juhasz, M. and Sharle, P. (2014) 'PPP in Hungary' in A. Roumboutsos, S. Farrel and K. Verhoest (2014) (Eds) *COST Action TU1001 – Public Private Partnerships in Transport: Trends & Theory: 2014 Discussion Series: Country Profiles & Case Studies*. ISBN 978-88-6922-009-8, COST Office, Brussels. Available online at: www.ppptransport.eu

Kania, M. (Ed.) (2013) *Partnerstwo publiczno-prywatne: teoria i praktyka*. Warszawa: Difin

Krajanová, D. (2014) 'PPP se vracia̋, štát už hladá poradcu' *Sme*, No 116, p. 10, 25 May 2014

Lember, V. (2013) 'PPP in Estonia' in: K. Verhoest, N. Carbonara, V. Lember, O. H. Petersen, W. Scherrer and M. van den Hurk (Eds) *COST Action TU1001 Public Private Partnerships in Transport: Trends & Theory P3T3, 2013 Discussion Papers Part I Country Profiles*. ISBN: 978-88-97781-60-8, COST Office, Brussels. Available online at: www.ppptransport.eu

Leviäkangas, P., Nokkala, M., Rönty, J., Talvitie, A., Pakkala, P., Haapasalo, H., Herrala, M. and Finnilä, K. (2011) *Ownership and governance of Finnish infrastructure networks*. VTT Publications 777: VTT, Espoo

Leviäkangas, P. (2013) 'PPP in Finland' in: K. Verhoest, N. Carbonara, V. Lember, O. H. Petersen, W. Scherrer and M. van den Hurk (Eds) *COST Action TU1001 Public Private Partnerships in Transport: Trends & Theory P3T3, 2013 Discussion Papers Part I Country Profiles*. ISBN: 978-88-97781-60-8, COST Office, Brussels. Available online at: www.ppptransport.eu

Lukasiewicz, A. (2014) 'PPP in Poland' in: K. Verhoest, N. Carbonara, V. Lember, O. H. Petersen, W. Scherrer and M. van den Hurk (Eds) *COST Action TU1001 Public Private Partnerships in Transport: Trends & Theory P3T3, 2014 Discussion Papers Part I Country Profiles*. ISBN: 978-88-6922-009-8, COST Office, Brussels. Available online at: www.ppptransport.eu

OECD (2011) *Public Procurement: Concessions and PPP*. Paris: OECD

Majszyk, K. (2013) 'GDDKiA może zapłacić dwa razy za projekt odcinka A1. Strata może sięgnąć 144 milionów złotych. *Gazeta Prawna*

Mälkönen, V. (2006) 'Eri hankintamuodot julkisissa investoinneissa' [Different procurement methods in public investments]. *VATT Discussion Papers 398*. Government Institute for Economic Research

Meyer-Sahling, J.-H. (2008) 'The changing colours of the post-communist state: the politicisation of the senior civil service in Hungary'. *European Journal of Political Research* 47(1), pp. 1–33

Ministry of Finance of Latvia (2014) *PPP Policy and Institutions*. Information brochure published by the ministry, 24 January 2014

Ministry of Transport and Communications Finland (2007) *Developing Financing Models for Transport Investments*. Publications of the Ministry of Transport and Communications 72/2008 [in Finnish only, English abstract]

Ministry of Transport and Communications Finland (2010a) *Finance Models for Transport Investments – Application Principles*. Publications of the Ministry of Transport and Communications 19/2010 [in Finnish only, English abstract]

Ministry of Transport and Communications Finland (2010b) *International Trends in Public Private Partnerships*. Publications of the Ministry of Transport and Communications 27/2010 [in Finnish only, English abstract]

Mladenovic, G. and Vajdic, N. (2013) 'PPP in Serbia' in: K. Verhoest, N. Carbonara, V. Lember, O. H. Petersen, W. Scherrer and M. van den Hurk (Eds) *COST Action TU1001 Public Private Partnerships in Transport: Trends & Theory P3T3, 2013 Discussion Papers Part I Country Profiles*. ISBN: 978-88-97781-60-8, COST Office, Brussels. Available online at: www.ppptransport.eu

Nunberg, B. (Ed.) (1999) *The State after Communism: Administrative Transitions in Central and Eastern Europe*. Washington, DC: The World Bank

Panasiuk, A. (2009) *Koncesja na roboty budowlane lub usługi. Partnerstwo publiczno-prywatne – Komentarz*. Warszawa: C. H. Beck

Roumboutsos, A., Nikolaidis, N. and Witz, P. (2013) 'Post-crisis Public-Private Partnerships models for transport infrastructure'. Rio de Janeiro: WCTRS Conference

Sajo, A. (1998) 'Corruption, clientalism, and the future of the constitutional state in Eastern Europe'. *East European Constitutional Review*, 7, 2, Spring

Sejm, R. P. (2013) 'Internetowy System Aktów Prawnych'. Available online at: http://isip.sejm.gov.pl/RelatedServlet?id=WDU20040190177&type=12&isNew=true

Szekeres, K. (2013) 'PPP in Slovakia' in: K. Verhoest, N. Carbonara, V. Lember, O. H. Petersen, W. Scherrer and M. van den Hurk (Eds) *COST Action TU1001 Public Private Partnerships in Transport: Trends & Theory P3T3, 2013 Discussion Papers Part I Country Profiles*. ISBN: 978-88-97781-60-8, COST Office, Brussels. Available online at: www.ppptransport.eu

The Government Office (2011) 'Jyrki Katainen's Government Program'. Helsinki, 22.6.2011

Transparency International (2009) '*Partnerství veřejného a soukromého sektoru v ČR*'. TIC: Prague

Verheijen, T. (Ed.) (2001) *Politico-administrative Relations: Who Rules?* Bratislava: NISPAcee

Witz, P. (2013a) 'Adapting governance of Public-Private Partnerships to the post-new public management regime: challenges to British, Czech and Spanish approaches'. International conference 'PPP Body of Knowledge (P3Book)', Preston UK

Witz, P. (2013b) 'PPP in the Czech Republic' in: K. Verhoest, N. Carbonara, V. Lember, O. H. Petersen, W. Scherrer and M. van den Hurk (Eds) *COST Action TU1001 Public Private Partnerships in Transport: Trends & Theory P3T3, 2013 Discussion Papers Part I Country Profiles*. ISBN: 978-88-97781-60-8, COST Office, Brussels. Available online at: www.ppptransport.eu

World Economic Forum (WEF) (2013) *Global Competitiveness Report 2013–2014*. Centre of Global Competitiveness and Performance, WEF. Available online from: www.wef.org

Zabko, O. (2013) 'PPP policy development in Latvia: experience of the first ten years and further perspectives'. Paper presented at the conference 'Global challenges in PPP' in Antwerp, November 2013

5 National contexts for PPPs in Europe

Conclusions and policy recommendations

*Koen Verhoest, Ole Helby Petersen,
Walter Scherrer, Murwantara Soecipto,
Veiko Lember, Pekka Leviäkangas,
Martijn van den Hurk, Tom Willems,
Petr Witz and Robert Ågren*

Public Private Partnerships (PPPs) in the form we know them in Europe are clearly facing a turning point. On the one hand, the budgetary situation of European governments is such that, in the years to come, additional financing from the private sector will be needed to be able to make investments. Moreover, there are such grand-scale social challenges that require cooperation between governments, citizens, non-profit and private companies. On the other hand, interest in PPPs, both in Europe and internationally, is under pressure. There is an image that PPPs are complex and that it is risky business for governments if they are not properly equipped to deal with PPPs. Moreover, the financial crisis has made (financial and other) actors averse to risk which, in turn, makes financing PPPs all the more difficult. Finally, there is a lack of actual transparency and empirical evaluation of PPPs, which may cause public support to be undermined.

Emerging findings

In this perspective, studying the national context across European countries is of crucial importance, in order to understand the different take-up of PPPs in the past and the prospects for the future. Based on the cross-country data collection carried out within COST Action TU1001, the three chapters which precede this chapter aimed to compare countries in terms of their context for PPPs. The three chapters are complementary to each other as they use partially different approaches and have a different focus. Whereas the chapter by Soecipto *et al.* focuses on policies, regulation and supporting arrangements as crucial elements of governmental support for PPPs across 20 countries and uses cluster analysis and a refined coding as analytical method, the chapter by Oliveira *et al.* uses multiple correspondence analysis with binary coding on data of 17 countries in order to develop a broader concept of institutional maturity, including some elements of government support but adding other elements like the maturity of financial capital, thereby referring to different levels of PPP context (see Figure 1.1 in the chapter by Verhoest *et al.* in this Part). Both chapters show that, despite a growing convergence in the PPP policy rhetoric across Europe, there is a widespread and enduring divergence in the actual policies, regulations and supporting arrangements enacted by governments to support (or hinder) the uptake of PPP across countries.

Given their different focus, approach and coverage of countries it is logical that both chapters result in partially different clustering and labelling of countries in terms of PPP context. In the chapter by Soecipto *et al.* the 20 countries are grouped into four clusters in terms of their governmental support for PPPs. Cluster 1 refers to countries with well-developed policies, political commitment and supporting arrangements (the UK, Netherlands, Germany and Belgium-Flanders). Greece, Portugal and France are grouped as strong legal and regulatory supporters of PPPs as their governmental support emphasises the articulation of a largely supportive legal and regulatory framework (cluster 2). Countries in cluster 3 have developed most elements of governmental support of PPPs but at a more limited or moderate scale (Switzerland, Czech Republic, Denmark, Italy and Slovak Republic). Cluster 4 comprises eight countries, being Austria, Estonia, Sweden, Finland, Serbia, Slovenia, Cyprus and Hungary, which are the least articulated providers of government support for PPP on all the three dimensions of governmental support.

The chapter by Oliveira *et al.* classifies 17 countries into two groups each with two clusters. Group 1 (cluster C1 and C2) includes Belgium (Flanders), United Kingdom (UK) and The Netherlands as cluster 1, and France, Greece, Italy, Portugal, and Serbia as cluster 2. Both clusters represent countries that are similar in terms of having established a central PPP unit, a formal knowledge centre and using PPP in more than four sectors. The two clusters mainly differ in terms of maturity in the dimension related to financial capital. Less PPP enthusiastic countries are in Group 2, encompassing cluster C3 with Cyprus, Slovak Republic, and cluster C4 with Austria, Finland, Denmark, Switzerland and Czech Republic. Countries in Group 2 are similar in two aspects: none have a PPP law (except for Slovenia) and all countries have a learning structure to capture and diffuse PPP knowledge in government. The main dissimilarities between clusters C3 and C4 seem to be in the level of scepticism towards PPP. In addition, Estonia and Sweden are considered as being outliers, since both countries have shown very little interest in PPP with no specific PPP policies.

Both chapters agree in their observation that the sample of PPP-enthusiastic countries seems to be distinguished in more policy-oriented countries versus countries investing in specific PPP legislation (see also Verhoest *et al.* 2015). Oliveira *et al.* (this volume) distinguish these groups as, respectively, organisational countries and regulatory countries, although the latter group develops less PPP specific regulation than the former group (possibly supported by the general procurement law and regulations). The first group of policy-oriented countries includes countries marked by a PPP institutional model dependent on supporting arrangements and clear policies and political commitment, while the second group consists of countries in which PPP routines are mostly supported by extensive PPP-specific legal frameworks (incl. PPP laws) besides institutionalised PPP supporting arrangements. Oliveira *et al.* (this volume) launch the hypothesis that

PPP policy and PPP law might be performing similar functions in different institutional contexts. Moreover, they hypothesise that countries, which appear enthusiastic with the PPP delivery format and invest in the development of PPP laws, may be doing this in a 'leap frog' process of catching up.

The third chapter by Witz *et al.* (this volume) presents the findings from a comparison of eight Central and East European countries with focus on their government support (i.e. political commitment, legal framework and institutional setting) as well as transparency of contracts and project performance and the public perception of PPPs. The chapter compares countries with transition economies, being Czech Republic, Estonia, Hungary, Latvia, Poland, Serbia and Slovakia on the one hand, and Finland as benchmarking country on the other hand. The chapter draws a very heterogeneous picture of PPP implementation processes in the countries 'east of Elbe', ranging from the financial and political failure in Hungary to a relatively thriving PPP market in Poland, with the rest as being intermediate based on the number of realised projects. The latter group can be further divided into countries with a consistent approach to PPP over time represented by Finland, Latvia or Estonia, and countries with a rather unstable PPP policy and unsettled PPP environment represented by the Czech Republic, Slovakia and Serbia. In terms of approaches to PPP, the chapter illustrates that each country in the region has its autonomous and specific PPP policy and procedures for PPP implementation influenced by deeply rooted patterns of governance, although there are common features. The expectation that the countries with certain historical reservations to the diffusion of market mechanisms in the public sector will reject PPP as incompatible with their development strategies seems to be reliably refuted. At the same time, though, the assumption that transition countries may face greater problems implementing PPPs than countries characterised by long-established institutions has proven to be largely justified. As the authors state 'certain transition countries, burdened with the legacy of public mismanagement under the previous regime, still struggle not just with PPP but with principles of good governance in general' (Witz *et al.* this volume). In sum, the chapter shows that countries' PPP failure rate seems to correspond rather well with the strength of their institutions as measured by international organisations (like the World Economic Forum).

Further research

The chapters presented here invite further research on several topics. Comparative data about the PPP policy contexts in different countries can be used in different ways to increase our knowledge. First, going beyond the efforts of Witz *et al.* (this volume), we might aim to further understand the emergence of PPP policies, regulation and supporting institutions, as well as their similarities and differences across countries and politico-administrative systems, by referring to international isomorphic pressures as well as country specific macro-institutional variables like culture, legal tradition, polity, economic-financial evolutions and actor constellations. We might study policy diffusion and transfer processes to understand the spread of PPP-propagating policies, regulations and supporting institutions.

Second, we may study the relation between the PPP policy, regulation and supporting institutions on the one hand and the extent to which PPP projects have been initiated, progressed or failed in various countries. Contrary to intuitive insights, this relationship is not so straightforward, with some countries with 'incomplete' institutional frameworks having a relatively large take-up of PPP, or countries with highly elaborated policies, regulations and supporting institutions experiencing a high failure rate of PPP projects (see Verhoest *et al.* 2015 for a preliminary and partial analysis for the period 2010-2012). Moreover, in spite of the inconclusive empirical evidence of PPP performance (see, for example, Hodge and Greve 2007) and difficulties arising from the global financial crisis, PPPs remains high on the political agenda in several European countries. By looking at the contextual factors, we will be better positioned to understand why PPPs continue to be popular in these countries in spite of such mixed results.

In sum, material presented in this chapter might be used in further research to draw insights on how and why governments working under different contextual settings develop institutional frameworks, policies and regulations that are meant to guide and steer the development and implementation of PPPs and, by linking these institutional frameworks to project-specific information on PPP practices, to study how they actually work.

Policy recommendations

In the remainder of this chapter, we now turn to the policy recommendations that were developed within the Working Group on National Context within COST Action TU1001 based on the comparative analyses of governmental support for PPP across countries. Our research has shown that a country's preparedness for PPP is influenced by the dimensions political support for PPP, legal environment for PPP and PPP-supporting organisational environment. A survey of 20 countries suggests that the degree of government support for PPPs varies strongly across dimensions and countries. Governments and public agencies could use such information to benchmark their own efforts to stimulate PPPs with the efforts of other governments. Moreover, investors might benefit from getting information on the PPP-enhancing context in different countries based on comparative country profiles and indices that map the governmental support and other aspects of the PPP environment in a country. In order to accomplish this transparency and evaluation of policies it is essential to, and even partly a prerequisite for, shaping a political, legal and organisational environment that is supportive of the development of PPP. We develop policy recommendations for these different dimensions of government support in the next three sections.

Policy recommendations on policies and political environment for PPP

The comparative research presented in the preceding chapters illustrates that political commitment and clear policies are important for establishing an environment that is supportive of the take-up of PPP. Given the long duration of PPP contracts, the most important precondition for a successful implementation of PPP policy is a stable political commitment to assure potential investors and to give them trust in the process. In the later phases of the procurement process and realisation phase of PPP projects, political influence may have an adverse effect on, for example, viable PPP deals signed by political opponents or promotion of projects that are not viable at all. Thus, on the project level, there is a need to depoliticise and objectivise the selection of projects and the procurement process.

At the level of PPP policies we recommend the following points:

- PPP as a government policy should not be launched unless there is broad cross-party support for using the model in the long run because instable political support might jeopardise the possible benefits of long-term partnerships.
- Proper guidelines should be created, together with either special dedicated units or general procurement units that are empowered to manage the PPP implementation processes.

At the level of PPP projects we recommend the following points:

- The PPP procurement process should be objectivised and depoliticised by strengthening the institutional framework for PPP and the affiliated decision-making based on proper evaluation and assessment of individual projects by independent government organisations that should be directly responsible for their decisions during the entire lifecycle of the project.
- PPP implementation should be shielded from changing political interests and clientelism by requiring that individual PPP deals over a certain threshold value be endorsed by national parliaments and by writing other relevant safeguards into the legal framework or into PPP guidelines.
- Parliaments should be informed about and involved in the development of multi-annual budgets that list the financial liabilities towards individual PPPs over time.

Research and international practice show that transparency and evaluation are useful in creating long-term support for PPPs. Therefore, it is crucial that additional tools are develpoed to further improve this transparency. Data and information are key prerequisites to move towards an investment environment that satisfies both the public and private sides. The public side is associated with nothing less than the involvement and engagement of citizens and different interest groups. The private side needs transparency too if the PPP market is to be made as efficient as possible. Opportunistic projects deliver uncertain results, whereas projects that are exposed to transparent scrutiny of the public, investors and media are much more likely to succeed in terms of generating outcomes that satisfy the multifaceted needs of public and private stakeholders in society.

One of the vital issues when governments are attempting to create a fertile ground for viable PPP projects is enhancing the transparency of past, existing and future PPP projects. In practice, digging into past projects by carrying out *ex-post* analysis (as often recommended by researchers and analysts) may be fruitful and provide relevant information for future decisions and projects. There are examples that are worth closer consideration. In Belgium the first steps in the direction of enhancing transparency and evaluation of PPP have been taken with the *ex-ante* added-value scan and reporting to the Flemish Parliament. In Australia and Canada the so-called reverse onus principle is already applied, which expands the transparency of PPP projects to the public as it shifts the onus of proof to the other (i.e. the private) partner. Another example of a fairly transparent PPP project and arrangement is the rail link connecting the centre of Stockholm with its international airport ('Arlandabanan'). Its website contains annual reports of the project company, the annual reports are by law made public (although a nominal fee has to be paid for detailed reports), the history of the project is well described with relevant milestones and related documents, and the corporate governance and ownership structure are clearly described.

These examples are worth pursuing in the quest to make PPP transparent and accountable to the public. Indeed, the increasing transparency of PPP projects is an issue not only associated with PPP, but also with the wider context of public investments and decision-making processes. Transparency created only for PPP requires dedicated rules and regulations, and, in practice, blocks the inevitable need to assess both PPP projects and other projects side by side. Hence, enhanced transparency requires more general practices to be adopted by countries to build an efficient infrastructure procurement market that is able to reflect a wide range of stakeholders' needs. If insufficiency of capital was ever one of the reasons why PPPs were taken into practice, transparency enhancement will now, after decades of experience with PPPs in Europe, serve a wider community of stakeholders including taxpayers and the public as a whole. New business models will emerge, new investors will enter the market, and innovative financing and procurement models will take their place and should be welcomed to the extent that they are transparent and accountable to society.

From our arguments we derive the following policy recommendations, as developed by the respective Working Group of COST Action TU1001 'PPP in Transport: Trends and Theory':

- *Ex-ante* evaluation instruments should be made more robust and be utilised more extensively and systematically. Also, current PPP projects should be subjected more systematically to *ex-post* evaluations, which should always be made available to the public.
- Confidentiality-based restrictions in PPP contracts should neither include elements like interest rates, return on investments and output specifications, nor the financial resources invested by public authorities.
- There should be full transparency in terms of governments' long-term financial engagements related to PPP contracts, and such engagements should be

placed on the government's balance sheet in order to avoid off-balance sheet accounting.

- During the course of a PPP contract, information stemming from the regular monitoring of the deliverables under the contract should be made publicly available and accessible.
- Public auditors and evaluators of PPP schemes should have adequate competences and resources to be able to perform the task of supervision.
- There is a need for continued effort to guarantee and reinforce the audit capacities and supervision by public authorities and parliaments at both national and sub-national levels where PPPs are being implemented.

Our research also shows that there is a significant lack of identifiable, measurable and reliable data on PPP activities both nationally and internationally. A lack of systematic, comparable and reliable data poses a serious hindrance to cross-national learning and distribution of best practice. It also emphasises the need for transparency to move into the next stage from procurement to implementation. If all PPP projects are liable to publish their financial information (the reporting requirement is there anyway), and if such a requirement is part of the PPP contract, market information relating to PPP companies is likely to become as transparent as that of other private companies. This will in turn allow analysts to investigate the projects and, also transmitted by the financial media, market information will become available and thus market efficiency will be increased. Consequently, there is a strong need for creating transparent and comparable cross-country data and make such data publicly available to benefit both public and private stakeholders.

We recommend establishing better data availability by taking the following steps:

- Data availability on PPP projects should be improved to increase transparency and accountability of all PPP projects, and a full list of PPPs with basic information should be made available at public websites.
- Data availability on PPP projects should be improved in order to allow for a better evaluation of PPP projects and should include PPP projects at national, regional and local levels.
- A comprehensive database of PPP projects should be built in order to underpin cross-national learning from best practice and support profound empirical analysis and research based on high-quality data.

Policy recommendations on the legal and regulatory framework for PPPs

The legal and regulatory framework for PPPs in countries may consist of a general public procurement regulation (which, in European countries, is strongly harmonised by EU regulation) and specific regulations and laws on PPPs or concessions. The findings from our research suggest a correlation between the existence of a specific PPP law and the preparedness of a country's legal environment for taking up PPPs. Nevertheless, legal provisions, which are in line with EU procurement law, seem to be sufficient for the take-up of PPP as a form of transport infrastructure delivery, and there are several countries with widespread PPP activity (such as the UK) that have not implemented a specific PPP law.

We recommend the following in relation to the legal and regulatory framework for PPP:

- Formulating a specific PPP law might have a weaker impact than expected. In most countries legal provisions, which are in line with EU procurement law, seem to be sufficient for the take-up of PPP as a form of transport infrastructure delivery. Therefore, the need for a specific PPP law should be assessed with great care.
- However, it is implied through research that specific PPP laws could serve their purpose when there is a strong need for harmonisation of PPPs, their processing through administration and final implementation and operation. Well-designed PPP acts have proven to be helpful in transition countries with challenges in public sector management and a high level of legal and political uncertainty. Specific PPP laws may alleviate legal uncertainties within adjacent policy fields such as spatial planning or land use rights.
- PPP-specific laws that are issued merely because of legitimisation reasons or to comply with normative pressures from international bodies like the OECD, the EU and the World Bank, or to give a strong signal of PPP interest to investors, should be carefully considered in terms of their relation with public procurement regulations and other regulatory frameworks.
- The public procurement regulation can facilitate PPPs within a country. Hence, instead of PPP-specific regulation, the public procurement legal framework could be expanded (or revised) to enable PPPs where they are seen as necessary.
- Today, most TEN-T investments still occur at national level and mainly serve national contexts. Benchmarking of PPPs and their contexts at European level should be implemented in a way that paves the way for pan-European investments to develop transport infrastructure across national borders.

Policy recommendations on PPP-supporting arrangements

PPP-supporting arrangements comprise dedicated PPP support units and standardisation efforts concerning contracts, contract procedures, risk allocation schemes and project content. While our analysis focuses on PPP support organisations at the central government level in their respective countries, it is important to note that in most countries that actually have a dedicated PPP unit the central government units serves procuring authorities at both the central and local level, while regional PPP units are absent in most cases.

With regard to their overall level of involvement and thus their importance within the whole PPP-supporting system, PPP units show noteworthy differences between countries ranging from both *de facto* and *de jure* strong institutions to countries without any dedicated PPP units. In general, the significance of PPP units tended to be overrated in the past: they have been good at promoting PPPs, but that may sometimes lead to overlooking alternatives and imply a certain pro-PPP bias. Moreover, our research shows that PPP units have in some instances mainly been established for formal reasons, not for reasons of political necessity.

As PPP units function alongside and are affected by a number of factors, which are either conducive or constraining to the development of PPPs, their *de facto* role might differ from their *de jure* role. Some PPP-supporting units have become powerful players and carry out important functions associated with project implementation, which makes them drivers of PPP policy (for example, MAPPP in France). On the other hand, examples from the study have shown that even if a unit is strong in formal terms, other factors can shape PPP policy and implementation and marginalise the role of a unit (for example, in the Serbian Commission for PPPs). An investigation of this difference between formal rules and rules-in-use would enable a further assessment of the role of PPP-supporting units.

Finally, applying standardisation of contracts, contract procedures, risk allocation schemes, and project content could allow for clustering of projects and thus reducing costs and reaping the benefits of economies of scale. Yet, a balance must be found between standardisation on the one hand and differentiation and customisation on the other hand.

We recommend the following in relation to PPP-supporting arrangements:

- PPP-supporting units require strong political support as well as a stable mandate if they are to fulfil a position that cannot be neglected. Thus, whereas political whims may be required to establish PPP-supporting units, their role can only be relevant in the longer term if those political whims are put at a distance once a unit has been established.
- There should be more attention placed on strengthening the *de facto* effectiveness of PPP units rather than only focusing on their formal role. PPP units should have a powerful mandate and political support. The political support at the establishment phase is much needed. Due to political and private interests, PPP units have often not been able to influence policy.
- Knowledge of PPP in most European countries is dispersed or even fragmented over various ministries and levels of government. Our advice is that this knowledge is pooled by the current knowledge centres, that there is a supporting service and that sector cells cooperate even more closely (for example, IAVA holding company model in Belgium).
- In a broader context, we suggest that instead of a specialised PPP unit, one can opt generally to group the expertise related to government investments into an 'infrastructure unit' or in procurement units that can decide on the appropriate procurement method (PPP units may push for PPP although they may not be the best solution on offer). The advantage of such a structure is that, for such a unit, PPP is only one of the possible forms in which a poject can be

implemented and that a more neutral assessment can be made as to whether PPP or traditional procurement is the best solution for the specific task.

- Adequate support should not only be provided to public bodies at central government level but equally so to regional and local authorities in order to advance proper project planning and implementation.

References

Hodge, G. A. and Greve, C. (2007) 'Public–Private Partnerships: an international performance review'. *Public Administration Review*, 67(3), pp. 545–558

Verhoest, K., Petersen, O. H., Scherrer, W. and Soecipto, R. M. (2015) 'How do governments support the development of Public Private Partnerships? Measuring and comparing PPP governmental support across 20 European countries'. *Transport Reviews*, 35(2), 118–139

Part 2

Decision models

6 Decision models in Public Private Partnerships

Introduction

Nunzia Carbonara

Although PPPs are now widely used for procuring public sector infrastructure around the world, their performance could be affected by a number of factors and their interactions, which might cause the inefficiency and ineffectiveness of the projects.

The critical failure factors of PPPs may be traced back to the lack of both a well-structured and feasible decision framework and analytical models that help both parties to make the best decisions – decisions that do not erode the savings achieved through PPP, undermine the expected benefits in PPP, and that take into account the multifarious and sometimes conflicting interests of different stakeholders involved in the PPP.

In order to address and resolve these issues the current research activity in PPPs reports some interesting studies, particularly those produced within the framework of COST Action TU1001 that provide useful guidelines to support the PPP decision-making process so assuring a more effective use of the PPP delivery model. The overview of this research and its complementarity is presented in the conclusions of Part 2.

The emphasis of the COST Action TU1001 working group on decision models has been on identifying relevant aspects of the decision process in PPPs and analysing them through suitable theories and models. Key theories and methodological tools used have been transaction cost theory, real-option theory, game theory, Monte Carlo simulation, Delphi and other surveys.

A most important contribution has been the organisation of all decisions within an overall framework, which has been gradually populated with models and methodologies.

Specifically, Chapter 7 reports the PPP Decision System (DS) framework developed by Carbonara *et al.* that represents the PPP decision-making process in a tree structure that identifies six areas of decision, each of them treated at a macro- and a micro-level. The framework allows the identification of the basic components of the PPP decision-making process, namely the phase of the PPP life-cycle in which the decision should be taken (When), the area of decision (What), the issues to deal with to take the decision (Which), the instruments/ processes to be used to take the decision (How), and the actors involved in the decision (Who).

The other two contributions to this Part concern an alternative conceptual model of selecting the appropriate tendering process and a discussion on innovative financing instruments.

More specifically, Chapter 8 presents the model developed by Pellegrino *et al.* for choosing the tendering procedure in PPPs that minimises the transaction costs borne by the public sector. Specifically, the model relates the level of transaction costs and the information managed during the tendering process and allows the identification of the best tendering procedure that minimises the transaction costs, namely one that includes the phase of tenderers' prequalification and the bid evaluation carried out by using complex methods – i.e. multi-criteria and composite methods, etc.

Finally, in Chapter 9, Syriopoulos discusses a number of innovative, dynamic and flexible financing and risk management instruments that can be appropriate for PPP ventures. The author, focusing on two key financial instruments, namely municipal bonds and interest rate swaps, highlights that the former can provide a source of alternative funding to expand PPP financing choices and the latter can contribute to financial risk dispersion and control.

7 Improving PPP decision-making processes

A decision support framework

Nunzia Carbonara, Sergio Domingues,
Louis Gunnigan, Aristeidis Pantelias,
Roberta Pellegrino and
Thierry Vanelslander

Introduction

Identifying, developing and implementing an infrastructure project as a Public Private Partnership (PPP) involves different steps and different actors. Numerous studies to date have demonstrated that to successfully implement PPPs it is necessary to manage the interaction of multiple factors during the life cycle of the project including, but not limited to, cost, quality, schedule, management ability and so forth, by taking appropriate decisions. These decisions should not be limited only to the 'front end' of the project nor to any other specific stage (such as planning, preconstruction, construction or operation), but should instead be extended to the whole life cycle of PPP projects. According to Koppenjan (2005) one of the main critical failure factors of PPPs is the lack of interaction within or insufficient embedding of the broader decision-making context. A well-structured and feasible decision framework is necessary to make PPPs more efficient (Zhang *et al.* 2002).

Decision-making in a PPP context is a demanding task because of a number of challenges:

1   the process needs to engage a wide range of stakeholders with different roles and objectives;
2   various decisions need to be made at different times and by different organisations;
3   many decisions have long-term effects and are based on long-term forecasts that are subject to great uncertainty.

The above challenges have motivated broad research interests in PPP decision-making during recent years. Relevant areas that have been investigated in the literature include tender/project team selection (Kumaraswamy and Anvuur 2008), concession models (Shen *et al.* 2002, 2007; Shen and Wu 2005), as well as specific risk analysis in politics (Wang *et al.* 2000) and financing (Wibowo and Kochendorfer 2005; Alonso-Conde *et al.* 2006). However, previous research efforts have been primarily aimed at resolving decision problems at the 'front end' and, more specifically, at the stage of procurement without paying attention to the integration and interaction of factors during the entire PPP life-cycle.

The aim of this chapter is to provide useful guidelines for supporting the PPP decision-making process in a structured way from the perspective of the relevant public sector authority. In order to achieve this aim a Decision Support (DS) framework has been developed with the intention to identify the main decisions to be taken during a PPP project, the actors involved in each of them, and the main instruments and methods used to support them. The DS framework is developed by framing practical and empirical knowledge on PPP decision processes within the theoretical model of business process modelling borrowed from the literature. A similar approach could also be developed for the relevant decisions of the various private sector stakeholders in such projects, i.e. the sponsors, the lenders and the financial investors. Modelling private sector decisions is outside the scope of this study and is included as a topic for further research.

The rationale for exploring further the public sector PPP decision space, despite the significant body of already existing literature, is that, with the exception of the consideration of unsolicited proposals (generated by the private sector), the public sector is in all cases the party that drives the delivery of such projects by undertaking multiple roles through their life-cycle from 'cradle to grave', i.e. owner, promoter, procurer, client (for the services provided), supervisor and contract co-manager. Furthermore, it is ultimately the public sector that has a vested interest in the delivery of such projects, due to the usual 'public good' nature of services to be provided, which makes its capacity for objective, efficient and effective decision-making a critical pre-requisite for the successful implementation of these projects.

As a first step towards making a contribution in this area, and in order to avoid 'reinventing the wheel', a screening of several existing instruments supporting public sector PPP decision processes was initially conducted, considering namely:

- *The PPP Guide* developed by the European PPP Expertise Centre (EPEC) of the European Investment Bank (EIB);
- *The Toolkit for Public-Private Partnerships in Roads and Highways* developed by the World Bank and the Public-Private Infrastructure Advisory Facility (PPIAF);
- *The PPP Toolkit* developed by the Ministry of Finance of the Indian Government (MFIG).

The results of this screening were combined with practical experience provided by PPP experts (from both industry and academia) during several brainstorming sessions. This process led to the identification of the areas of decision-making characterising each phase of the PPP life-cycle as well as the different issues to be dealt with within each area. The above efforts have culminated in the development of the 'PPP Decision Tree', with two levels of detail – a macro- and a micro-level. At the macro-level the different areas of decision-making for each phase of the PPP life cycle have been identified. At the micro-level, for each individual area of decision-making in each phase of the PPP life cycle, the different issues that warrant taking a decision have been further identified and characterised.

The remainder of this chapter is structured as follows: an overview of issues related to the PPP life-cycle is presented, followed by a discussion on PPP decisions. Then the proposed DS framework is introduced and discussed. The chapter ends with conclusions and topics for further research.

PPP project life cycle

The consideration of certain fundamental characteristics of PPP arrangements, i.e. the long-term nature of the agreement, the public sector's aim to contract a service (or deliver a 'public good') rather than just procure an infrastructure asset, the time variation of risks, as well as the interrelated nature of various project activities, has naturally led several scholars and practitioners to adopt a life-cycle approach when describing the PPP delivery process.

On the practitioner side, the review of the three aforementioned PPP guides provides further validation of this approach. For example, the Indian Government organises the PPP delivery process into a sequence of four phases: (1) project identification and needs analysis; (2) PPP decision, project appraisal and clearance; (3) final approval and procurement; (4) implementation and monitoring. Additionally, *The Toolkit for Public-Private Partnerships in Roads and Highways* developed by the World Bank and the PPIAF (2009) identifies five key stages in the delivery process, from the selection of highway projects, through contract award and until the facilities are transferred back to the public authority: (1) identification, prioritisation and selection of the PPP project; (2) due diligence and feasibility studies; (3) procurement; (4) contract award; and (5) contract management. Finally, according to the EIB, the PPP life-cycle is defined by four phases: (1) project identification; (2) detailed preparation; (3) procurement; and (4) project implementation.

On the academic side, several authors (Tiong 1990; Aoust *et al.* 2000; Thomas *et al.* 2003; Carbonara *et al.* 2013) have also adopted the project life-cycle approach in order to identify and analyse PPP risks. This is important, since it is widely recognised that the magnitude of the impact of a risk materialising decreases over time, while its probability of occurrence increases over time due to the increase of uncertainty in the long run. Other scholars have modelled PPP by using a life-cycle approach in order to identify critical success factors and related key performance indicators. According to Yuan *et al.* (2009) the life-cycle of a typical PPP project is characterised by six stages: (1) needs for PPP; (2) design and building; (3) transfer management; (4) procurement; (5) operation; (6) post-transfer.

Furthermore, Demirag *et al.* (2004) have also employed a life-cycle approach in order to develop a system for evaluating the implications of accountability and value-for-money (VfM) decisions in private finance initiative (PFI) projects, not only during the projects' initial stages but also throughout their implementation.

In particular they define five stages in the PPP delivery process: initiation; set-up; implementation; internal monitoring; and external monitoring.

In this study, public sector decisions within the PPP life-cycle will be analysed according to the EIB EPEC guide, i.e. by considering the following four phases: project identification, detailed preparation, procurement and project implementation. The involvement of the public sector in the context of these four phases is briefly described as follows:

- Project identification takes place before the preparation and procurement phases. It determines whether the selected project can (and/or should) be delivered as a PPP instead of using traditional public procurement. It involves two stages: project selection and assessment of the PPP option. In this phase the projects are identified, ranked and prioritised. The best projects, with the highest potential for delivery through the PPP route, have to meet a wide range of criteria: for example, strong economic and social need, robust economic and financial viability with no (or minor) need for public aid, manageable risks and limited negative environmental and social impacts, among others.
- The detailed preparation phase takes place before launching the tender. This phase includes activities and studies to ensure the selected project is well designed and can be successfully tendered and implemented. It involves intensive stakeholder consultation to ensure that the eventual final design will be guided by a robust set of output specifications.
- Procurement starts with the publication of the procurement notice and ends with financial close, the point at which project activities (beginning with detailed design and construction) can start. It includes two stages: the bidding process and the period from the selection of the preferred bidder to financial close.
- Project implementation covers the period during which the PPP project is being implemented (i.e. from financial close to the expiry of the PPP contract). It involves regular monitoring of performance and requires taking appropriate actions in accordance with the terms of the PPP contract. This phase consists of two stages: contract management and *ex-post* evaluation.

The four aforementioned phases follow a sequential time path. However, they are not completely isolated from one another and there are likely to be feedback loops and other interrelations between them based on the issues that may arise within the PPP life-cycle. For example, a possible backloop may be due to a tender failure, which may have resulted from weak project preparation or because the project is just not appropriate for delivery through the PPP route and should be returned to the public procurement programme. In the first case the backloop is between phase 3 and phase 2 while in the second case between phase 3 and phase 1 of the PPP life-cycle. Such backloops are, in practice, very costly and in many cases tarnish the reputation of public sector authorities that are in charge of delivering these types of projects. Being able to streamline and rationalise the decision process in order to minimise or completely avoid such backloops is an additional aim of the analysis presented in this study.

Decisions in PPP projects

Implementing PPP projects requires taking a sequence of decisions along the entire PPP life-cycle that clearly affect the best possible VfM of the projects and, more generally, the PPP success (Yuan *et al.* 2009).

First and foremost, decisions need to be taken for the identification and prioritisation of PPP projects. The public sector should be aware that the PPP route is not a panacea and may not be appropriate for all infrastructure projects. The government should conduct a comprehensive feasibility study to examine the economic viability as well as the applicability of the PPP approach for a specific infrastructure project before it is implemented, by assessing the business objectives, needs and constraints, including the issue of affordability. An outline business case, specifying the output requirements, is prepared by the public-sector authority in consultation with PPP stakeholders. It involves the assessment of costs and benefits of the various options including do nothing, do minimum, traditional procurement and PPP (Kwak *et al.* 2009). Additionally, when several projects are intended to be developed under PPP, the government should also prioritise these projects by considering their economic and financial strengths and weaknesses, the required public sector support, social acceptance, and environmental and social impacts.

The success of a PPP project depends largely on the selection of the most suitable private concessionaire, which requires a well-structured tendering process, an appropriate concessionaire evaluation method, and a set of objective evaluation criteria (Miller 2000). In particular, a well-structured tendering process that can minimise tendering costs and ensure sufficient competition between private bidders is necessary, since it is widely recognised that the tendering process of PPP is more complicated and more costly than that of traditional public infrastructure development[1]. Many governments adopt a multi-stage tendering process composed of stages such as inviting expressions of interest, prequalifying tenders, evaluating tenders, and negotiating with the preferred bidder(s) to select the most suitable concessionaire. This is not sufficient, however, to guarantee an optimum selection. According to HM Treasury[2], a tender should only be selected as the preferred tender and subsequently be awarded the contract when it satisfies criteria including: meeting output specifications, whole life VfM, acceptance of key contract terms and required transfer of risks, confirmation of access to finance, unitary charge affordable to the public client (if applicable), and a cohesive consortium (Zhang 2004a; Zhang 2004b). Towards this end, a number of tender evaluation methods and criteria have been developed to assist governments in selecting the best concessionaire (Zhang 2005; Zhang *et al.* 2002).

Other significant decisions concern risk management and, more specifically, risk allocation between the contractual parties, as well as the selection of suitable risk mitigation strategies. The accurate allocation and mitigation of risks are major assignments for the success of PPP projects (Li *et al.* 2005) and this is why, in recent years, an interesting volume of literature on risk management in PPP projects has been developed, both from academic (Bing *et al.* 2005; Li 2003; Grimsey and Lewis 2004; Ng and Loosemore 2007) as well as industry authors (see, for instance, technical reports provided on the US Federal Highway Administration website). Effectively, in order to assist the public sector with decisions related to risk allocation in PPP projects, various standardised risk allocation matrices have been developed (Milner 2004; Smith 1996). With respect to the identification of suitable strategies to mitigate risks, most of the relevant studies have had a very specific focus, i.e. proposing specific strategies to mitigate specific types of risk. In particular, there are a number of risk mitigation strategies for technical risks. These mitigation strategies are, in general, defined as clauses in the agreement and usually take the form of guarantees provided by one of the participants. For example, to mitigate construction risks, Pfeffer (2010) proposes a Guaranteed Maximum Price agreement, while Nevitt and Fabozzi (2005) propose completion guarantee extension to debt maturity. Several strategies have been proposed to mitigate commercial risks, either in the form of guarantees, options (i.e., to expand or contract project capacity), or other mechanisms. Finally, specific mitigation strategies are proposed for economic and financial risks. For example, an interest rate guarantee may be released by government in order to ensure the project's financial close (Wibowo 2004). A step toward the development of a comprehensive tool for supporting the decision makers in the selection of appropriate risk mitigation strategies has been undertaken by Carbonara *et al.* (2013) through the development of a framework that allows the association of risks encountered in PPP projects with suitable risk mitigation strategies.

Many other decisions characterise the whole PPP life-cycle, such as the selection of the appropriate concession period, the determination of the project's financial structure, and the establishment of key performance indicators to monitor the project's implementation and operation. All of these decisions are interrelated and should take into consideration the multifarious and sometimes conflicting interests of different stakeholders involved in the project.

Given the obvious importance of all the aforementioned decisions in the success of PPP projects, in recent years a number of useful PPP decision-support instruments have been produced by various organisations, such as the ones considered in this study. These instruments intend to help overcome the lack of standardisation that causes many PPP decisions to be left to the discretionary power of relevant public decision-makers. This lack of standardisation, often combined with a lack of experience and specialist skills by public decision makers, can negatively affect projects delivered via the PPP route.

In spite of the positive contribution of the decision support instruments that have been developed to date, there are some critical issues that are still left unattended. In particular, current decision tools are predominantly based on financial concepts of VfM, while the individual perspectives and objectives of the different stakeholders are often disregarded. However, it is widely recognised that most of the PPP-related decisions taken by public authorities are not driven solely by economic principles. In fact, besides economic criteria, public authorities have to comply with a complex framework of legal regulations and laws (Essig and Batran 2005) and to appraise the feasibility of the project in relation to the environmental, societal, political, legislative and financial context of the country (and/ or sector) within which a project is being developed. Furthermore, most of the decision tools provided correspond to the project's early stages. However, as previously explained, it is important to recognise that decisions are taken across all phases of the PPP life cycle.

In order to provide useful guidelines for supporting the PPP decision-making process to cope with the above critical issues, a DS framework is proposed that identifies the main decisions to be taken during a PPP project, the actors involved in each of them, and the main instruments and methods used to support them.

The decision support framework

The PPP decision tree

The analysis of the existing body of knowledge on PPP decision processes involved the review of existing instruments supporting PPP decision processes as well as related academic literature. The outcomes of this review were combined with practical experience provided by PPP experts (from both academia and the industry) during thorough brainstorming sessions. Through this two-tiered analysis it was possible to identify the areas of decision-making that characterise each phase of the PPP life-cycle as well as the different issues to be dealt with within each area. This process has resulted in the development of a PPP Decision Tree, with two levels of detail, a macro- and a micro-level.

At the macro-level the different areas of decision-making for each phase of the PPP life cycle have been identified in aggregate form. Six areas of decisions have been used, namely: economic/financial, technical, social, legal, environmental and political, all of which have been associated with each phase of the PPP life cycle (Figure 7.1).

At the micro-level, for each individual area of decision-making in each phase of the PPP life cycle, the different issues that warrant taking a decision have been further identified. Figure 7.2 shows an example of the micro-level of the PPP Decision Tree for the phase 'Detailed Preparation'.

The PPP DS framework

Following the identification of the different issues embraced by each area of decision in each phase of the PPP life-cycle, a modelling effort was undertaken

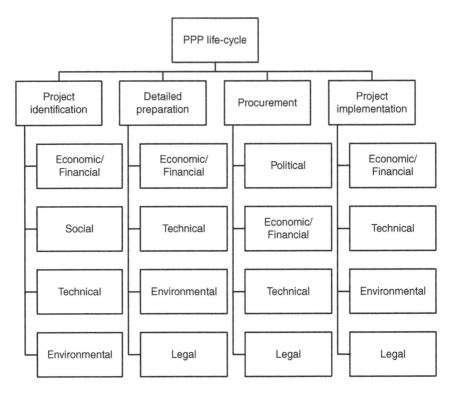

Figure 7.1 Decision areas in each phase of the PPP life-cycle.

aiming at developing an efficient PPP DS framework. Decision process modelling, in fact, provides decision-makers with the necessary standardised knowledge to systematically manage the decisions that need to be made across all phases of the PPP life cycle.

There is an extensive amount of literature in the field of Organisation and Management that deals with the analysis of decision processes and, even wider, with the analysis of business processes. These studies propose different techniques and approaches to characterise and model the business and decision processes. The literature review shows that business processes as well as decision processes can be described at different levels of detail depending on the purpose of the analysis. Furthermore, good modelling practices also suggest that the decision-making process needs to be described through its components (Szykman *et al.* 2001).

Lardeur and Longueville (2004) define four such components: the structure of the decision (which is usually described by design rationale methodologies), the result of the decision (what is to be decided?), the activities of the decision within the overall decision-making process, and the organisation of the actors involved in the process. According to Curtis *et al.* (1992), the components of the process to

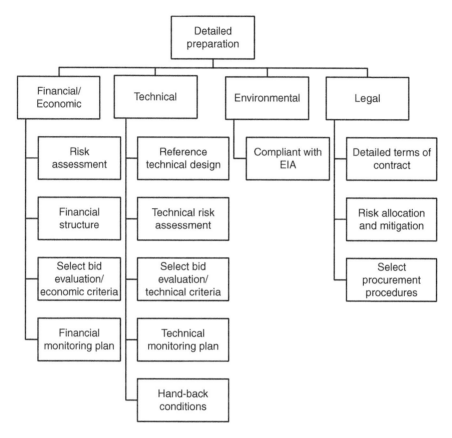

Figure 7.2 Decisions in the phase detailed preparation.

be considered depend on the perspective used in the representation. The authors identify four different perspectives in processes representation:

- Functional perspective: representing what process elements (activities) are being performed, and what flows of informational entities (for example, data, artefacts, products, etc.), are relevant to these process elements.
- Behavioural perspective: representing when process elements are performed (for example, sequencing), as well as aspects of how they are performed through feedback loops, iteration, complex decision-making conditions, entry and exit criteria, and so forth.
- Organisational perspective: representing where and by whom (which agents) in the organisation process elements are performed, the physical communication mechanisms used for the transfer of entities, and the physical media and locations used for storing entities.

• Informational perspective: representing the informational entities produced or manipulated by a process and their interrelationships; these entities include data, artefacts, products (intermediate and end), and objects; this perspective includes both the structure of informational entities and the relationships among them.

The above concepts were taken into consideration for the development of the PPP DS framework where each decision process is described through the following components:

When: PPP life-cycle phase
What: area of decisions
Which: issues to deal with
How: what instruments/processes are used to take the decision
Who: actors involved in the decision.

The characterisation of each decision process according to the first level-components (When, What, Who) can be graphically viewed as a cube (Figure 7.3).

Each part of the cube shows the main issues (What) that warrant a decision that a specific actor has to deal with in each project phase on a specific decision area. For example, during the 'Project Identification' phase, economic/financial decisions are based on evaluations of the project affordability (i.e. the capacity of the authority or the users to pay for the project), the compliance (or not) with the

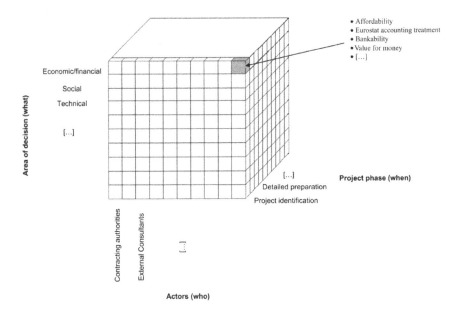

Figure 7.3 Modelling components of PPP decision processes.

Eurostat accounting treatment, the project bankability, and the overall VFM evaluation. Each issue is addressed by a specific actor who has to answer a set of relevant questions. Table 7.1 identifies, for each PPP decision process, the two categories of actors involved in the decision (Who), namely those that support the decision process and those who take the decision.

Once the main issues relevant to taking the decision (Which) have been identified, the instruments used to process the information (How) are also defined for each issue. Tables 7.2–7.5 show the characterisation of the decision processes in the four phases of the PPP life-cycle. The first column shows the issues to be addressed in each area of decision (Which), the second column contains the set of questions that need to be answered to take the corresponding decision, while the third column reports the tools/instruments used to process the information and support the decision (How).

Table 7.1 Actors involved in the PPP decision processes

Decision processes	Who supports the decision process?	Who takes the decision?
Phase 1: Project Identification		
Area of Decision: Financial/Economic		
1.1.1　Affordability	Ministry of Finance; Contracting authority; Sponsoring agency	Minister of Finance
1.1.2　Feasibility	Contracting authority; Sponsoring agency	Contracting authority/ Minister of Finance
1.1.3　Bankability	Financial advisors	Contracting authority/ Minister of Finance
1.1.4　VfM analysis	Contracting authority, Sponsoring agency	Contracting authority/ relevant Ministry
1.1.5　Accounting regulation	Contracting authority; Accounting advisors	Minister of Finance
Area of Decision: Social		
1.2.1　Social acceptance of PPP as a means of providing the infrastructure	External consultant; Public stakeholders	Contracting authority
Area of Decision: Technical		
1.3.1　Size/scope	Contracting authority	Contracting authority
1.3.2　Output specification/ user requirements	Contracting authority	Contracting authority
1.3.3　Alternative solutions	Contracting authority; External consultants	Contracting authority
Area of Decision: Environmental		
1.4.1　Environmental Impact Assessment (EIA)	External consultants	Contracting authority

(*Continued*)

Table 7.1 Actors involved in the PPP decision processes (Continued)

Decision processes	*Who supports the decision process?*	*Who takes the decision?*
Area of Decision: Legal		
1.5.1 Term of the contract: concession period, compensation	PPP expert team; Contracting authority	Contracting authority
Phase 2: Detailed Preparation		
Area of Decision: Financial/Economic		
2.1.1 Risk assessment	External advisors; Contracting authority	Contracting authority
2.1.2 Financial structure	External advisors; Contracting authority	Minister of Finance; Contracting authority
2.1.3 Select Bid evaluation/ Economic criteria	External advisors; Contracting authority	Contracting authority
2.1.4 Financial monitoring plan	External advisors; Contracting authority	Contracting authority
Area of Decision: Technical		
2.2.1 Reference technical design	External advisors; Contracting authority	Contracting authority
2.2.2 Technical risk assessment	External advisors; Contracting authority	Contracting authority
2.2.3 Select Bid evaluation/ Technical criteria	External advisors; Contracting authority	Contracting authority
2.2.4 Technical monitoring plan	External advisors; Contracting authority	Contracting authority
2.2.5 Hand-back conditions	External advisors; Contracting authority	Contracting authority
Area of Decision: Environmental		
2.3.1 Compliant with EIA	External consultant	Contracting authority
Area of Decision: Legal		
2.4.1 Detailed terms of contract	External advisors; Contracting authority	Contracting authority
2.4.2 Risk allocation and mitigation	External advisors; Contracting authority	Contracting authority
2.4.3 Select procurement procedures	External advisors; Contracting authority	Contracting authority
Phase 3: Procurement		
Area of Decision: Political		
3.1.1 Political decision to go to tender	Contracting authority	Relevant ministry/ Parliament
3.1.2 Political decision to sign the contract	Contracting authority	Relevant ministry/ Parliament

(*Continued*)

Table 7.1 Actors involved in the PPP decision processes (Continued)

Decision processes	Who supports the decision process?	Who takes the decision?
Area of Decision: Financial		
3.2.1 Financial evaluation of bids	External advisors; Contracting authority; PPP support unit	Contracting authority
3.2.2 Financial negotiation with bidders	External advisors; Contracting authority; Bidders	Contracting authority
Area of Decision: Technical		
3.3.1 Technical evaluation of bids	External advisors; Contracting authority	Contracting authority
3.3.2 Clarifications of technical requirements	External advisors; Contracting authority	Contracting authority
Area of Decision: Legal		
3.4.1 Bid evaluation	External advisors; Contracting authority	Contracting authority
3.4.2 Negotiation of agreement	External advisors; Contracting authority; Bidders	Contracting authority
3.4.3 Finalisation of agreement	External advisors; Contracting authority; Selected bidder	Contracting authority
Phase 4: Project Implementation		
Area of Decision: Financial/Economic		
4.1.1 Financial monitoring	Contracting authority; Concessionaire	Concessionaire; Contracting authority
4.1.2 Refinancing	Contracting authority; Concessionaire	Contracting authority; Concessionaire
Area of Decision: Technical		
4.2.1 Technical monitoring of construction and operating	Contracting authority; Concessionaire	Contracting authority; Concessionaire
4.2.2 Design/construction evaluation	Contracting authority; Concessionaire	Contracting authority; Concessionaire
4.2.3 Hand-back	Contracting authority; Concessionaire; External advisors	Contracting authority; Concessionaire; External advisors
Area of Decision: Environmental		
4.3.1 Comply and update EIA	Contracting authority; Concessionaire	Contracting authority; Concessionaire
Area of Decision: Legal		
4.4.1 Contract monitoring and enforcement	Contracting authority; Concessionaire	Contracting authority; Concessionaire
4.4.2 Dispute resolution	Contracting authority; Concessionaire	Arbiter
4.4.3 Renegotiation	Contracting authority; Concessionaire; External advisors	Contracting authority; Concessionaire

Table 7.2 Decision processes in the project identification phase

1	Phase: Project Identification	Set of questions that need to be answered	How
1.1	**Area of Decision: Financial/Economic**		
1.1.1	Affordability (Government budget)	Is it affordable by the government? Are there evident social-economic returns? Which project will be prioritised?	Cost-Benefit Analysis; IRR; prioritisation analysis; political negotiation.
1.1.2	Feasibility (project budget)	Is it financially sustainable? If not, are public subsidies a viable option? What will the payment mechanism options be? What will the length of the contract be?	Cost-Benefit Analysis; EIRR; Discounted Cash Flow analysis; FRR.
1.1.3	Bankability	Is the project financially attractive to the market?	Market sounding (Cash-Flow Analysis; Simulations; Cover ratios).
1.1.4	VfM analysis	Is the project delivering good VfM? Is PPP the most appropriate form of procurement for the project?	Public Sector Comparator; Public Private Comparator.
1.1.5	Accounting regulation (Eurostat95)	Does the project meet the accounting regulation? Will the project be considered on- or off- the authority's balance sheet?	Specific legislation (EU legislation).
1.2	**Area of Decision: Social**		
1.2.1	Social acceptance of PPP as a means of providing the infrastructure	What is the impact on the different interest groups of stakeholders (community, environmental, etc.)? What is the public perception of the project? Is there sufficient public support/acceptance for the project?	Social Impact Index; Social impact assessment; Public consultation; ESIA study/report.
1.3	**Area of Decision: Technical**		
1.3.1	Size/scope	For which users and for which purpose will the infrastructure be built? What are the capacity requirements (present and future)?	Simulations; Sector masterplan; Government goals.
1.3.2	Output specification/ user requirements	What Level of Service is expected?	International best practices; local restrictions due to legislation.
1.3.3	Alternative solutions	Are there any other viable solutions?	Simulation analysis; Technical feasibility study.

(Continued)

Table 7.2 Decision processes in the project identification phase (Continued)

1	Phase: Project Identification	Set of questions that need to be answered	How
1.4	**Area of Decision: Environmental**		
1.4.1	Environmental Impact Assessment (EIA)	What are the environmental impacts of the project? How can they be mitigated and/or compensated?	E(S)IA study.
1.5	**Area of Decision: Legal**		
1.5.1	Term of the contract: concession period, compensation	Should the concession period be fixed or variable? What will the type of contract be? What will the payment mechanism be?	DCF analysis; CB analysis; legislation constraints; public consultation.

Table 7.3 Decision processes in the detailed preparation phase

2	Phase: Detailed Preparation	Set of questions that need to be answered	How
2.1	**Area of Decision: Financial/Economic**		
2.1.1	Risk assessment	What risks can affect the project? What is the impact/likelihood of these risks on the project CF?	Simulation analysis; Sensitivity analysis.
2.1.2	Financial structure	Which discount rates? Which WACC? Which Debt/Equity ratio? Is the payment mechanism sufficiently robust? Are there governmental guarantees or tax incentives? Which funding mechanisms? Which incentives/penalties? Under what conditions should the project be refinanced?	Discounted Cash Flow Analysis; Financial simulation.
2.1.3	Select bid evaluation/Economic criteria	What are the economic/financial criteria to be used in the evaluation of bids? What weighting is given to financial/economic criteria?	Multi-criteria Analysis; International best practices.
2.1.4	Financial monitoring plan	Which economic/financial KPIs could be monitored throughout the project's lifecycle?	International best practices.
2.2	**Area of Decision: Technical**		
2.2.1	Reference technical design	What is the reference technical design? What room for flexibility can be allowed in the project?	Simulation analysis; Technical feasibility studies; International best practices.

(Continued)

Table 7.3 Decision processes in the detailed preparation phase (Continued)

2	Phase: Detailed Preparation	Set of questions that need to be answered	How
2.2.2	Technical risk assessment	What are the technical risks of the project? What is the impact/likelihood of these risks on project performance?	Simulation analysis; Risk workshop; Risk registers.
2.2.3	Select bid evaluation/ Technical criteria	What are the technical criteria to be used in the evaluation of bids? What weighting is given to technical criteria?	Multi-criteria Analysis; International best practices.
2.2.4	Technical monitoring plan	Which technical KPIs could be monitored throughout the project's lifecycle?	International best practices.
2.2.5	Hand-back conditions	What will the project's hand-back requirements be?	International best practices.
2.3	**Area of Decision: Environmental**		
2.3.1	Compliant with EIA	Is the initial EIA respected? Should it be updated?	E(S)IA review and validation.
2.4	**Area of Decision: Legal**		
2.4.1	Detailed terms of contract	What is the contract's performance regime (which KPIs to include in contract and how to enforce performance)? What are events of default? What are compensation events? What are relief events? What are force majeure events? Which elements should trigger renegotiation? Which conflict resolution process could be adopted?	International best practices.
2.4.2	Risk allocation and mitigation	Which is the party more capable of bearing the risk? What are the available risk mitigation strategies?	International best practices; Risk register; Risk allocation matrix; Risk workshop.
2.4.3	Select procurement procedures	Which are the most suitable procedures among: competitive dialogue *vs.* open procedure *vs.* restricted *vs.* negotiated, etc.? Which bid evaluation criteria (technical, economic) should be adopted?	International best practices; Analysis of the legal framework.

Table 7.4 Decision processes in the procurement phase

3	Phase: Procurement	Set of questions that need to be answered	How
3.1	**Area of Decision: Political**		
3.1.1	Political decision to go to tender	Is the project mature enough (completed reference design, completed financial, risk assessment, etc.) to go to the tender?	Government consultation; Parliament hearing.
3.1.2.	Political decision to sign the contract	Are all the processes completed correctly?	Government consultation; Parliament hearing.
3.2	**Area of Decision: Financial**		
3.2.1	Financial evaluation of bids	Who is the preferred bidder (financial criteria)?	International best practices.
3.2.2	Financial negotiation with bidders	Have all the financial elements of the tender been fully addressed? Is the project bankable?	International best practices.
3.3	**Area of Decision: Technical**		
3.3.1	Technical evaluation of bids	Who is the preferred bidder (technical criteria)?	International best practices.
3.3.2	Clarifications of technical requirements	Are there any clarifications required by the bidders? Have the clarifications been communicated to all the bidders?	International best practices.
3.4	**Area of Decision: Legal**		
3.4.1	Bid evaluation	Are the bids submitted and evaluated according to the procurement process? Are there any complaints?	International best practices.
3.4.2	Negotiation of agreement	Are there any additional considerations? Has the process reached a BAFO*?	International best practices.
3.4.3	Finalisation of agreement	Are both parties fully satisfied with the final agreement documents?	International best practices.

*best and final offer

Conclusion

This chapter is a first step in an effort to further clarify and standardise (to the extent possible) the PPP decision-making process as part of a longer-term goal to eventually extend and upgrade this framework to a true decision support system (DSS). The proposed framework draws from already existing literature on decision support systems and their analysis, while the breakdown of the PPP life-cycle into various phases follows the structure suggested in the EPEC PPP Guide

Table 7.5 Decision processes in the project implementation phase

4	Phase: Project Implementation	Set of questions that need to be answered	How
4.1	**Area of Decision: Financial/Economic**		
4.1.1	Financial monitoring	Is the project performing financially as planned? Are the financial KPIs being met? Are there any relevant decisions/ changes to be made?	Reporting of revenues and costs; variation analysis.
4.1.2	Refinancing	Is the refinancing being carried out in accordance with the agreement?	Concession agreement.
4.2	**Area of Decision: Technical**		
4.2.1	Technical monitoring of construction and operating	Are levels of service and KPIs being met? Are deviations penalised and the performance regime enforced?	Periodic reports.
4.2.2	Design/construction evaluation	Are quality standards and deadlines being met?	Periodic reports.
4.2.3	Hand-back	Are project hand-back requirements being met?	Hand-back process and criteria.
4.3	**Area of Decision: Environmental**		
4.3.1	Comply and update EIA	Is the E(S)IA being respected? Should it be updated?	Periodic reports.
4.4	**Area of Decision: Legal**		
4.4.1	Contract monitoring and enforcement	Is the contract being followed? Are both parties conforming to their contractual responsibilities?	Periodic reports.
4.4.2	Dispute resolution	Are there any issues that require arbitration/adjudication?	Adjudication/ arbitration.
4.4.3	Renegotiation	Has the contract failed? Can any form of opportunistic behaviour be detected in the request for renegotiation? Can disputes be resolved in good faith? What is the impact of renegotiation on the public budget? What is the impact of renegotiation on the project?	Project monitoring; Contract monitoring.

by the EIB. The PPP DS framework is founded on the representation of PPP decisions in a tree structure that identifies six areas of decision-making, each of them treated at a macro- and a micro-level. The framework aims at providing answers to three basic questions (When? What? Who?) that form the basic components of the PPP decision-making process, leading to a three-dimensional graphical representation of the PPP decision-making space.

More research is needed in order to further complement and validate the results of this study, especially considering that due to the uniqueness of these projects there is no 'one size fits all' approach to them when considering how decisions that have been made during the course of their life-cycle have ultimately impacted on their eventual success or failure. Additionally, this effort aims to model and clarify the decision-making process from the perspective of the public sector authority. A useful extension of this study would be to model in a similar way the decision processes of the various private sector stakeholders and then map the interactions between their decisions and the ones from the public sector side. By mapping the entire universe of decisions from both sides, it could then be possible to identify synergies or obvious areas of conflict and/or arbitrage that are currently unidentified or not properly accounted for. Nevertheless it is anticipated that the work presented in this chapter will strongly contribute to the streamlining of the PPP decision-making process, ultimately leading to better structured and more successful projects.

Notes

1 For example, Birnie found that tender costs for PFI projects in the UK ranged from 0.48-0.62 per cent of the total project costs, which are much higher than those for design-build projects (0.18-0.32 per cent) and traditional design-bid-build projects (0.04-0.15 per cent).
2 Technical Note No. 4, 'How to Appoint and Work with a Preferred Bidder', Treasury Taskforce-Private Finance, London, 1999.

References

Alonso-Conde, A. B., Brown, C. and Rojo-Suarez, J. (2006) 'Public Private Partnerships: incentives, risk transfer and real options'. *Review of Financial Economics*, 16(4), pp. 335–49

Aoust, J. M., Bennett, T. C. and Fiszelson, R. (2000) 'Risk analysis and sharing: the key to a successful Public-Private Partnership' in: J. Y. Perrot and G. Chatelus (Eds.) *Financing of Major Infrastructure and Public Service Projects: Public-Private Partnership*. Éditions Lavoisier

Bing, L., Akintoye, A., Edwards, P. J. and Hardcastle, C. (2005) 'The allocation of risk in PPP/PFI construction projects in the UK'. *International Journal of Project Management*, 23, pp. 25–35

Birnie, J. (1997) 'Risk allocation to the construction firm within a Private Finance Initiative (PFI) project'. *ARCOM Conference Proceedings*, pp. 527–534

Carbonara, N., Pellegrino, R. and Vajdic, N. (2013) 'Real option theory for risk mitigation in transport PPPs'. Built Environment Project and Asset Management (*BEPAM*), 3 (2)

Curtis, B., Kellner, M. I. and Over, J. (1992) 'Process Modeling'. *Communication of ACM*, September, 35(9)

Demirag, I., Dubnick, M. and Khadaroo, M. I. (2004) 'A framework for examining accountability and value for money in the UK's Private Finance Initiative'. *JCC*, 15 Autumn, pp. 63–76

EIB (2012) *The European PPP Expertise Centre (EPEC) PPP Guide*. Available online at: www.eib.org/epec/g2g/index.htm

Essig, M. and Batran, A. (2005) 'Public–Private Partnership – development of long-term relationships in public procurement in Germany'. *Journal of Purchasing and Supply Management*, *11*(5–6), pp. 221–231

Government of India (2010) *Developing Toolkits for Improving PPP Decision Making Process: User Guide*. Department of Economic Affairs, Ministry of Finance, Government of India. Available online at http://toolkit.pppinindia.com/pdf/ppp_toolkit_user_guide.pdf

Grimsey, D. and Lewis, M. K. (2004) *Public Private Partnerships*. Cheltenham UK: Edward Elgar

HM Treasury Taskforce (1999) 'How to Appoint and Work with a Preferred Bidder', Technical Note No. 4, London. Available online at www.treasuryprojects-taskforce.gov.uk

Koppenjan, J. F. M. (2005) 'The formation of Public–Private Partnerships: lessons from nine transportation infrastructure projects in the Netherlands'. *Public Administration*, 83(1), pp. 135–57

Kumaraswamy, M. M. and Anvuur, A. M. (2008) 'Selecting sustainable teams for PPP projects'. *Building and Environment*, 43(6), pp. 999–1009

Kwak, Y. H., Chih, Y. and Ibbs, C. W. (2009) 'Towards a comprehensive understanding of Public Private Partnerships for infrastructure development'. *California Management Review*, 51 (2), pp. 51–78

Lardeur, E. and Longueville, B. (2004) 'Mutual enhancement of systems engineering and decision-making through process modeling: toward an integrated framework'. *Computers in Industry*, 55, pp. 269–282

Li, B. (2003) 'Risk management of Public/Private Partnership projects'. Unpublished PhD thesis. School of the Built and Natural Environment, Glasgow Caledonian University, Glasgow, Scotland

Li, B., Akintoye, A., Edwards, P. J. and Hardcastle, C. (2005) 'Perceptions of positive and negative factors influencing the attractiveness of PPP/PFI procurement for construction projects in the UK'. *Engineering, Construction and Architectural Management*, 12(2), pp. 125–148

Miller, J. B. (2000) *Principles of Public and Private Infrastructure Delivery*. New York, NY: Springer

Milner, M. (2004) 'Eurotunnel car traffic declines'. The *Guardian*, 21 March, p. 14

Nevitt, P. K. and Fabozzi F. J. (2005) *Project Financing* (7th Ed.). Euromoney Books: London

Ng, A. and Loosemore, M. (2007) 'Risk allocation in the private provision of public infrastructure'. *International Journal of Project Management*, 25, pp. 66–76

Pfeffer, D. J. (2010) 'The construction contract: lump sum *vs.* cost plus'. *The New York Law Journal*, December 28

PPIAF/World Bank (2009) *Toolkit for Public-Private Partnerships in Roads and Highways*. World Bank and Public Private Infrastructure Advisory Facility, Washington, DC. Available online at www.ppiaf.org/sites/ppiaf.org/files/documents/toolkits/highwaystoolkit/index.html

Shen, L. Y., Li, H. and Li, Q. M. (2002) 'Alternative concession model for build operate transfer contract projects'. *Journal of Construction Engineering and Management*, 128 (4), pp. 326–330

Shen, L. Y. and Wu, Y. Z. (2005) 'Risk concession model for build/operate/transfer contract projects'. *Journal of Construction Engineering and Management*, 131 (2), pp. 211–220

Shen, L.Y., Bao, H. J., Wu, Y. Z. and Lu, W. S. (2007) 'Using bargaining-game theory for negotiating concession period for BOT-type contract'. *Journal of Construction Engineering and Management*, 133(5), pp. 385–392

Smith, N. J. (1996) *Engineering Project Management.* Oxford: Blackwell Scientific Publications

Szykman, S., Sriram, R. D. and Regli, W. C. (2001) 'The role of knowledge in next-generation product development systems'. *Journal of Computation and Information Science in Engineering*, 1 (1)

Thomas, A.V., Kalidindi, S. and Ananthanarayanan, K. (2003) 'Identification of risk factors and risk management strategies for BOT road projects in India'. *Indian Highways*, 31(12), pp. 53–75

Tiong, R. L. K. (1990) 'BOT projects: risk and securities'. *Construction Management & Economics*, 8, pp. 315–328

World Bank and the PPIAF (2009) *Toolkit for Public-Private Partnerships in Roads and Highways.*

Wang, S. Q., Tiong, R. L. K., Ting, S. K. and Ashley, D. (2000) 'Evaluation and management of political risks in China's BOT projects'. *Journal of Construction Engineering and Management*, 126(3), pp. 242–50

Wibowo, A. (2004) 'Valuing guarantees in a BOT infrastructure project'. *Engineering, Construction and Architectural Management*, Vol. 11, No. 6, pp. 395–403

Wibowo, A. and Kochendorfer, B. (2005) 'Financial risk analysis of project finance in Indonesian toll roads'. *Journal of Construction Engineering and Management*, 131(9), pp. 963–72

Yuan, J., Yajun Zeng, A., Skibniewski, M. J. and Li, Q. (2009) 'Selection of performance objectives and key performance indicators in Public–Private Partnership projects to achieve value for money'. *Construction Management and Economics*, 27, pp. 253–270

Zhang, X. Q. (2004a) 'Concessionaire selection: methods and criteria'. *Journal of Construction Engineering and Management*, 130(2), pp. 235–244

Zhang, X. Q. (2004b) 'Improving concessionaire selection protocols in public/private partnered infrastructure projects'. *Journal of Construction Engineering and Management*, 130(5), pp. 670–679

Zhang, X. Q. (2005) 'Criteria for selecting the private-sector partner in Public-Private Partnerships'. *Journal of Construction Engineering and Management*, 131(6), pp. 631–644

Zhang, X. Q., Kumaraswamy, M. M., Zheng, W. and Palaneeswaran, E. (2002) 'Concessionaire selection for build-operate-transfer tunnel projects in Hong Kong'. *Journal of Construction Engineering and Management*, 128(2), pp. 155–163

8 Designing the tendering process in PPP

A transaction cost-based approach

*Nunzia Carbonara, Nicola Costantino
and Roberta Pellegrino*

Introduction

In the last few decades, due to the public budget constraints and the severe need for new or upgraded infrastructure, more and more governments have fostered private sector involvement in public investment projects. For this reason, Public Private Partnership (PPP) has become a major scheme in delivering public infrastructure (Walker and Smith 1995). The adoption of PPP is also supported by the belief that PPP can bring cost and time-savings and efficiencies on project delivery and operations (FHWA 2007). Governments, in addition to transferring the financial burden to private partners, can exploit their technical expertise and managerial competences in managing infrastructures.

Generally, the private party of a PPP is awarded by means of a public tender. The tendering processes of PPP seem to be more complicated and more costly than those of conventional procurement for two main reasons. First, the transaction in PPP involves not only the design and construction of the infrastructure but also the finance and the future operations and management, so requiring that the evaluation and selection are based on a wide set of parameters. Second, governments should ensure wider competition among private participants, so increasing the number of potential bidders to be evaluated. Birnie (1997) finds that tender costs for Public Finance Initiative (PFI) projects in the UK ranged from 0.48–0.62 per cent of the total project costs, which are higher than those for conventional procurement (i.e., design-build projects (0.18–0.32 per cent) and traditional design-bid-build projects (0.04–0.15 per cent)). Other estimates with respect to PPP tendering costs are even higher, with some estimates at 10 per cent or greater (Zhang 2005b, Dudkin and Välilä 2005). Furthermore, the inner characteristics of PPP, such as the huge amount of investment, the long life cycle of the agreements, the uniqueness of each project, increase the uncertainty of the transaction and require a great effort in contract design and monitoring.

Therefore, although PPP can help governments fill the gap between available public finding and needed resources and may offer considerable benefits and significant savings over the entire life cycle of the project, they may increase the cost of procuring, monitoring and enforcing contracts, i.e. transaction costs, much more than traditional procurement of public investment projects (Soliño and de Santos 2010). In fact, transaction costs vary on the basis of the amount of information to be processed and codified during the procurement process. The higher the amount of information to be managed, the higher the level of transaction costs. PPPs are characterised by a greater uncertainty and complexity than the conventional procurement, and then by a higher level of information to be managed (Soliño and de Santos 2010).

The rationale for the search of the 'best' tendering approach in PPP lies in finding ways to minimise transaction costs that can erode cost savings achieved through them and thus undermine efficiency gains (Soliño and de Santos 2010). For this reason contracting authorities have to design the tendering process carefully in order to maximise their outcomes, by increasing the competition in the market, by shortening the time of the entire procedure, and by keeping the current and future transaction costs low (Kwak *et al.* 2009).

Transaction cost economics (TCE) has frequently provided scholars with an analytical framework for the study of public/private contracting. Parker and Hartley (2003) develop a framework to assess if the use of PPP necessarily leads to improved economic efficiency, with a particular focus on military procurement. They consider the economics of PPP and, more specifically, the roles of transaction costs, trust and relational contracting in the achievement of successful PPPs. Their study concludes that PPPs involve significant transaction costs that must be set against any benefits in terms of economic efficiency incentives. Zitron (2006) posits an initial model of how the private sector bidders decide whether to bid for a contract by developing an empirical study. Roumboutsos and Sciancalepore (2014), based on an analytical model, predict the maximum number of potential bidders with respect to tender transaction costs. Among others they identified that increased transaction costs limit market competition, with the usual number of bidders not exceeding three.

Even if the body of theoretical knowledge to analyse PPP seems to be well developed, it is less focused on the tendering process with respect to minimising transaction costs at this stage and seems more aimed at standardising the tendering process. On the other side, Soliño and de Santos (2010), focusing more specifically on the tendering process, provide some empirical evidence on transaction costs in PPP transport infrastructure projects. Their study analyses the relationship between transaction costs of PPP transport infrastructure projects and the procurement procedure used to launch those projects. Focusing on transaction costs, Soliño and de Santos (2012) compare negotiated procedures with the open procedure. They find that it is difficult to justify the employment of negotiated procedures in most PPP contracts. However, some issues are still open. How do you structure the tendering process in PPP in order to minimise transaction costs? Which phases and awarding methods should be used in the tendering process? How do specific factors, such as the size of the project, the number of bidders, the complexity of the project, affect the choice of the tendering procedure?

In response, the present chapter develops a decision model for choosing the tendering procedure in PPP that minimises transaction costs. In particular, according to the total cost of ownership approach proposed by Ellram (1995), we attend to transaction costs as the most important or significant cost in the acquisition, possession, use and subsequent disposition of a good or service beyond the price of a purchase. Although transaction costs are highly relevant for both parties involved in the transaction, i.e., public sector and bidding companies, we focus on the transaction costs borne by the public sector that is responsible for designing the tendering procedure.

A conceptual model that explains the relationship between transaction costs and the level of information for every considered tendering procedure is developed here. According to the amount of information characterising different types of tendering procedures in PPP, the model allows the identification of the tendering procedure that minimises transaction costs. This baseline conceptual model is also used to analyse the effect of specific factors, namely the size of the project, the number of bidders, and the project complexity, on the choice of the tendering procedure.

The chapter is structured as follows. The second section presents the relevant aspects characterising the structure of tendering process in PPP. The third discusses the transaction costs generally associated with PPP. The following two sections present the baseline conceptual model to use to choose the tendering procedure that minimises transaction costs and its application to contexts characterised by different values of specific factors affecting the level of transaction costs. Finally, conclusions end the chapter.

Procedures for PPP tendering

An overview of the existing literature on the theme shows two relevant aspects characterising the structure of the tendering process in PPPs. The first one concerns the phases of the tendering process and the second concerns the awarding methods used to rank candidate partners for PPPs and choose the best one.

On the basis of the choices on the characteristics of these two aspects it is possible to design different types of tendering procedures. As regards the first aspect, the following three main phases can characterise and be distinguished in many tendering procedures (Tiong and Alum 1997):

- Pre-qualification of bidders. The aim of the pre-qualification phase is to reduce the number of interested bidders to a shortlist, which consists only of reputable and experienced ones that are able to take over project risks. Unnecessary tendering costs of weaker bidders are avoided.
- Bid evaluation. This phase consists of the selection of one or more among qualified bidders. Tenderers on the shortlist are invited to submit detailed proposals that are evaluated in accordance with the predefined evaluation criteria.
- Negotiation with preferred tenderers. This phase consists of the negotiation prior to the final awarding with one or a few preferred tenderers. At this stage,

provisions in agreements are carefully reviewed. Once the agreement is signed, a contract award notice will be published and the contract is implemented.

Tendering processes in PPPs show a variety of types of tendering procedures based on a different adoption of these phases. For instance, the pre-qualification phase is missing in some Asian countries like Hong Kong, Thailand and Malaysia, while it is adopted by many other contracting authorities in countries like Australia, Canada, Philippines, USA, UK (Tiong and Alum 1997; To and Ozawa 2007). Also the negotiation phase can be missing, as in the case of procedures followed in the Philippines (To and Ozawa 2007). The UK's PFI procurement process is indeed an example of a multi-stage tendering process, which includes all or almost all the stages (Kwak *et al.* 2009), as shown in Figure 8.1.

The procurement processes for the award of public contracts adopted in the EU are five (as described in the new Public Contracts Directive), rather than the existing four (Directive 2004/18/EC of the European Parliament and Council on the coordination of procedures for the award of public works contracts, public supply contracts and public service contracts (European Union 2004)). They are: open procedures, restricted procedures, competitive procedure with negotiation (negotiated procedures), competitive dialogue procedure and innovation partnership procedure. According to the Directive, open procedures miss both the

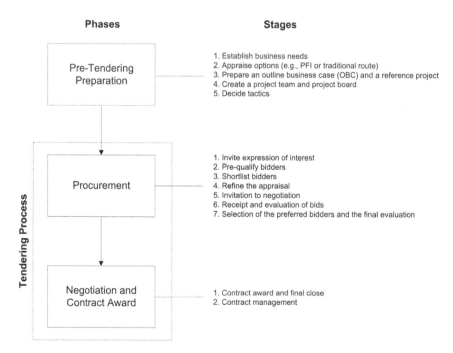

Figure 8.1 UK's PFI procurement process (Kwak *et al.* 2009).

pre-qualification and negotiation phases. In fact, any interested economic operator may submit a tender. Their proposals are binding and thus cannot be changed or negotiated during the procedure. The contract is awarded on the basis of the 'most economically advantageous tender'. That is to say that the proposal can also include, in addition to economic values, improvements of the technical, time-related and managerial contents of the project. Restricted procedure includes pre-qualification: only a limited number of economic operators invited by the contracting authority may submit a tender (always according to the 'most economically advantageous tender' criterion). Negotiated procedures are those where the contracting authorities consult the selected economic operators and negotiate the terms of contract with one or more of them. Negotiated procedures are structured into different phases (pre-qualification, invitation to negotiate, best and final offer, preferred bidder). The competitive dialogue is quite a new procedure in which any economic operator may request to participate and whereby the contracting authority conducts a dialogue with the candidates admitted to the procedure, with the aim of developing one or more suitable alternatives capable of meeting its requirements, on the basis of which the chosen candidates are invited to tender (Soliño and de Santos 2010). Finally, the innovation partnership procedure is the new procedure introduced by the new Public Contracts Directive (2014) under which a selection is made of those who respond to the advertisement and the contracting authority uses a negotiated approach to invite suppliers to submit ideas to develop innovative works, supplies or services aimed at meeting a need for which there is no suitable existing 'product' on the market. The contracting authority is allowed to award partnerships to more than one supplier.

For the more innovative projects, it is possible to integrate the competitive dialogue with the recent Pre-Commercial Procurement (PCP) approach, which is not concerned with the procurement of existing products or services on the market but with the purchase of research and development (R&D) services by the public sector, namely solution exploration and design, prototyping, up to the original development of a limited volume of first products or services (Lucas *et al.* 2013).

The analysis of the tendering procedures adopted all over the world reveals that the public procurement regulation can influence the design of the tendering procedure by restricting the use of options. For instance, the EU Directive outlines the use of the different procurement procedures for the award of public contracts. Generally speaking, public contracts in the EU are awarded by applying either open or restricted procedures. However, articles 29 and 30 of the cited Directive highlight specific circumstances in which contracting authorities may award public contracts by means of the competitive dialogue or the negotiated procedures (European Union 2004).

As regarding the awarding methods used to rank candidate partners for PPP, these can be classified on the basis of the phase in which they are used (Zhang 2004; Wang and Dai 2010). In particular, a set of methods can be used for the tenderers' pre-qualification and another one in the bid evaluation.

Table 8.1 Methods for bidder pre-qualification and bid evaluations

	Significant methods	*Sources*
Pre-qualification	• Binary method • Simple scoring • Multi-attribute methods	Zhang (2004)
Bid evaluation	• Simple scoring • NPV • Multi-attribute analysis • Two envelope method • NPV + simple scoring • Binary method + NPV • Lowest price • Shortest concession period • Kepnoe-Tregoe technique • Least Present Value of Revenues	Zhang (2004), Wang and Dai (2010)

Table 8.1 summarises the most common methods used for pre-qualification of bidders and bid evaluation.

The above methods can use different evaluation criteria on which to base the selection of a private partner. Even in this case, some authors have proposed a different set of criteria to be adopted in the pre-qualification phase, while many others proposed criteria for choosing the best among the candidate partners to be used in the bid evaluation phase. Table 8.2 shows a summary of significant criteria selected in the literature.

Table 8.2 Criteria for bid evaluations

	Significant criteria	*Sources*

Financial and
Economic
criteria
	• Sound financial analysis
	• Reasonable source and structure of funds
	• Innovation of financing method
	• Net Present Value
	• Tariff/toll setting up and adjustment
	  mechanism
	• Ability to address commercial risk
	  (e.g., supply and demand risks)
	• Minimal financial risks to the client
	• Internal rate of return
	• Financial strength of the participants in
	  the project company
	• Financial guarantee
	• Total investment schedule
	• Concession period
	• Strong financial commitments from
	  shareholders
	• Pay-Back Period
	• Profitability Index
		Zhang (2005a),
		Rudzianskaite
		et al. (2010)

(Continued)

Table 8.2 Criteria for bid evaluations (Continued)

	Significant criteria	*Sources*
Technical criteria	• Qualifications and experiences of key design and construction personnel • Experience in similar projects • Conforming to client's requirements • Competencies of designer/sub-designers • Contractor/subcontractors • Conforming to design requirements • Construction programmes and abilities to meet them • Design and construction quality control schemes • Use of advanced technologies • Maintainability • Design life • Design standard • Quality management and assurance systems	Zhang (2005a), Wang *et al.* (2007)
Safety, Health & Environmental criteria	• Qualifications/experience of relevant personnel • Management system of safety, health and environment • Conformance to laws and regulations • Construction/demolition waste disposal • Control of air and water pollution • Past environmental performance • Protection of items of cultural/ archeological value • Management safety accountability • Noise reduction and dust reduction	Wang *et al.* (2007), Zhang (2005a), Rudzianskaite *et al.* (2010)
Social criteria	• Importance of the project for public transport	Rudzianskaite *et al.* (2010)
Managerial criteria	• Project management skills • Constitution of the management, their qualifications and experience • Coordination system within the consortium • Success rate of cooperation among private consortium • Leadership and allocation of responsibilities in the consortium • Effective project controlling system • Working relationship among participants	Zhang (2005a), Wang *et al.* (2007)

Transaction costs in PPP

The international literature reports several definitions of transaction costs. Coase (1937), who first introduced the concept, defines transaction costs as the costs of using price mechanism due to the need for specifying, negotiating and enforcing contracts.

Wallis and North (1986) define transaction costs as the costs of making exchanges among people. Niehans (1969) defines transaction costs as the costs associated with the transfer of ownership from one individual to another. Williamson (1975; 1985) uses transaction costs to explain the different forms of organisation and contractual arrangements. He defines transaction costs as the costs of drafting, negotiation and safeguarding an agreement, and also the costs of haggling, costs of governance, bonding costs to secure commitments (Williamson 1985).

Transaction costs are usually divided into two categories: '*ex-ante*' or front-end transaction costs and '*ex-post*' or back-end transaction costs (Arrow 1974; Williamson 1985; Soliño and de Santos 2010). *Ex-ante* transaction costs refer to the tasks of defining, negotiating and maintaining an agreement. They include search and information costs, i.e., transaction costs incurred in determining whether the required good is available on the market, its lowest price and so on, and bargaining costs, i.e., costs to reach an agreement and draft an appropriate contract. *Ex-post* transaction costs include the monitoring and enforcing costs, due to the need for monitoring that the other party fulfils the terms of the contract and taking appropriate action if not.

In public procurement transaction costs borne by the public sector can be divided into two main categories: initiation/procurement costs and contract management costs. Initiation and procurement costs are related to the first two phases of the procurement process and are mainly due to the activities prior to signing the contract. Contract management costs are mainly related to the activities that occur after closing out procurement of the contract (after signing the contract) such as operations and maintenance quality controls, contract enforcement and dispute resolutions (Farajian and Cui 2010).

Transaction costs related to the various procurement situations vary on the basis of the amount of information to be processed and codified. The higher the customisation (i.e., uniqueness and uncertainty) of the supply, the more its transaction needs the exchange and sharing of uncodified (or less codified) knowledge and information. Quantity and level of codification, and therefore transaction cost, varies significantly according to what is transacted (Costantino and Pietroforte 2005). In fact, if we consider commodities (for example, standard supplies), their procurement process is characterised by a reduced amount of information flows with high levels of codification, a decreased risk of contractual hazard and opportunistic behaviour. On the other hand, if we consider customised supplies, their procurement process is characterised by an increased amount of information flows with varying extents of codification and an increased risk of contractual hazards and opportunistic behaviour.

Focusing on PPP, their characteristics, such as the rare occurrence of contracts, the long life-cycle of the agreements, the complex revenue streams, the uncertain demand, and the uniqueness of each project, determine procurement situations that are much more uncertain than those associated with conventional procurement, thus increasing the level of information to be managed (Soliño and de Santos 2010). This can often cause significant transaction costs (Ho and Tsui 2009).

In PPP, several entities with different goals participate in the transaction, so increasing the probability that opportunistic behaviour rises from all sides, making the negotiations more expensive. The complexity and uncertainty of trade relationships imply that it is impossible to plan for every potential contingency and that, even if every contingency could be predicted, it would probably be difficult to write down these plans in a contract between two parties that is enforceable by law. In other words, the contracts are incomplete and therefore must constantly be revised or renegotiated as time goes on (de Bettignies and Ross 2004).

Dudkin and Välilä (2005), focusing on PPP in UK, find that the costs related only to the process of procurement amount on average to well over 10 per cent of the capital value of the project. Public tendering process costs occur in both the pre-tendering preparation and the tendering process. The first are due to the evaluation of the possible tendering approaches and to the preparation of tendering documents; the others are incurred for the pre-qualification, bid evaluation and negotiation. The Federal Ministry of Economics and Technology in Germany estimates the amount of these costs at about 1.7 billion Euro for the preparation of tendering documents and about 3.5 billion Euro for the tendering process (www.bmwi.de). There are other major transaction costs that are hidden and not easily assessed, such as the opportunity costs due to renegotiation and hold-up problems (Ho 2006). All these costs may potentially erode the savings achieved through PPP, undermining the expected benefits in PPP. For this reason, an important challenge in PPP implementation is to reduce these transaction costs to an acceptable level. With this aim, contracting authorities may act on the pre-tendering preparation by getting organised and finalising all preparation before launching the tenders (EPEC 2011), and/or on the tendering process, through the design of the tendering procedure. In the following section, we develop a conceptual model to support the contracting authority in the design and choice of the tendering procedures in PPP.

A baseline conceptual model for choosing PPP tendering procedures: A transaction costs–based approach

As described in the previous section, during the selection of the private party the contracting authority can design different types of tendering procedures by choosing the phases to be implemented in the tendering process and the awarding methods for ranking candidate partners with the evaluation criteria. The resulting different types of tendering procedures will require the management of differing amounts of information (Lingard *et al.* 1998).

It is possible to classify three main types of tendering procedures on the basis of the phases included and the methods adopted.

- **Single Phase Procedure (SPP):** including only the phase of bid evaluation carried out by using simple methods, i.e. simple scoring method and best price;

- **Dual Phase Procedure (DPP):** including two phases: i) the pre-qualification of tenderers and ii) the bid evaluation carried out by using complex methods, i.e. multi-criteria and composite methods, etc.;
- **Three Phase Procedure (TPP):** including all the three phases: i) the pre-qualification of tenderers, ii) the bid evaluation carried out by using complex methods, i.e. multi-criteria and composite methods, etc., and iii) negotiation with preferred tenderers.

The identified tendering procedures are characterised by a different amount of information. In particular, procedure SPP deals with a low amount of information before the partner selection. In the absence of the pre-qualification phase, there is no need for reviewing the competences of all prospective bidders, thus causing the likelihood of having *ex-post* adaptation and changes to be an important feature of the transaction, and the need to manage *ex-post* a great amount of information.

Procedures DPP and TPP deal with a greater amount of *ex-ante* information since the pre-qualification phase requires the collection of prospective bidders' performance. In addition, for TPP, the negotiation with preferred tenderers leads to a more detailed contract. The greater the *ex-ante* information to be managed, the lower the amount of *ex-post* information requirements and the probability of *ex-post* adaptation and changes.

Figure 8.2 shows the amount of *ex-ante* and *ex-post* information characterising each type of tendering procedure.

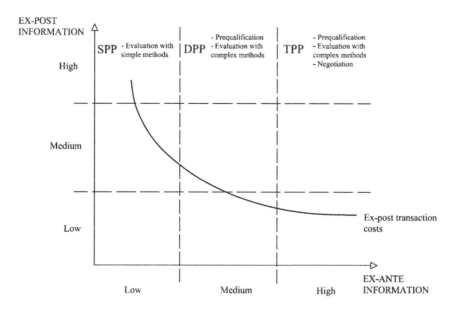

Figure 8.2 Ex-ante and *ex-post* information characterising tendering procedures.

As highlighted previously, information can be considered as a prime source of transaction costs (Casson 1994; Holmstrom and Tirole 1989). Therefore, each tendering procedure is characterised by different levels of transaction costs according to the amount of information managed.

TPP is characterised by high costs for collecting information on all prospective bidders for the purpose of making a partner selection decision (high level of *ex-ante* transaction costs). Gathering a great amount of information surely increases bargaining costs (costs to reach an agreement and drafting an appropriate contract). Contrarily, the *ex-post* costs for monitoring and eventually enforcing the contract will be reduced, since the incompleteness of the contracts is reduced and the selected partner would be less likely to engage in opportunistic behaviour. On the other hand, SPP manages little information about prospective bidders prior to the award of the contract, causing a low level of *ex-ante* transaction costs. However, it is likely that *ex-post* costs will be high, due to the need for close monitoring of private party activities and the increased possibility of costly legal disputes and claims.

Figure 8.3 shows the trend of *ex-ante* and *ex-post* transaction costs associated with each tendering procedure.

Considering the total transaction costs as the sum of the two components, the tendering procedure that minimises the transaction costs is DPP, as shown in Figure 8.4.

Factors affecting the choice of the PPP tendering procedure

The level of transactions costs in PPP projects is strongly affected by several factors, such as the size of the project, the number of bidders, and the level of complexity of the project (Farajian and Cui 2010). The proposed baseline model has been used to choose the tendering procedure in contexts characterised by different values of these factors with the aim of minimising the transaction costs, as discussed in the following sections.

The project size

Project size can be measured in terms of investments required by the project. According to the data collected on projects financed by the European Investment Bank, the level of transaction costs in the procurement of infrastructure in PPP projects is, on average, about 10 per cent of the capital value of the project, and the overall transaction cost of the project for the public sector is about 2–3 per cent of the capital value of the project. Empirical studies reveal that the *ex-ante* transaction costs borne by the public sector for small size projects (capital value below 25 million GBP) are significantly higher than those for bigger projects in terms of the percentage of the total capital value of the project (Dudkin and Välilä 2005; Farajian and Cui 2010). Such an inverse relationship occurs because many of the transaction activities included in the tendering procedure are the same and independent of project size. Therefore, the larger the size of the project, the lower is the

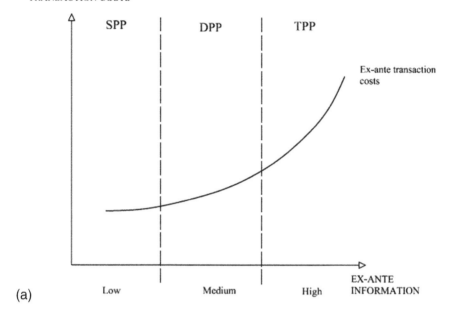

(a)

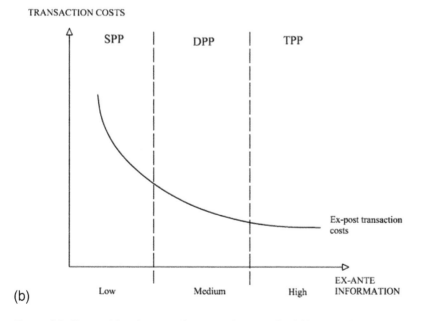

(b)

Figure 8.3 Ex-ante (a) and *ex-post* (b) transaction costs for different tendering procedures.

TRANSACTION COSTS

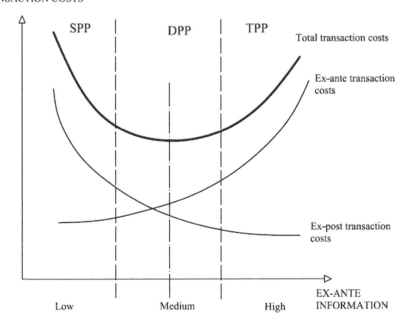

Figure 8.4 Tendering procedure that minimises the transaction costs.

incidence of *ex-ante* transaction costs. This is coherent to the widely accepted notion that the high transaction costs characterising PPP necessitate a minimum project size for a partnership to be a financially and economically viable option. On the contrary, *ex-post* transaction costs increase when the project size increases, due to the greater effort required by the public sector to monitor it (Torres and Pina 2001). Figure 8.5 depicts the effect of the project size on the transaction costs and reveals that when the project size increases the tendering procedure that minimises the transaction costs moves toward more complex procedures (i.e., TPP).

The number of bidders

Ex-ante transaction costs could be expected to increase when the number of bidders increases because of a higher amount of information to be managed during the project initiation and procurement process. *Ex-post* transaction costs are generally higher when the number of bidders is low, because the consequent absence of competition is likely to result in a higher probability of contract rene-gotiation during the project life cycle. At the same time, *ex-post* transaction costs increase with the number of bidders, because the high level of competition reduces the effort of the participants in preparing the bid as they perceive a low probability of winning the tender. There is a U-relationship between the *ex-post* transaction costs and the number of bidders (Dudkin and Välilä 2005). Empirical studies on real PPP projects (Dudkin and Välilä 2005; Estache *et al.* 2008) and

TRANSACTION COSTS

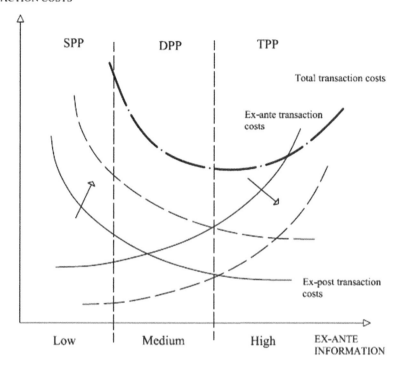

Figure 8.5 The effect of the project size on the transaction costs.

theory (Roumboutsos and Sciancalepore 2014) show that the average number of participants in a bidding process ranges mostly from 2 to 4. This is the reason why the rising part of U-relationship has not been considered. Figure 8.6 depicts the effect of the number of bidders on the transaction costs and reveals that when the number of bidders increases the tendering procedure that minimises the transaction costs moves toward more simple procedures (i.e., SPP).

The project complexity

Project complexity depends on a wide range of factors, namely technical, legal, political, and economic, embedded into the entire PPP project life-cycle (De Meyer *et al.* 2002; Luhman and Boje 2001; Müller and Geraldi 2007; Remington *et al.* 2009; Williams 2002). However, it is possible to identify two primary sources of complexity (Boushaala 2010; Geraldi 2008; Gidado 1996; Ng and Loosemore 2006):

- **Difficulty**: the complexity of the infrastructure project itself due to the design and technological complexity of the construction process;

TRANSACTION COSTS

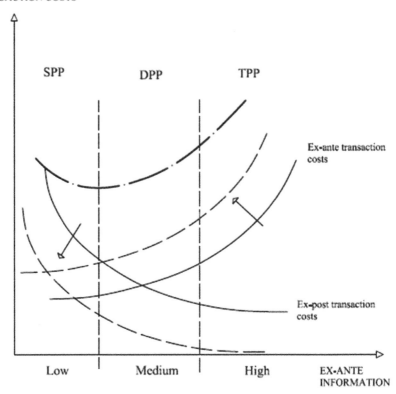

Figure 8.6 The effect of the number of bidders on the transaction costs.

- **Uncertainty**: the complexity of the operating phase due to the long time-frame of concession contracts that increases the uncertainty in business forecasting (revenue, costs, volume, etc.).

The complexity related to the design and construction process will require a great amount of information to be managed in the first phase of the procurement process (*ex-ante* information). The complexity of the operating phase will increase the effort in the monitoring process and the likelihood of having *ex-post* adaptation and changes (i.e., renegotiation). These increase the need to manage *ex-post* a great amount of information. As a result, the project complexity increases transaction costs.

Three different scenarios can be hypothesised:

1) *Ex-ante* and *ex-post* transaction costs increase in the same manner assuming a similar level of complexity in the construction process and

operating phase: the best tendering procedure that minimises the total transaction costs does not significantly change (Figure 8.7);

2) *Ex-ante* transaction costs increase more than *ex-post* transaction costs,
    assuming that the complexity of the construction process is higher than
    the complexity of the operating phase: the best tendering procedure that
    minimises the total transaction costs moves toward more simple procedures
    (i.e., SPP) (Figure 8.8);

3) *Ex-post* transaction costs increase more than *ex-ante* transaction costs,
    assuming that the complexity of the operating phase is higher than the com-
    plexity of the construction process: the best tendering procedure that
    minimises the total transaction costs moves toward more complex proce-
    dures (i.e. TPP) (Figure 8.9).

Conclusions

This chapter provides a conceptual tool to support the contracting authority in
the design and choice of the tendering procedures in PPP. The driver of such

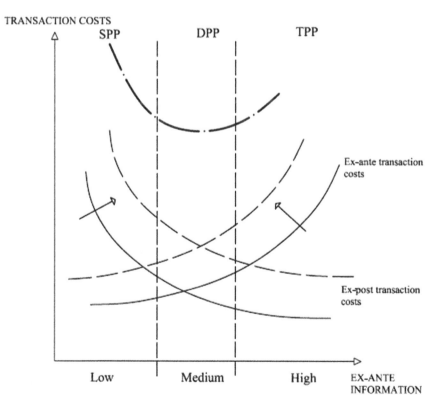

Figure 8.7 The effect of the project complexity on the transaction costs when *ex-ante* and
ex-post transaction costs increase in the same manner.

TRANSACTION COSTS

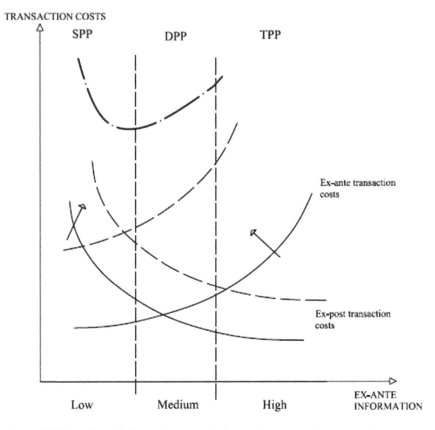

Figure 8.8 The effect of the project complexity on the transaction costs when *ex-ante* transaction costs increase more than *ex-post* transaction costs.

a decision process is the level of transaction costs borne by the public sector and its aim is the minimisation of the transaction costs.

On the basis of two relevant aspects characterising the structure of tendering process in PPP, namely the phases of tendering process and the awarding methods used to rank candidate partners for PPP and choose the best one, we have identified three main tendering procedures, each dealing with a different amount of information.

We have developed a baseline conceptual model that relates the level of transaction costs and the information managed during the tendering process and identifies the tendering procedure that minimises the transaction costs. We found that the best procedure includes the phase of tenderers' pre-qualification and the bid evaluation carried out by using complex methods, i.e. multi-criteria and composite methods, etc. (DPP).

We have further applied the proposed conceptual model to contexts character-ised by different values of project size, project complexity and number of bidders.

TRANSACTION COSTS

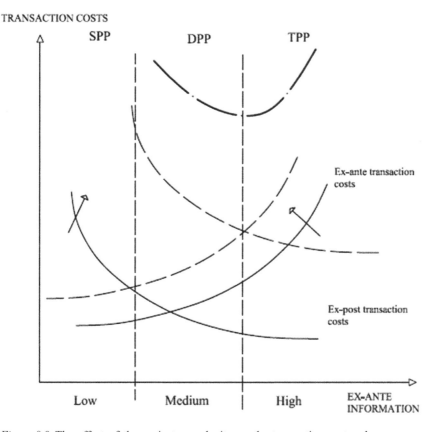

Figure 8.9 The effect of the project complexity on the transaction costs when *ex-post* transaction costs increase more than *ex-ante* transaction costs.

The results show that when the project size increases, the tendering procedure that minimises the transaction costs includes all the three phases: the pre-qualification of tenderers, the bid evaluation carried out by using complex methods, and negotiation with preferred tenderers (TPP). We found that when the number of bidders increases the best tendering procedure includes only the phase of bid evaluation carried out by using simple methods, i.e. simple scoring method and best price (SPP).

Finally, as concerns the effect of the project complexity on the choice of the tendering procedure, three scenarios have been identified on the basis of the level of complexity characterising the construction process and the operating phase:

- **Scenario 1:** same level of complexity in the construction and operations;
- **Scenario 2:** complexity in the construction higher than in operations;
- **Scenario 3:** complexity in operations higher than in the construction.

The optimal procedures are DPP, SPP and TPP in Scenarios 1, 2, and 3 respectively.

The main contribution of this study lies in offering a new conceptual approach, based on transaction costs, for supporting the public authority in the decision-making process about the tendering procedures in PPP without imposing the selection of a specific tendering method. The main limitation of this study is due to the conceptual nature of the proposed model. Further research will be devoted to develop an analytical model for testing the proposed conceptual model on real cases. To address this issue, there is a need to define proxies for measuring the amount of information and the level of transaction costs, analytical models explaining the relationships between these two variables, and how they are affected by the project size, the number of bidders, and the level of project complexity.

References

Arrow, K. J. (1974) *The Limits of Organization*. New York: Norton

Birnie, J. (1997) 'Risk Allocation to the Construction Firm within a Private Finance Initiative (PFI) Project'. *ARCOM Conference Proceedings*, pp. 527–534

Boushaala, A. A. (2010) 'Project complexity indices based on topology features'. *World Academy of Science, Engineering and Technology*, 69, pp. 49–54

Casson, M. (1994) 'Why are firms hierarchical?' *Journal of the Economics of Business*, 1, pp. 47–76

Coase, R. H. (1937) 'The nature of the firm'. *Economica*

Costantino, N. and Pietroforte, R. (2005) 'The diffusion of B2B in the construction market: organizational and technological determinants'. *CIB 2005*, Helsinki, Joint Symposium

de Bettignies, J. E. and Ross, T.W. (2004) 'The economics of Public-Private Partnerships'. *Canadian Public Policy*, 30(2), pp. 135–154

De Meyer, A., Loch, C.H. and Pich, M. T. (2002) 'Managing project uncertainty: from variation to chaos'. *MIT Sloan Management Review*, 43(2), pp. 60–67

Dudkin, G. and Välilä, T. (2005) *Transaction Cost in Public Private Partnerships: A First Look at the Evidence*. European Investment Bank

Ellram, L. M. (1995) 'Total cost of ownership: an analysis approach for purchasing'. *International Journal of Physical Distribution & Logistics Management*, 25(8), pp. 4–23

EPEC (2011) *The Guide to Guidance: How to Prepare, Procure and Deliver PPP Projects*

Estache, A., Guasch, J. L., Iimi, A. and Trujillo, L. (2008) *Multidimensionality and Renegotiation: Evidence from Transport-Sector Public-Private-Partnership Transactions in Latin America*. World Bank Policy Research Working Paper, N. 4665

European Union (2004) Directive 2004/18/EC of 31 March 2004 on the Coordination of Procedures for the Award of Public Works Contracts, Public Supply Contracts and Public Service Contracts. Brussels: European Union

European Union (2014) Directive 2014/24/EU of the European Parliament and of the Council of 26 February 2014 on public procurement and repealing Directive 2004/18/EC. Brussels: European Union

Farajian, M. and Cui, Q. (2010) 'Estimating transaction cost in Public-Private Partnerships'. *AEC Innovation Conference*, June 9–11, State College, PA

FHWA, J. D. (2007) Hearing on Innovative Contracting in Public-Private Partnerships before the Committee on Transportation and Infrastructure Subcommittee on Highways and Transit US House of Representatives

Geraldi, J. (2008) 'Patterns of complexity: the thermometer of complexity'. *Project Perspectives 2008, The Annual Publication of International Project Management Association*, 4–9

Gidado, K. I. (1996) 'Project complexity: the focal point of construction production planning'. *Construction Management and Economics*, 14, pp. 213–225

Ho, S. P. (2006) 'Model for financial renegotiation in Public-Private Partnership projects and its policy implications: game theoretic view'. *Journal of Construction Engineering and Management*, 132 (7), pp. 678–688

Ho, S. P. and Tsui, C. W. (2009) 'The transaction cost of Public Private Partnerships: implications on PPP Governance Design'. LEED 2009, Colorado

Holmstrom, B. R. and Tirole, J. (1989) 'The theory of the firm' in: R. Schmalensee and R. D. Willig *Handbook of Industrial Orgnanization, Vol. 1.* Amsterdam: Elsevier Science Publishers

Kwak, Y. H., Chih, Y-Y. and Ibbs, C.W. (2009) 'Towards a comprehensive understanding of Public Private Partnerships for infrastructure development'. *California Management Review*, 51(2), pp. 51–78

Lingard, H., Hughes, W. and Chinyio, E. (1998) 'The impact of contractor selection method on transaction costs: a review'. *Journal of Construction Procurement*, 4(2)

Lucas, R., Vulcano, A. and Jacobsen, B. (2013) *A Practical Guide to PCP Implementation or PROGR-EAST Pilots.* Available online at: www.innova-eu.net/publications/benchmarking-studies/13-benchmarking-studies/278-pre-commercial-procurement-pcp-manual-a-practical-guide-to-pcp-implementation-for-progr-east-pilots

Luhman, J. and Boje, D. (2001) 'What is complexity science? A possible answer from narrative research'. *Emergence: Complexity and Organization*, 3(1), pp. 158–168

Müller, R. and Geraldi, J. G. (2007) 'Linking complexity and leadership competences of project managers'. *IRNOP VIII Conference (International Research Network for Organizing by Projects)*, Brighton, UK

Ng, A. and Loosemore, M. (2006) 'Risk allocation in the private provision of public infrastructure'. *International Journal of Project Management*, 25, pp. 66–76

Niehans, J. (1969) 'Money in a static theory of optimal payments arrangements'. *Journal of Money, Credit, and Banking* (November), pp. 706–26

Parker, D. and Hartley, K. (2003) 'Transaction costs, relational contracting and Public Private Partnerships: a case study of UK defence'. *Journal of Purchasing & Supply Management*, 9, pp. 97–108

Remington, K., Zolin, R. and Turner, R. (2009) 'A model of project complexity: distinguishing dimensions of complexity from severity'. *Proceedings of the 9th International Research Network of Project Management Conference*, 11–13 October, Berlin

Roumboutsos, A. and Sciancalepore, F. (2014) 'PPP Tenders: optimising on competition'. Transportation Research Board, 2014 Annual Meeting, TRR 141489

Rudzianskaite-Kvaraciejiene R., Apanaviciene, R. and Butauskas A. (2010) 'Evaluation of road investment project effectiveness'. *Inzinerine Ekonomika* [Engineering Economics], Vol. 21, No. 4, pp. 368–376

Soliño, A. S. and de Santos, P. G. (2010) 'Transaction costs in transport Public–Private Partnerships: comparing procurement procedures'. *Transport Reviews: A Transnational Transdisciplinary Journal*, 30(3), pp. 389–406

Soliño, A. S. and de Santos, P. G. (2012) 'Propuesta para la mejora de los procedimientos de licitación en las colaboraciones público-privadas'. *Proceedings of XIX Encuentro de Economía Pública*, Santiago de Compostela, Spain, 26–27 January

Tiong R. L. K. and Alum, J. (1997) 'Evaluation of proposal for BOT projects'. *International Journal of Project Management*, 15(2), pp. 67–72

To, N. T. and Ozawa, K. (2007) 'Evaluation of procurement systems for BOT infrastructures in Asian countries'. *Proceedings of the International Symposium on Social Management*, March, Hubai (China), pp. 9–11

Torres, L. and Pina, V. (2001) 'Public-Private Partnership and private finance initiatives in the EU and Spanish local governments'. *The European Accounting Review*, 10(3), pp. 601–619

Walker, C. and Smith, A. J. (1995) *Privatized Infrastructure*. New York, NY: American Society of Civil Engineers

Wallis, J. and North, D. (1986) 'Measuring the transaction sector in the American economy, 1870–1970' in: S. Engerman and R. Gallman (Eds) (1986) *Long-term Factors in American Economic Growth, NBER Studies in Income and Wealth, 51*. Chicago: The University of Chicago Press

Wang, D. and Dai, D. (2010) 'Research on the concessionaire selection for build-operate-transfer projects. *Proceedings of International Conference on Management and Service Science (MASS)*, Wuhan (China), 24–26 August

Wang, W-X., Li, Q-M., Deng, X-P., Li, L-H. and Cai, Y. (2007) 'Selecting optimal private-sector partners in infrastructure projects under PPP model'. *Proceedings of International Conference on Management Science and Engineering (ICMSE 2007)*, Harbin (China), 20–22 August

Williams, T. (2002) *Modelling Complex Projects*. Chichester, UK: John Wiley & Sons, Ltd.

Williamson, O. E. (1975) *Markets and Hierarchies: Analysis and Antitrust Implications*. New York: The Free Press

Williamson, O. E. (1985) *The Economic Institutions of Capitalism*. New York: The Free Press

Zhang, X. (2004) 'Concessionaire selection: methods and criteria'. *Journal of Construction Engineering and Management*, 130(2), pp. 235–244

Zhang, X. (2005a) 'Criteria for selecting the private-sector partner in Public–Private Partnerships'. *Journal of Construction Engineering and Management*, 131(6), pp. 631–644

Zhang, X. (2005b) 'Critical success factors for Public–Private Partnerships in infrastructure development'. *Journal of Construction Engineering and Management*, 131(1), pp. 71–80

Zitron, J. (2006) 'Public–Private Partnership projects: towards a model of contractor bidding decision-making'. *Journal of Purchasing & Supply Management*, 12, pp. 53–62

9 Bonds and derivatives as financing and risk management instruments in PPPs

Theodore Syriopoulos

Introduction

Public Private Partnership (PPP) project financing and risk management decisions deserve increasing attention since they have critical implications for the efficient and uninterrupted operation and performance of PPP services for the end-users. PPPs bring together public and private partners to facilitate project construction, financing and management, as surplus capital resources are channelled from the private to the public sector in order to alleviate public sector financial constraints. Nevertheless, Public Private Partnerships involve typically complex contractual arrangements, cover a large spectrum of varying projects and services, assume varying governance and accountability arrangements and are evaluated to have both financial benefits but risk constraints as well (Akintoye *et al.* 2001; Institute of Public Policy Research 2001; Bovaird 2004; Davis 2005; Weihe 2006; Kleimeier and Versteeg 2010; Borgonovo *et al.* 2010).

Until recently, PPP financing in Europe has been predominantly supported by the banking sector (Hainz and Kleimeier 2012). However, severe adverse implications related to the global financial crisis, liquidity constraints, risks and uncertainties, extensive worldwide banking sector restructuring and recent conventions such as the Basel III directives, lead market players to search more emphatically for alternative financing sources and instruments, turning mainly to the international capital markets. Specifically, the bond market has long been the core capital market for debt fund raising, incorporated by governments, institutions, corporations and municipalities. Private parties usually take on risks if they can be appropriately priced, managed and mitigated. If the risks bear a significant probability of interrupting the payment stream to debt servicing, the private party (debt financiers) will demand a significant premium to accept that risk. This, in turn, significantly increases the cost of financing the project.

With a view to the transportation sector, prevailing trends indicate a shift from transport service to integrated network solutions which, in turn, exert stress on regional networks as they may be less attractive to strategic international investors (Glaister 1999). In this setting, the issue of regional or municipal project financing with bonds, especially municipal bonds, comes to the fore and is worth investigating further. In conjunction with this, flexible, dynamic risk management instruments, such as financial derivatives including interest rates swaps, can be conveniently adjusted and incorporated into PPP project financing to mitigate associated financial risk exposures.

This chapter focuses on discussing and explaining municipal bonds and interest rate swaps in particular. This is a useful task since, on the one hand, municipal bonds can provide financing alternatives to fund raising of municipal or regional projects and, on the other hand, financial risks, related in particular to interest rate swings and directly affecting project cost of finance, can be contained and hedged by interest rate swap derivatives. These instruments can contribute to materially improving the risk-return profile of the project under development.

The structure of the chapter develops as follows. The next section discusses innovative methods of PPP fund raising and explains the financing advantages of municipal bonds. The subsequent section deals with the critical issue of financial risk hedging and control in PPPs and explains the interest rate swap derivatives.

Municipal bonds as PPP financing instruments

Public and private sector PPP finance: Overview

The economic viability and robust cash flow streams of a project may permit financing either by own funding (organic financing) or, more frequently, by debt (external financing). However, the assessment of potential risks associated with the financial aspects of the project, such as revenue risk, may demand active public sector participation in order to efficiently allocate respective risks. This is particularly so in case the underlying services at stake are socially critical at a national or regional level and the State remains responsible for securing a minimum acceptable level of service.

Major transport infrastructure projects require a large initial investment that has to be raised in order to cover the initial costs of the project. The initial outlay typically accounts for about 70 per cent to 75 per cent of the total cost of the project (Profit 2001). In order to raise cash for finance investment activities, three financing forms are basically available:

- equity finance;
- debt finance;
- other finance (mixed, grants, subsidies etc.).

Public sector finance

The public sector can promote a range of measures to attract and facilitate private investments and minimise the private sector financing cost premiums. At one end of the spectrum stands equity financing that the public sector can fully provide. This may also take the form of infrastructure provision or support of

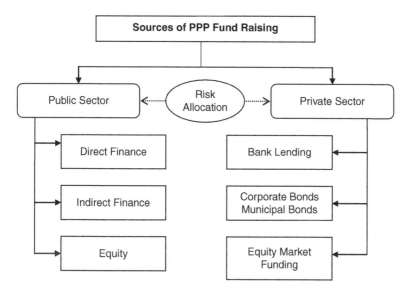

Figure 9.1 Sources of PPP financing.
Source: Adapted from Profit 2001.

a revenue-generating stream (for instance, toll revenues or other subsidies). Public equity creates an environment of mutual interest for both public and private sector partners and can contribute to debt raising at relatively attractive terms (improving debt-to-equity ratios). Subsequently, based on a successful track record, the project can be sold through a share flotation or a private placement with institutional investors.

At the other end of the spectrum stands the injection of direct finance (Figure 9.1). An intermediate combination is indirect government contributions, which cover a whole range of possible instruments from state guarantees to advantageous loan conditions (Profit 2001). State guarantees in project finance contribute in general to a lower cost of capital for the private sector.

The provision of indirect financing by the public sector can enhance the project's attractiveness and result in financial risk mitigation. The public sector can support this objective on the basis of a range of financial instruments. Focusing on transportation projects, these indirect financial tools include, selectively, the following (Profit 2001):

- revenue guarantees;
- loan guarantees;
- banding shadow tolls;
- other types of guarantees;
- tax holidays;

- tax reduction/corporation tax advantages;
- structurally subordinated loans;
- early operational stage loans;
- transfer of rights;
- fiscal advantages:

  ○ reduction (or exclusion) of VAT on construction (and/or maintenance costs);
  ○ exemption from withholding tax, results in lower financing costs;
  ○ reduction of corporate income tax.

The role of guarantees is to increase the attractiveness of a project for the banks by providing the following benefits: (1) credit enhancement; and/or (2) extension of the loan repayment period; thereby, (3) reducing financing costs. The percentage of guaranteed loans is a critical factor for banks to participate in debt financing of a project. The higher the ratio of guaranteed loans to normal loans, the higher the probability of banks financing the project. In addition to national governments, international bodies participate in project financing by offering loans and guarantees. Two such bodies in the EU include: (1) the European Investment Bank (EIB) and (2) the European Investment Fund (EIF).

Private sector finance

The sources of finance available to the private sector include, broadly, equity funding and debt. The debt-to-equity ratio (gearing) is determined basically by the risk profile of the project. The riskier the project the larger the equity share demanded by lenders. Most commonly, large infrastructure projects are dependent on external financing (debt), which can take a variety of forms, including indicatively:

- bank lending;
- syndicated loans;
- bond issuing;
- municipal bonds;
- credit facilities, etc.

The attainment of positive cash flows in the project can be a strong advantage to attract investors' funding. Thus, the equity base can be enhanced by:

- share flotation of the project;
- participation of strategic investors;
- promotion of private placement;
- participation of institutional investors (funds, etc.).

Issuing municipal bonds to finance PPPs

Despite the fact that the bond market is one of the fastest growing capital market segments worldwide (Fabozzi 2008), the advantages of this instrument have not been fully exploited in PPPs as yet. A bond is essentially a form of long-term debt (term horizon of up to 30 years) and can be conceived as a type of lending, since investors transfer funds to the bond issuer (PPP project) for a certain interest rate (bond coupon). Depending on the type of the issuer and/or the term horizon, bonds can be defined as government bonds, municipal bonds, corporate bonds and treasury bills. The issuer of the bond (borrower) undertakes the responsibility to meet a number of interest (coupon) payments to bondholders (lenders/investors) at regular time intervals. The original amount borrowed (principal) is then repaid at the end of the bond's term horizon.

From the borrower's viewpoint, bonds can be a financing instrument of relatively lower cost when compared with bank lending. In the context of a project, the borrower can make long-term plans, assessing the project's long-term cost of capital. For this reason, bonds can be an attractive fund-raising instrument for PPPs in major transportation projects, where risks can be higher (relative to contract-led projects, such as Power Projects). Bond investors can attain considerable liquidity to buy and sell publicly listed bonds as and when they choose. Furthermore, it can be an attractive instrument for certain types of institutional investors, such as pension funds, which often look for investments that match their long-term liabilities, based on a conservative risk-return investment profile.

Traditionally, government and corporate bonds have proven to be flexible tools in financing investment projects undertaken by governments and corporations. On top of that, municipal bonds exhibit robust growth rates over recent years, as a financing method to infrastructure requirements at the regional or local community level. Municipal securities are debt securities issued mainly by states, municipalities, cities, townships, counties, and their associated authorities and agencies. The capital raised by these securities is used to cover a diversified range of social needs including, for instance, extending a county highway spur through a rural area, building a new school, constructing a water purification plant, or even just refunding an earlier debt issue. The municipal bond market has seen robust growth rates since the 1970s, predominantly in the US. The insuperable financial constraints (close to bankruptcy) experienced by New York City, following the rapid increase of its outstanding debt and leading to the default of a note issue (1975), have been a critical milestone for the persistent growth of the municipal bond market since.

When a municipality needs more funding than it receives from tax and other regular revenues, it has the option of borrowing against future tax revenues; the loan can take the form of a municipal bond issue. Municipal bonds provide the finances that support growth and generate income for local governments and can be divided into (Zipf 2002):

- **public purpose bonds**, issued directly by the State or local government and used for traditional municipal projects (transportation, schools, etc.);
- **private activity bonds**, even if they are issued by the State, local government or an agency, they supply funds for 'private' projects (for example, sports arena, shopping mall, etc.);

- **non-governmental purpose bonds**, raise funds for 'non-governmental' (but not private) uses (for example, housing, student funding, etc.).

Municipal bonds can be divided into two broad categories:

- **General Obligation (GO) bonds**, which include limited tax bonds and special assessment bonds

  ○ all GO bonds are backed by the taxing counties, hence only an issuer with the power to tax may issue GO bonds; principal and interest are paid regularly;
  ○ when a legal limit is imposed on the taxing power of the issuer, general obligation bonds are then 'limited tax' bonds;
  ○ 'special assessment' bonds are secured by an assessment of those who benefit directly from the project (e.g. the residents of the area where a bridge is built).

- **Revenue bonds**, which include industrial development bonds, special tax bonds and public housing authority bonds

  ○ revenue bonds may be issued by an agency, commission or authority in order to construct a 'facility' (such as toll bridge, airport, port, turnpike, hospital, university or water and electricity districts);
  ○ the fees, taxes or toll charges for the use of this facility ultimately pay off the debt;
  ○ since the municipality itself does not back such bonds, they are usually riskier than general obligation bonds, and pay a relatively higher interest rate; defaults are rare but can occur.

Using municipal bond insurance is one way to reduce credit risk on this instrument. This includes an agreement by an insurance company to pay debt service that is not paid by the bond issuer. In other words, municipal bond insurance guarantees that the issuer will pay interest and principal on the insured bonds as they become due, if the issuer fails to make the payments. Most municipal bonds are insured at issue and insurance is sold as part of the new issue. A typical structure of a municipal bond set-up is summarised in Figure 9.2.

Municipal bond credit rating

Credit rating is considered to be the most important factor in the pricing of bonds and significant correlation has been detected between rating and bond spreads (Fridson and Garman 1998). Most institutional investors, underwriters and traders use the municipal bond rating provided by international rating agencies, such as Moody's, Standard and Poor's (S&P's), Fitch and Duff & Phelps, in order to evaluate investment creditworthiness of the underlying assets. Based on rating agencies' evaluation, bonds are rated either as of investment or non-investment grade ('high yield' or 'junk' bonds).

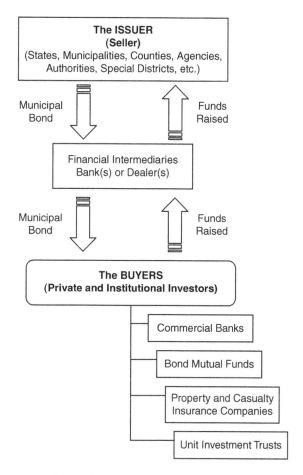

Figure 9.2 Typical structure of a municipal bond set-up.
Source: Adapted from Zipf 2002.

The municipal bond rating system used by Moody's grades the investment quality of municipal bonds in a nine-symbol system that ranges from the highest (Aaa) to the lowest (C) investment quality. The municipal bond rating system used by Standard and Poor's grades the investment quality of municipal bonds in a ten-symbol system that ranges from the highest (AAA) to the lowest (D) investment quality. More specifically, bonds rated in the range of Aaa/AAA (Moody's/ S&P's) to Baa/BBB (Moody's/S&P's) are considered as 'investment grade'. Any bonds rated B (Moody's/S&P's) or below are included in the 'high yield' class (see Table 9.1). Adjustments can be made within a rating category by adding a + or – (Moody's) or 1, 2 and 3 (S&P's) to indicate a higher or lower issue in its class. Major factors that credit rating agencies take into account when they

Table 9.1 Typical credit rating grades

Moody's	S&P's	Characteristics	Comment	Class
Aaa	AAA	Highest grade	Maximum safety	*Investment Grade*
Aa	AA	High grade	Slightly lower standards	
A	A	Upper medium	Favorable but possible future problems	
Baa	BBB	Medium grade	Moderate security and protection	
Ba	BB	Moderate protection	Contain speculative elements	*Speculative*
B	B	Potentially undesirable	Low assurance of future payments	*'High Yield'*
Caa	CCC	Danger of default	Dangerous elements present	*or 'Junk' Bonds*
Ca	CC	Likely in or to default	Highly speculative	
CC	C	Lowest class	Extremely poor prospects	
C	D	Bottom-most grade	Unlikely to attain any standing	
NR	NR	Not ranked	No evaluation available	

Source: Adapted from Feldstein *et al.* 2008.

evaluate a bond issue include: sovereign/macroeconomic issues, issuer structure, industry outlook, management quality, operating position, financial position, and issuer characteristics.

Market participants pay particular attention to rating as a key factor that affects spreads and municipal bond value. Since rating indicates competitive credit risk of any two investments within the group of rated instruments, rating also can support forecasts of 'probability of default'. Lower rated issues are associated with higher default probabilities. This is perceived as an indicator of investors' protection in case a bond issuer faces adverse long-term economic conditions. In the context of maritime transportation, for instance, respective bond rating takes into account a number of issues including: the impact of cyclicality and volatility on shipping markets; the uncertainty about the future direction of freight rates; the business percentage allocation into spot or chartered markets; the ability of the issuer to attain sustainable future cash flows; and the issuer's vulnerability to economic cycles and the implications for interest and principal payment.

Callability of a municipal bond implies that the issuer has a call option embedded and the issuer retains the right to retire (call back) the bond at specified prices before maturity. This option is of value in the case of lower interest rate expectations, since the issuer may have the opportunity to refinance debt with a lower interest rate instrument, thus improving the issuer's debt terms. However, investors are exposed to reinvestment risk and, consequently, they would target higher returns for that. Furthermore, municipal bond pricing may be affected by the maturity horizon of a bond and where a negative relationship between maturity and spread is anticipated. The float (issue amount) of a municipal bond indicates the liquidity of the issue. Larger bond issues are expected to have lower risk premiums than smaller issues traded in thinner markets. An inverse relationship between float and spread (smaller issues – larger spreads) is anticipated.

The 'default rate' is a measure of credit risk in the municipal bond market that reflects the relative likelihood that there may be a difference between what investors were promised and what they actually receive from the bond issuer. That is, a default implies any missed or delayed disbursement of interest or principal. It includes, furthermore, 'forced exchange', in case a bond issuer has offered a new instrument containing a diminished financial obligation, such as preferred or common stock or debt with a lower coupon or par amount (Fabozzi 2008). Since higher default rates are associated with higher risk premium and investors demand a higher spread for compensation, a positive relationship between default rate and spreads would be plausible. The spread is also affected by subordination (in terms of debt claims priority) and is related to whether debt is secured (collateralised by assets) or unsecured; unsecured bond issues are expected to carry wider spreads.

In this setting, the characteristics and structure of municipal bonds could be adjusted to the specific financial requirement of a PPP project, thus offering an attractive alternative source of funding. The (PPP) issuer's creditworthiness could be secured by an embedded State, municipal or public agency participation in the project and could be further insured to guarantee the issuer will pay interest and principal on the (PPP) bond.

Depending on the attractiveness and risk characteristics of the PPP project under development, bond pricing could bear a higher or lower spread on its coupon. The spread is defined as the difference between the yield to maturity on a coupon-paying (municipal/PPP) bond and the yield to maturity on a coupon-paying government bond of the same maturity. Furthermore, the amount to be raised, in conjunction with PPP project characteristics, could have a significant impact on (PPP) bond's liquidity, affecting its attractiveness to investors. What is more, PPP partners could proceed to a rating agency and have this bond issue rated, thus enhancing the creditworthiness and transparency of the issue, increasing the project's visibility and facilitating investors' capital contribution substantially.

Risk management in PPPs

Risk allocation and control in PPPs

PPP projects bear a high degree of uncertainty and involve a wide range of risks, including those in the areas of design and development, construction, finance, operation and ownership (Lewis 2002; Ball *et al.* 2003; Hodge 2004; Ng and Loosemore 2007). Consequently, efficient risk evaluation, allocation and management remains a key issue. As the public sector holds the leading role, this is the partner in an advantageous position to take action towards risk control. An efficient risk allocation approach should focus on transferring to each partner only those risk components that can be best managed.

The concept of risk in PPP projects is complex and multifaceted. The interest in this chapter focuses on innovative financial instruments for fund raising in PPP ventures and the associated financial risk. The probability of an undesirable event occurring indicates the level of risk exposure in a project. From a financial measurement viewpoint, risk is depicted by the statistical variance (or standard deviation) of possible financial outcomes from their mean. Modern finance decomposes risk into two components: (1) systematic (market) risk and (2) (project) specific risk. Major risk categories include the following (Oldfield and Santomero 1997): credit risk, counterparty risk, operational risk, legal risk.

A number of quantitative tools and approaches can be used in the case of PPPs to measure financial risks, including:

- volatility analysis;
- factor sensitivity analysis;
- value-at-risk;
- credit risk measurement;
- asset/liability analysis;
- z-score measurement;
- the capital asset pricing model (CAPM).

Since PPP funding bears a high risk element, the risk components involved in a project should be monitored and evaluated frequently (in risk maps, risk matrices, etc.).

Financial instruments to risk management

A set of specialised financial derivatives to support risk hedging and control can be conveniently adapted to usefully apply to PPP financial risk management. Three broad types of financial derivatives can be distinguished:

Forwards and futures contracts

Forward or futures contracts are based on the obligation to buy or sell the underlying asset at/until a specific future date (maturity date) and at a pre-specified price (exercise price).

Options (calls/puts)

Option contracts provide the right to the bearer (but not the obligation) to buy (call option) or sell (put option) the underlying asset at/until a specific future date (maturity date) and at a pre-specified price (exercise price).

Swaps

Swaps refer to the mutual sale and purchase of cash flows related to underlying interest rates, currencies or other financial assets between two counterparties.

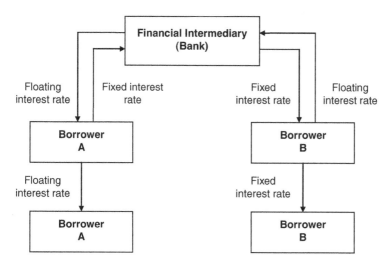

Figure 9.3 Structure of an interest rate swap.
Source: Adapted from Marshall and Kapner 1993.

Interest rate and currency swaps include two legs of cash flows with differing interest rate or currency characteristics. Swaps can also apply to liability or asset cash flows (liability or asset swap). Interest rate swaps present the most popular swap type and they usually involve swap of fixed rate cash flows with floating rate cash flows (plain vanilla swap). Other widely employed swap types include equity swaps and commodity swaps (Marshall and Kapner 1993).

Figure 9.3 describes a typical interest rate swap structure that is flexible and applicable to PPPs on the basis of the following assumptions:

(a) Borrower A has a loan to service in floating interest rate (floating rate) whereas Borrower B has a fixed interest rate loan (fixed rate);
(b) Due to capital market conditions and a different stance of banks towards the two borrowers

   (i) borrower A would prefer to have the loan in fixed interest rate and borrower B in floating interest rates;
   (ii) the two borrowers would be prepared to accept a swap of their interest payments; and,
   (iii) the bank would be keen to intermediate in this swap at a fee.

(c) The intermediating bank then pays borrower A the floating rate against the fixed rate and also pays borrower B the fixed rate against the floating rate; the bank can flexibly cancel out potential losses and gains through this matching procedure.

Conclusion

PPP ventures exhibit persistently robust growth trends as a dynamic alternative vehicle to finance infrastructure projects, including transportation. The joint partnership of public and private agents can apply to a wide spectrum of projects and services but it is complex and bears both financial benefits and risks.

This chapter has discussed critical issues relating to alternative PPP financing tools, in particular municipal bonds, and selective financial risk hedging instruments, that is interest rate swaps. These issues are interrelated, as the financing instruments employed have considerable impact on the financial risks, pricing and risk management of a PPP venture.

As funding requirements of PPP projects can frequently surpass private investors' financing capacity apart from bank lending, global capital markets – including equity and bond markets – can offer a range of attractive alternative fund raising sources, departing from traditional bank lending practices. To this end, credit rating was argued to be a critical factor for the attractiveness, risk-return profile and pricing of a bond issue that could be incorporated in PPP finance.

PPP projects are consistently in need of innovative financial instruments and risk mitigation and hedging tools. Real options analysis has attempted more recently to provide a dynamic valuation alternative to standard valuation methods, such as Net Present Value, blending standard investment appraisal criteria with financial derivatives practices. Recent developments in capital markets and sophisticated structured finance products can provide interesting alternatives to PPP project funding and risk management.

References

Akintoye, A., Beck, M., Hardcastle, C., Chinyio, E. and Assenova, D. (2001) 'A framework for risk assessment and management of private finance initiative projects'. *Working Paper*, Glasgow Caledonian University

Ball, R., Heafey, M. and King, D. (2003) 'Risk transfer and value for money in PFI projects'. *Public Management Review*, 5(2), pp. 279–290

Borgonovo, E., Gatti, S. and Peccati, L. (2010) 'What drives value creation in investment projects? An application of sensitivity analysis to project finance transactions'. *European Journal of Operational Research*, 205, pp. 227–236

Bovaird, T. (2004) 'Public-Private Partnerships: from contested concepts to prevalent practice'. *International Review of Administrative Sciences*, 70(2), pp. 199–215

Davis, K. (2005) 'PPP and infrastructure investment'. *Australian Economic Review*, 38(4), pp. 439–444

Fabozzi, F. (Ed.) (2008) *The Handbook of Fixed Income Securities* (8th Ed.). New York: McGraw-Hill Publications

Feldstein, S. G., Fabozzi, F. and Kennedy, P. (2008) 'Municipal Bonds' in: Fabozzi, F. (Ed.) *The Handbook of Fixed Income Securities* (8th Ed.). New York: McGraw-Hill Publications

Fridson, M. and Garman, C. (1998) 'Determinants of spreads on new high yield bonds'. *Financial Analysts Journal*, March/April, pp. 28–39

Glaister, S. (1999) 'Past abuses and future uses of private finance and Public Private Partnerships in transport'. *Public Money & Management*, 19(3), pp. 29–36

Hainz, C. and Kleimeier, S. (2012) 'Political risk, project finance, and the participation of development banks in syndicated lending'. *Journal of Financial Intermediation*, 21, pp. 287–314

Hodge, G. A. (2004) 'The risky business of Public-Private Partnerships'. *Australian Journal of Public Administration*, 63(4), pp. 37–49

Institute of Public Policy Research (IPPR) (2001) *Building Better Partnerships: The Final Report of the Commission on Public Private Partnerships.* London: Institute of Public Policy Research

Kleimeier, S. and Versteeg, R. (2010) 'Project finance as a driver of economic growth in low-income countries'. *Review of Financial Economics*, 19, pp. 49–59

Lewis, M. K. (2002) 'Risk management in Public Private Partnerships'. *Working Paper*, University of South Australia

Marshall, J. F. and Kapner, K. R. (1993) *Understanding Swaps.* New York: J. Wiley & Sons

Ng, A. and Loosemore, M. (2007) 'Risk allocation in the private provision of public infrastructure'. *International Journal of Project Management*, 25, pp. 66–76

Oldfield, G. S. and Santomero, A. M. (1997) 'Risk management in financial institutions'. *Sloan Management Review*, Fall, pp. 33–46

Profit (2001) *Private Operations and Financing of TEN's, EC Project.* Rotterdam: NEI Transport

Weihe, G. (2006) 'Public-Private Partnerships: addressing a nebulous concept'. *Working Paper*, Copenhagen Business School

Zipf, R. (2002) *How the Bond Market Works* (3rd Ed.). New York: New York Institute of Finance

Glossary

Table 9.2 summarises and explains briefly a set of key concepts and terms in relation to bond financing and derivatives risk management.

Table 9.2 Glossary: explanation of key financial terms

Term	Explanation
Asset backed bond	A secured bond backed by collateral; the bondholder has the right to take possession of and sell this collateral if the bond issuer fails to make full interest and principal payments when due.
Bond	A debt (fixed-income) instrument (security) issued by institutions (mainly governments, companies, municipalities) for the purpose of raising capital; a bond entitles the holder (obliges the issuer) to repayment of the principal sum, plus interest, at maturity.
Bond rating	Bond rating agencies (e.g. Moody's, Standard & Poor's, Fitch) provide a service to investors by grading fixed income securities; the rating system indicates the likelihood that the issuer may default either on interest or capital payments.
Callable bond	A bond issued with call provisions can be redeemed (or called) at the option of the issuer prior to the maturity date; issuers will often seek to redeem outstanding bonds when interest rates decline, so they can pay off the bonds and reissue them at a lower interest rate.

(Continued)

Table 9.2 Glossary: explanation of key financial terms (Continued)

Term	Explanation
Common stock	The most usual and commonly held form of stock in a company (also known as common or ordinary shares); shareholders of common stock have voting rights in corporate decisions.
Corporate bond	A bond issued by a corporation; it usually pays a higher interest rate than government bonds since it bears higher risk.
Credit Default Swap (CDS)	A swap designed to transfer the credit exposure of fixed income products between parties (credit derivative); it is an agreement between a protection buyer and a protection seller, whereby the buyer pays a periodic fee in return for a contingent payment by the seller upon a credit event (default) happening in the reference entity; a CDS is often used as an insurance policy or hedge for the debtholder.
Debenture	A bond that is not secured by specific property or collateral (backed by the full faith and credit of the issuer); and bondholders have a general claim on assets that are not pledged to other debt.
Debt	A debt is created when a creditor agrees to lend a sum of assets to a debtor; it is usually granted with expected repayment plus interest; numerous types of debt including basic loans, syndicated loans, bonds and promissory notes.
Derivatives (financial)	A financial instrument derived from an underlying asset's value; rather than trade or exchange the asset itself, market participants enter into an agreement to exchange money, assets or some other value at some future date based on the underlying asset; most frequent derivative products include futures, options and swaps.
Futures	Financial contracts giving the buyer an obligation to purchase an underlying asset and the seller an obligation to sell that asset, at a set price at a future point in time.
Government bond	A bond issued by a national government, denominated in the country's own currency (bonds issued in foreign currencies are normally referred to as sovereign bonds); it is usually considered as a risk-free security.
Means of financing	Financing a company (project) through the sale of stock is known as equity financing; alternatively, debt financing (for instance, by issuing bonds) can be chosen to avoid ownership dilution; unofficial financing (known as trade financing) is provided by vendors and suppliers and constitutes the major part of working capital (operational needs); equity and debt financing are usually used for longer-term investment projects.
Mezzanine capital/ Debt (finance)	This is a broad financial term that refers to unsecured, high-yield, subordinated debt or preferred stock that represents a claim on a company's assets that is senior only to that of a company's shareholders; it refers to that layer of financing between a company's senior debt and equity, filling the gap between the two; structurally, it is subordinate in priority of payment to senior debt but senior in rank to common stock or equity; in a broader sense, mezzanine finance may take the form of convertible debt, senior subordinated debt or private 'mezzanine' securities (debt with warrants or preferred equity).

(Continued)

Table 9.2 Glossary: explanation of key financial terms (Continued)

Term	Explanation
Municipal bond	A debt obligation issued by a state, city or local government to finance governmental needs or special projects; two general categories: revenue bonds (backed by revenues generated by a specific project or agency); general obligation bonds (backed by full faith and credit or taxing power of issuer); also, two primary groups of municipal bonds: public purpose bonds (tax-exempt bonds); private purpose bonds (taxable unless specifically exempted).
Options	A right (not an obligation) to buy (call) or sell (put) an underlying asset at a specific price (exercise price).
Subordinated debt	A loan (or security) that ranks below other loans (or securities) with regard to claims on assets or earnings (also known as 'junior security' or 'subordinated loan'); in the case of default, creditors with subordinated debt would not get paid out until after the senior debtholders were paid in full; hence, subordinated debt has a higher expected rate of return but is more risky than unsubordinated debt.
Swap	An agreement between two counter-parties to exchange (swap) two streams of cash flows; it is an offer to pay a value (based on an index or fixed value) and receive another value (based on an index or fixed value); typically, the owner will offer to swap a fixed price position for a floating position or vice versa; payment is determined by the difference between the two legs once the prices can be determined (cash-settled over-the-counter derivative).
Swaption	An option on a forward start swap that provides the purchaser the right to either pay or receive a fixed rate (payers'/receivers' swaption); it can be used as a hedging vehicle for fixed debt, floating debt or swaps.
Syndication	A group of individuals or companies that has formed a venture to undertake a project that would not be feasible to pursue alone; it usually refers to doing an underwriting or private placement for a public (listed) company.
Treasury Bill	A short-term, government-backed, debt obligation with a maturity of less than one year (usually 1-, 3-, 6-months); it is issued at a discount from par, meaning that (rather than paying fixed interest payments like conventional bonds) the appreciation of the bond provides the return to the holder; it is considered to be the most risk-free financial product.
Value-at-Risk (VaR)	A measure of market risk (maximum amount at risk to be lost from an investment), indicating how the market value of an asset (or a portfolio) is likely to decrease over a certain time period (usually over 1 or 10 days) under 'normal' conditions; VaR has three parameters: time-horizon (holding period); confidence level at which the estimate is made; unit of currency that will be used to denominate the value at risk.

10 Decision models in Public Private Partnerships

Conclusions, future research and policy recommendations

Nunzia Carbonara

An overview

Implementing PPP projects requires taking a sequence of decisions along the entire PPP life-cycle that clearly affect the success of a PPP (Yuan *et al.* 2009). These decisions range from the selection of the appropriate concession period to the determination of the project's financial structure, from the selection of the most suitable private concessionaire to the establishment of key performance indicators to monitor the project's implementation and operation, and from the selection of suitable risk mitigation strategies to the prioritisation of PPP projects.

Some of the above mentioned decisions are strongly affected by the regulatory framework, others are policy-driven, and others are supported by very well-consolidated decision tools. However, there are areas of decision that require the support of analytical models to guide the decision-maker in the effort to strike a balance between safeguarding the potential to achieve savings through PPP and secure expected social benefits, and to take into account the multifarious and often conflicting interests of different stakeholders involved in the PPP. Among these relevant decisions, those more complex that strongly affect the success of a PPP project concern the selection of the concessionaire and the definition of the contractual terms, as they impact the entire PPP life-cycle.

The selection of the most suitable private concessionaire requires a well-structured tendering process, an appropriate concessionaire evaluation method, and a set of objective evaluation criteria (Miller 2000). In particular, a well-structured tendering process that can minimise tendering costs and ensure sufficient competition between private bidders is necessary, since it is widely recognised that the tendering process of PPP is more complicated and more costly than that of traditional public infrastructure development.

The existing literature on the theme focuses on two relevant aspects characterising the structure of the tendering process in PPP. The first one concerns the phases of the tendering process; the second concerns the awarding methods used to rank candidate partners for PPP and to choose the best one. However, some issues are still open: how to structure the tendering process in PPP in order to minimise transaction costs? Which phases and awarding methods should be used in the tendering process? How do specific factors such as the size of the project, the number of bidders, the complexity of the project, affect the choice of the tendering procedure?

The tendering process is the responsibility of the public procuring authority. Project size, project complexity, the number of potential bidders impact the amount of information processed and relate to the transaction costs borne by the public authority. The selection of the appropriate tendering procedure is influenced by the effort to reduce and minimise related transaction costs. Chapter 8 of this Part addresses this issue. More specifically, Carbonara *et al.*[1] propose a baseline conceptual model that relates the level of transaction costs and the information managed during the tendering process to identify the tendering procedure that minimises the transaction costs for the public sector.

However, when designing the tendering process, the potential number and the existing competition is also a factor to be considered. Roumboutsos and Sciancalepore[1] (2014) take an alternative approach to the topics of competition, tendering and transaction costs. They reverse the common question of 'how to improve competition in the market through the tendering procedure' to 'how to exploit all existing competition in the market through the tendering procedure', therefore designing efficient tendering procedures. Their analytical game model produces a map correlating level of transaction costs versus number of potential bidders upon which areas of optimum and suboptimum market conditions are identified, allowing public procurement authorities to select the appropriate tendering process based on the number of potential bidders and the acceptable private sector transaction costs. The model predicts that optimality is reached with 2-3 bidders. Interestingly, while there are tendering processes designed to reduce the number of bidders (for example, by introducing a preselection phase), the optimal situation when there are fewer bidders is reached by increasing transaction costs. This suggests that the private authority should either tender more complex projects or that tendering procedures with increased transaction costs (such as competitive dialogue) may (or should be) introduced.

The latter finding combines with research undertaken by Hoezen *et al.*[1] (2012a) with respect to the dynamics in a competitive dialogue procedure; with emphasis on the contracting dynamics (Hoezen *et al.*[1] 2012b); its formal and informal side as it is driven through the negotiation process (Hoezen *et al.*[1] 2013); leading to how complex projects may be procured through the competitive dialogue procedure (Hoezen *et al.*[1] 2014).

Closely related to the tendering process, the contracting holds a whole new set of decisions. Risk allocation and management are at the heart of this process, considered to be the cornerstone in the justification of the PPP model. Specifically, in order to assist the public sector with decisions related to risk allocation in PPP projects, various standardised risk allocation matrices have been developed (Milner 2004; Smith 1995). Roumboutsos *et al.*[1] (2012) study the particular risks related to transport PPP projects indicating that transport PPP key risks are related to demand risks concentrated around the level of natural or contractual monopoly, the network effects and how demand risk may be balanced within the revenue risk through the bundling of other business activities (Roumboutsos 2013a[1]; 2013b[1]; Roumboutsos and Temeljotov[1] 2013).

Furthermore, the contractual setting and how it influences a party's ability to manage risk should be the guiding principle in risk allocation (Loosemore *et al.* 2006). However, Roumboutsos and Pantelias[1] (2015) find that risk management principles are not always identified in practice. Various measures to financially secure the project are put forward. Many efforts are centred on guarantees. Notably, while guarantees and, especially, minimum revenue ones (MRG), may improve the financiability of a PPP project, defining their optimum value is a critical issue. Carbonara *et al.*[1] (2014) propose a tool for setting the revenue guarantee level secured by the government, which balances the interests of both parties and uses the concept of fairness for structuring MRGs. In particular, expanding on the studies already undertaken in this field, the authors develop a real option-based model that supports the decision-maker in finding the optimal value of the 'revenue cap' (the minimum amount of revenue secured by the government) that is able to satisfy the interest of the private sector by guaranteeing a minimum revenue, and the interest of the public sector by ensuring that the investment can be considered off-balance sheet. At the same time, this optimal value of the 'revenue cap' ensures a fair risk allocation between parties, in terms of probability that the interests of the two parties are not satisfied. Monte Carlo simulation has been used as the option pricing method, rather than existing analytical methods developed for financial options, thus overcoming the limitations that the latter methods present in modelling and valuing real options.

However, apart from risk allocation, acknowledging the potential to manage risks over time and introducing suitable strategies to mitigate risks is equally important. Most of the relevant studies have had a very specific focus, i.e. proposing specific strategies to mitigate specific types of risk (Pfeffer 2010; Nevitt and Fabozzi 2005). However, the literature review reveals two main gaps. First, the studies lack a comprehensive tool for supporting the decision-makers in the selection of appropriate risk mitigation strategies. Secondly, none of the existing models has the capability to support governmental decision-making in the choice of risk mitigation strategies that satisfy the interests of both parties by taking into account unforeseen risks and uncertainties and that allows for fair risk sharing between parties. More specifically, the success of a PPP project often depends on the ability of the project participant to manage the project risks. These risks are not only challenges but also opportunities for the private concessionaire as well as for the government. Traditional risk management techniques tend to ignore the manager's ability to recognise and exploit opportunities, which arise as uncertainties that could be resolved over time and which could potentially increase the project's value. Therefore it is necessary for the risk management process to take into account managerial flexibility. To address this issue Pellegrino *et al.*[1] (2013) adopt a real option-based approach, where real options represent the possibility (the right, not the obligation) of taking actions in the future by incurring a certain cost to acquire this right. In particular, focusing on transport PPP, an option-based risk management framework is proposed that associates to each PPP risk the related mitigation strategies expressed in terms of real options. The framework provides valid support for decision-makers in finding the most cost-effective combination of mitigation strategies to embed in a PPP investment in order to optimally control risk and maximise investment value.

Progressing on this topic and recognising that the relevance of risks, the establishment of an acceptable risk allocation scheme, and the choice of the appropriate risk mitigation strategies depend on the specific PPP sector, Carbonara *et al.*[1] (2014), focusing on the motorway sector and on the basis of the results of a Delphi survey, provide a guideline for both public and private parties in defining a list of significant risks in PPP motorway projects, preparing a practical risk allocation framework and identifying the most suitable mitigation strategies.

Risk mitigation is also accomplished through the financing structure. Syriopoulos in Chapter 9 discusses two financial instruments that can be appropriate for PPP transport ventures: municipal bonds and interest rate swaps.

Contractual terms are usually the result of a negotiation process between the public and private party. Studies on PPP projects identify contract negotiation as an important step in improving PPP, since it allows a satisfactory agreement to be reached between the parties. Research on this topic addresses different issues, usually under negotiation. Specifically, a stream of studies focuses on the concession period and develops methodologies for calculating a reasonable concession period. Most of the proposed models determine the concession period considering only the maximisation of concessionaire benefits (Engle *et al.* 2001; Vassallo 2006), while only few models adopt a win-win approach, in the sense that the concession period is determined in order to maximise the benefits to both the government and the concessionaire (Shen *et al.* 2002; Zhang and AbouRizk, 2006). However, none of the models proposed in literature has the capability to support the governmental decision-making in the choice of a concession period that satisfies the interests of both parties by taking into account unforeseen risks and uncertainties, and that allows a fair risk sharing between the parties. Notably, a key factor of a PPP project is the agreement on the length of concession period. The concession period is one of the most important decision variables for arranging a successful PPP contract because its value decides when ownership of a project will be transferred from the investor to the government, thereby demarcating the authority, responsibility and benefits between the private party and the government. Carbonara *et al.*[1] (2014) provide a new model for calculating the concession period as the best instant of time that creates a 'win–win' solution for both project sponsor and the host government and allows for fair risk sharing between the two parties. In other words, the concession period is able to satisfy the private party and the government by guaranteeing for both parties a minimum profit and, at the same time, to fairly allocate the risks between parties. In order to take into account the uncertainty that affects the PPP projects, the Monte Carlo simulation technique is adopted. A case study on a BOT port project is used to check the applicability of the proposed model for determining the reasonable length of the concession period that safeguards the multiple interests of the public sector and the profit-making interest of the private sector, and that allows for fair risk sharing between the public and private sectors by minimising the difference between the risks of loss borne by the two parties. The application shows that the developed model can be a valid tool for supporting the public authority in the decision-making process about the length of the concession period.

Finally, it is acknowledged that PPP contracts are inherently incomplete. Renegotiations are, in many cases, unavoidable and present the risk of hold up due to residual ownership rights, asymmetry in information and strategic behaviour of counterparties (see Nikolaidis and Roumboutsos[1] 2013). However, Domingues and Zlatkovic[1] (2015) show how, by strengthening partnering, optimum conditions may be reached.

Given the obvious importance of all the aforementioned decisions in the success of PPP projects, in recent years a number of useful PPP decision-support instruments have been produced by various organisations in order to overcome the lack of standardisation that causes many PPP decisions to be left to the discretionary power of relevant decision-makers. This lack of standardisation, often combined with a lack of experience and specialist skills by public decision-makers, can negatively affect projects delivered via the PPP route. In spite of the positive contribution of the decision-support instruments that have been developed to date, there are some critical issues that are still left unattended. In particular, current decision tools are predominantly based on financial concepts of VfM, while the individual perspectives and objectives of the different stakeholders are often disregarded. However, it is widely recognised that most of the PPP-related decisions taken by public authorities are not driven solely by economic principles. In fact, besides economic criteria, public authorities have to comply with a complex framework of regulations and laws (Essig and Batran 2005) and to appraise the feasibility of the project in relation to the environmental, societal, political, legislative and financial context of the country (and/or sector) within which a project is being developed. Furthermore, most of the decision tools provided correspond to the project's early stages. However, it is important to recognise that decisions are taken across all phases of the PPP life cycle. It is also important to consider how decisions impact the future, especially with respect to government liabilities (see Sfakianakis and van de Laar[1] 2013).

In order to provide useful guidelines to support the PPP decision-making process a toolkit has been developed that is formed of two components: 1) PPP Decision Tree; 2) PPP Decision Support (DS) framework (see Chapter 7). The proposed framework draws from already existing literature on decision-support systems and their analysis, while the breakdown of the PPP life-cycle into various phases follows the structure suggested in the EPEC PPP Guide by the EIB. The PPP DS framework is founded on the representation of the PPP decision processes in a tree structure that identifies six areas of decision, each of them treated at a macro- and a micro-level. The framework aims at providing answers to three basic questions (When? What? Who?) that form the basic components of the PPP decision-making process, leading to a three-dimensional graphical representation of the PPP decision-making space.

Future research

Stemming from the last contribution, it is evident that a large body of knowledge and decision models exist that are not always linked with the entire process of decision-making in PPP transport and other sectors. Identifying their potential impact on the PPP life-cycle and correlating them to performance indicators is an important step in their validation and assessment. Within this process, it is also important to identify the impact the various decisions have on the PPP risk profile and their allocation.

Another point is that the decision process is usually studied from the public contracting authority point of view. Admittedly, many decisions are linked to the public party, especially in the pre-award stage. However, many decisions can be well effected if they can account for a win-win perspective. In other words, decisions should take into account the interests of the private party more. The latter, in fact, sustains high transaction and tendering costs that are not priced in the PPP project value.

Finally, PPPs represent inherently incomplete contracts. Identifying appropriate mechanisms that increase the level of contractual flexibility and that allow for an on-going renegotiation are important to the success of the PPP undertaking.

Policy recommendations

A key role should be played by the public sector in implementing research findings in PPP practice, so assuring a more effective use of PPP delivery. This requires the improvement of competences and know-how of public administrators involved in the PPP decision-making processes. In turn this will improve the assessment of the feasibility, affordability and sustainability of PPP projects, the selection of bidders, and the adoption of risk management practices to efficiently allocate and mitigate risks.

Following a standard process of decisions, as proposed by Carbonara *et al.*[1] in Chapter 7, is supportive when the public sector does not possess the full scale of competences and experience needed. It should, however, be considered as a means rather than a scope, as it is also important to consider both the incompleteness of the PPP contracts and the flexibility requirements.

Public sector competence will also improve the proposed 'win-win' perspective and introduce managerial flexibility allowing for an 'on-going' renegotiation process. Its success requires transparency with respect to the impact of the various decisions and trust between parties.

Note

1 Research carried out within the working group on decision models of COST Action TU1001.

References

Carbonara, N., Costantino, N., Gunnigan, L. and Pellegrino, R. (2014) 'Risk Management in PPP projects: an empirical study on the motorway sector'. *Proceedings of the POMS Conference*, 9–12 May, Atlanta (USA)

Carbonara, N., Costantino, N. and Pellegrino, R. (2014a) 'Concession period for PPP: a win-win model for a fair risk sharing'. *International Journal of Project Management*, 32, pp. 1223–1232

Carbonara, N., Costantino, N. and Pellegrino, R. (2014b) 'Revenue guarantee in PPP: a fair risk allocation model'. *Construction Management and Economics*, 32(4), pp. 403–415

Domingues, S. and Zlatkovic, D. (2015) 'Renegotiating PPP contracts: reinforcing the "P" in Partnership'. *Transport Reviews*, DOI: 10.1080/01441647.2014.992495

Engle, E. M. R. A., Fischer, R. D. and Galetovic, A. (2001) 'Least-Present-Value of revenue auctions and highway franchising'. *Journal of Political Economy*, 109 (5), pp. 993–1020

Essig, M. and Batran, A. (2005) 'Public–Private Partnership: development of long-term relationships in public procurement in Germany'. *Journal of Purchasing and Supply Management*, 11(5–6), pp. 221–231

Hoezen, M. E. L., Voordijk, J. T. and Dewulf, G. P. M. R. (2012a) 'Contracting dynamics in the competitive dialogue procedure'. *Built Environment Project and Asset Management*, 2, pp. 6–24

Hoezen, M. E. L., Voordijk, J. T. and Dewulf, G. P. M. R. (2012b) 'Formal and informal contracting processes in the competitive dialogue procedure: a multiple case-study'. *Engineering Project Organization Journal*, 2 (3), pp. 145–158

Hoezen, M. E. L., Voordijk, J. T. and Dewulf, G. P. M. R. (2013) 'Formal bargaining and informal sense making in the competitive dialogue procedure: an event-driven explanation'. *International Journal of Managing Projects in Business*, 6 (4) pp. 674–694

Hoezen, M. E. L., Voordijk, H. and Dewulf, G. (2014) 'Procuring complex projects using the competitive dialogue'. *International Journal of Project Organisation and Management*, 6 (4), pp. 319–335

Loosemore, M., Raftery, J., Reilly, C. and Higgon, D. (2006) *Risk Management in Projects*. London: Taylor & Francis

Miller, J. B. (2000) *Principles of Public and Private Infrastructure Delivery*. New York, NY: Springer

Milner, M. (2004) 'Eurotunnel car traffic declines'. The *Guardian*, 21 March

Nevitt, P. K. and Fabozzi, F. J. (2005) *Project Financing* (7th Ed.). London: Euromoney Books

Nikolaidis N. and Roumboutsos A. (2013) 'A PPP renegotiation framework: a road concession in Greece'. *Built Environment Project and Asset Management Journal*, Vol 3, No. 2, pp. 264–278

Pellegrino, R., Carbonara, N. and Vajdic, N. (2013) 'Real option theory for risk mitigation in transport PPP'. *Built Environment Project and Asset Management*, 3(2)

Pfeffer, D. J. (2010) 'The construction contract: lump sum *vs.* cost plus'. *The New York Law Journal*, 28 December

Roumboutsos, A. (2013a) 'The need for integrated transport system Public Private Partnerships'. 2013 Innovation in Public Finance (IPF) Conference, Milano, Italy, 17-19 June

Roumboutsos, A. (2013b) 'Anticipating and managing risks of an integrated infrastructure system'. International

Roumboutsos, A. and Pantelias, A. (2015) 'Allocating revenue risk in transport infrastructure Public–Private Partnership projects: how it matters'. *Transport Reviews*, DOI: 10.1080/01441647.2014.988306

Roumboutsos, A. and Sciancalepore, F. (2014) 'PPP Tenders: optimising on competition'. *Transportation Research Records*, TRR – 14489

Roumboutsos A., Pellegrino, R., Vanelslander, T. and Macario, R. (2012) 'Risks and risk allocation in transport PPP projects: a literature review' in: A. Roumboutsos and N. Carbonara *COST Action TU1001, Public Private Partnerships: Trends & Theory, 2011 Discussion Papers*. COST Office, Brussels, ISBN 978-88-97781-04-2 Conference on PPP Body of Knowledge, Preston, UK, 18-20 March

Roumboutsos, A. and Temeljotov-Salaj, A. (2013) 'Entrepreneurial models of Public Private Partnerships in local development'. International Conference on PPP Body of Knowledge, Preston, UK, 18-20 March

Sfakianakis, E. and van de Laar, M. (2013) 'Fiscal effects and public risk in Public-Private Partnerships'. *Built Environment Project and Asset Management*, 3(2), pp. 181–198

Shen, L. Y., Li, H. and Li, Q. M. (2002) 'Alternative concession model for build operate transfer contract projects'. *Journal of Construction Engineering and Management*, 128(4), pp. 326–330

Smith, N. I. (1995) *Engineering Project Management*. Boston, USA: Blackwell Science

Vassallo, J. M. (2006) 'Traffic risk mitigation in highway concession projects'. *Journal of Transport Economics and Policy*, 40(3), pp. 359–381

Yuan, J., Yajun Zeng, A., Skibniewski, M. J. and Li, Q. (2009) 'Selection of performance objectives and key performance indicators in Public–Private Partnership projects to achieve value for money'. *Construction Management and Economics*, 27, pp. 253–270

Zhang, X.Q. and AbouRizk, S. M. (2006) 'Determining a reasonable concession period for private sector provision of public works and services'. *Canadian Journal of Civil Engineering*, 33(5), pp. 622–631

Part 3

Performance

11 Performance monitoring and assessment

Introduction

Champika Liyanage

Introduction

This chapter is based on findings emerged as part of COST Action TU1001. The findings particularly focus on Critical Success Factors (CSFs) and Key Performance Indicators (KPIs), in order to identify success factors leading to successful projects and assess KPIs that are able to monitor performance as conducted by the respective Working Group. In fulfilling the aforementioned tasks a qualitative methodology has, in the main, been adopted in the chapters presented in this Part. These are discussed in the following sections.

Identifying different levels of performance

The definition of 'performance' can be viewed differently according to different types of PPP, types of stakeholders, different modes of transport, etc. After some corroboration with the literature and the PPP project context, the following different levels of performance for PPP transport projects were identified to define performance (please refer to Figure 11.1). As per Figure 11.1, the KPIs (and CSFs) differ according to the different stages of a PPP. More specifically, with respect to the design, construction, operation and/or maintenance stage, different stakeholders have a different set of KPIs and factors that they consider significant for the success of a project. In addition, KPIs used in a road project could slightly (or largely) differ from those of a rail or port project; they could also differ according to different types of PPP, for example, Built-Operate-Transfer (BOT) or Private Finance Initiatives (PFI).

Defining and assessing performance of a project considering all the above-mentioned levels can be a daunting task. For the purpose of this Part and in order to fulfil the objectives mentioned in the previous section, the stakeholder point of view was taken as the main basis for the measurement of performance. This does not mean the other levels are ignored, as these are considered from the different stakeholder perspectives. In a PPP project, there can be various stakeholders ranging from client, construction contractor, facilities management contractors,

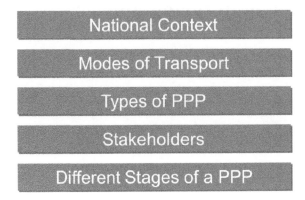

Figure 11.1 Different levels of performance.

financiers and suppliers to users. They may be grouped into three categories: public sector, private sector and users. Herein, the public sector includes any public administration that acts as promoter, contracting or regulating at any level; the private sector includes the different private participants in a PPP project, mainly land owners, constructors, operators, financiers and advisory firms.

The stakeholder view is important when measuring the success of projects (Bryde and Brown 2005; Pinto and Slevin 1988; Savindo *et al.* 1992). This is even more important for a PPP project, as it is a long-term partnership between the public and private sector; and users are either directly or indirectly involved within the payment process of the PPP project. Some PPP projects can be very successful in terms of reaping benefits from the private sector point of view; however, it may be a costly provision in the view of users. Therefore, to measure the success of a PPP project, it is important to examine success from all stakeholder perspectives.

For the purpose of this study, based on the aforementioned three categories, a literature review was carried out to develop a set of CSFs and KPIs that are applicable for PPP transport projects. This is discussed below.

Literature review

A literature review served as a literature database. The compiled database consisted of 67 individual articles (mainly journals) that were written particularly on performance of PPPs in the transport sector (www.ppptransport.eu). A snapshot view of the database is given in Figure 11.2. The literature review analysis was then carried out using content analysis – particularly with the use of frequency of 'mentions' (i.e. how many times the CSFs and KPIs have been mentioned within the literature review database). The latter helped in recognising 'Key' indicators and 'Significant' factors that are applicable for PPP transport projects. Findings obtained from the literature review will be discussed in some

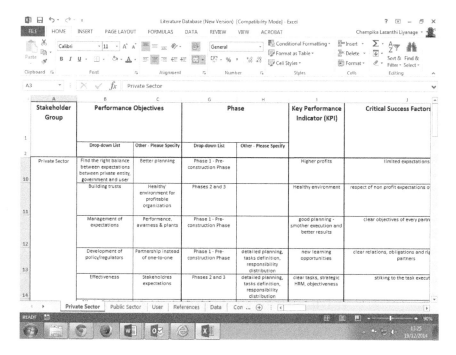

Figure 11.2 Snapshot of the literature review template.

of the chapters presented in this Part, for example, Voordjik *et al.*, Ribeiro *et al.* and Liyanage *et al.*

Based on the findings and analysis, it was decided to carry out a case study approach for empirical data collection.

Case study approach

The case study approach has been a key research method in the research of PPP in transport within COST Action TU1001 and with respect to identifying Critical Success Factors in particular. This is discussed in depth in the Appendix. More specifically, a case study template was developed for the purpose of data collection to maintain consistency. A section called 'performance monitoring' was added to the template to identify the CSFs and KPIs. Once the first set of case study data was collected, due to the large number of cases (30+) and the enormity of information received from each case study, different analysis methods were employed to derive findings and conclusions on different aspects of performance. The four chapters presented in this Part put forward findings that have been obtained applying different case analysis methods and methodologies. A KPIs table developed as part of the case analysis formed the basis for two analysis methods presented in the chapters (Liyanage *et al.* and Voordjik *et al.*). The KPIs table

Table 11.1 KPIs and performance measures

KPIs	Performance measures – criteria	Scale	Success max. value
Objectives	1. Are the objectives specified in the contract SMART? Specific, Measurable, Achievable, Realistic and Time bound.	1 to 5	5
	2. To what extent have the objectives been achieved?	1 to 5	5
	3. Have/will user benefits been/be monitored?	1 to 5	5
	4. Have user benefits been as large as expected?	–2 to 2	2
2. Risks	5. How much risk has been transferred to the private sector?	1 to 5	5
	6. Was risk allocation agreed quickly?	1 to 5	5
3. Contract project specifications	7. Have the deliverables been specified clearly in the contract?	1 to 5	5
	8. Are the roles and responsibilities of different parties involved in the contract clearly defined?	1 to 5	5
	9. Are minimum standards for condition of infrastructure and equipment specified in the contract?	1 to 5	5
	10. Are there any performance targets?	1 to 5	5
	11. Is the method of measuring performance targets clearly defined?	1 to 5	5
	12. Are there penalties for non-compliance?	1 to 5	5
	13. Does the contract have procedures for amendments, dispute resolution or termination?	Yes/No	Yes
	14. Has the contract proceeded without renegotiations?	Yes/No	Yes*
	15. Are there any guarantees specified in the contract?	Yes/No	Yes
4. Tendering process	16. No. of bidders (negotiation *vs.* final)	1 to 3	3
	17. Time from tender notice to financial close < 3 years?	Yes/No	Yes
	18. Legal challenges to outcome?	Yes/No	No
5. Construction phase	19. Was the project completed on time?	Yes/No	Yes
	20. Was the project completed within budget?	Yes/No	Yes
	21. Was the project completed according to the specifications and design?	Yes/No	Yes
	22. Are there any penalties for non-compliance?	Yes/No	Yes
6. Operations	23. Were the services specified in the contract delivered?	1 to 5	5
7. Maintenance	24. Are the deliverable standards for infrastructure and equipment being met?	1 to 5	5
8. Monitoring and evaluation	25. Is there a formal monitoring procedure in place?	1 to 5	5
9. Finance	26. Was finance available when needed?	1 to 5	5
	27. Was the project cash flow sufficient to make expected payments to all parties?	1 to 5	5
	28. Did the project result in financial benefits to users (e.g. in terms of charges, etc.)?	–2 to 2	2
	29. Has the financial outcome been equal or better than expected for the private partner?	–2 to 2	2

(Continued)

Table 11.1 KPIs and performance measures (Continued)

KPIs	Performance measures – criteria	Scale	Success max. value
10. Actual traffic and revenue	30. Traffic Actual/Forecast? (*)	1 to 3	3
	31. Revenue Actual/Forecast? (*)	1 to 3	3
11. Downturn impact	32. Revenue Impact from 2008-2013? (*)	1 to 3	3

*Yes – unless renegotiation is due to success or due to change of context

(Table 11.1) has been developed using QSR NVivo analysis (NVivo is a qualitative data analysis computer software package produced by QSR International).

The KPIs table includes 9 KPIs and 29 performance measures that can be used to measure performance of PPP transport projects. The data collected from the case study templates were then populated onto this KPIs table (please see Table 11.2). The main idea of the KPIs table was to identify the scale of success in each and every project in terms of the given KPIs and performance measures. Assessments were made using appropriate Likert scales or a colour-coded theme (i.e. red – failure, yellow – neither success nor a failure, green – success). The data in Table 11.2 was then analysed/interpreted using different methodologies/approaches. For example, manual pattern matching was adopted, *inter alia*, to derive findings from this KPIs table (in Voordjik *et al.*). The Delphi method is another method that was used to assess the performance of case studies (in Liyanage *et al.*).

Contributions

From the methods discussed above, four are presented in this Part. Vanelslander and Farrell (Chapter 12) aim to answer the research question 'are there contextual

Table 11.2 Filling in the KPIs table

KPIs	Criterion	Success	Remarks	MST - Metro Sul do Tejo (Portugal)	Manchester Metrolink	A50	A55	TIA ALBANIA (Public Works and Service	CTV (SGS) ALBANIA (Public Service Concession	BR (ex of t i An
Tendering Process	No. of bidders (negotiation vs. final)	More than one bidder	* Likert scale of 3: Red - 1 and 0, Yellow - 2, Green - 3 or more.	2	3	4	4	4	3	
	Time from tender notice to financial close	Less than 03 years		Yes		Yes		Yes	Yes	
	Legal challenges to outcome	No legal disputes/challenges		Yes	Yes.	no	no	No	No	
Contract project specifications	Has the deliverables specified clearly in the contract?	Yes (** Likert scale - 4 and 5)	Please specify whether the deliverables are given in-depth.	4	5	4	5	5	5	
	Are the roles and responsiblities of different parties involved in the contract are clearly defined?	Yes (** Likert scale - 4 and 5)	Are there any deviations in terms of the roles and responsiblities ? if yes, Why? What was the outcomes (succuess/failure)?	5	4	4	4	5	5	

characteristics that are similar across different port PPP settings leading to similar PPP outcomes?'. To do that, a methodology stemming from fuzzy logic employing the case study template development has been applied. This contribution allows a comparison of seven different port cases, all from different EU countries, through an in-depth cross-case analysis.

Voordjik, Liyanage and Temeljotov-Salaj in Chapter 13 assess CSFs that are applicable at different stages of delivery of PPP transport infrastructure. Findings are extracted from an in-depth analysis of 34 transport projects in the EU. Taking the case study protocol presented in the Appendix into consideration, the authors specifically focus on the 'which-way' aspect of the PPP cases, i.e. the key characteristics of the tendering process and the contractual agreement. Findings are mainly derived using a pattern matching method.

In Chapter 14 Ribeiro, Couchinho, Macario and Liyanage assess the CSFs of PPP projects in the context of four urban rail PPP. The selected projects are the Metro Sul do Tejo (MST) in Portugal, the TVR Caen in France, the Metrolink in the UK and the Brabo1 in Belgium. The authors adopt a 3-step approach in assessing the CSFs relating to the four urban rail projects. They discuss the respective CSFs and also focus on the deviations and issues relating to success factors in PPP urban rail projects.

The final contribution (Chapter 15) is also a joint paper by Liyanage, Villalba-Romero and Njuangang. The chapter presents the findings of the qualitative content analysis and a three-stage Delphi process. These findings have then been refined and analysed to measure success or level of performance of PPP transport projects. This has been performed by particularly focusing on 13 road transport projects in the EU. Detailed descriptions of the cases are provided in the paper, as well as a comprehensive cross-case analysis of the success of all 13 projects.

References

Bryde, D. J. and Brown, D. (2005) 'The influence of project performance measurement system on the success of a contract for maintaining motorways and trunk roads'. *Project Management Journal*, 35(4), pp. 57–65

Pinto, J. K. and Slevin, D. P. (1988) 'Critical success factors across the project life cycle'. *Project Management Journal*, 19 (3), pp. 67–75

Savindo, V., Grobler, F., Parfitt, K., Guvenis, M. and Coyle, M. (1992) 'Critical success factors for construction projects'. *Journal of Construction Engineering and Management*, 118 (1), pp. 94–111

12 Main challenges in PPP for port development

Thierry Vanelslander and Sheila Farrell

Introduction

Seaports in various locations of the world are experiencing increasing growth in traffic volumes, and in related needs of expanding capacity, hard as well as soft. That means they have to invest, not only in maritime infrastructure but also in terminal capacity and adequate hinterland connections (Vanelslander 2014).

Ports however are organised in very different ways. Decision-taking and financial independence on the one hand and unity of command and integrated commercial management on the other hand, are the main dimensions used to distinguish between port organisational models with an impact on container handling supply and demand. With respect to decision-taking and financial independence, five organisational types are distinguished: sea-port authority bodies under direct national jurisdiction; sea-port authority bodies under sub-national jurisdiction; self-governing public sea-port authorities; privately owned and operated sea-port authorities; and corporate sea-port authorities. With respect to unity of command and integrated commercial management, three port organisational types are distinguished: land-lord sea-port; limited-operating (tool) sea-port; and comprehensive operating (or service) port authorities.

It should not be forgotten that sea-port categorisation is not static. Over time, sea ports shift over the categories set out by Suykens and Van de Voorde (1998). The typical national preferences often disappear so that sea-port type dispersion is getting larger: countries traditionally applying one of the systems above have often introduced different structures for newly developed ports, often for budgetary reasons. The Latin type with its strong central government control used to be applied in all countries denominated as 'Latin' in culture, which are generally southern-European and Latin-American countries. Some of these have now lessened the extent of central control. In Belgium, for instance, there was a notable shift from municipal port departments towards autonomous port authorities as, for example, in Ghent and Ostend, and even to corporatised ports as, for example, in Antwerp and Zeebruges. These dynamics make the traditional comparisons among countries much more complex than before (Verhoeven 2014; Vanelslander 2005).

Lately there has been a further shift, among other things, due to the application of PPP. The traditional financing of port infrastructure works has reached its limits, especially because of limited financial means. To cover up for the lack of financing, more and more alternative financing methods are sought. Globally, three types can be distinguished: alternative financing methods considered by the investing government to be a purely financial operation; a non-financial PPP (where financing is not the primary purpose); and the privatisation of infrastructure elements (Meersman *et al.*, 2014; 2010).

Given the variety in seaport organisational forms, it would be interesting to learn, from the application of PPP in concrete situations, what settings work well and are most frequently used. This comparison aims at answering the main research question of this chapter 'are there contextual characteristics that are similar across different port PPP settings and lead to similar PPP outcomes?'

The present chapter takes the above-mentioned research a step further. In the next section, it performs a literature review on existing analyses of PPP in seaports, and on methods that can be applied to deal with the analysis. The following section introduces the data used for the analysis. Then the results of the in-depth analysis of each of the selected PPP dimensions are presented. Finally, a summary of observations on the various dimensions is presented and lessons are drawn from the summary, with the goal of discussing the findings with respect to similarities and differences as well as the potential for knowledge transfer. Furthermore, directions for further research are given.

Literature review and methodology selection

Academic articles on PPP in transport are often in the form of case studies of individual projects, or describe the evolution of policy for one mode of transport in one particular country (for example, Castillo-Manzano and Ascencio-Flores 2012; Lipovich 2008; Marques and Fonseca 2010) or continent (for example, Chin and Waldron 2014; Farrell 2014; Theofanis and Boilé 2014; Verhoeven 2014). The most far-reaching analysis for seaports is by the Organisation for Economic Cooperation and Development (2011), which deals with port organisation and responsibilities in its member countries from a competition and regulation perspective.

Sector-wide studies for seaports (for example, De Langen and Heij 2014; Meersman *et al.* 2010; Notteboom *et al.* 2012; Pigna 2014) are growing in number, but they look inwards at variations in PPP practice within each mode, rather than relating them across the various modes of transport.

Books and reports about PPP in transport also tend to deal separately with each mode (for example, Asian Development Bank 2001, Estache and de Rus 2003), or discuss generic issues such as risk sharing, contract design and regulation, using appropriate examples from different modes of transport (for example, Guasch 2004; Macário 2014). If any conclusion can be drawn it is that differences between countries are likely to be at least as important as differences between modes in explaining variations in PPP structures.

Vanelslander *et al.* (2013) apply a fuzzy logic approach in comparing PPP settings for three cases from the urban, road and port areas respectively. Fuzzy logic is a precise logic for dealing with imprecision and approximate reasoning. It reflects human behaviour in so far as it allows reasoning and rational decision-making in an environment of imperfect information (Zadeh 2008). At the core of fuzzy logic are the concepts of graduation and granulation. In fuzzy logic, everything is or is allowed to be granulated, with a granule being a clump of attribute-values drawn together by indistinguishability, similarity, proximity or functionality (Zadeh 2008).

Like Vanelslander *et al.* (2013), this chapter applies the 'Contextual Ws Risk Analysis framework' (Roumboutsos 2010). This approach highlights the basic structural elements of a PPP project and the surrounding macroeconomic environment, and how they impact on the port sector, which is the core topic of analysis in this chapter. The granular value of each W is expressed through a set of linguistic variables. Each linguistic variable has been chosen to reflect the source of the impact on the W granular value. The methodology and the required data are further explained in the next section.

Methodology development and data collection

Eight 'W' granules are distinguished in this chapter: What, Where, When, Who, Whom, Why, Which Way and the Whole.

As to the 'What', the chapter considers consecutively the following characteristics of the projects under review:

- The function: what role does the project play in the overall port system and the entire supply chain?
- The brownfield/greenfield/mixed character: whether the project is predominantly brownfield (i.e. giving new life to outdated estates within an existing port footprint), greenfield (i.e. developing new estates outside of the previous footprint), or a combination of both.
- The physical characteristics: what infrastructure and superstructure are we talking about?
- The budget: what amount of financing is involved?
- The level of exclusiveness: to what extent does the project enjoy a monopoly (natural or contractual) or is competing with other projects serving the same market partially or entirely?
- The TEN-T character: whether the project is part of the European TEN-T network and, as such, receives funding from EU funds or, in general, political support.

'Where' refers to the geographical location of the project: is the project located in a Northern- or Southern-European port, and close to its market or further away. The 'When' of the project designates the timeframe in which the project was set up, and hence also its maturity. 'Who' identifies the public authority that acts as the project principal and initiated the project. Reference is made to the relevant level of government. The 'Whom' is the private entity that enjoys the project and, in particular, its nature: an existing market that gets served or a new market that gets developed. 'Why' indicates the reasons for the project to be developed as a PPP, the two extremes being either a quality of service purpose or a financing purpose. 'Which Way' deals with the contractual agreement and its characteristics. It consequently involves the financing and funding structure, the tendering and awarding process, the contract duration and the risk division among the parties involved (Roumboutsos *et al.* 2012). The latter can go from the extreme of solely the private sector assuming the specific risk to the other extreme of solely the public sector taking it up. The 'Whole' finally considers the wider environment and macro-economic conditions in which the project develops.

The linguistic variables, and their potential values, are summarised per granule in Table 12.1.

The analysis in this chapter remains at a 'pre-fuzzy' stage. The sample of port cases is rather limited: seven cases are used, from the ports of Antwerp, Durres, Koper, Piraeus, Rijeka, Sines and Valencia. Values for all variables and for all cases were collected as part of the COST Action TU1001 on *Public Private Partnerships in Transport: Trends and Theory*. The information was gathered through a review of literature and documents, complemented with interviews with key executives from both the public and private sector. The interviews in most cases turned out to be crucial to get behind real motivations, to get a complete overview of the actors involved directly and indirectly, and make linkages between the actors. The summary of the information for each of the cases is available through Roumboutsos *et al.* (2013 and 2014).

The chapter tests for each of the granules and the underlying linguistic variables, whether the hypothesis holds that the value marked grey in Table 12.1 is the most likely to occur for port PPP projects. The analysis of the cases, which is the basis for the testing, is done in the next part of this chapter. The actual hypothesis testing is done in the following section.

Granular Ws contextual analysis

A discursive method is used to value the different Ws as described in the previous section. The method was useful to extract information, which cannot be gained through cross-sectional studies, longitudinal designs, event sequence studies, and conversation analysis (McPhee *et al.* 2009). Because the sample size is rather small (seven projects), one needs to stress that this section is simply intended to illustrate the methodology. Conclusions can be drawn with a higher degree of confidence as the sample size expands in future research.

'What' – Mapping projects in the transport arena

Nature

Of the considered cases, only the **Valencia** project was meant to serve passengers. All of the others were cargo-oriented (Table 12.2). This is consistent with the view that seaports overall still serve cargo in the first place, and that passenger

Table 12.1 Linguistic variables and their possible values of granular units of the Ws Contextual Framework

Linguistic Variable	Variable Range					
Granule: What – The project						
Nature	Cargo		Passenger		Mixed	
Function		Local hinterland		Hinterland gateway	Transhipment hub	Transhipment + hinterland
Brownfield / greenfield	Brownfield		Greenfield		Mixed	
Physical characteristics	Berth only	Terminal superstructure only	Cranes only	Berth and terminal superstructure	Terminal superstructure and cranes	Berth, terminal superstructure and cranes
Budget	Small		Medium		Large	
Level of exclusiveness	Competitive environment	Not exclusive	Quite not exclusive	Somewhat exclusive	Rather exclusive	Exclusive
TEN-T	Not included in TEN-T		Included in TEN-T	TEN-T priority project	TEN-T core project	TEN-T peripheral project
Granule: Where – Project Location						
Geographical		Northern-European		Southern-European		
Market		Close to market		Rather distant from market		
Granule: When – Project (Investment) Timing						
Maturity	Recent			Older		
Granule: Who – the Public Initiator						
National-Port driven	Nation-driven		Region-driven	Municipality-driven		Port-driven
Granule: Whom – User						
Business developer / servicer	Business servicer	Mostly business servicer	More business servicer	More business developer	Mostly business developer	Business developer

(Continued)

Table 12.1 Linguistic variables and their possible values of granular units of the W's Contextual Framework (Continued)

Linguistic Variable	Variable Range					
	Solely service-based approach	Mostly service-based approach	More service-based approach	More finance-based approach	Mostly finance-based approach	Solely finance-based approach
Granule: Why – the Scope of PPP						
Finance – Service Based Approach	Solely service-based approach	Mostly service-based approach	More service-based approach	More finance-based approach	Mostly finance-based approach	Solely finance-based approach
Granule: Which way – strategy with respect to the contractual agreement (Risk Allocation & Payment Structure)						
Funding	Availability fees and subsidy	Availability fees	Shadow tolls and subsidy	Shadow tolls/no subsidy	User fees and subsidy	User fees no subsidy
Majority financing	Nation	Region	Municipality	Port	Bank	SPV
Tendering	Competitive			Negotiated		
Awarding	One stage			Several stages		
Duration	Short		Medium		Long	
Design and construction risks	Totally private	Mostly private	More private	More public	Mostly public	Totally public
Maintenance risk	Totally private	Mostly private	More private	More public	Mostly public	Totally public
Risk of exploitation	Totally private	Mostly private	More private	More public	Mostly public	Totally public
Commercial revenue risk	Totally private	Mostly private	More private	More public	Mostly public	Totally public
Financial risk	Totally private	Mostly private	More private	More public	Mostly public	Totally public
Regulatory risk	Totally private	Mostly private	More private	More public	Mostly public	Totally public
Force majeure	Totally private	Mostly private	More private	More public	Mostly public	Totally public
Granule: Whole						
Impact /influence of macro-environment	No exposure / influence of macro-environment	Very little exposure to macro-environment	Little exposure to macro-environment	Some exposure to macro-environment	Significant exposure to macro-environment	Extreme exposure to macro-environment

Table 12.2 Function of the considered PPP projects

Port	Antwerp	Durres	Koper	Piraeus	Rijeka	Sines	Valencia
Function	Cargo	Cargo	Cargo	Cargo	Cargo	Cargo	Passenger

ferry services remain concentrated in a rather limited number of ports, while the cruise business has only recently begun expanding geographically.

Function

It turns out that most of the considered projects are hinterland gateway ones (Table 12.3). The only 'local' project is the one at **Durres**. The only project really linking with transhipment activities is **Piraeus**[1]. It is to be stressed that the function is strictly tied to the considered project: it may well be that the ports where the projects are located are of a different nature for different types of traffic, while specific projects deviate from the port's overall functions. The port of **Antwerp**, for instance, has an important transhipment function as far as containers are concerned, but the lock project considered here serves an area that hosts only local-bound non-container traffic. The new Antwerp lock feeds into the Waasland channel. From there, shipping traffic has quick access to the other Left Bank docks: the Doeldok, the Verrebroekdok, the Vrasenedok and the Noordelijk en Zuidelijk Insteekdok. The area is well-connected to its hinterland.

The port of **Durres** is connected with the main road and railway network of Albania.

Luka **Koper** lacks state investments on public connecting infrastructure and sufficient provision of infrastructural connections with the hinterland such as, for example, the delay in the modernisation of the Slovenian railway network, standstills in the construction of the second Koper-Divaca track, unsuitable policies for the systematic arrangement of rail transport implementation in the light of transport liberalization, and insufficient competitiveness of the public railway infrastructure in comparison with other transport routes.

Most of the container traffic through Greece is discharged in **Piraeus**, and either stripped there or transferred to trucks for onward transport to end locations. **Rijeka** is a gateway for Corridor Vb. **Sines** is connected to the Portuguese hinterland, but is not that well connected yet to the more distant cross-border Spanish hinterland, which it is trying to serve. The **Valencia** project involves a terminal, which, on the one hand, aims at bringing in visiting cruise passengers to the city

Table 12.3 Function of the considered PPP projects

Port	Antwerp	Durres	Koper	Piraeus	Rijeka	Sines	Valencia
Function	Hinterland gateway	Local hinterland	Hinterland gateway	Transhipment + hinterland	Hinterland gateway	Hinterland gateway	Hinterland gateway

Table 12.4 Brownfield/greenfield character of the considered PPP projects

Port	Antwerp	Durres	Koper	Piraeus	Rijeka	Sines	Valencia
Brownfield / greenfield	Mixed	Mixed	Mixed	Mixed	Mixed	Greenfield	Mixed

but, on the other hand, also functions as an important embarkation point for Spanish passengers.

Brownfield/greenfield character

All projects except for **Sines** are mixed brown – and greenfield projects (Table 12.4). The **Sines** project is a greenfield one, with a totally new site to be developed.

Physical characteristics

The only case not involving a pure berth project is the **Antwerp** one (Table 12.5). The Deurganckdock lock will have the same dimensions as the Berendrecht lock (68m x 500m), that is for the moment the biggest sea lock in the world, but it will be deeper (-17,80m C-CD). All other projects either involve terminal development and operations (terminal and cranes) or are all-encompassing (berth, terminal superstructure and cranes). This is because the operations component is important in most port PPP.

The berth and terminal projects vary substantially in size. **Durres** Port East Terminal has an area of 20ha, and two aprons accounting for 25 per cent of the total overall quay length of the port of **Durres**. The **Koper** project encompasses 48.4ha of indoor warehouses on 290ha of land area, 109.6ha of outdoor warehouses and 28 ship moorings on 3,282m of shore line.

The capacity of Pier II at **Piraeus** was to be increased from 1.7m TEU to 2.7m TEU p.a., mainly through equipment upgrades and an increase in the container stacking density. The proposed Pier III has a quay length of 600m, a water depth up to 18m, and a planned throughput of 1.0m TEU.

In **Rijeka**, various terminals are involved, including a general cargo terminal (**Rijeka**, 2.5m tons), a cereal terminal (Silos, 800,000 tons), a bulk cargo terminal (Bakar, 4.5m tons), a terminal for liquid cargo (Omišalj, 24m tons), a general

Table 12.5 Physical characteristics of the considered PPP projects

Port	Antwerp	Durres	Koper	Piraeus	Rijeka	Sines	Valencia
Physical characteristics	Berth only	Terminal superstructure and cranes	Terminal superstructure and cranes	Berth, terminal superstructure and cranes	Terminal superstructure and cranes	Berth, terminal superstructure and cranes	Berth, terminal superstructure and cranes

Table 12.6 Budget of the considered PPP projects

Port	Antwerp	Durres	Koper	Piraeus	Rijeka	Sines	Valencia
Budget	€ 382.3 m	?	€ 430 m	€ 500 m	?	€ 332 m	€ 59.6 m

cargo terminal (Raša-Bršica, 1m tons) and a container terminal (Brajdica, 250,000 TEUs).

The objective of the PPP project in **Sines** was to build in four stages a container terminal with an eventual quay length of 940m, a back-up area of 36.4ha, and a capacity of 1.5m TEU p.a.

In **Valencia**, a 1,700 metre long berth line with a draught of 14m and a surface area of 5.3ha is to be built. Four additional berthing points will be dedicated to cruise ships calls and a new cruise terminal will be built.

Budget

From Table 12.6, it can be deduced that more or less all projects are of the same order of magnitude in terms of budget (total project cost including finance and other expenses). Only **Valencia** has a cheaper project, while the amounts for **Durres** and Rijeka have not been disclosed.

Level of exclusiveness

All projects seem to enjoy a substantial to high degree of exclusiveness, with only **Valencia** being a competitive project (Table 12.7). Notably, the ports of **Koper** and **Rijeka** compete with each other and with the other North Adriatic ports (Venice and Trieste), Piraeus competes for transhipment traffic with other East Mediterranean transhipment hubs like Suez East and Gioia Tauro, and **Antwerp** competes with Rotterdam, even though the considered PPP projects themselves have a high degree of exclusivity within the public authority's capacity of assignment.

TEN-T character

All selected projects were included in the TEN-T, except for **Rijeka**, which is not included, and **Koper**, which is included but as the only considered project with a priority status (Table 12.8).

Table 12.7 Level of exclusiveness of the considered PPP projects

Port	Antwerp	Durres	Koper	Piraeus	Rijeka	Sines	Valencia
Level of exclusiveness	Exclusive	Somewhat exclusive	Exclusive	Somewhat exclusive	Exclusive	Exclusive	Competitive environment

Table 12.8 TEN-T character of the considered PPP projects

Port	Antwerp	Durres	Koper	Piraeus	Rijeka	Sines	Valencia
TEN-T character	Included in TEN-T	Included in TEN-T	TEN-T priority project	Included in TEN-T	Not included in TEN-T	Included in TEN-T	Included in TEN-T

'Where'

Geographical location

Of the selected projects, only **Antwerp** is located in Northern Europe. All of the others are in Southern Europe, most on the Mediterranean Sea (Table 12.9). This supports the observations of, among others, Sys *et al.* (2014) that Mediterranean ports are particularly active in seaport expansion projects, some of them more successful than others (Sys *et al.* 2014). Given budget constraints that particularly hit Southern-European governments, the call for private support is an obvious solution, changing the Latin port management nature those ports typically featured.

Market location

The market location looks at the position of the specific PPP project – whether the project is located close to the market or at a distance from it. In the latter case, the availability of good hinterland connections is of crucial importance, which decreases the so-called 'time distance'.

The port of **Antwerp** in 2012 handled 183.8m tonnes of goods (Table 12.10). 10.8m tonnes of conventional cargo were unloaded and loaded, along with 4.8m tonnes of RoRo cargo. The number of cars handled in 2012 was over 1.2m, while liquid bulk goods totalled 45.2m tonnes. All of these volumes are linked to a close-by hinterland, either located right in the port itself (Figure 12.1a), or within a range of about 40 kms (Figure 12.1b).

Durres East Terminal (DET) is located in Durres city, in an urban environment in the Tirana-Durres region, connected with important national and international transportation nodes in Albania. The port of **Koper** is one of the most relevant generators of transport for its region. **Piraeus** is the largest port in Greece, located only a few miles from the capital Athens. It handles around three quarters of the country's container trade and is the main hub for domestic

Table 12.9 Geographical location of the considered PPP projects

Port	Antwerp	Durres	Koper	Piraeus	Rijeka	Sines	Valencia
Geographical location	Northern Europe	Southern Europe	Southern Europe	Southern Europe	Southern Europe	Southern Europe	Southern Europe

Table 12.10 Market location of the considered PPP projects

Port	Antwerp	Durres	Koper	Piraeus	Rijeka	Sines	Valencia
Market location	Close to market	Close to market	Rather distant from market	Close to market	Rather distant from market	Rather distant from market	Close to market

shipping services to the Greek islands. Because of its position, the port of **Rijeka** usually provides a shorter and faster land transport route to some markets of the highly developed countries compared with a number of other established ports in the region.

The **Sines** container terminal was originally intended to handle mainly transhipment traffic, in which case it would also have been competing with two much larger transhipment hubs at Algeciras (Southern Spain) and Tanger Med (Morocco). Because of competition from these two much larger hubs, the **Sines** container terminal has been able to attract very little transhipment traffic and, as a result, serves mainly the Portuguese market and Western Spain. That market is of course much more limited.

The port of **Valencia** over the last decade, and especially during the last five years, has succeeded in attracting a new market of international cruise passengers. The city of Valencia is becoming an attractive tourist destination by itself

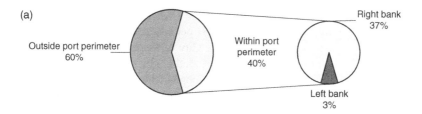

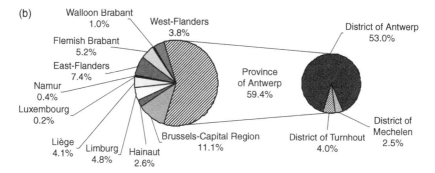

Figure 12.1 Market location Port of Antwerp (in value added).

Source: Coppens *et al.* 2007.

so the Port of Valencia has the opportunity to become an essential call for cruise liners operating in the Mediterranean.

'When' – maturity

As can be observed, all recorded PPP projects are of rather recent dates (Table 12.11). That confirms the general view that PPPs have been stimulated by shrinking government budgets, and a desire to get more private sector involvement in order to increase efficiency and quality of operations.

'Who' – public initiator

In all cases, the national governments seem to have been the prime drivers for the port PPP projects. **Antwerp** is a somewhat special case as all territorial competencies in Belgium, including ports, are in the hands of the regions – Flanders in this case.

Further on in most cases, special purpose vehicles are developed through which the projects get executed. In **Antwerp**, NV Vlaamse Havens was established, which later on, together with the Port of **Antwerp**, created the NV Deurganckdoksluis for building the specific **Antwerp** project. The sponsor for **Durres** Port East Terminal (EMS APO Ltd) is the German company 'EMS Shipping and Trading GMBH' formed by the merger of two subsidiaries: Albania Stevedoring Company (ASC) and GALA – German and Albanian Logistic Agency Ltd. The Port of **Koper** group is a public limited company and operates as a holding company. The ownership structure is divided between the largest shareholder, the Republic of Slovenia with a 51 per cent equity stake, some financial, investment or insurance companies, the City of Koper and others. The ten largest shareholders control 76.05 per cent of total equity stake. A similar situation is encountered with 'Luka **Rijeka**', supplemented with its subsidiary 'Jadranska Vrata'. **Sines** does feature a special purpose vehicle. In **Valencia**, the contract is still to be concluded.

'Whom' – user

In **Antwerp**, the development on the Left Bank of the Port of Antwerp dates back to the 1970s and started from the Waasland channel with the construction of the north and south docks. The Kallo Lock, operational since 1983, is the only access way to the Waasland port. The lock is heavily occupied: 8,800 shifts per year (123,389,866 tonnes of cargo per year). Waiting times amount to 3.5 hours. The

Table 12.11 Maturity of the considered PPP projects

Port	Antwerp	Durres	Koper	Piraeus	Rijeka	Sines	Valencia
Maturity	2010	2013	2008	2008	2011	2004	2007-2008

Table 12.12 Users of the considered PPP projects

Port	Antwerp	Durres	Koper	Piraeus	Rijeka	Sines	Valencia
Usership	Mostly business servicer	Mostly business servicer	Mostly business developer	Mostly business developer	Mostly business developer	Mostly business developer	Mostly business servicer

capacity increase of the Kallo Lock is due to increasing sea traffic and an increased use of the lock by inland navigation. The direct lock users will be shipping companies and goods handlers in the docks behind the lock. Hence, the PPP project is mainly meant for business servicing (Table 12.12).

Durres port is regarded as having considerable growth potential. Politically, economically and socially, Albania is assumed to steadily integrate into the European Union. Key users in the East Terminal of the Port of Durres will be the companies shipping goods and the owners of vessels for the transportation of export-import goods such as coal, steel and scrap metal, cement, etc.

Users of the container terminal at Luka **Koper** are ship-owners and shipping agents and freight forwarders, and less often importers/exporters. The port holds a leading position in the North Adriatic area in terms of container throughput and is the second in the Mediterranean area in terms of car throughput. It performs most of its services for hinterland countries such as Austria, Italy, Hungary, Slovakia, the Czech Republic, Poland, Germany, Serbia, Switzerland, Croatia, Bosnia and Herzegovina, Ukraine and Russia. In this case, the new terminal is mainly meant to upscale the port's activities and attract new volumes.

The new Piraeus terminal will serve container shipping lines, importers/exporters and freight forwarders. The project was needed in order to improve the port's competitive position. However, an *ex-post* evaluation indicates that there was sufficient capacity in the port to handle Greek domestic traffic for at least several more years. The attraction of more transhipment traffic brings some local economic benefits, but these are likely to be relatively small.

The port of **Rijeka** provides a gateway to the sea for Croatia, Hungary, Austria, Czech Republic, Slovakia, Bosnia and Herzegovina, west Ukraine, south Poland and south Germany. At **Sines**, target users are container shipping lines, importers/exporters and freight forwarders. Portuguese container traffic was fairly small, at just over 1.4m TEU in 2010. Indicative investment commitments were made, which were to be triggered by specified amounts of traffic growth.

In **Valencia**, the main users are cruise lines and cruise passengers. Given the traffic forecasts, the number of berthing points needed in 2027 would range from four, in the low case scenario (organic growth), to seven in the most optimistic scenario, with Valencia acting as a home port for international cruise ships.

'Why' – scope of PPP

The motivations behind the use of PPP for the various projects are varied, ranging between solely finance-based to more service-based (Table 12.13). Hence, all

Table 12.13 Scope of the considered PPP projects

Port	Antwerp	Durres	Koper	Piraeus	Rijeka	Sines	Valencia
Scope	Mostly finance-based	Mostly finance-based	More service-based approach	More finance-based approach	More service-based approach	Solely finance-based approach	Mostly finance-based approach

projects feature at least a finance component. The main motivations are the following, each of them applying to some or all of the projects:

- a possibility of spread payments from private to public partner, untaxed on value added;
- a possibility not to have to consolidate the investment into the government's budget since the construction is ESA- (European System of National and Regional Accounts) neutral;
- a limitation of the risks (demand risk, construction risk, availability risk, including eventual supplementary expenses).

At **Antwerp**, the use of a special purpose vehicle allowed all expenses and revenues related to the lock construction to be identified and controlled. This legal body is responsible in a transparent way for optimising the extension of maritime access to the port areas, which is said to offer the best guarantees for the coordination of the project and its quick execution.

At the request of the Antwerp Port Authority, a scenario was also investigated in which the port authority, as construction master, took care of lock construction and financing. In the comparison of the PPP track with construction by the Port of **Antwerp**, the following elements were considered: juridical responsibility, neutrality with respect to ESA, legislation on government procurement, VAT regulations, etc. In terms of the physical outcome, both scenarios are equivalent. The construction and financing via the NV Vlaamse Havens and its daughter subsidiary company Deurganckdoksluis NV delivered the following advantages and/or opportunities compared with the materialisation of the project via the port authorities:

- maintaining the philosophy of the Port Decree by placing important aspects of port policy (building infrastructure) at the level of the Flemish Region;
- more guarantees in terms of equal operational conditions for the Flemish ports;
- a high level of transparency in terms of the financing port infrastructure.

Paying attention to the fact that building the locks is a core activity of the Flemish Region, the formula of delegated building responsibility was not retained and the choice was made for the current PPP setting.

'Which Way'

Funding

In **Antwerp**, the NV Deurganckdoksluis will provide the lock to the port authority, which will then exploit the lock. In exchange, the Antwerp Port Authority pays an availability fee. The annual concession fee to be paid by the Antwerp Port Authority will only be determined after the construction has been completed, based on the effective building and financing cost. The fee amounts, according to current estimations, to €20.88m. In return for the fee, the Flemish Region gives the port authority a subsidy for using the lock, linked to a number of conditions related to the operation of the lock. The subsidy is apart from building the lock and amounts to €18m on an annual basis. **Antwerp** seems to be the only one of the case studies with an availability fee in place: all other cases seem to feature a user fee (Table 12.14).

In **Durres**, a concession applies, the value of which comprises:

- concession fee of 2 per cent of annual revenues;
- royalty (I) of 11 per cent of all processing fees for the types of goods handled;
- royalty (II) of a fixed percentage of turnover;
- annual terminal leasing fee: €3.89/m²/year;
- operator investments that will be required during the first ten years of the concession for the reconstruction of infrastructure and machinery equipment.

In **Koper**, the agreed concession fee is 3.5 per cent of the company's operating revenues, reduced by received port dues. The concession fee also includes rent and wayleave rights, and encompasses water rights, the water fee and other dues related to usage of the water area.

In **Piraeus**, use is made of a concession fee too, comprising:

- a lump sum fee of €50m, of which €2.9m was for the transfer of the spares inventory;
- a percentage of gross revenue increasing from 21 per cent in years 1-8 to 24.5 per cent from year 9 onwards, to be paid in monthly instalments; this is subject to minimum payments based on the minimum throughput guarantees;
- an annual lease payment linked to the length of quay available (€1,800 per metre p.a.);
- an annual lease payment linked to the container yard area (€4.00 per m² p.a.).

Table 12.14 Funding of the considered PPP projects

Port	Antwerp	Durres	Koper	Piraeus	Rijeka	Sines	Valencia
Funding	Availability fees and subsidy	User fees no subsidy	User fees no subsidy	User fees no subsidy	User fees no subsidy	User fees no subsidy	User fees no subsidy

Both of the lease payments are to increase over time at an annual rate, which is 2 per cent higher than the Greek Consumer Price Index.

Rijeka applies concession fees, but it was not possible to identify their structure. For the **Sines** PPP project, the concession agreement did not include any allowance for non-transport related activities, so no additional sources of income were available apart from container handling. The concession fees paid by PSA to the port authority are entirely in the form of royalties per TEU of throughput. Unusually, the concession agreement does not appear to have included any provisions for ground rent.

In **Valencia**, finally, the private operator will have to pay the following port charges to the Port Authority of Valencia:

- 'tasa de actividad', a charge for using the port domain to generate private income; this will be 2 per cent of turnover or 20 per cent of the 'tasa de ocupación', whichever is highest, and is estimated as equivalent to €0.13 per passenger in year 2;
- 'tasa de ocupación', an annual lease payment equivalent to €0.39 per passenger in year 2.

The following rebates will be applied according to law:

- 95 per cent rebate of 'tasa de ocupación' during the construction period;
- 15 per cent rebate of 'tasa de actividad' for good environmental practices;
- 15 per cent rebate of 'tasa de actividad' for quality control certification.

Financing

A mixture of port and bank financing is encountered in the selected PPP cases. For the **Antwerp** case, ParticipatieMaatschappij Vlaanderen (PMV) has, on instruction by NV Vlaamse Havens and NV Deurganckdoksluis, led negotiations with the EIB. The EIB has financed 50 per cent of the total construction price, up to a maximum of €160.5m. Next to that, the KBC Bank also provides a credit line of €81m (Table 12.15). The remaining amount is put on the table by the Antwerp Municipal Port Authority and the Flemish Government.

In the **Durres** case, it was agreed that the operator should arrange the financing of the required and agreed investments and operations, and should bear all costs for technically upgrading the terminal facility, providing equipment, computer systems, manpower, and all direct and indirect expenses relating to the obligation to provide cargo terminal services. This includes, *inter alia*, all costs for

Table 12.15 Majority financing of the considered PPP projects

Port	Antwerp	Durres	Koper	Piraeus	Rijeka	Sines	Valencia
Financing	Bank	Bank	Port	Bank	Port	Bank	Bank

management and staff, maintenance and repair, security, energy, fuel, electricity, water, communications, safety, cleaning and waste management, staff training, etc.

At **Koper**, investments in port infrastructure are made by the concessionaire in agreement with the Republic of Slovenia, based on port infrastructure development programmes. Maintenance of the port infrastructure dedicated to transport is financed from port dues, while Luka Koper takes care of the financing for all of the other investments in the port infrastructure.

At **Piraeus**, around half of the costs not covered by the terminal's operating cash flow are expected to be covered by equity contributions and around half by debt. Like most of the other large international terminal operators, Cosco Pacific is likely to use corporate debt – bonds or senior loans secured by parent company assets – rather than project-specific non-recourse financing.

Rijeka features a situation where the planned development projects are financed from several sources: the Port of Rijeka Authority's own funds, budget subsidies and a loan granted by the IBRD.

At **Sines**, the investments undertaken up to 31 December 2009 – public and private – received a grant of €25.5m from the EU Structural Funds, and €9m from central government, within a total expenditure of €137m.

At **Valencia**, the Port Authority of Valencia is responsible for building the breakwaters, dredging, building the docks, maintenance of the access to the port, navigation aids and navigation safety, and making sure that private companies will provide marine services (pilotage and towage), while the private operator is responsible for the construction and maintenance of the terminal building, the provision of equipment, and operating the terminal during the concession period.

Tendering

In **Antwerp**, following a public tender, six applications were submitted on 2 February 2011. In **Durres**, the Ministry of Public Works and Transport (MPWT) transferred to the private sector through public tendering the management, operation and maintenance of the East Terminal in the Port of Durres under a concession agreement (Table 12.16). At **Koper**, for the first 35 years, the concession was given directly to Luka Koper d.d. by a governmental Decree on the administration of the freight port of **Koper**. After this period, an open tender is required under PPP regulations.

At **Piraeus**, before proceeding to the tender stage, the Ministry of Merchant Marine had already approached several terminal operating companies, including Cosco Pacific, HPH, DP World, APM Terminals, MSC, and Zim, and held discussions with other governments (China and Korea) that had expressed

Table 12.16 Tendering of the considered PPP projects

Port	Antwerp	Durres	Koper	Piraeus	Rijeka	Sines	Valencia
Tendering	Competitive	Competitive	Negotiations	Negotiations	Competitive	Competitive	Competitive

interest in investing in port facilities at Piraeus (and Thessaloniki). Although the government eventually committed itself to open competitive tendering, in line with best international practice, there were fears that the port might end up with the 'wrong' partner – the government had spent some time negotiating with Cosco Pacific on a non-competitive basis.

In **Rijeka**, tendering procedures are promulgated by the Concessions Act (NN 143/2012) passed by the Croatian Parliament. This Act regulates the procedures for the award of concessions, termination of concessions, and other related issues.

At **Sines**, a 'blueprint' tender based on studies was sent to 32 possible concessionaires and published in seven international journals, to test the market. An initial response was obtained from nine companies, four of which – Liscont, ECT, HMM and Kashi International – dropped out quite rapidly. The five potential partners remaining in the frame were a very mixed group, comprising PSA Corp and P&O Ports (large international terminal operators), Mitsui (an industrial conglomerate with shipping and engineering interests), Chemical Bank (an institutional investor) and Portsines (a multi-purpose terminal operator already established at Sines).

At **Valencia**, before proceeding to the tender stage, the Port Authority of **Valencia** approached most cruise terminal operating companies and cruise liners that could have an interest in the project and informed them about the characteristics of the infrastructure and the tendering procedures. It held discussions with them to assess the level of private sector interest in the concession before a competitively tendered concession call was launched in the second half of 2013.

Awarding

In **Antwerp**, the contract was granted to THV Waaslandsluis (Table 12.17). In **Durres**, selection of the winners was made based on the offer presented only by the German Company 'EMS Shipping and Trading GMBH'.

At **Koper**, as mentioned, for the first 35 years, the concession was given directly to Luka Koper.

At **Piraeus**, the percentage of gross revenue offered was one of the main award criteria for the concession. Cosco offered 21 per cent for the first eight years and then 24.5 per cent with the second bidder (HPH) offering 19 per cent. HPH – the clear winner at Thessaloniki and a close second at Piraeus – had already proved to be a tough negotiator, and its willingness to walk away from the Thessaloniki concession put additional pressure on the Greek Government to conclude an early agreement with Cosco Pacific.

Table 12.17 Awarding of the considered PPP projects

Port	Antwerp	Durres	Koper	Piraeus	Rijeka	Sines	Valencia
Awarding	One stage	Two stages	One stage	Two stages	One stage	Two stages	One stage

In **Rijeka**, all economic activities have been taken over by concessionaires. Among the five main concessionaires, Luka Rijeka d.d., a mixed public-private company, is the one that uses most of the **Rijeka** port area.

At **Sines**, although the original intention had been to request formal expressions of interest and then build a financial model of the concession, which would provide a basis for negotiations with each of these potential partners, this was not done. PSA was more proactive than the other potential partners, and the port authority was under pressure from the government to act quickly in order to secure a partner with such a strong international reputation. So after PSA Corp presented its proposals for a JV on 13 June 1998, it was given exclusive rights to participate in the proposed JV, and access to confidential information that would allow it to undertake its own technical studies and due diligence work. In August 1998, PSA Corp submitted a formal proposal for a JV between itself (67 per cent) and the port authority (33 per cent). The Tribunal de Contas, which later reviewed the award process, found no evidence to suggest that this bid was objectively evaluated by either the port authority or its parent ministry. In March 1999, after further studies, PSA Corp submitted a revised proposal that was radically different from its first one, abandoning the JV concept in favour of a more conventional concession in which the public sector would provide the breakwater and road and rail access, and the private sector would provide the quay wall, superstructure and equipment. The new proposal formed the basis for the agreement on principles signed in June 1999, and for the concession agreement itself, which was signed in September 1999. The port authority's non-competitive approach to the selection of a partner was expressly authorised by Decreto Lei 384A/1999 in September 1999, three days before the concession agreement was signed.

At **Valencia**, the selection of the private sector operator for Valencia cruise terminal took place following the port's normal competitive procurement procedures.

Duration

All seven selected PPP projects have contract durations of between 25 and 35 years (Table 12.18). At **Piraeus**, an automatic extension option of five years conditional on the completion of the Pier III investment was scheduled. In **Rijeka**, the initial contract was from 2000 to 2012, while the renewal of the concession period to another 30 years started in 2012, running until 2042. All of these can be considered long durations.

Table 12.18 Exposure to macro-environment of the considered PPP projects

Port	Antwerp	Durres	Koper	Piraeus	Rijeka	Sines	Valencia
Duration (years)	20	35	35	30	42	30	25

Table 12.19 Risk division of the considered PPP projects

Port	Antwerp	Durres	Koper	Piraeus	Rijeka	Sines	Valencia
Design and construction risks	Mostly public	Mostly private	More private	Mostly private	Totally public	More public	More public
Maintenance risk	Mostly public	Totally private	Totally private	Mostly private	Totally public	More public	More private
Risk of exploitation	Mostly public	Totally private	Totally private			Mostly private	Mostly private
Commercial revenue risk	Mostly public	Totally private	Totally private	Mostly private	Mostly private	Mostly private	More private
Financial risk		Mostly private	Totally private	Mostly private	Mostly private	Mostly public	More private
Regulatory risk		Mostly public	Totally public			Totally public	More private
Force majeure		Mostly public				Totally public	

Risk allocation

As to risk allocation, a varied picture is found (Table 12.19). **Antwerp** is the only case where most of the risks are absorbed by the public sector. This probably has to do with the nature of the project: a lock, not a commercial terminal. **Durres**, **Koper** and **Piraeus** have a stronger private focus.

'The Whole'

The port of **Antwerp** is Belgium's largest port and Europe's second in terms of freight volume and value added. Although the port is known for its diversity, it is mainly the container throughput that has grown in recent years. Given the moderate growth prospects for Western Europe, business opportunities for port operators are mainly in emerging countries. China is getting ever stronger, and other Asian countries such as India and countries like Poland, Russia and Turkey expect higher than average export growth. **Antwerp**, being an export-driven port, can benefit from this upheaval, being one of the fewer ports concentrating European export traffic. During the coming ten years, the Belgian port expects additional competitive pressure from Rotterdam, through the delivery of the Tweede Maasvlakte. Furthermore, Bremen also has the potential, through its geographical position, to develop into an important competitor (Table 12.20).

Table 12.20 Exposure to macro-environment of the considered PPP projects

Port	Antwerp	Durres	Koper	Piraeus	Rijeka	Sines	Valencia
The whole	Extreme exposure to macro-environment	Significant exposure to macro-environment	Significant exposure to macro-environment	Extreme exposure to macro-environment	Significant exposure to macro-environment	Significant exposure to macro-environment	Extreme exposure to macro-environment

Durres Port is regarded as having growth potential as Albania is steadily integrated into the European Union.

The port of **Koper** is one of the most powerful generators of transport activity in its region. The multiplier effects of port activity are reflected in the port's direct surroundings and wider environment (Trupac and Twrdy 2010). The Central and Eastern Europe market is particularly important.

Piraeus is the largest port in Greece, located only a few miles from the capital Athens. It handles around three quarters of the country's container trade, and is the main hub for domestic shipping services to the Greek islands. It is also the only port in Greece with large amounts of transhipment traffic which, in 2007 – the year in which the PPP was tendered – accounted for 37 per cent of its throughput. At the beginning of the decade, Piraeus had been one of the largest container transhipment hubs for the East Mediterranean but, by the time of the tender, it was facing growing competition from newer ports such as Suez Canal East (Egypt) and Ambarli (Turkey).

Because of its position, the port of **Rijeka** has many advantages, from the water depth and shelter to relatively short and fast land transport routes to the markets of the more developed countries further north.

As indicated previously in the section on 'market location', the port of **Sines** was intended to compete with transhipment ports such as Algeciras and Tanger Med. The government identified the need for Portugal to develop a deep-water port capable of accommodating larger container ships than its existing ports could handle. Because Sines had no existing container traffic, and was located in an area that was not likely to generate much local container traffic (at least initially), transhipment traffic was seen as the key to building up the critical level of traffic needed to attract shipping lines and create connectivity to the outside world.

Over the last decade, and especially during the last five years, the port of **Valencia** has succeeded in attracting a new market of international cruise passengers. The city of Valencia is becoming an attractive tourist destination by itself so the port of Valencia has the opportunity of becoming an essential call for cruise liners operating in the Mediterranean. This fact would have a significant economic impact on both the city and the region with a feedback effect on the tourist sector, even though Northern America continues to be the clear leader of the cruise sector. However, in the last five years, the European market has experienced significant growth while Asia has kept its relatively low growth rates and small presence in the industry. Although the European market will probably keep on growing at similar rates in the medium and long term, additional new challenges must be faced. According to the World Tourism Organisation, the number of tourists in Europe will grow by 3.1 per cent, the forecast for 2020 being 717 million visitors to the continent. All destinations will need to take into consideration the total number of tourists when planning and making decisions concerning new cruise packages. New high value destinations may be able to sell new cruise itineraries that will help alleviate congestion in certain key Mediterranean ports. In this context, Valencia needs to position itself with infrastructure capable of competing as a home port, providing additional capacity which complements that of Barcelona.

Summary

This section summarises the results obtained for each of the granular units and their linguistic variables for the seven port cases analysed in this chapter.

Of the hypotheses brought forward in Table 12.1, a number were confirmed (rows with only grey cells in Table 12.21):

- Cargo PPP projects are by far the most frequently occurring ones.
- At least four of the seven projects feature large investment amounts. For two projects, the amount is not known.
- Most projects are included in TEN-T. One is even a priority project.
- Half plus one of the projects are located close to their hinterland markets.
- All but one project date back no longer than six years.
- Tendering was done competitively in all but two cases.
- Four cases featured a one-stage award procedure.
- Typically, ports have long contract periods, which may be linked to the size of the investments to be undertaken.
- The predominance of private sector responsibility for maintenance, exploitation and commercial risks was confirmed, although for the exploitation risk, the risk division could not be indicated for two cases.

The following hypotheses were not confirmed, or at least not fully (rows with black and grey cells or only black ones):

- Most of the selected projects are not transhipment hubs but hinterland gateways.
- All but one projects are of mixed brownfield/greenfield nature, whereas greenfield was hypothesised to be the most frequently occurring.
- Only three projects involve berth, terminal superstructure and cranes, whereas it was assumed the majority would do so. Three others actually involved only terminal superstructure and cranes.
- The hypothesis was that the majority of identified projects would be competitive, but only one turned out to be so. Most projects ranged from 'somewhat exclusive' to 'exclusive'.
- Although it was thought that the majority of the projects would have been port-driven, in fact it was national governments that were pushing for the projects in all cases.
- The hypothesis was more or less right that most of the project sponsors would be business developers, at least for four of the seven cases, even though it was never to the full extent, hence we do not consider the hypothesis to be strongly met.
- Equally, it was more or less correctly hypothesised that port PPP projects would be mostly finance-oriented, although the degree was stronger than expected, so we also do not consider this hypothesis to be strongly met. Only two cases inclined more towards a service-based nature.

Table 12.21 Actual values for linguistic variables of the Ws Contextual Framework

Linguistic Variable	Variable Range					
Granule: What – the project						
Nature	Cargo		Passenger	Mixed		
Function	Local hinterland		Hinterland gateway	Transhipment hub		Transhipment + hinterland
Brownfield/greenfield	Brownfield		Greenfield	Mixed		
Physical characteristics	Berth only	Terminal superstructure only	Cranes only	Berth and terminal superstructure	Terminal superstructure and cranes	Berth, terminal superstructure and cranes
Budget	Small		Medium		Large	
Level of exclusiveness	Competitive environment	Not exclusive	Quite not exclusive	Somewhat exclusive	Rather Exclusive	Exclusive
TEN-T	Not included in TEN-T		Included in TEN-T	TEN-T priority project	TEN-T core project	TEN-T peripheral project
Granule: Where – project location						
Geographical	Northern-European			Southern-European		
Market	Close to market			Rather distant from market		
Granule: When – project (investment) timing						
Maturity	Recent			Older		
Granule: Who – the public initiator						
National-Port driven	Nation-driven		Region-driven	Municipality-driven		Port-driven
Granule: Whom – user						
Business developer / servicer	Business servicer	Mostly Business servicer	More business servicer	More business developer	Mostly business developer	Business developer

(Continued)

Table 12.21 Actual values for linguistic variables of the Ws Contextual Framework (Continued)

Linguistic Variable	Variable Range					
Granule: Why – the scope of PPP						
Finance – service-based approach	Solely service-based approach	Mostly service-based approach	More service-based approach	More finance-based approach	Mostly finance-based approach	Solely finance-based approach
Granule: Which way – strategy with respect to the contractual agreement (risk allocation & payment structure)						
Funding	Availability fees and subsidy	Availability fees	Shadow tolls and subsidy	Shadow tolls/No subsidy	User fees and subsidy	User fees no subsidy
Majority financing	Nation	Region	Municipality	Port	Bank	SPV
Tendering	Competitive			Negotiated		
Awarding	One stage			Several stages		
Duration	Short		Medium		Long	
Design and construction risks	Totally private	Mostly private	More private	More public	Mostly public	Totally public
Maintenance risk	Totally private	Mostly private	More private	More public	Mostly public	Totally public
Risk of exploitation	Totally private	Mostly private	More private	More public	Mostly public	Totally public
Commercial revenue risk	Totally private	Mostly private	More private	More public	Mostly public	Totally public
Financial risk	Totally private	Mostly private	More private	More public	Mostly public	Totally public
Regulatory risk	Totally private	Mostly private	More private	More public	Mostly public	Totally public
Force majeure	Totally private	Mostly private	More private	More public	Mostly public	Totally public
Granule: Whole						
Impact /influence of macro-environment	No exposure / influence of macro-environment	Very little exposure to macro-environment	Little exposure to macro-environment	Some exposure to macro-environment	Significant exposure to macro-environment	Extreme exposure to macro-environment

- As to funding, whereas other sectors such as roads are often funded by avail-ability fees, in the ports sector the opposite turned out to be true, with all but one of the projects applying user fees (without subsidies).
- In all but two cases, bank loans were the major source of finance, and not national government budgets as presumed.
- Design and construction risk is typically more public sector than was previously assumed.
- Financial risk turned out to be predominantly with the private partner, with the public sector having a much smaller role.
- Regulatory risk is predominantly with the public side, although in one case it is on the private side; three cases do not disclose this risk division.
- For two cases, the force majeure risk seemed to lie with the public sector. For all of the others, the division could not be identified.
- Finally, exposure to the macro-environment turned out to be quite strong, but not extreme, as opposed to what was hypothesised. The main reason for this is that the considered ports are less purely transhipment projects than was stated as a hypothesis.

Conclusions and future research

It is observed that PPP are increasingly being used to finance seaport projects. One of the purposes of this research was to try and find commonalities among seaport PPP projects. To do that, a methodology stemming from fuzzy logic with an assessment of granulation based on a risk analysis contextual framework was applied, as summarised in Table 12.1. This allows for a comparison of seven different cases, all from different countries in Europe.

Most projects seem to deal with cargo transfer, and the majority involve a hinterland gateway function. Not all are greenfield, as might be presumed. They involve various combinations of either berth, terminal superstructure and/or cranes. Budgets are typically large and operations exclusive. Most port PPP projects are also part of TEN-T programme corridors.

Most developments are also found in Southern Europe, where the expansion needs are highest and government budgets are most constrained. That is also an explanation of why most such projects are of recent origin. The big drivers behind the projects are national governments, most likely because of the strategic importance of the projects and governments' lack of finance. For that reason, the PPP option is most often motived by financial and not service arguments. Projects are typically located close to the markets they serve. They are also meant to expand the business.

Most projects recover costs through user fees without subsidies. Bank loans are the major source of finance. Tendering typically is competitive, though involving some negotiation, and award of contract is done in one stage.

Project duration is typically long. Maintenance, exploitation, commercial and financial risks turn out to be mostly private. Design, regulatory and force majeure risks are mostly public. Finally, the impact of the macro-environment is strong in all cases.

The analysis is pre-fuzzy and hence preliminary. It is a first test applied to a set of port cases, with interesting and sometimes surprising results. Extension is possible in various ways. First of all, it would be interesting to include more cases, not only from within Europe, but also from other continents. It might, in that respect, be interesting to include cases from less-developed regions, from regions with booming economic growth, and from more centrally-planned countries. Furthermore, it would be interesting to make cross-modal comparisons, so as to transfer best practices from ports to other modes or vice versa. Finally, it would be interesting to further codify the values of the various linguistic variables, so as to allow for quantitative analysis.

Acknowledgement

The authors are grateful to the COST TU1001 members who helped collect data as part of the case database build-up: Maša Čertalič, Ali Dedej, Sheila Farrell, Sandra Juretic, Vera Shiko, Alenka Temeljotov-Salaj, Athena Roumboutsos, Thierry Vanelslander and Céline Vannieuwenhuysen.

Note

1 Sines was intended to be a transhipment port, but failed to attract the necessary traffic.

References

Asian Development Bank (2001) *Developing Best Practices for Promoting Private Sector Investment in Infrastructure: Ports*. Manila: Asian Development Bank

Castillo-Manzano, J. I. and Ascencio-Flores, J. P. (2012) 'Competition between new port governance models on the Iberian Peninsula'. *Transport Reviews: A Transnational Transdisciplinary Journal*, 32, pp. 519–537

Chin, A. and Waldron, S. (2014) 'Financing options for ports: observations from Asia' in: H. Meersman, E. Van de Voorde and T. Vanelslander (Eds) *Port Infrastructure Finance* (pp. 141–162). Abingdon, UK: Routledge

Coppens, F., Lagneaux, F., Meersman, H., Sellekaerts, N., Van de Voorde, E., van Gastel, G., Vanelslander, T. and Verhetsel, A. (2007) *Economic Impact of Port Activity: A Disaggregate Analysis*. Brussels: National Bank of Belgium

De Langen, P. and Heij, C. (2014) 'Corporatisation and performance: a literature review and an analysis of the performance effects of the corporatisation of Port of Rotterdam Authority. *Transport Reviews: A Transnational Transdisciplinary Journal*, 34, pp. 396–414

Estache, A. and de Rus, G. (2003) *Privatization and Regulation of Transport Infrastructure: Guidelines for Policymakers and Regulators*. Washington: World Bank Institute

Farrell, S. (2014) 'Attracting private finance in African ports' in: H. Meersman, E. Van de Voorde and T. Vanelslander (Eds) *Port Infrastructure Finance* (pp. 181–210). Abingdon, UK: Routledge

Guasch, J. L. (2004) *Granting and Renegotiating Infrastructure Concessions: Doing it Right*. Washington: World Bank

Lipovich, G. (2008) 'The privatization of Argentine airports'. *Journal of Air Transport Management*, 14, pp. 8–15

Macário, R. (2014) 'Public-Private Partnerships in ports: where are we?' in: H. Meersman, E. Van de Voorde and T. Vanelslander (Eds) *Port Infrastructure Finance* (pp. 55–68). Abingdon, UK: Routledge

Marques, R. C. and Fonseca, A. (2010) 'Market structure, privatisation and regulation of Portuguese seaports'. *Maritime Policy & Management*, 37, pp. 145–161

McPhee, R., Corman, S. and Dooley, K. (2009) 'Characteristic Processes and Discursive Methods in the Study of Organizational Knowledge'. Available online at: www.researchgate.net/publication/2390665_Characteristic_Processes_and_Discursive_Methods_in_the_Study_of_Organizational_Knowledge

Meersman, H., Pauwels, T., Van de Voorde, E. and Vanelslander, T. (2010) 'Applying SMC pricing in PPPs for the maritime sector'. *Research in Transportation Economics*, 30 (1) pp. 87–101

Meersman, H., Van de Voorde, E. and Vanelslander, T. (2014) 'Future port infrastructure finance: lessons and recommendations' in: H. Meersman, E. Van de Voorde and T. Vanelslander (Eds) *Port Infrastructure Finance* (pp. 229–237). Abingdon, UK: Routledge

Notteboom, T. E., Pallis, A. and Farrell, S. (Eds) (2012) 'Special issue on port concessions'. *Maritime Policy & Management*, 39(1) pp. 27–43

Organisation for Economic Cooperation and Development (2011) *Competition Concerns in Ports and Port Services*. Paris: OECD Competition Committee

Pigna, F. (2014) 'Port authority corporitisation – leading towards their privatisation?' in H. Meersman, E. Van de Voorde and T. Vanelslander (Eds) *Port Infrastructure Finance* (pp. 141–162). Abingdon: Routledge

Roumboutsos, A. (2010) 'A Ws Contextual Risk Analysis framework: mapping knowledge transfer potential between road and port Public Private Partnerships'. *Proceedings of the CIB World Congress*, Salford Quays, United Kingdom

Roumboutsos, A., Pellegrino, R., Vanelslander, T. and Macário, R. (2012) 'Transport PPP Projects: a literature review'. *COST Action TU1001: Public Private Partnerships in Transport: Trends and Theory; 2011 Discussion Papers*. ISBN 978-88-97781-04-2, COST Office, Brussels. Available online at: www.ppptransport.eu

Roumboutsos, A., Farrell, S., Liyanage, C. L. and Macário, R. (2013) *COST Action TU1001 Public Private Partnerships in Transport: Trends & Theory P3T3, 2013 Discussion Papers Part II Case Studies*. ISBN 978-88-97781-61-5. Available online at: www.ppptransport.eu

Roumboutsos, A., Farrel, S. and Verhoest, K. (Eds) (2014) *COST Action TU1001 – Public Private Partnerships in Transport: Trends & Theory: 2014 Discussion Series: Country Profiles & Case Studies*. ISBN 978-88-6922-009-8, COST Office, Brussels. Available online at: www.ppptransport.eu

Suykens, F. and Van de Voorde, E. (1998) 'A quarter of a century of port management in Europe: objectives and tools. *Maritime Policy and Management* 25(3), pp. 251–261

Sys, C., Vanelslander, T., Adriaenssens, M. and Van Rillaer, I. (2014) 'International emission regulation in sea transport: economic feasibility and impacts'. *Proceedings of the International Conference: 'Climate Change and Transport'*, Karlsruhe

Theofanis, S. and Boilé, M. (2014) 'Experiences with bond financing and innovative transport project financing: some evidence from ports and port-related projects' in: H. Meersman, E. Van de Voorde and T. Vanelslander (Eds) *Port Infrastructure Finance* (pp. 163–180). Abingdon, UK: Routledge

Trupac, I. and Twrdy, E. (2010) 'More competitiveness of the Port of Koper through supply chain integration'. *Promet – Traffic & Transportation* 22(4), pp. 251–257

Vanelslander, T. (2005) 'The economics behind co-operation and competition in sea-port container handling'. PhD, University of Antwerp

Vanelslander, T., Chomat, G., Roumboutso, A. and Bonnet, G. (2013) 'Cross-sectoral comparison of concessions in transport: urban, road and port pre-fuzzy assessment'. *Built Environment Project and Asset Management* 4(1), pp. 22–39

Vanelslander, T. (2014) 'Port infrastructure: what are we talking about?' in H. Meersman, E. Van de Voorde and T. Vanelslander (Eds) *Port Infrastructure Finance* (pp. 5–32). Abingdon, UK: Routledge

Verhoeven, P. (2014) 'Port privatisation in the United Kingdom and Continental Europe: an evaluation of past experience and new drivers' in: H. Meersman, E. Van de Voorde and T. Vanelslander (Eds) *Port Infrastructure Finance* (pp. 111–140). Abingdon: Routledge

Verhoeven, P. and Vanoutrive, T. (2012) 'A quantitative analysis of European port governance'. *Maritime Economics and Logistics* 14(2), pp. 178–203

Zadeh, L. A. (2008) 'Is there a need for fuzzy logic?' *Information Sciences* 178, pp. 2751–2779

13 Critical success factors in different stages of delivery in PPP transport infrastructure projects

Johannes T. Voordijk,
Champika Liyanage and
Alenka Temeljotov-Salaj

Introduction

The use of the Public Private Partnership (PPP) models for project delivery, especially for infrastructure projects, has increased over the past decades. Their growing economic importance for society has triggered research interest with respect to private involvement in project delivery and financing of public infrastructure and social projects. A Public Private Partnership is a legal framework under a PPP act, defined as a relationship involving private capital in a public project. These projects are in the public interest, based on relationships between public and private partners and focused on the construction, maintenance and operation of public infrastructure and the associated provision of commercial and other public services or activities. PPP structures are typically more complex than traditional public procurement. There are often more parties involved in a project, the financing costs of PPP are generally higher and the different parties have to share the risks involved in a PPP.

The focus of this study is to identify and evaluate critical success factors (CSFs) in the different stages of delivery of PPP transport infrastructure. The objectives are (1) to enhance understanding of which factors in the different stages of delivery across different countries and different types of PPP transport projects are considered important for the success of these projects; and (2) to identify areas that PPP stakeholders should pay special attention to in the future in order to achieve success of projects.

The aforementioned objectives were fulfilled within the context of COST Action TU1001 on 'Public Private Partnerships in Transport: Trends and Theory' (P3T3). The work presented particularly focuses on findings of the Working Group (WG) on identification of CSFs and KPIs for improved PPP performance. In Figure 13.1 below, the general framework of the steps in ascertaining PPP performance in transport projects executed by WG is given. This paper focuses on steps 2 and 3. A list of performance criteria and CSFs for PPP performance in transport was based on analysing case studies and the compilation of reported

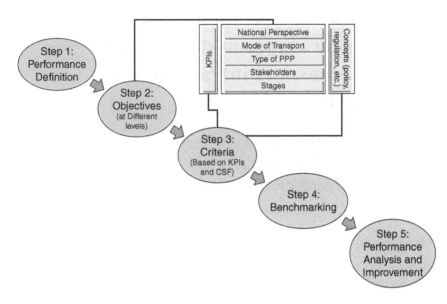

Figure 13.1 PPP performance in the transport sector.

research (Qiao *et al.* 2001; Bing *et al.* 2005a; Zhang 2005). More specifically, a PPP literature database and case study database on CSFs and KPIs on PPP performance was developed. The focus was on the prime stages of PPP: the pre-contract (tender) stage, contractual agreement, project contractual monitoring, project transfer and the partnership.

In the next section, the research methodology used to achieve the objectives mentioned above is outlined. Next, the results of preliminary investigations on performance criteria from different stakeholders' perspectives (i.e. users, private party and public party) in the context of PPP transport infrastructure are presented. Subsequently, the case protocols are presented and data analysis of CSFs is demonstrated and discussed. Finally, conclusions are drawn including addressing the limitations of this study and recommendations for further research.

Methodology

According to Yin (2009), case studies are a preferred research method when a 'how' or 'why' question is being asked about a contemporary set of events over which a researcher has little or no control. Case research may be on a single case (Flyvbjerg 2006) or multiple cases. In this study, Eisenhardt's (1989) approach of building theory based on case study research to answer the research questions is used. The various steps adopted for this approach are described below (see also Table 13.1).

Table 13.1 Building theory from case study research (based on Eisenhardt 1989, p. 533)

Key tasks	#	Step	Activity (according to Eisenhardt 1989)	COST Action WG2
Getting started	1	Getting started	Definition of research question *A priori* constructs	Focus on CSFs in different stages of delivery of PPP transport infrastructure. Definition of stakeholders' performance objectives by reviewing existing CSFs and KPIs.
Data collection	2	Selecting cases	Specified population	Defining the type of cases: European PPP in transport infrastructure for transport modes.
	3	Crafting instruments and protocols	Multiple data collection methods.	Case study collection method procedure considering all key aspects of the PPP arrangements: W7 model.
	4	Entering the field	Overlap data collection and data analysis. Flexible data collection methods.	Describing CSFs in the different stages of delivery in the WG2 Case: CSFs mentioned in the database.
	5	Analysing data	Within-case analysis. Cross-case pattern search.	Within-case: column-by-column analysis. Cross-case: line-by-line analysis – analysis based on horizontal comparison of the data.
Data analysis	6	Shaping propositions	Replication, not sampling, logic across cases. Search evidence for the 'why' behind relationships.	Some general conclusions based on the case analysis.
	7	Enfolding literature	Comparison with conflicting literature. Comparison with similar literature.	Reflection on CSFs in the delivery of PPP transport infrastructure.
	8	Reaching closure	Theoretical saturation when possible.	

Getting started (Step 1)

For this research project, the major research question is: what are the critical success factors (CSFs) in the different stages of delivery of PPP transport infrastructure? In a preliminary investigation, some '*a priori* constructs' have been generated. Herein, the focus is on performance objectives and criteria from the different stakeholders' perspectives (i.e. users, private party and public party) in the context of PPP transport infrastructure. Selected literature and papers were reviewed during the initial stages of the project. Most of these papers and reports represented successful contracts or contracts with good solutions at some stage. The literature review aimed at identifying CSFs, KPIs and different methods of measuring KPIs in different types of PPP projects and during different phases of PPP projects, i.e. design, construction, operation and maintenance.

Data collection (Steps 2-4)

The comparison of a set of PPP cases requires a systematic protocol, which may describe all features of a PPP arrangement. This also takes into account the specificities of the asset delivered, which creates difficulties for transport projects, not only because of the multiplicity of contractual arrangements but also due to the individual characteristics of the various subsectors. It is also important to identify the suitability for knowledge transfer between transport subsectors and across other sectors where PPPs are applied. This effort leads to the development of a case protocol (Step 2) suitable to describe PPP in transportation. Its key characteristic is the ability to compare seemingly different cases across different modes, different regions and different countries. Eisenhardt (1989) supports the use of multiple data collection methods in order to strengthen the triangulation of evidence/findings. Therefore, in Step 3, crafting instruments and protocols were carried out using two templates as guides for the case research method proposed. The first provides a 'story telling' basis for the case study as it considers all key aspects of the PPP arrangement (Roumboutsos and Liyanage 2013). The second focuses on the identification and evaluation of CSFs in the different stages of delivery of PPP transport infrastructure through a comparative study of 34 cases. Step 4 involved a combination of data collection and analysis (i.e. entering the field). A flexible data collection was proposed herein, because it allowed investigators to take advantage of emergent themes and unique case features.

Data analysis (Steps 5-8)

In Step 5 (i.e. analysing data), 'within-case analysis' and 'cross-case analyses' were carried out. A cross-case analysis through a line-by-line analysis and a horizontal comparison of the data helped to identify relevant CSFs in the different stages of delivery of PPP transport infrastructure. The column-by-column analysis was applied in vertical within-case analysis. The cross-case analysis highlights the key similarities and differences between the different cases. In Step 6 (i.e. shaping propositions), preliminary propositions for the analysis were formulated. It is important to emphasise that these propositions are based on 34 case studies and that more evidence is needed to confidently generalise the outcomes and provide support for the formulated propositions. In Step 7 (i.e. enfolding literature), the findings and propositions were discussed in terms of supportive and conflicting literature. Ideally, closure is reached when theoretical saturation occurs (Step 8).

Getting started (step 1)

The performance of PPP projects is affected by a number of factors, their interactions during the projects' life cycle, and is linked to different stakeholder perspectives. At the beginning, in the WG2, discussions were carried out on different definitions of performance criteria and objectives, including various stakeholder perspectives and a performance measurement system. The performance objectives are used to identify the strengths and weaknesses of PPP projects and are seen as useful tools for effective PPP project performance management. These objectives are expected to be fulfilled by the PPP project, from project planning to operation. Their significance depends on stakeholder perspective (public partner, private partner and users). In terms of defining a successful PPP, a two-layered approach was defined: the first one based on general definition of project success principles and the other related to elements of stakeholder success objectives (Mladenovic *et al.* 2013) (see Table 13.2). Defining successful PPP was based on the fulfilment of the ultimate objectives of each stakeholder, i.e. profitability and customer and owner satisfaction for private sector, value for money, effectiveness, efficiency and environmental impact for public sector, and level of service and environmental impact for users.

The performance objectives developed by the WG2 group were grouped according to their contexts and area of relevance. The following categories of performance objectives were identified: PPP environment (political, legal, economic, institutional); partners' strengths and skills; relationship between partners; technology transfer and innovation; project risk and risk allocation; project economic and financial characteristics, project general characteristics and impact; project procurement; and implementation.

Data collection (steps 2-4)

Selecting cases

In the case study analysis 34 PPP cases were taken into consideration from 12 countries: Albania, Austria, Belgium, Cyprus, Czech Republic, France, Greece, the Netherlands, Portugal, Serbia, Spain and the UK (see Table 13.3). The largest group, 17 cases in total, are road and motorway projects, while nine are rail projects or urban transport projects and the rest are on ports and airports. The cases presented a range from conventional motorways through to road tunnels, financed by different payment methods. In terms of PPP, rail projects appear to be not that attractive for private investors because of their complexity and high investment, but PPPs in urban public transport, on the other hand, are dominated by franchises, management contracts for networks, different investment schemes for light rail and metro. Ports and airports are the most attractive for private financing because of profitable terminal operation and generating revenue.

Table 13.2 Performance objectives according to different stakeholder perspectives

Public sector	Private sector	User
Environment (political, legal, institutional, economic)		
Institutional reform.	Institutional reform.	Public awareness.
Development of policy/ regulators.	Regulatory framework.	Social responsibility.
Effectiveness.		
Liberalisation of the market.		
Introduction of user charging.		
Partners' strengths and skills		
Import skills from the market.	Increase of business.	
Service differentiation.	Diversification into service provision.	
Relationship between partners		
Building trust.	Building trust/long term relationship.	
Management of expectations.	Management of expectations.	
Find the right balance between expectations of private entity, government and user.	Leverage.	
Forming long-term relationship.		
Technology transfer and innovation		
Effective technology transfer.	Innovation (develop innovative solutions).	
Innovation (come up with innovative solutions).		
Project risk and risk allocation		
Risk allocation.	Risk allocation, risk reward ration.	
Risk reward ration.	Traffic risks (for example, Greece).	
Traffic risks.		
Project economic and financial characteristics		
Efficiency (whole life cycle costing).	Internal Rate of Return (IRR).	Minimisation of Vehicle Operating Costs (VOC).
To minimise costs, maximise user benefits.	Repayment on equity.	Value for money.
Value for money.	Revenue.	
Project general characteristics and impact		
Health and safety.	Health and safety.	Accessibility.
User satisfaction.	User satisfaction.	Availability.
		Comfort.
		Reliability.
		Safety.
Project procurement and implementation		
Specialise in regulations/ procurement.	Transparency/acquiring right set of info.	Public awareness.
Ongoing monitoring.	Ongoing monitoring.	Social responsibility.
Project management skills/ experience.	Project management skills/experience.	

Source: Mladenovic *et al.* 2013.

Table 13.3 Overview of case studies

Country	Roads and motorways	Rail and urban public transport	Ports and airports
UK	A19 Dishforth.* BNRR M6 Toll Road.* M80 Haggs to Stepps.* A50 Road.** A55 Road**.	Manchester Metrolink.** London Underground.	
Greece	Attika Tollway.* Ionia Odos Motorway.* Olympia Odos Motorway.* Rio Anttirio Bridge.**		Piraeus Container Terminal*
Serbia	Horgos – Pozega Tollway.*		
Belgium	Via Invest Zaventem.	Brabo 1.*	Deurganck dock lock.*

Portugal	A23 Motorway Beira.**	FERTAGUS Train.*
		MST Metro Sul do
		  Tejo.*
			Alcantra Container
			  Terminal.
			Sines Container
			  Terminal.*

Poland	Highway A2.**		
Spain	Eje Aerpuerto Motorway.** Radial 2 Highway.** M45 Motorway.**	SEVICI.*	
Netherlands	Coen Tunnel.*		
Austria		Guterterminal Werndorf.*	
France		Caen TVR.* Reims Tramway.*	

Czech Rep.		Central Public
		  Transport Depot
		  Pilsen.*	

Albania			Durres Port East
			  Terminal.**
			Tirana International
			  Airport.*
			CTV (SGS).

Source: COST Action TU1001, 2013* and 2014**.

The transport PPP case study protocol

Roumboutsos (2010) presented a contextual framework based on the transport PPP context for risk analysis in order to compare and identify the potential of knowledge transfer between the road and port transport subsectors. This contextual framework describes the 'who', 'why', 'whom', 'who-for', 'which-way', 'what', 'where', 'when' and the 'whole' elements of a PPP. The framework provides a story-telling basis for a case study considering the different aspects of the PPP arrangement (see Chapter 11 and Appendix).

Because the main objective of this study is to enhance understanding of which factors in the different stages of delivery of PPP transport projects are considered important for the success of these projects, the focus here is on the 'which-way' element, i.e. key characteristics of the tendering process and contractual agreement. With respect to the tendering process, there are a variety of procedures that may be followed. 'Which-way' includes the principal factor of PPP: the way risks are allocated between public and private parties (Roumboutsos *et al.* 2012). Herein the key 'factor' is the level of 'openness', which is registered by the number of bidders per stage and total tendering duration. The description of the contractual agreement concerns the description of the level of involvement of the public and private sector in the project, the payment scheme and the existence of guarantees and renegotiation clauses. Other characteristics are risk allocation, construction duration and financial issues. The protocol also includes key performance indicators (KPIs) included in the contract. The assessment measures are defined by three types of Likert Scales (Table 13.4). Besides the contract and financial issues, the focus is on CSFs in different stages of project delivery: construction, operations, maintenance, monitoring and evaluation. The importance of these CSFs in different stages can be compared with each other within the case or CSFs of one stage can be compared between cases.

Data analysis (steps 5-8)

Data analysis is focused on identifying CSFs in PPP cases: the factors of considerable influence on the success or failure of PPP. In Table 13.4, the most interesting results from the pattern method research of 34 PPP cases in transport are shown and outcomes are discussed.

Horizontally, negative assessments of factors are mostly connected with the Tendering process and Construction phase. For example, with regard to tendering process, ten negative assessments concern legal challenges to outcome, which means ten of the 34 projects have had legal issues one way or another within the tendering process of the PPP project. In addition, there were nine negative assessments for the duration between tender notice to financial close, which means nine projects have had increased transaction costs during the tendering stage of the PPP project. Regarding the construction phase, nine of the 34 projects were not completed on time because of different reasons on the public or private side such as: administrative changes, project changes or that they included a long negotiation period. Eight projects were not completed within budget because of different reasons such as higher cost overruns due to long negotiation periods, project redesigning or because of financing issues during the recession.

The most positive assessments of factors were given for some connected to contract project specification. In 31 of the 34 cases it was found that deliverables were specified clearly in the contract. In 30 cases the roles and responsibilities of each member were clearly defined in the contract. In 27 cases the minimum standards with respect to the condition of infrastructure were highly ranked (4 or 5) – the equipment and materials were used in compliance with national and/or international codes of practice.

Table 13.4 Critical success factors in the stages of delivery of transport infrastructure

Stages	Success measurement	Outcomes
Tendering process	Success by more than one bidder.	In 13 cases: only 1 or 2 bidders.
	Time from tender notice to financial close.	In 9 cases time lasted more than 3 years. Delays caused by change in municipal government. Several delays explained by problems with final clause and legal challenges.
	Number of legal disputes/challenges.	In 10 of the 34 cases there were legal challenges. In some cases different governmental levels challenged the project. In one case the project was legally challenged by the provincial government. In another case, the project faced strong opposition from ministry of finance, trade unions and the leading opposition.
Contract project specifications	Deliverables specified clearly in the contract.	In 31 of the 34 cases it was said the deliverables were specified clearly in the contract.
	Roles and responsibilities of different parties involved in the contract clearly defined.	In most cases (30) the roles and responsibilities of each member are clearly defined in contract and external regulation.
	Minimum standards for condition of infrastructure and equipment specified in the contract.	In 27 cases the standards were evaluated with score 4 or 5. It was written that equipment and materials are used in compliance with national codes of practice.
	Performance targets.	In 23 cases, the score was 4 or 5. The most mentioned KPIs were: technical parameters, safety impacts, availability, carriage way performance, supply capacity, delays, operational performance and, specifically for urban transportation: number of passengers, punctuality, passenger satisfaction, regularity.
	Method of measuring performance targets clearly defined.	18 cases got scores of 4 or 5, 3 are not clear enough, 4 are neutral and for 7 information is not available. Methods mentioned: sold tickets, number of trains, safety parameters as road accident index, automatic incident detector system, response time, satisfaction of users conducted by different surveys, technical parameters.
	Penalties for non-compliance.	In 3 cases a score of 1 or 2, 8 neutral, 6 do not know, 16 cases got the score 4 or 5.

(Continued)

Table 13.4 Critical success factors in the stages of delivery of transport infrastructure (Continued)

Stages	Success measurement	Outcomes
	Procedures for amendments, dispute resolution or termination.	27 cases were evaluated with a score of 4 or 5. Procedures depend on country rules. In France it is obligatory by the Procurement Law for Public Service Concessions. In Greece, the contract is ratified by parliament defining in detail in one case the design, construction, financing, maintenance and operation of the bridge. It describes the various rights and obligations of each participant together with their respective commitments and it provides a precise procedure and required authorisations in case of departures from the base case. We found 6 reds: for Greece cases – every change has to follow law-changing procedures by the parliament rules and for Spanish ones – open negotiations were needed to restore initial conditions.
	Proceeding the contract without renegotiations.	In 13 cases renegotiations were needed for different reasons: construction cost overrun, traffic deviation, expropriation costs, additional investment, improvement of employment conditions, user tariff, etc.
	Guarantees specified in the contract.	The guarantees were not mentioned in 3 cases only.
Construction phase	Project completed on time.	9 reds – reasons were on public and private sides, because of administrative changes, project changes, long negotiation period.
	Project completed within budget.	8 reds – reasons are compensation for overrun cost because of long negotiation, redesigning, the recession. In the case of London Underground the inability to complete the work within budget was the main cause of the PPP failure.
	Project completed according to the specifications and design.	Only 1 red (London Underground), some investments (4) are still under construction, but the others were completed.
	Penalties for non-compliance?	In 17 cases, they couldn't be found (don't know) and in 4 cases penalties for non-compliance were not included.
Operation	Services specified in the contract.	Only 1 red – because of brown field with limited services, 4 are neutral and 6 do not know.
Maintenance	Standards for infrastructure and equipment being met.	10 do not know, 2 reds. All the others are green: in some cases the maintenance regime has been implemented; in some cases the information about bad performance couldn't be found. In one case the high maintenance standards were incorporated in order to sustain the infrastructure in excellent condition. In another case problems with vandalism and lack of qualified maintenance staff were reported.

Monitoring and evaluation	Formal monitoring procedure in place.	6 x do not know, 6 neutral, 3 red. Annual reports are produced by the concessionaire on the content specified in the contract. The public authority monitors the network. There is no formal conclusive reporting on the performance of the project itself. Annual customer satisfaction surveys are conducted.
Finance	Finance available when needed.	4 x no, 1 do not know. Rest of the cases: yes. In one case bank finance failed; in two Greek cases the brown field toll contribution reduced banks; in the London Underground case bank finance seems to have been available when needed, but the returns on equity were not high enough and there were serious cash flow problems.
	Project cash flow sufficient for expected payments to all parties.	6 x no – the above-mentioned cases and the two Spanish cases, for which it was reported that cash flow just covered operating costs – 8 do not know, 1 neutral.
	Project resulted in financial benefits to users.	In 14 cases the answer is neutral, 5 red/no, 2 do not know. In rail and urban transport cases the big increase of users' benefits were found out in connection with slight or not any increase of user charges. The benefits in road cases are evaluated through reduction of time – the reds are connected with increase of direct user toll.
	Financial outcome has been equal or better than expected for the private partner,	In 11 cases it is not known, 7 x no, 3 neutral. Red answers are connected with the financial problems because of bad performance, such as: experiencing losses in revenue and user numbers; economic crisis; the public transport operator has less money than expected; poor financial performance has resulted from lower than expected traffic growth; concession losses, no dividend, contingent shareholders' payments to cover debt service.
Risks	Risks have been transferred to the private sector.	In 11 cases it is not known, 3 x no, 3 x neutral. Various cases, various risks: design, construction, maintenance, commercial/revenue, exploitation, financial or demand risk. It was reported that the projects in which the entire risk was transferred to the private sector was one of main reasons for failure.
	Was risk allocation agreed quickly?	Different discussions were on-going, the longer and tougher ones especially connected with the unexpected situations, for example: deciding who will take the risk for damaging the existing tunnel; due to the financial-economic crisis not only banks but also the public sector partner were highly risk-averse in the initial negotiation stages.

(Continued)

Table 13.4 Critical success factors in the stages of delivery of transport infrastructure (Continued)

Stages	Success measurement	Outcomes
Network parameters	Project has competition with the network.	In 31 cases: yes.
	Effects of alternatives on outcomes.	In 24 cases, respondents do not know. In some road projects the user decrease was reported, because of toll prizes and other alternatives.
Objectives	Objectives in the contract specified SMART.	In 23 cases: yes, 5 x no. Specific, Measurable, Achievable, Realistic and Time bound.
	Objectives being achieved.	13 do not know, 4 neutral, 6 no – some of them were fully achieved, for some the increase of supply and use was achieved, some of them reported lack of quality and continuity of service, expensive public charge and the others complained of lack of demands for the infrastructure or failure.
	User benefits monitored.	9 do not know, 3 neutral, 5 no or red.
	User benefits as large as expected.	4 do not know, 1 neutral, 9 no/red: periodic non-availability of the supplier, low user capacity; high cost for users though the accessibility is better.

Three Likert Scales that have been used for the matrix above:
* Likert Scale 1 to 3: 1 – Red (Tenderers either 1 or 0), 2 – Yellow (2 Tenderers), 3 – Green (Tenderers 3 or more);
** Likert Scale 1 to 5: 1 – Red (being negative) and 5 – Green (being positive);
*** Likert Scale -2, -1, 0, 1 and 2: -2- Red (being negative) and 2 – Green (being positive).

It was difficult to find clear-cut assessments on some factors. For example, in seven of the 34 cases, methods for measuring the performance targets could not be identified in the contract project specifications. In a number of other cases, there were not any penalties for noncompliance specified in the contract. Furthermore, some cases lacked information on maintenance standards and agreements on risk transfer.

Discussion

In the road sector, especially in the countries where the economic situation has had a negative influence on private partners' finance (for example, the Ionia and Olympia Odos Motorway in Greece) the PPP performance indicators are found to be critically evaluated throughout the entire project. In the mentioned projects we evidenced within the tender process a small number of bidders and delays from the beginning of tender notice to financial close. In the contract, project specification performance targets were weakly marked, methods of measuring performance targets were not defined and procedures for amendments were very long, because of the national rules: each contract was ratified by parliament, so every change has to follow national law-changing procedures. All these facts resulted in long renegotiation processes, the construction phase was suspended, finance was not available when needed, project cash flow was not sufficient. All together it was evaluated that projects have not resulted in financial benefits to users.

In his study, Chan (2010) has identified 18 CSFs that make a PPP successful, which were then categorised into five main elements of success, i.e. stable macro-economic environment; shared responsibility between public and private sectors; transparent and efficient procurement process; stable political and social environment; and judicious government. However, during the case analysis for COST TU1001, it was apparent in the selected cases that three elements were absent as success categories, i.e., an unstable macroeconomic environment, no shared responsibility (renegotiation on 2013 increased governmental participation) and an unstable political and social environment (renegotiation procedure lasted from 2010-2013).

A stable macro-economic, political and institutional environment is a key factor for PPP success. Mahalingam and Kapur (2009) state that political willingness proves to be a key environment factor to determine whether PPP will survive in the long term. An institutional environment becomes more mature under the influence of positive political willingness and a clear rationale, which pushes towards increased public capacity to identify, award and govern projects (Matos Castaño 2011). This increased public capacity allows governments to develop other institutional capabilities such as predictability, public and private sector commitment, and risk allocation mechanisms. Moreover, in mature environments, governments understand the importance of planning and procurement for PPP project success and, therefore, they maximise efforts in these stages of project development. For this reason, problems tend to be less severe in these stages of PPP projects in more mature institutional environments.

In many cases (for example, Ionia Odos Motorway and Olympia Odos Motorway, Radial 2 Highway and Eje Aerpuerto Motorway, Brabo 1, London Underground and Horgos Pozega Motorway) financial risks are shown to be the strongest factor for the project success/failure, especially the 'debt servicing risk' in Greek and Spanish cases. Because of that, also 'site risk' as delay of completion and failure to meet performance criteria, and 'revenue risk' could be exposed. Matos Castaño (2011) concluded that trustworthy risk and financing mechanisms shorten negotiations for planning and procurement and foster private sector commitment during project development. However, strict financial requirements might also obstruct private sector capacity enhancement.

From the tendering process of the cases, we found that a small number of bidders have not influenced the success of the project if the other parameters were positively measured (i.e. the Caen case) but, combined with delays and legal disputes, the success or failure depends on a strong public partner and political will, like in Portugal, Poland and Albania. It is also noted that Roumboutsos and Sciancalepore (2014) found, based on transaction cost theory, that depending on bidder entry costs, the optimum number of bidders in a competitive market cannot be greater than three.

For the element of 'contract project specification' (see Table 13.4) in most cases deliverables are clearly specified, partners' roles and responsibilities are clearly defined, and minimum standards are specified. In terms of performance, performance targets were highly evaluated only in 67 per cent of projects. Further, methods of measuring performance are mentioned only in 53 per cent of projects, while procedures for contract amendments, dispute resolution or termination in some projects differ according to national rules. Thirty eight per cent of the projects have gone through renegotiation processes, and guaranties have been mentioned in almost all cases.

In the cases where performance indicators are mentioned (for example, technical requirements, safety impacts, availability, carriageway performance, supply capacity, delays, operational performance, environmental constrains and, specifically for urban transportation, number of passengers, punctuality, passenger satisfaction, regularity), the indicators are usually measured quantitatively or with the use of technical measurements. For example, sold tickets (for number of passengers), number of trains (for supply capacity), road accidents (as a safety parameter), automatic incident detector system (as a safety parameter), response time (for operational performance), satisfaction of users measured by different surveys (for passenger satisfaction), etc. In the Attika Tollway case in Greece, 35 performance indicators were put on all major factors of operation: traffic management, toll operation, infrastructure maintenance, human resources and violation enforcement.

Bing *et al.* (2005b) states that the opportunity to adopt strategic measures to address project success is best exploited in the early stages of a project. For the 'construction phase' it was found that 30 per cent of the projects have not been completed on time (excluding the ones that are not finished yet), seven per cent were finished a few months before the schedule, and 26 per cent were not completed within the budget. Specifications were changed most in the projects that were delayed. In 50 per cent of cases, penalties for non-compliance were not found.

Regarding monitoring and evaluation of the maintenance stage, the case study analysis shows that annual reports by the concessionaire include no mention of project performance. Usually user satisfaction surveys are conducted in rail and tramway projects.

Conclusion

Usage of PPP procurement methods, especially for infrastructure projects, has increased over the past decades. The adoption of such arrangements enables governments to deliver infrastructure, enabling the growth of the wider economy without impacting upon the public budget. Due to the large and complex nature of the PPP delivery and the project itself, it becomes difficult to gather data from a range of infrastructure projects and study them against a common basis. However, as part of the COST Action TU1001 on PPP, there was a need to scrutinise the different arrangements that different projects have used in procuring infrastructure projects using PPP. Case research has been identified as the best method in fulfilling the aforementioned need. In this study, two case protocols for transport PPP were used to collect data on PPP cases. The empirical part of this study focused on the 'which-way' issues: the key characteristics of the tendering process and the contractual agreement.

Through the case study research, it was found that in mature institutional environments, problems tend to be less severe in the planning and procurement stages of PPP projects. In the cases with small numbers of bidders, with tendering process delays and legal disputes, the success or failure of the project depended on the strong political will of the public partner. Moreover, a stable macro-economic, political and institutional environment is considered a key factor for PPP success. While contract specifications were of a high quality for transport PPP, performance indicators were not always present.

Looking at the CSF analysis, it can be suggested that specifying clear performance targets and methods of measuring in the contract would avoid potentially long (re)negotiation procedures in the future. Performance measurement should include all major factors/elements of PPP operation.

The long-term nature of a PPP, inevitably, make PPP contracts sensitive to a changing economic environment. This results mainly in financing and funding issues. Thus, more research is needed on issues relating to the vulnerable nature of long-term contracts such as PPP on financing and funding issues. This is not only with respect to transport projects, but also for PPP projects in general.

References

Akintoye, A., Beck, M. and Hardcastle, C. (2003) *Public-Private Partnerships: Managing Risks and Opportunities*. Oxford: Blackwell Science

Bing, L., Akintoye, A., Edwards, P. J. and Hardcastle, H. (2005a) 'Critical success factors for PPP/PFI projects in the UK construction industry'. *Construction Management & Economics*, 23(5), pp. 459–471

Bing, L., Akintoye, A., Edwards, P. J. and Hardcastle, H. (2005b) 'The allocation of risk in PPP/PFI projects in UK construction industry'. *International Journal of Project Management*, 23(1), pp. 25–35

Chan, A., Lam, P., Chan, D., Cheung, E. and Ke, Y. (2010) 'Critical success factors for PPP in infrastructure developments: Chinese perspective'. *Journal of Construction Engineering and Management*, 136(5), pp. 484–494

Chung, D., Hensher, D. A. and Rose, J. M. (2010) 'Toward the betterment of risk allocation: investigating risk perceptions of Australian stakeholder groups to Public Private-Partnership toll road projects'. *Research in Transportation Economics*, 30(1), pp. 43–58

Eisenhardt, K. M. (1989) 'Building theories from case study research'. *Academy of Management Review*, 14(4), pp. 532–550

Flyvbjerg, B. (2006) 'Five misunderstandings about case-study research'. *Qualitative Inquiry*, 12(2), pp. 219–245

Galilea, P. and Medda, F. (2010) 'Does the political and economic context influence the success of a transport project?' *Research in Transportation Economics* 30(1), pp. 102–109

Li, B., Akintoye, A., Edwards, P.J. and Hardcastle, C. (2005) 'Critical success factors for PPP/PFI projects in the UK construction industry'. *Construction Management and Economics*, 23(5), pp. 459–471

Mahalingam, A. and Kapur, V. (2009) 'Institutional capacity and governance for PPP projects in India'. LEAD 2009 Conference, South Lake Tahoe, CA, USA. Available online at: www.epossociety.org/LEAD2009/Mahalingham_Kapur.pdf

Matos Castaño, J. (2011) *Impact of the Institutional Environment on the Development of Public Private Partnerships in the Road Sector*. Enschede: Twente University

Mladenovic, G., Vajdic, N., Wundsch, B. and Temeljotov, S. A. (2013) 'Use of key performance indicators for PPP transport projects to meet stakeholders' performance objectives'. *Built Environment Project and Asset Management*, 3(2), pp. 228–249

Qiao, L., Wang, S. Q., Tiong, R. L. K. and Chan T.-S. (2001) 'Framework for critical success factors of BOT projects in China'. *The Journal of Structured Finance*, 7(1), pp. 53–61

Roumboutsos, A. (2010) 'A Ws Contextual Risk Analysis framework: mapping knowledge transfer potential between road and port Public Private Partnerships' in: *CIB Task Group TG72 – Public Private Partnerships*. CIB World Congress, The Lowry, Salford Quays, United Kingdom, (pp. 68–79)

Roumboutsos, A. and Liyanage, L. C. (2013) 'Public Private Partnerships in transport: case study structure' in: A. Roumboutsos, S. Farrell, C. L. Liyanage and R. Macário *Public Private Partnerships in Transport: Trends & Theory (P3T3). COST Action TU 1001 in 2013 Discussion Papers Part II Case Studies* (pp. 11–18). ISBN 978-88-97781-61-5, COST Office, Brussels. Available online at: www.ppptransport.eu

Roumboutsos, A., Farrell, S., Liyanage, C. L. and Macário, R. (Eds) (2013) *COST Action TU1001 Public Private Partnerships in Transport: Trends & Theory P3T3: 2013 Discussion Papers Part II Case Studies*. ISBN 978-88-97781-61-5, COST Office, Brussels. Available online at www.ppptransport.eu

Roumboutsos, A., Farrell, S. and Verhoest, K. (Eds) (2014) *COST Action TU1001 – Public Private Partnerships in Transport: Trends & Theory 2014 Discussion Series:*

Country Profiles & Case Studies. ISBN 978-88-6922-009-8, COST Office, Brussels. Available online at: www.ppptransport.eu

Roumboutsos A., Pellegrino, R., Vanelslander, T. and Macario, R. (2012) 'Risks and risk allocation in transport PPP projects: a literature review' in: A. Roumboutsos and N. Carbonara (Eds) *COST Action TU1001, Public Private Partnerships: Trends & Theory, 2011 Discussion Papers* (pp. 15–41). ISBN 978-88-97781-04-2, COST Office, Brussels. Available online at: www.ppptransport.eu

Roumboutsos, A. and Sciancalepore, F. (2014) 'PPP Tenders: Optimising on Competition'. Transportation Research Board 2014 Annual Meeting, TRR 141489

Taylor, J., Dossick, C. and Garvin, M. (2009) 'Conducting research with case studies' in: *Proceedings of the 2009 Construction Research Congress*. Construction Institute, American Society of Civil Engineers (ASCE), Seattle, WA, Reston, VA, 5–7 April, pp. 1469–1478

Yin, R. K. (2009) *Case Study Research: Design and Methods. Applied Social Research Methods*. Los Angeles, California: Sage Publications

Zhang, Z. (2005) 'Critical success factors for Public-Private Partnerships in infrastructure development'. *Journal of Construction Engineering and Management*, 131(1), pp. 3–14

14 Cross-country analysis of PPPs

The case of urban light rail projects

*Joana Ribeiro, Rui Couchinho, Rosário
Macário and Champika Liyanage*

Introduction

Public Private Partnerships (PPPs) have been increasingly used by governments around the world as a way of funding and promoting public investment, particularly in providing public transport infrastructure. This remains a widespread tendency all over the world and particularly in Europe. As an example, Portugal, France, the United Kingdom (UK) and Belgium currently have vast experience in the PPP infrastructure market, acquired over a few decades. Infrastructure projects are inherently large and complex and absorb a vast amount of resources in terms of time and money. To add to that, and essentially in urban light rail projects involving very complicated relationships among various stakeholder groups such as government, the public, private industry and financial institutions coming together when forming a PPP, compromise and risk will be prevalent, thus requiring better management. The needs and benefits for these groups differ greatly and this can create conflicts, which in turn leads to failure rather than to a successful project. According to Zou *et al.* (2014), the quality of the relationship between the public and private sector has been identified as a key contributor to the success of a PPP project.

If, on the one hand, planning, organising, motivating, influencing, communicating, monitoring and controlling are key management functions truly important for the effective, efficient and cooperative management of urban regeneration projects (such as urban light rail projects), on the other hand, the urban characteristics and context of these specific projects inevitably affect the success of project management and the project itself (Yu and Kwon 2011).

It is important, therefore, to understand which factors will help manage a project better to achieve the project objectives, while bringing value not only to the stakeholders but also to the wider social, economic and environmental contexts.

The purpose of this chapter is to understand the main factors of success. This will be identified in the context of four PPP contracts in urban light rail projects. The selected cases are: the Metro Sul do Tejo (MST) in Lisbon, Portugal; the Transport sur Voie Réservée (TVR) in Caen, France; the Metrolink in Manchester, UK; and the Brabo1 in Antwerp, Belgium.

To understand how the critical success factors (CSFs) are reflected in the case studies, first a brief description of the four case studies regarding identification of stakeholders, along with the type of project and some basic information such as contract duration, contract PPP model and budget, are presented. Then, in the context of *ex-post* analysis, the first step of this work was to identify the conflicts/problems that have occurred in all cases and the respective phase in which they occurred. Risk sharing and risk allocation are also addressed in this work. Finally, CSFs reported in literature are analysed against the four case studies, taking into account the relevant phase and their absence when problematic issues are present.

The chapter is based on research conducted within the framework of COST Action TU1001 – Public Private Partnerships in Transport: Trends and Theory (P3T3). It is composed of this introduction, followed by a literature review section focused on CSFs; the methodology including the case study analysis; findings; their discussion; and it ends with conclusions, limitations and suggestions on the next steps of this research.

Literature review

Critical success factors

The exploration of the factors affecting the success of infrastructure projects has been carried out by many researchers and practitioners. The specific term 'Critical Success Factor (CSF)' refers to an element that is necessary for an organisation or a project to achieve its mission. CSFs are those few things that must go well to ensure success of a project/entity/organisation and, therefore, they represent those managerial or enterprise areas that must be given special and continual attention to bring about high performance. The identification of CSFs is an important step forward to the development of a workable and efficient PPP procurement protocol (Zhang 2005).

There has been much work done in the past to collate CSFs within PPP procedures and in practice to create a comprehensive list that is relevant to all (Qiao *et al*. 2001; Hardcastle *et al*. 2006; Zhang 2005). The critical factors for success are, in many papers, grouped into larger elements that inevitably follow the route of the execution of a project from consideration and inception to the design and construction, and onto operation. Another approach is the categorisation of factors according to political, social, economic and environmental factors that are related to PPPs. This grouping can be extended by including technological, legal and risk factors as well, due to their importance within a wider stakeholder environment. Consideration of these factors for the success of a project is important as they influence the 'project environment'. In a more recent study (Zou *et al*. 2014), CSFs for relationship management in PPP projects were also identified. As mentioned in the introduction section, the idea of this chapter is to highlight the CSFs in the urban light rail context. Regarding urban projects, Yu and Kwon

(2011) identified and confirmed ten CSFs and determined their priority according to the project phase in urban regeneration projects in Korea.

From the literature review, the following table presents a summary of CSFs related to:

1) urban regeneration projects;
2) relationship management (RM) in PPPs;
3) PPP/PFI projects in the construction industry;
4) transport-related (road projects); and
5) project environment.

Not neglecting the importance of the project environment and context, social, cultural, economic and political factors were added in this research, since they are not at all unique to projects and some of these are unpredictable 'no matter how well or comprehensively the projects are planned' (Gow and Morss 1988).

Based on the CSFs identified from theory, the following section presents the methodology used to investigate how those CSFs were reflected on four urban light rail cases in different stages of the project.

Methodology: Case study analysis

Using case study analysis is appropriate when a research addresses either a descriptive question such as 'what happened' or an explanatory question such as 'how or why did something happen' (Yin 2009). Considering that the main research question in this chapter is 'How CSFs reported in literature are reflected in the four case studies', the case study method was considered the best option to develop this research. Creating a study through selected examples can be a useful tool to understand the concepts and decisions involved in the issue. Additionally, this type of research can be used to achieve various research aims such as to provide a description of phenomena, to develop or test a theory, and to explore hypotheses.

Regarding cross-country studies, it is useful to form a class of research methods that involve observation of some subset events of items, in which groups/ entities can be compared at different moments with respect to independent variables/situations. Cross-country data refers to data collected by observing many subjects (firms/entities/organisations in different countries/regions) at the same point of time, or without regard to differences in time.

Hence, the findings presented in this chapter are based on a four-year COST Action TU1001 on Public Private Partnerships in Transport: Trends and Theory (P3T3). The COST Action used an exploratory case study approach in achieving, *inter alia*, the objective of the chapter. The data collection of the case studies was carried out using a detailed template, which included both descriptive and quantitative data (with a Likert-scale). Of the case studies conducted, four cases of urban transport were particularly chosen for this chapter: the Metro Sul do Tejo (MST) in Lisbon, Portugal; the TVR in Caen, France; the Metrolink in

Table 14.1 Summary of CSF from theory

Urban regeneration project in Korea (Yu and Kwon, 2011)	Relationship management in PPPs (Zou et al. 2014)	PPP/PFI projects in the UK construction industry (Li et al. 2005)		Transport projects (Qiao et al. 2001)	Project environment
Minimisation of conflict between stakeholders.	Commitment and participation of senior executives.	Transparent procurement process.	Strong and good private consortium.	Appropriate project identification.	Stable political and social environment.
Optimisation of legal and administrative services.	Multidisciplinary team responsible for implementation of the RM.	Competitive procurement process.	Favourable legal framework.	Stable political and economic situation.	Transparent and predictable legal framework.
Standardisation of decision-making process.	Defining the value objectives to be achieved with the implementation of the RM strategy.	Good governance.	Government involvement by providing guarantees.	Attractive financial package.	A favourable investment climate.
Good communication and information sharing.	Integration of the different divisions of the organisation so as to meet the general RM objectives of the company and of each of the groups.	Well-organised and committed public agency.	Multi-benefit objectives.	Acceptable toll/tariff levels.	A stable macroeconomic environment.
Reasonability of project master and implementation plans.	Disseminating the objectives, benefits and implications of the project to all the staff.	Social support.	Political support.	Reasonable risk allocation.	Actual existence of transportation infrastructure needs.
Suitability of project management system.	Staff's commitment to the RM strategy.	Shared authority between the public and private sector.	Stable macro-economic conditions.	Selection of suitable subcontractors.	

(Continued)

Table 14.1 Summary of CSF from theory (Continued)

Urban regeneration project in Korea (Yu and Kwon, 2011)	Relationship management in PPPs (Zou et al. 2014)	PPP/PFI projects in the UK construction industry (Li et al. 2005)	Transport projects (Qiao et al. 2001)	Project environment
Establishment of appropriate organisational structure.	Integrating IS for consistency and availability of information related to RM in the organisation.	Thorough and realistic cost/benefits assessment.	Management control.	Sound economic policy.
Cooperativeness of stakeholders on project.	Effective communication approaches/channels between the PPP main parties.	Project technical feasibility.	Technology transfer.	Available financial market.
Performance management at each phase.		Appropriate risk allocation and risk sharing.		Commitment/responsibility of public/private sectors.
Balanced adjustment between the public and the private interests.				

Manchester, UK; and the Brabol in Antwerp, Belgium. This is to maintain consistency and to ensure robust comparison of CSFs as projects similar in context are analysed. The data collected from the case studies were then analysed using the following three-step methodology:

1. identification of conflicts and problems per project phase;
2. risk sharing and allocation;
3. how CSFs reported in literature are reflected in the four case studies.

The three steps are discussed in the following sections, following a brief description of the four case studies.

The analysis

In this section a brief description of the four case studies is presented, followed by the results of each step: 1) conflicts/problems and respective phase; 2) risk sharing and risk allocation; and finally 3) how CSFs reported in literature are reflected in the four case studies.

Case studies description

A brief description of the four case studies regarding identification of stakeholders, along with the type of project and some basic information such as contract duration, contract PPP model and budget, are given below in Table 14.2.

The **Metro Sul do Tejo (MST)** in the Lisbon region is a brownfield and a greenfield project. It is indeed an urban regeneration project since, besides the light rail transit (LRT) itself, it comprises the complete renovation of roads and public spaces, including the construction of corridors for buses and private vehicles, wider pavements, parking lots, street furniture and new water drainage. The agreement between the Government and MST is a Design, Build, Operate, Finance and Maintain (DBOFM) contract where MST develops its activity under concession, for the design, construction, equipment supply and rolling stock, financing, operation, maintenance and upkeep of the entire network of light rail at the south bank of the Tagus (Macário *et al.* 2013; Tavares 2012).

The **TVR** in Caen is also a brownfield and a greenfield project, comprising the construction of a guided tyre tramway system and operation of the entire urban public network of Caen city and metropolitan area. This project lies at the very heart of Caen's public transport regeneration. New routes have also been set up, including three east-west routes that cross the TVR Caen axis, two inter-district services, local routes and two express routes providing a direct link between Caen city centre and some of the nearby towns. With respect to contractual obligations, the concessionaire is responsible for the design, financing, building, operation and maintenance of the TVR Caen system; operation of the overall urban transport network (TVR Caen LRT and buses); and maintenance and renewal of assets allocated to public service. In addition, at the end of the concession period, the

Table 14.2 Brief description of case studies

Case studies	MST	TVR	Metrolink	Brabo 1
Country	Portugal	France	UK	Belgium
Type of project	Brownfield and greenfield.	Brownfield and greenfield.	Brownfield and greenfield. Phase 1: 15, Phase 2: 17, Phase 3: 10.	Greenfield.
Contract duration (years)	30	30		35
Budget	284 M€ (construction), 55M€ (rolling stock and ticketing equipment).	230 M€ (construction).	GBP 1,000 M.	125 M€ (design and build).
PPP model	DBOFM[1]	DBFOT[2]	DBOM[3]/DBFO[4]	DBFM[5]
Stakeholders	**Public** Portuguese government; Municipalities of Almada, Seixal and Barreiro; Refer; IMTT (now IMT) **Private** SPV MST **Final users**	**Public** French government; Municipality of Caen; SMTCAC (now Viacités) – Syndicat Mixte des Transports en Commun de l'Agglomération **Private** STVR – Société des Transport sur Voie Réservée **Final users**	**Public** British government; GMPTE – Greater Manchester Transport Executive **Private** TfGM – Transport for Greater Manchester RATP – Régie Autonome des Transports Parisiens **Final users**	**Public** Flemish Government; City of Antwerp; **Private** SPV Brabo 1 **Final users and citizens**

1 DBOFM: Design, Build, Operate, Finance and Maintain
2 DBFOT: Design, Build, Finance, Operate and Transfer
3 DBOM: Design, Build, Operate and Maintain
4 DBFO: Design, Build, Finance and Operate
5 DBFM: Design, Build, Finance and Maintain

TVR Caen project is to be transferred back to the responsible public authority – SMTCAC (Bonnet and Chomat 2013).

Again, the **Metrolink** in Manchester is also a brownfield and greenfield project. The system uses in part the existing suburban heavy rail infrastructure, creating a specific LRT corridor. The purpose of the Metrolink is to link the northern and the southern suburbs in which the vast majority of population live and where the commercial and leisure areas of the city are located (Villalba-Romero and Liyanage 2014). Metrolink is a PPP between TfGM and private transport firms and has used different types of contract in its three phases. In phase 1 there was a 15-year DBOM concession contract. Between 1992 and 2007 Metrolink was operated and maintained as a concession by Serco Group. Phase 2 was also a DBOM concession contract of 17 years granted to a new consortium. From 2007 until 2011 it was operated and maintained by Altram, a consortium including John Laing, Serco and Ansaldo Trasporti. In phase 3, an operating and maintenance 10-year contract, along with a separate design and built public procurement contract, was established.

The **Brabo 1** in Antwerp, which is a greenfield project, was the first PPP for public transport in the Flanders region. The project involved the design, financing, construction and maintenance of the civil, mechanical and electrical infrastructure associated with two separate tramway extensions in the eastern part of the Antwerp city: the Antwerp-Deume section was extended to Wijnegem and the Antwerp-Mortsel section was extended to Boechout. Both trajectories were extended for a comprehensive renewal of all associated street infrastructure (including pavements and street furniture) for motor traffic, cyclists and pedestrians. A substantial stabling and maintenance depot, located on one of the lines, was also included (van den Hurk and Van Gestel 2013). It is also a case of urban regeneration.

First step: Identification of conflicts/problems and respective phase

As mentioned before, CSFs in PPPs are important elements for the development of any project. CSFs should be identified at two different moments of the life cycle: *ex-ante* and *ex-post* the contractual award. The *ex-post* form is the most common approach and seeks, following the conclusion of the contract, to identify which factors could have influenced the observed results. On the other hand, the *ex-ante* form is the exercise of anticipating contractual clauses able to guarantee the control of expected risks, barriers and other failures. These two moments represent different approaches and both originate from the antagonistic relation between risk, barriers, failures and success in any project. Either by contractual elaboration, reform or review, the identification of success factors starts with the possible or real conflicts/problems in the project. Therefore, in the context of *ex-post* analysis, the first step of this work is to identify the conflicts/problems that have occurred in all cases and the respective phase they occurred in. For the four cases studied these issues are presented in Table 14.3.

Table 14.3 Identification of conflicts/problems for the case studies and respective phase

Project	Conflict/problem	Phase
MST	**A.1 Risk Allocation:** The concession model of the MST is established in traffic bands for financial feasibility of the project, where the Government assumes much of the central risk in this concession. Demand risk has had a major impact due to optimistic forecasts, and has materialised into large compensations to be paid by the Portuguese State to the private partner.	Contract and Operation Phase.
	A.2 Communication problems: A renegotiation process motivated by delay in construction was initiated in 2004 and resulted in a financial rebalancing agreement that entitles MTS, S.A. to a 77,5 M€ compensation (between CMA and Portuguese State).	Construction Phase.
	A.3 No economic viability: With the current tariff and under contractually defined terms, the economic viability of the MST is only possible with the support of the State, since the tariffs are 'social', which does not support the operating and financial costs of the project.	Operation Phase.
	A.4 Poor contract management: The current model of management does not follow any best practices or use important management tools, compromising the objectives and VfM.	Operation and Maintenance Phase.
	A.5 Asymmetry of information: Dispersion of functions and responsibilities of the public party (IMTT, GMST and REFER) resulting in asymmetry of information between the public and private partners since, in the renegotiation process, it was difficult to adopt solutions that safeguard the public interest.	Operation and Maintenance Phase.
TVR Caen	**B.1 Delay in tender call:** The TVR Caen project was conceived in 1998. However the tender call only opened 5 years after; the second tendering process had some delay linked to political changes in the municipality of Caen.	Tender Phase.
	B.2 Technical problems: The project was appointed as rather a failure, even if traffic is in compliance with the forecast, due to a lot of technical problems.	Maintenance Phase.
	B.3 End of contract: Two concession contracts were put to an end (20 years in advance) by the decision of the public part.	Operation Phase.

Metrolink	**C.1 Discussion about alternatives:** 10 years' delay from project conception to construction phase	Project conception.
	C.2 Schemes costs: After a national Audit Office report, the government revised the costs as those of schemes such as the Metrolink increased.	Operation Phase.
	C.3 Termination of the 2nd concession and increase in fares: Robust demand allowed operator (in phase 2) to raise fares significantly. Some critics speculated that it was an attempt to 'price off' demand and avoid additional purchases of rolling stock. However, GMPTA sought to maximise ridership. The conflicting objectives contributed to the concession's eventual termination.	Operation Phase.
	C.4 Costs overruns: Design, construction and maintenance risks are supposed to be totally private but, in practice, private party asks for additional compensation.	Design and Construction and Maintenance Phases.
Brabo 1	**D.1 Financial economic crisis in 2008:** This event delayed the procurement process. As bidders failed to find the required external financing for their best and final offers, tendering procedure stood still for approximately six months.	Tender Phase.
	D.2 Lawsuit by one of the bidders: Another postponement-inducing event was a lawsuit that was filed by one of the bidders (TRAVANT), with legal challenges to outcome, as it was excluded unfairly from the tender procedure. There has also been contestation on behalf of local politicians.	Tender Phase.
	D.3 Delay in construction due to citizens' complaints: For a certain period of time, the construction of the Brabo 1 project was stopped. A full judicial procedure had to be followed in order to continue the works again, and this has led to some extra costs.	Construction Phase.

Second step: Risk sharing and risk allocation

Risk sharing analysis is a systematic assessment of the decision variables that are subject to risk and uncertainty. This analysis comprises the establishment of probabilities of occurrences of adverse events, the setting of assumptive bounds to associated uncertainties, and the management of the potential impact of risk event outcomes (Edwards and Bowen 1998). The objective of such analysis is to capture all feasible options and to analyse various outcomes of any decision. The risk allocation option enables parties to optimise the management of each risk factor associated with a PPP project. In the allocation of PPP risk factors, the main issues that need to be considered are the nature and size of the risk, and their impact on each of the stakeholders of the project (Li *et al.* 2004).

According to Grimsey and Lewis (2005), the risks should be allocated to the party that can manage them more efficiently at a lower cost. Furthermore, the risk-sharing agreement should be an incentive for the private party to be more efficient (Kwak *et al.* 2009). This agreement is not easy since each project is unique and, therefore, there is not a standard approach to risk allocation that can be applied to all projects. Usually, in PPP arrangements, the public sector transfers risks to the private sector for more efficient management of costs since the private sector has an incentive to manage risks as efficiently and innovatively as possible in order to control costs (Bracey and Moldovan 2007). Risk allocation is therefore a means to give appropriate incentives for the private partner to perform according to the contract terms, achieving value for money (World Bank 2007). Risk allocation strategies in PPPs will depend on the context and the project, but general principles can be found in the literature recommending that risks external to the project should be borne by the public partner, while the private partner bears the risks related to the project, and that the remaining risks, uncontrollable by either partner, be shared (Froud 2003; Ng and Loosemore 2007, cited by Kwak *et al.* 2009).

Regarding risk sharing, a cross-case comparative analysis is presented in the Table 14.4. The risks identified are categorised into design and construction, maintenance, exploitation, commercial/revenue, financial, regulatory and force Majeure.

Table 14.4 Risk sharing of the four case studies

Risks	MST	TVR Caen	Metrolink	Brabo 1
Design and Construction	Private	Private	Private	Private
Maintenance	Private	Private	Private	Shared
Exploitation	Public	Private	Private	Public
Commercial / Revenue	Private	Private	Shared	Public
Financial	Public	Private	Public	Shared
Regulatory	Public	Public	Public	Public
Force Majeure	Public	Public	Public	Shared

Third step: How CSFs reported in literature are reflected in the four case studies

Given the discussions in the previous sections, Table 14.5 summarises how CSFs reported in the literature are reflected in the four case studies. The analysis takes into account the relevant phases of the CSFs and where the issues identified were present or absent.

Discussion

Based on the three steps discussed above and the findings of the case study analysis presented in Table 14.5, this section discusses the results for each project.

MST

The first identified problem in the MST case was an inappropriate risk allocation decided in the contract. However, this was only perceived during the operation phase. The MST concession contract was defined through traffic bands for financial feasibility of the project, where the Government assumed much of the central risk. In this case, the private party assumed the risk of construction, and should also have assumed the full risk of passenger traffic associated with the operation of the service, which did not happen in this contract. This occurrence leads to no incentive efficiency on the part of the contract private party. Moreover, demand risk has had a major impact due to optimistic forecasts, and has materialised as large compensations to be paid by the Portuguese State to the private partner.

Another problem was a renegotiation process motivated by delay in construction. The discovery of archaeological remains and changes imposed by the public party to the track layout caused delays, which led to the renegotiation of the contract resulting in high costs to the public party. A disagreement between the government and the Municipality of Almada aggravated the situation. In this conflict several types of CSFs were visible, such as the urban regeneration, PPP, RM and environment-related.

The three other identified problems were during the Operation and Maintenance phases. One of them was related to tariff levels. With the current tariff and under contractually defined terms, the economic viability of the MST is only possible with the support of the State, since the tariffs are considered social, which does not support the operating and financial costs of the project. Moreover, the current model of management does not follow any best practices or use important management tools, compromising the objectives of the project and the value for money.

Furthermore, there is a dispersion of functions and responsibilities on the part of public bodies such as IMTT, the GMST and REFER, which resulted in difficulties in adopting solutions that safeguard the public interest, both in the renegotiation and in the asymmetry of information between the public and private partners. It should also be noted that public entities do not provide data regarding

Table 14.5 How CSFs from theory are reflected in the four case studies

Phase	Conflict/ problem	CSF	Type	Ref.
Project conceiving	C.1	Thorough and realistic cost/benefits assessment	PPP/PFI	(Li et al., 2005)
Tender Phase	B.1	Political support	PPP/PFI	(Li et al., 2005)
		Stable political and social environment	Project environment	
	D.1	Stable macro-economic conditions; Available financial market	PPP/PFI	(Li et al., 2005)
		Stable political and economic situation	Transport	(Qiao et al., 2001)
		A stable macroeconomic environment; A favorable investment climate; Stable political and social environment	Project environment	
Contract Phase	D.2	Transparency procurement process	PPP/PFI	(Li et al., 2005)
	A.1	Appropriate risk allocation and risk sharing; Government involvement by providing guarantees	PPP/PFI	(Li et al., 2005)
		Appropriate project identification; Reasonable risk allocation	Transport	(Qiao et al., 2001)
		Actual existence of transportation infrastructure needs	Project environment	(Li et al., 2005)
Design Phase	C.4	Appropriate risk allocation and risk sharing; Government involvement by providing guarantees	PPP/PFI	(Li et al., 2005)
		Reasonable risk allocation	Transport	(Qiao et al., 2001)
Construction Phase	A.2	Minimisation of conflict between stakeholders; Good communication and information sharing; Reasonability of project master and implementation plans; Cooperativeness of stakeholders on project; Balanced adjustment between the public and the private interests;	Urban regeneration	(Yu & Kwon, 2011)
		Integration of the different divisions of the organisation so as to meet the general RM objectives of the company and of each of the division/groups; Effective communication approaches/channels between the PPP main parties	Relationship management	(Zou et al., 2014)
		Commitment/responsibility of public/private sectors	PPP/PFI	(Li et al., 2005)
		Stable political and social environment	Project environment	
	C.4	See above		
	D.3	Minimisation of conflict between stakeholders	Urban regeneration	(Yu & Kwon, 2011)
		Social support	PPP/PFI	(Li et al., 2005)
		Appropriate project identification	Transport	(Qiao et al., 2001)

Phase	Code	Critical success factor	Project environment	References
Operation & Maintenance Phase	A.1	Stable political and social environment See above		
	A.3	Acceptable toll/tariff levels	Transport Urban regeneration	(Qiao et al., 2001) (Yu & Kwon, 2011)
	A.4	Suitability of project management system; Performance management at each phase	Relationship management	(Zou et al., 2014)
	A.5	Integration of the different divisions of the organisation so as to meet the general RM objectives of the company and of each of the division/groups Management control Good communication and information sharing	Transport Urban regeneration Relationship management	(Qiao et al., 2001) (Yu & Kwon, 2011) (Zou et al., 2014)
	B.2	Integrating Information Systems for consistency and availability of information related to RM in the organization Well-organised and committed public agency Performance management at each phase	PPP/PFI Urban regeneration PPP/PFI	(Li et al., 2005) (Yu & Kwon, 2011) (Li et al., 2005)
	B.3	Project technical feasibility; Appropriate risk allocation and risk sharing; Strong and good private consortium Technology transfer Minimisation of conflict between stakeholders; Cooperativeness of stakeholders on project; Balanced adjustment between the public and the private interests	Transport Urban regeneration	(Qiao et al., 2001) (Yu & Kwon, 2011)
	C.2	Political support Reasonable risk allocation	PPP/PFI Transport	(Li et al., 2005) (Qiao et al., 2001)
	C.3	Acceptable toll/tariff levels	Transport	(Qiao et al., 2001)
	C.4	Minimisation of conflict between stakeholders; Cooperativeness of stakeholders on project; Balanced adjustment between the public and the private interests; See above	Urban regeneration	(Yu & Kwon, 2011)

this contract, which shows that the obligation of transparency to the citizens is not being met in the best way (Tavares 2012).

TVR

The first identified problem in the TVR case was a delay in the tender call. The TVR Caen project was conceived in 1998, however the tender call only opened five years later. Moreover, it should be noted that the second tendering process had some delays linked to political changes in the municipality of Caen. For some time there was some uncertainty about the realisation of the project, although in the end it went ahead (*Chambre régionale des comptes*, 2004). The critical aspect here was due to the lack of a stable political environment.

During the operation phase, at the end of 2011, there was an announcement by the public body regarding its intention to conclude the agreement in advance. Although the traffic is in compliance with the forecast, the project was determined to be rather a failure, since there were many technical problems and, as a consequence, the concession contracts were brought to an end by the decision of the public party. Here, again, there was not an appropriate risk allocation, since it was the private partner who totally assumed the innovation risks. In the end, the quality of the relationship between public and private sector was the key contributor to the success (or in this case failure) of a PPP project, as Zou *et al.* (2014) conclude.

Metrolink

Regarding Metrolink, it took 10 years from project conception to the construction phase. During this period there was discussion about alternatives, which suggest that a thorough and realistic cost/benefits assessment was developed. Despite this, costs overruns occurred in the design and construction and maintenance phases. Those risks were supposed to be totally private (see Table 14.4) but, in practice, the private party asked for additional compensation from the State. Contrasting this situation, during the operation phase, the government revised the costs as those of schemes such as the Metrolink increased, after a national Audit Office report. This is intimately linked with an appropriate risk allocation, since the risks related to unilateral decisions are private. The private partner is not the party who can best manage this, since it has no power over government decisions. Moreover, a robust demand allowed the operator (in phase 2) to raise fares significantly. Some critics speculated that it was an attempt to 'price off' demand and avoid additional purchases of rolling stock. However, GMPTA sought to maximise ridership. The conflicting objectives contributed to the concession's eventual termination, suggesting two critical factors: acceptable tariffs, and cooperation and trust between stakeholders.

Despite these conflicts and problems, the Metrolink is seen as a resounding success as measured by usage, performance and also by the adoption of the PPP model. Phases 2, 3, 4-6 are perceived to increase the regional GDP by 259m GBP and, nowadays, the Metrolink has been referenced as a profitable model.

Brabo 1

In the case of Brabo 1, there were two conflicts/problems during the tender phase. The first one was triggered by financial crisis in 2008. This event delayed the procurement process, as bidders failed to find the required external financing for their best and final offers. Consequently, the tendering procedure stood still for approximately six months. Here, the lack of a stable macroeconomic environment as well as a favourable investment climate and a stable political and social environment were the main critical factors. Moreover, another postponement-inducing event in this phase was a lawsuit that was filed by one of the bidders (TRAVANT), with legal challenges to outcome, as it was excluded unfairly from the tender procedure. This situation suggests a lack of a transparent procurement process as well as the lack of trust between stakeholders.

The last problem identified in the Brabo 1 case was a delay during the construction phase. For a certain period of time, the construction of the Brabo 1 project stopped due to citizens' complaints. A full judicial procedure had to be followed in order to continue the works again, and this has led to some extra costs. This situation suggests the lack of some critical success factors such as minimisation of conflict between stakeholders, as well as the lack of the support of the community, which leads us to think that there was not an appropriate project identification process (at earlier stages) and a bad decision process.

According to Yu and Kwon (2011), 'minimization of conflict between stakeholders' is the most crucial CSF, implying that considerable management effort should be exerted for the analysis and prevention of potential conflicts, which seems to be the case in Brabo 1. Moreover, another conclusion of the study of Yu and Kwon (2011) was that the earlier phases of an urban regeneration project deserve more managerial efforts for overall project success, which is also the case in Brabo 1 where the main conflicts occurred during the tender phase. Although those conflicts and the official reports are not publicly available, the Brabo 1 project is generally considered a success, also in the current operational phase.

Among the CSFs, a common problem seems to have been repeated in the four cases. This was relating to the interaction and the relationships of the stakeholders, especially between the government and different stakeholders. The CSFs identified in the four case studies of this study are not all exclusively for PPP projects but, according to De Schepper *et al.* (2014), the stakeholder environment of a PPP becomes more complex to manage compared with the context of traditional public infrastructure projects.

It is interesting to note that the more balanced risk allocation between the public and private partners presented in the Metrolink and Brabo 1 cases resulted in more success than the unbalanced risk allocation presented in MST and TVR cases (see Table 14.4).

Conclusions

The main objective of this chapter was to understand how CSFs from theory were reflected in four PPPs in the context of urban light rail sector in different countries. Five CSFs related to 1) urban regeneration; 2) RM in PPP; 3) PPP/PFI; 4) transport and 5) environment context were considered in this work.

Among the CSFs, three main groups of CSFs have appeared in the case studies:

- **Poor stakeholder interaction.** This was relating to the interaction and the relationships of the actors, especially between the government and different stakeholders. The CSFs identified in the four case studies of this study are not all exclusively for PPP projects but, according to De Schepper *et al.* (2014), the stakeholder environment of a PPP becomes more complex to manage compared with the context of traditional public infrastructure projects. Moreover, urban regeneration projects have a higher possibility of uncertainty and complexity than other construction projects. According to Yu and Kwon (2011), 'minimization of conflict between stakeholders' is the most crucial CSF, implying that considerable management effort should be exerted for the analysis and prevention of potential conflicts. Another conclusion of this study was that the earlier phases of an urban regeneration project deserve more managerial efforts for overall project success. This was the case in Brabo 1 as most of the CSFs appeared during the tender phase. The main CSFs during the construction and operation and maintenance phases were not related to the PPP model of delivery, but to conflicts resulting from the normal urban life such as construction works or cost of expropriation.
- **Inappropriate risk allocation.** Indeed, the main CSFs of a PPP are the appropriate risk allocation, transparency and a competitive and efficient procurement process. It is interesting to note that Metrolink and Brabo 1 are the only cases where a more balanced risk allocation between the public and private partners had occurred, resulting in more success than in the MST and TVR cases. In the latter two cases the risk allocation was unbalanced and not appropriate. According to Grimsey and Lewis (2005), the risks should be allocated to the party that can manage them more efficiently at a lower cost. Furthermore, the risk-sharing agreement should be an incentive for the private party to be more efficient (Kwak *et al.* 2009), which did not happen in the cases of MST and TVR.
- **Unstable context in terms of political, social and economic situation.** In all cases, with the exception of Metrolink, some factors related to project context were identified. In the case of Brabo 1, it was particularly visible that the problems (for example, complaints from the public) have occurred during the financial crisis in 2008. In this case, it shows that the project environment and context, especially in terms of social, cultural, economic and political factors, are not at all unique to projects and some of these are unpredictable 'no matter how well or comprehensively the projects are planned' (Gow and Morss 1988).

Apart from the aforementioned critical factors, there were also conflicts between stakeholders that are not all exclusively for PPP project context. However, managing stakeholders of a PPP project is more complex and complicated compared with the context of traditional public infrastructure projects. Another important factor was related to the context of the case study itself with regard to their relevant political, economic and financial aspects.

It is worthwhile adding more urban light rail projects to the aforementioned analysis to come up with an extended comparative analysis and to deduce further conclusions. Also, further research is needed within the context of CSFs to understand the behaviour of these CSFs, not only within urban rail but also within other modes of transport.

Acknowledgments

We would like to thank Gilles Chomat from CERTU for his availability during the development of this work. We would also like to thank COST Action TU001 Chair, Professor Athena Roumboutsos for her continuous support and encouragement. We would also like to thank Dr Champika Liyanage, the host of our COST Action Short Term Scientific Mission, for the opportunity to exchange knowledge during our stay in University of Central Lancashire, Preston, UK in May 2013.

References

Bonnet, G. and Chomat, G. (2013) 'The Caen' TVR, France' in: A. Roumboutsos, S. Farrel, C. L. Liyanage and R. Macário (Eds) (2013) *COST action TU1001 – 2013 Discussion Chapters: Part II Case Studies.* COST Office, Brussels

Bracey, N. and Moldovan, S. (2007) 'Public-Private Partnerships: risks to the public and private sector'. Communication to The Louis Berger Group, Inc. 6th Global Conference on Business and Economics, Boston, Massachusetts. 2006

Court of Auditors (2011). *Auditoria de Seguimento à Concessão Metro Sul do Tejo.* Report no. 22/2011

De Schepper, S., Dooms, M. and Haezendonck, E. (2014) 'Stakeholder dynamics and responsibilities in Public–Private Partnerships: a mixed experience'. *International Journal of Project Management* 32 (2014), pp. 1210–1222

Edwards, P. J. and Bowen, P. A. (1998) 'Risk and risk management in construction: a review and future directions for research'. *Engineering, Construction and Architectural Management* 5(4), pp. 339–349

Eisenhardt, K. M. (1989) 'Building theories from case study research'. *Academy of Management Review*, Vol. 14, No. 4, pp. 532–550

Gow, D. D. and Morss, E. R. (1988) 'The notorious nine: critical problems in project implementation'. *World Development* 16 (12), pp. 1399–1418

Grimsey, D. and Lewis, M. (2005) 'Are Public Private Partnerships value for money? Evaluating alternative approaches and comparing academic and practitioner views'. *Accounting Forum* 4(29 December), pp. 345–78

Hardcastle, C., Edwards, P. J., Akintoye, A. and Li, B. (2006) 'Critical success factors for PPP/PFI projects in the UK construction industry: a factor analysis approach' in T. S. Ng (Ed.) *Public Private Partnerships: Opportunities and Challenges.* Hong Kong: University of Hong Kong, Centre for Infrastructure and Construction Industry Development

Kwak, Y. H., Chih, Y. Y. and Ibbs, C. W. (2009) 'Towards a Comprehensive Understanding of Public Private Partnerships for Infrastructure Development'. *California Management Review*, Vol. 51, No. 2, Winter 2009

Li, B., Akintoye, A. and Hardcastle, C. (2004) *Risk Analysis and Allocation in Public Private Partnership Projects.* Glasgow: Department of Building and Surveying, Glasgow Caledonian University

Li, B., Akintoye, A., Edwards, P. and Hardcastle, C. (2005) 'Critical Success Factors for PPP/PFI projects in the UK construction industry: a factor analysis approach'. *Construction Management and Economics*, 23 (5), pp. 1–9

Macário, R., Couchinho, R., Costa, J. and Ribeiro, J. (2013) 'Cross-sectorial comparative analysis of four transport case studies'. Presented at the international conference Global Challenges in PPP: Cross-sectorial and cross-disciplinary solutions? in Nov 2013

Macário, R., Ribeiro, J. and Couchinho, C. (2013) 'Metro Sul do Tejo, Portugal' in: A. Roumboutsos, S. Farrel, C. L. Liyanage and R. Macário (Eds) (2013). *COST action TU1001 – 2013 Discussion Chapters: Part II Case Studies.* COST Office, Brussels

Qiao, L., Wang, S., Tiong, R. and Chan, T. (2001) 'Framework for Critical Success Factors of BOT projects in China. *The Journal of Project Finance*, 7 (1), pp. 53–61

Rockart, J. F. (1982) 'The changing role of the information systems executive. A Critical Success Factors perspective'. *Sloan Management Review*, 24/1 (Fall 1982), pp. 3–13

Tavares, S. (2012) *Gestão de Contratos em Parceria Público – Privada.* Masters Thesis from Instituto Superior Técnico, Universidade de Lisboa, Portugal

UTAP (2012) *Relatório Anual das PPP – 2012.* Unidade Técnica de Acompanhamento de Projetos. Ministério das Finanças, Portugal

van den Hurk, M. and Van Gestel, K. (2013) 'Brabo 1, Flanders, Belgium' in: A. Roumboutsos, S. Farrel, C. L. Liyanage and R. Macário (Eds) (2013) *COST action TU1001 – 2013 Discussion Chapters: Part II Case Studies.* COST Office, Brussels

Verhoest, K., Carbonara, N., Lember, V., Petersen, O. H., Scherrer, W. and Hurk, M. V. D. (2013) *Public Private Partnerships in Transport: Trends and Theory P3T3, 2013 Discussion Chapters Part I Country Level.* COST Office, Brussels

Villalba-Romero, F. and Liyanage, C. (2014) 'Metrolink Light Rail Transport, Manchester United Kingdom' in: A. Roumboutsos, S. Farrel and K. Verhoest (Eds) (2014) *COST action TU1001 – 2014 Discussion Chapters Country Profiles and Case Studies.* COST Office, Brussels

World Bank (2007) *Best Practices on Contract Design in Public-Private Partnerships.* Report prepared for the World Bank by Iossa, E., Spagnolo, G. and Vellez, M.

Yin, R. K. (2009) *Case Study Research: Design and Methods* (4th Ed.), *Applied Social Research Methods V.5.* London: Sage Publications Inc.

Yu, J. H. and Kwon, H. R. (2011) 'Critical success factors for urban regeneration projects in Korea'. *International Journal of Project Management*, 29 (2011), pp. 889–899

Zhang, X. Q. (2005) 'Critical Success Factors for the Public Private Partnerships in infrastructure development'. *Journal of Construction Engineering and Management*, 131/1 (January 2005), pp. 3–14

Zou, W., Kumaraswamy, M., Chung, J. and Wong, J. (2014) Identifying the critical success factors for relationship management in PPP projects. *International Journal of Project Management*, 32 (2014), pp. 265–274

15 Measuring success in PPP road projects in Europe

A performance measurement system (PMS)

Champika Liyanage, Stanley Njuangang and Felix Villalba-Romero

Introduction

There are many studies carried out that aim to search for the most appropriate approach to conceptualise and measure the success of Public Private Partnership (PPP) projects in infrastructure. The concept of a project success is commonly referred to in the academic literature as broad criteria including diverse Critical Success Factors (CSFs), and the way to measure the criteria usually includes diverse elements known as Key Performance Indicators (KPIs). Although analysis of success could vary according to the type of sector and class of project, there is no clear consensus about the method of measuring the success of projects using KPIs.

Many authors define project success in different ways. Ashley *et al.* (1987) describe project success as 'achieving results much better than expected or normally observed in terms of cost, schedule, quality, safety, and participant satisfaction'. Shenhar *et al.* (1997) indicate that project success should be perceived as major vehicles for organisational and societal prosperity. Shaoul *et al.* (2007) conclude that success should be determined at a micro level in terms of technical achievements, but that social and financial objectives should also be considered. Likewise, defining the 'success' of a project can differ according to the different contextual factors of a project. It takes on more of a subjective form depending on what someone wants to look at in a project. For example, a project can be successful in terms of achieving cost targets, however it may be unsuccessful in the view of time targets. Similarly, a project can be successful from a private partner point of view but it may not be a success from a user's perspective.

A project has traditionally been considered successful when it has satisfactorily met the 'iron triangle' measures: time – finished on time; cost – within budget; and quality – finished according to specifications (Atkinson 1999; Khosravi and Afshari 2011); or a good combination of these measures (Phua 2004). Nguyen *et al.* (2004) have measured the success of a project using this traditional approach, but they also include the measurement of project development in accordance with stakeholders' satisfaction. Furthermore, Savindo *et al.* (1992) base the success of the project on the achievement of expectations of different stakeholders, such as the owner, the planner and engineers, the constructor or the operator; introducing, therefore, the participants' requirements. Authors such as Pinto and Slevin (1988) and Bryde and Brown (2005) also identify the main element of project success as the satisfaction of the stakeholders. Cox *et al.* (2003), however, have evaluated project success based on contract specification; not only technical specifications but also other quantitative measures. On the other hand, Freeman and Beale (1992) and Toor and Ogunlana (2008) have identified process performance (efficiency and effectiveness of different processes involved in a project) as the main criteria of project success. Likewise, there are many other researchers who have identified different ways and means of measuring project success either in general, or specifically with regard to PPP (Aziz 2007; Takim and Adnan 2008; Takim *et al.* 2004; Li *et al.* 2005; Farinde and Sillars 2012; Zhang 2005; Chan 2001).

Although attempts such as those above remain, according to Hodge and Greve (2007) strong and independent evaluation of PPP has been sparse. As Hodge and Greve further affirm, it appears that insufficient research has been undertaken to be fully informed on the outcome of the PPP to date. Thus, there is a serious need for a rigorous assessment of PPP. Therefore, the main purpose of this chapter is to fill this gap by presenting a robust assessment of the success of PPP. This assessment is presented as a Performance Measurement System (PMS) and the PMS is tested using 13 selected case studies. The selected case studies have been taken from the case database of the P3T3 COST TU1001 action *Public Private Partnership in Transport: Trend and Theory* networking project.

Assessment of success – A performance measurement system (PMS)

The assessment of the success of PPP projects is carried out in this chapter using a performance measurement system. It is presented using a step-by-step approach as discussed below:

Step 1: Use of a case study approach;
Step 2: Case descriptions;
Step 3: Development of the KPIs and performance measures (PMs);
Step 4: Three-stage Delphi approach to refine and prioritise the KPIs and PMs;
Step 5: Assigning mean zones (M);
Step 6: Filling in the KPIs table;
Step 7: Calculation of the weighted score (WS);
Step 8: Calculating the overall level of performance;
Step 9: Interpretation of the performance results.

These steps are discussed in detail in the subsequent sections.

Step 1: Use of a case study approach

According to Yin (2009), case studies are the preferred research strategy when, 'a "how" or "why" question is being asked about a contemporary set of events, over which the investigator has little or no control'. Taylor *et al.* (2009) suggest that case study research should attempt to achieve depth by including multiple, polar cases and including multiple, analytically similar cases. What is achieved through this approach is the element of verification or testing of theory as it shifts from deductive to inductive, or the need to apply replication logic (Eisenhardt 1989). Considering the main research question of this chapter, 'how to measure success in transport projects?', there was a need to adopt an exploratory approach with the use of in-depth case study research. The present work draws on that of Yin (2009) and Voss *et al.* (2002).

The case study methodology used a template developed by P3T3 COST Action (TU1001), which included questions ranging from actors and project specifics to performance monitoring (please refer to Chapter 11). Primary data for this study are obtained from these filled (descriptive) templates. The case study templates have been completed using both semi-structured interviews and secondary data. Secondary data was widely available on the web and some information was collected from related project reports. Overall, 13 PPP road projects were chosen for the analysis of success. Choosing a particular type/mode of project makes the cross-case analysis and synthesis consistent, reliable and valid. All the selected road projects represent the most prominent development in their respective countries. The choice of countries (UK, Spain, Greece, Portugal, Belgium and the Netherlands) where these case studies operate were also an added advantage to maintain consistency and reliability. All the countries selected are considered as 'active' users of the model of PPP. Other than the case studies selected, there were four other road projects in the P3T3 case study database. However, these were not taken into consideration due to incompleteness of the templates. The 13 projects selected for the success analysis are:

1. The Coen Tunnel, Netherlands;
2. M6 Toll Road, UK;
3. M80 Haggs, UK;
4. A19 Dishforth, UK;
5. Via-Invest Zaventem, Belgium;
6. A-23 Beira Interior, Portugal;
7. Olympia Odos Motorway, Greece;
8. Attica Tollway, Greece;
9. Ionia Odos Motorway, Greece;
10. Rio-Antirio Bridge, Greece;
11. Radial 2, Spain;
12. The Eje Aeropuerto Toll Road, M-12, Spain;
13. M-45 Semi Loop Road, Spain.

Brief descriptions of each project are given in the following section.

Step 2: Case study descriptions

The Coen Tunnel (Netherlands) is a combination of both brownfield and greenfield projects. The project involves the maintenance of an existing tunnel (expanding the capacity from two to three lanes in each direction, two reversion lanes and the widening of 14 km of road at the north and south entrance of the tunnel), the construction of a new one alongside the previous one, and construction of some facilities (parking and fuel station) located in the northern conurbation of the Dutch Randstad in The Netherlands. The project is part of a series of infrastructure capacity enlargements to improve access to the main road network. The construction of the project was carried out by five main contractors and a key subcontractor. The PPP agreement is under a Design, Build, Finance and Operate (DBFO) contract. The project is the first project that used the Competitive Dialogue approach in the Netherlands. The concessionaire is the Coen Tunnel Company. They are responsible for the design, construction and maintenance of the tunnel. For more information on Coen Tunnel, please refer to Voordijk (2013).

The M6 Toll Road (UK) was originally called the Birmingham North Relief Road (BNRR). It is a greenfield project that connects M6 Junction 4 at the NEC to M6 Junction 11A at Wolverhampton in the area of Birmingham, UK. This is a six-lane motorway that is 27 miles long (43km). The agreement is a Concession contract, a Build, Operate and Transfer (BOT) model with direct toll, which is often included within the Private Finance Initiative (PFI) in the UK. For more information on the M6 Toll Road, UK, please refer to Boles and Liyanage (2013).

The M80 Haggs (UK) can be considered as a mixed brownfield and greenfield project in the UK. This project forms part of the strategic road network between Glasgow, Stirling and the North East of Scotland. The construction works include around 8km of new dual two-lane motorway and hard shoulders between Stepps and Mollinsburn, the upgrading of 3km of the existing M80 road to three-lane motorways between Mollinsburg and Auchenkilns, and the upgrade to dual two-lane motorway of 7km of the existing A80 between Auchenkilns to Haggs. The agreement is a PPP under a Design, Build, Finance and Operate (DBFO) contract. This was the first and largest project that used the Competitive Dialogue procurement route in Scotland. The concessionaire is Highways Management Ltd. The project is currently totally owned by Bilfinger Berger though, originally, John Graham and Northstone participated in the shareholding with 10 per cent each. For more information on M80 Haggs, please refer to Boles and Liyanage (2013).

The A19 Dishforth (UK) is a brownfield project that consists of two- and three-lane carriageways located in the North East of England, UK. This project provides the main link between three main areas, i.e. Newcastle, Sunderland and Middleborough. This road is 118km in length. The project agreement is on a Design, Build, Finance and Operate (DBFO) procurement model. The project was one of the PFI road projects introduced in the mid-1990s and is identified as part of Tranche 1A PFIs. The owner of the SPV is Sir Robert McAlpine Ltd.

The concessionaire is Autolink Concessionaries, UK. For more information on the A19, please refer to Boles and Liyanage (2013).

The Via-Invest Zaventem project (Belgium) is a mixed greenfield and brownfield project. The project involves a range of works: i.e. adaptation and extension of a junction in Machelen; conversion of Luchthavenlaan main road; building a viaduct over the existing road; construction of a cycle bridge and tunnel; maintenance of the existing bridge; and overhauling car park and bridge installations. The project is integrated into the Diabolo railway project, although it is a separate one. The contract is a Design, Build, Finance and Maintain (DBFM) model, which includes a hybrid structure of the Dutch and English PFI standards for DBFM agreements. Construction costs are only around €70m, out of the €220m total cost of the project. The concessionaire is Via Invest Zaventem NV. The private contractor is mainly responsible for the main part of the maintenance of the infrastructure. The Flemish region keeps some of the functions related to service and crisis management. For more information on Via-Invest, please refer to Van der Hurk and Van Gestel (2013).

The A-23 Beira Interior Toll Road Project (Portugal) is a combination of some existing infrastructure and the construction of a new toll road in the centre of Portugal, linking the north-south axis of the A1 near the Spanish border. The contract is Build, Operate and Transfer (BOT). The concessionaire is SCUTVIAS – Auto Estradas da Beira Interior, S.A. – for most of the length of the project (178 out of 217km) and it is responsible for the design, construction, operation and maintenance during the concession period. The remaining section is managed by the national road institute, Instituto das Estradas de Portugal (IEP). For more information on A-23, please refer to Costa *et al.* (2014).

The Olympia Odos Motorway (Greece) is a mixed greenfield and brownfield project. The road is about 365km in length in the northern of the Peloponnese region, Greece. The road consists of dual carriage lanes, over forty interchanges and 4.5km of tunnels in four sections: Elefsina-Korinthos (63.6km), an existing three-lane toll motorway to be upgraded and maintained; Korinthos-Patra (120km), an existing one-lane per direction toll road to be expanded and maintained as a toll motorway; Patras Bypass section (18.3km), an existing non-tolled motorway with two lanes and a tunnel of 4.7km to be maintained without revenues; and Patra-Pyrgos-Tsakona (163.3km), a new toll road to be built and maintained. The whole project is part of the PATHE (Patra-Athens-Thessaloniki) corridor and Trans European network. The model is a Design, Build, Finance and Operate (DBFO) contract, which mixes maintaining and operating existing infrastructure and building new toll roads, partially using traffic revenues from the existing roads and new financing with strong public support from the Greek State and EU funds. The concessionaire is Olympia Odos. Both operating concessionaire and the construction SPV are owned by the sponsors, led by the French construction company VINCI. For more information on Olympia Odos, please refer to Nikolaidis and Roumboutsos (2013).

The Athens Ring Road, i.e. the Attica Tollway (Greece) is a greenfield project consisting of a three-lane ring road around the city of Athens in Greece.

It extends along 65km and connects the 30 municipalities of the Attica basin. This is part of the Trans-European network. The construction of the project was performed in parallel with flood protection works as it passes through three large hydrographic basins. It is a hybrid structure of a PPP project under a Build, Operate and Transfer (BOT) contract with strong public financial support. The concessionaire is Athiki Odos, more commonly known as Attica Tollway. They are responsible for the construction and operation of the road. It has established back-to-back contracts with the concession agreement, with Attiki Odos Construction Joint Venture for the project construction and Attikes Diadromes, S. A. for the operation and maintenance of the project. For more information on Attica, please refer to Halkias *et al.* (2013).

The Ionia Odos Motorway (Greece) is a mixed greenfield and brownfield project. The project consists of three-sections: a 160km long new motorway in western region, a 30km bypass around Agrinio city and a 175km long existing motorway along the PATHE (Patra-Athens-Thessaloniki) way that was constructed by the Greek state under a public procurement scheme. The project includes over 42 interchanges and over 7km of tunnels and is part of the Trans-European network. The model is a Design, Build, Finance and Operate (DBFO) contract with strong emphasis on maintaining and operating existing infrastructure based on user toll. Its financing is also partially supported by the EU and the Greek State. The operating concessionaire is Nea Odos, S.A. For more information on Ionia Odos, please refer to Nikolaidis and Roumboutsos (2013).

The Rio-Antirio Bridge (Greece) is a mixed greenfield and brownfield project, which connects the regions of Aetoloakarnania and Achaia. The road is 2,880 metres long and 28 metres wide. It is a two-lane road each way that includes a pedestrian walkway and an emergency lane. It is the world's second longest cable-stayed deck and it received the Outstanding Structure Award in 2006 from the International Bridge and Structural Engineer (IABSE), among other recognitions. This project is part of the Patras-Athens-Thessaloniki, Trans-European network (PATHE TEN-T). The project is a Design, Build, Finance and Operate (DBFO) contract based on toll revenues with strong financial support from the Greek State and the EU Community Structural Funds. The concession-aire is GEFYRA, S.A. led by the French construction company VINCI and five main Greek builders. For the construction, a joint venture named Kinopraxia GEFYRA, S.A. has been created. For more information on Rio-Antirio, please refer to Papanikolas *et al.* (2014).

The Radial 2 Toll Road (R-2, Spain) is a greenfield project in the Northeast area of Madrid, Spain. The road is 80.7km long and includes the toll road R-2 for 62.3km and an 18.4km section of the M-50 loop between the existing A-2 and A-4. The PPP option of the project is a Build, Operate and Transfer (BOT) contract. The concessionaire, named as HENARSA, S.A., is responsible for the construction, operation and financing of the road (through a financing SPV) and is entitled to receive revenues for the services provided. For more information on R-2, please refer to Villalba-Romero and Liyanage (2014).

The Eje Aeropuerto Toll Road (Airport axis) M-12 (Spain) is a greenfield project, which provides access to the new Terminal 4 of Madrid Barajas Airport and connects the national motorways A-1 and A-2 at the intersection of the M-40 ring road in Spain. It roams the east part of Madrid and has become an alternative route to connect new neighbourhoods in the area. The road is 9.4km long and runs in a double tube tunnel for nearly 2km in a unique way, consisting of two lanes that could be expanded to three-lane roads. In 2006 the tunnel was named the best tunnel in Europe by the EuroTAP Program. The PPP model is a Build, Operate and Transfer (BOT) contract in which the investment is recovered by user tolls. The concessionaire is Eje Aeropuerto, C.E.S.A. They are responsible for the maintenance and operation during the concession period. The project uses a financing SPV and sole shareholder, named Aeropistas, S.L. For more information on M-12 please refer to Villalba-Romero and Liyanage (2014).

The M-45 Semi Loop Road (Spain) is a greenfield project that is divided into three sections. Overall, the road length is 37.1km, going from the east to the south area of Madrid municipalities, between the national motorway A-2 (to Barcelona) and the A-5 (to Extremadura). Most parts of the road have three lanes. The PPP model is a Build, Operate and Transfer (BOT) contract, based on shadow tolls to be paid by the grantor. This is the first project that introduced the shadow repayment mechanism in Spain. The three concessionaires are Concesionarias de Madrid, S.A., Euroglosa 45, S.A., and Trados-45, S.A. For more information on M-45, please refer to Villalba-Romero and Liyanage (2014).

Taking all the aforementioned into consideration, the following table (Table 15.1) can be presented to show the summary of the main details/features of the projects chosen.

Step 3: Development of KPIs

The case study data on the 13 projects mentioned above were analysed using qualitative content analysis. During this process, different categories and codes were developed to make the case studies comparable. The categorisation and coding was done using QSR NVivo (NVivo is a qualitative data analysis computer software package produced by QSR International). The main categories developed for the case study data emerged from the different sections of the case template itself. The categories and codes were then transferred to a tabular format. The codes were given a Likert scale to easily quantify the results (Liyanage and Villalba-Romero 2015).

The categories developed were identified as Key Performance Indicators (KPIs) and the codes developed within them were identified as performance measures to define the success criteria of a project. The developed indicators and measures were then refined, revised and weighted using a three-stage Delphi Study. These were subsequently assessed to identify the overall level of performance of each project as discussed below.

Table 15.1 Summary of the case studies

PROJECT NAME	Coen Tunnel	M6	M80 Hagg	A19 Dishforth	Via-Invest Zaventem Airport	A23-Beira Interior
COUNTRY	Netherland	UK	UK	UK	Belgium	Portugal
Identification						
Geographical region	Noordelijke Randstad, Netherland	Midlands UK	Scotland, UK	North East of England, UK	Brussels, Belgium	Beiras, Portugal
Cost	€ 500 mill.	£485 mill.	£320 mill.	£ 29,4 mill.	€ 220 mill.	€ 628 mill.
Contract Duration	30 yrs	53 yrs	33 yrs	30 yrs	30 yrs	30 yrs
Tender call	2005	2007	1992	1995	2006	Oct. 1997
Contract approval	2008	2009	2000	1996	2007	13/09/1999
Operational start	2013	08/12/2003	01/11/2011	02/09/1998	01/02/2012	27/07/2003 (Completion date)
Public Authorities						
Government Sponsor	Dutch Minister of Transport	Department of Transport	Scottish Government	Department of Transport	Flemish Government	Ministry of Public Facilities
Commissioning Authority	Dutch Highways Agency	DFT/ Highways Agency	Transport Scotland	DFT/Highways Agency	Via Invest Vlaanderen NV	National Road Institute
Private Contract holder						
Name Consortia/ Contractor	Coen Tunnel	Midland Expressway Ltd	Highways Management	Autolink Concessionaries UK	Via Invest Zaventem NV	Auto Estradas da Beira Interior, S.A.
No. partners Consortium	7	2	3	1	2	6
Details	Dura Vermeer and others	Macquarie	Bilfinger Berger	Robert Mc. Alpine Ltd.	Perticipatiemaa tschappij Vlaanderen	Soares da Costa, ES Concessões, Globalvia, Alves
No of contractors	5	4	3	N/A	5	6
Financial Details						
No. Banks/ Bond Holders	5 Bank + EIB	1 Bank	Banks and EIB / Capital	2 Bank	1 Bank	EIB + >10 banks
Method of payment						
Toll	Availability fees	Direct	Availability / Shadow	Shadow	Shadow	Direct/ Availability. (Initially Shadow)

Olympia Odos	Attica Tollway	Ionia Odos	Rio-Antirio Bridge	Radial 2	M-12 Airport Axis
Greece	Greece	Greece	Greece	Spain	Spain
Northern Peloponeso, Greece	Athens, Greece	Western Greece	Patras Gulf, Greece	Madrid, Spain	Madrid, Spain
€ 2,200 mill.	€ 1,300 mill.	€ 1,200 mill.	€ 815 mill.	€ 500 mill.	€ 382 mill.
30 yrs	25 yrs (or before)	30 yrs	42 yrs (or before)	25 yrs (Ext. to 39)	25 – 26 yrs
2001	18/02/1995	2001	1991	04/02/2000	05/03/2002
20/12/2007	23/05/1996	19/12/2006	03/01/1996	02/01/2001	08/11/2002
Partial start, project not finished	18/03/2001	Partial start, project not finished	12/08/2004	06/10/2003	June 2005
Ministry of Development and Infrastructure Transport	Ministry of Development and Infrastructure Transport	Ministry of Development and Infrastructure Transport	Ministry of Development and Infrastructure Transport	Ministry of Public Works	Ministry of Public Works
L.S.E.P	L.S.E.P	L.S.E.P	L.S.E.P	Infrastructure Secretariat	Infrastructure Secretariat
Olympia Odos	Attiki Odos	Nea Odos, S.A	GEFYRA, S.A.	HENARSA, S.A.C.E.	Eje Aeropuerto, C.E.S.A.
6	3	3	6	5	2
Vinci Concessions	Ellaktor	Ferrovial, ACS, and GEK Terna	Vinci Concessions	ACS Group	OHL Group
3	14 originally	3	6	2	1
EIB + >10 banks	EIB + >10 banks	EIB + >10 banks	EIB + >10 banks	EIB + >10 banks	Holding loan, Banks backed
Direct	Direct	Direct	Direct	Direct	Direct

Step 4: Three-stage Delphi approach

A three-stage Delphi study was conducted to refine the KPIs and performance measures and then to prioritise them in accordance with their level of importance (based on a Likert scale). The initial set of KPIs and performance measures were refined using a focus group. This was considered as the first Delphi round. The focus group was conducted in June 2013 in University of Twente, Netherlands. The focus group included members from the COST TU1001 project. Eleven members were present during the focus group discussions. All the members have in-depth knowledge and experiences on the subject of PPP. Altogether nine KPIs and 29 performance measures were developed (and refined) using the qualitative content analysis described in Step 3 and the focus group. Table 15.2 shows the nine KPIs and 29 performance measures developed. For ease of reference, all the 29 performance measures were assigned codes. These indicators and measures were then prioritised/assigned weightings using the level of consensus achieved during the second and third rounds of Delphi exercises. The method for arriving at a consensus, assigning weights and calculating the level of importance of the performance measures are similar to the methodology adopted by Njuangang *et al.* (2014).

Table 15.2 Mean scores and ranks of performance measures

KPI and performance measures – PM	Code	Mean score	Rank
Objectives	**KPI-1**		
Are the objectives specified in the contract SMART?	PM-1	3.1765	25
To what extent have the objectives been achieved?	PM-2	4.3514	2
Have/will user benefits been/be monitored?	PM-3	4.1765	8
Have user benefits been as large as expected?	PM-4	3.6471	20
Risk	**KPI-2**		
How much risk has been transferred to the private sector?	PM-5	3.9730	13
Was risk allocation agreed quickly?	PM-6	3.3529	23
Specifications (contract project)	**KPI-3**		
Have the deliverables been specified clearly in the contract?	PM7	4.1892	7
Are the roles and responsibilities of different parties involved in the contract clearly defined?	PM-8	4.3243	3
Are minimum standards for the condition of infrastructure and equipment specified in the contract?	PM-9	3.7778	18
Are there any performance targets?	PM-10	3.9091	15
Is the method of measuring performance targets clearly defined?	PM-11	3.2500	24
Are there penalties for non-compliance?	PM-12	4.5556	1
Does the contract have procedures for amendments, dispute resolution or termination?	PM-13	3.8919	16
Has the contract proceeded without renegotiations?	PM-14	3.0606	27
Are there any guarantees specified in the contract?	PM-15	3.7188	19

(Continued)

Table 15.2 Mean scores and ranks of performance measures (Continued)

KPI and performance measures – PM	Code	Mean score	Rank
Tendering process	**KPI-4**		
No. of bidders (negotiation *vs.* final).	PM-16	2.8788	**28**
Time from tender notice to financial close.	PM-17	2.3824	**29**
Legal challenges to outcome.	PM-18	3.0909	**26**
Construction phase	**KPI-5**		
Was the project completed on time?	PM-19	4.0270	**12**
Was the project completed within budget?	PM-20	4.1389	**9**
Was the project completed according to the specifications and design?	PM-21	4.2432	**5**
Are there any penalties for non-compliance?	PM-22	4.0541	**11**
Operations	**KPI-6**		
Were the services specified in the contract delivered?	PM-23	4.2973	**4**
Maintenance	**KPI-7**		
Are the deliverable standards for infrastructure and equipment being met?	PM-24	4.2162	**6**
Monitoring and evaluation	**KPI-8**		
Is there a formal monitoring procedure in place?	PM-25	3.8919	**16**
Finance	**KPI-9**		
Was finance available when needed?	PM-26	3.9189	**14**
Was the project cash flow sufficient to make expected payments to all parties?	PM-27	4.1351	**10**
Did the project result in financial benefits to users (e.g. in terms of charges)?	PM-28	3.5000	**22**
Has the financial outcome been equal or better than expected for the private partner?	PM-29	3.5135	**21**

Step 5: Assigning mean zones (M)

Based on the mean score results of the Delphi exercises, the performance measures (PM1 – PM29) were ranked in varying levels of importance in PPP transport projects. The ranking of the performance measures provided a clear indication that some performance measures contributed more to the success of PPP transport projects than others did. Therefore, to distinguish the performance measures according to levels of importance, they were categorised into four mean zones. If the mean score of the performance measure is X, the mean zone it belongs to is identified using the following scale:

$$\leq 4.28 \text{ to } \geq 5; \quad \leq 4.01 \text{ to } > 4.28; \quad \leq 3.75 \text{ to } > 4.01; \quad \text{and} < 3.75$$

The mean zones were also assigned weightings on a range of 4 to 1, where 4 and 1 represent the highest and lowest mean scores respectively.

Step 6: Filing in the KPIs table

Having established different weightings, which was achieved through the second and third rounds of Delphi, the next step was to adopt the weightings to measure the level of performance of the 13 PPP transport projects. For this, the level of performance for each KPI and performance measure was to be identified. This was identified by filling in the KPIs table (Table 15.2) on a Likert scale. The table was filled in by the different author/s that initially developed the respective case studies. This assures validity and reliability of the data, as they are the ones who have the knowledge/information of the particular case(s). To maintain consistency and accuracy an example was given initially to all case study authors to fill in the KPIs table. The main idea of the KPIs table was to identify the scale of success in every project in terms of the given KPIs and performance measures. This was identified not only using different Likert scales but also using a colour-coded theme (i.e. Red – failure, Yellow – neither success nor a failure, Green – success). This is discussed in detail in the introductory chapter in this Part.

Step 7: Calculation of weighted score (WS)

Since the performance measures have varying levels of importance towards the success of PPP transport projects, a weighted score for each performance measure was calculated by multiplying the level of performance (L – filled in during Step 3) against the weight (W – identified during Step 3). Please refer to Table 15.3 for more information. The weight assigned to a mean zone, i.e. WS_A, is the same for all the performance measures that are categorised in that mean zone.

Step 8: Calculating the overall level of performance

Having assigned the weighted score (L×W) for all 29 performance measures (refer to Table 15.3), the next step was to establish the overall level of performance of the 13 PPP transport projects. This was achieved by adding the weighted score for all the 29 performance measures that are categorised under each of the PPP transport projects. As shown in the formula provided in Table 15.3, the total weighted score of a PPP transport project can be calculated by adding together the scores of the four mean zones. Alternatively, all the weighted scores under a particular case study can be added together. Whatever the method adopted, the overall results can then be divided by the total number of performance measures in the mean zones and multiplied by their respective maximum weighted scores. The weights of the performance measures are the same in the mean zones across the PPP transport projects. Therefore, the maximum weighted score for all the projects is calculated as WS_A (20*4) + WS_B (15*8) + WS_C (10*7) + WS_D (5*10) = 320. Finally the overall performance has been identified using the following formula (Njuangang *et al.* 2014: 236):

$$\frac{\sum \left(WS_A + WS_B + WS_C + WS_D\right) \times 100}{\left[N(P_A) \times 20\right] + \left[N(P_B) \times 15\right] + \left[N(P_C) \times 10\right] + \left[N(P_D) \times 5\right]}$$

Where:
N (P) = Number of performance measures in a mean zone

Table 15.3 Overall level of performance of PPP transport projects

Performance Level Rating (L)
1 – Very Poor, 2 – Poor, 3 – Average, 4 – Good, 5 – Excellent

Weighted Score (WS) = (L × W)

Mean Zones	Weight (W)	Performance Measures (PM)	Coen Tunnel (Netherlands)	M 6 (UK)	M 80 (UK)	A 19 (UK)	Via Invest Zav. (Belgium)	A 23 (Portugal)	Olympia Odos (Greece)	Attica (Greece)	Iona Odos (Greece)	Rio Antirio (Greece)	R-2 (Spain)	Eje Aeropuerto (Spain)	M-45 (Spain)	Total WS for each PM	Overall Level of Performance per PM
WS$_A$ ≤ 4.28 to ≥ 5	**4**	PM-12	20	12	20	0	20	16	–	12	–	–	12	12	20	**144**	**55%**
		PM-2	20	–	–	–	–	16	–	20	–	20	8	4	16	**104**	**40%**
		PM-8	16	20	20	20	20	20	12	12	16	20	16	16	20	**228**	**88%**
		PM-23	20	20	20	20	–	20	–	20	8	16	20	20	20	**204**	**78%**
WS$_B$ ≤ 4.01 to > 4.28	**3**	PM-3	15	15	15	–	–	12	–	15	–	–	6	6	12	**96**	**49%**
		PM-7	9	12	12	12	12	12	12	12	12	15	12	12	15	**159**	**82%**
		PM-19	15	15	15	15	15	15	3	15	3	15	3	3	–	**132**	**68%**
		PM-20	15	15	15	15	3	15	3	15	3	15	3	3	3	**123**	**63%**
		PM-21	15	15	15	15	15	15	3	15	–	15	15	15	15	**165**	**85%**
		PM-22	15	–	–	–	15	15	3	15	3	3	15	15	15	**114**	**58%**
		PM-24	15	15	15	15	–	15	6	12	3	12	15	15	15	**153**	**78%**
		PM-27	15	15	15	–	15	12	3	9	3	15	3	3	15	**123**	**63%**
WS$_C$ ≤ 3.75 to > 4.01	**2**	PM-5	–	–	–	–	–	8	–	–	–	–	10	10	8	**36**	**28%**
		PM-9	10	10	10	10	–	10	8	8	8	10	8	8	10	**110**	**85%**
		PM-10	8	2	8	6	6	8	4	8	4	2	8	8	10	**82**	**63%**
		PM-13	10	10	10	10	10	10	2	2	2	10	2	2	2	**82**	**63%**
		PM-15	10	10	8	–	10	10	10	10	10	8	10	10	10	**110**	**85%**
		PM-25	10	4	8	0	6	10	6	10	2	8	6	6	6	**82**	**63%**
		PM-26	8	8	10	8	10	10	2	6	2	10	8	8	10	**100**	**77%**

(Continued)

Table 15.3 Overall level of performance of PPP transport projects (Continued)

Performance Level Rating (L)
1 – Very Poor, 2 – Poor, 3 – Average,
4 – Good, 5 – Excellent

Weighted Score (WS) = (L×W)

Mean Zones	Weight (W)	Performance Measures (PM)	Coen Tunnel (Netherlands)	M 6 (UK)	M 80 (UK)	A 19 (UK)	Via Invest Zav. (Belgium)	A 23 (Portugal)	Olympia Odos (Greece)	Attica (Greece)	Iona Odos (Greece)	Rio Antirio (Greece)	R-2 (Spain)	Eje Aeropuerto (Spain)	M-45 (Spain)	Total WS for each PM	Overall Level of Performance per PM
WS_D <3.75	1	PM-1	4	1	4	–	4	5	4	4	4	5	2	2	4	43	66%
		PM-4	5	2	–	–	–	5	1	5	1	–	2	2	5	28	43%
		PM-6	1	4	4	5	3	4	4	4	4	4	4	4	5	50	77%
		PM-11	5	1	4	4	–	5	2	4	2	3	3	3	5	41	63%
		PM-14	5	5	5	1	5	5	1	1	1	5	1	1	1	37	57%
		PM-16	3	3	3	–	4	2	2	3	2	2	3	3	3	33	51%
		PM-17	1	1	5	5	5	5	1	1	1	1	5	5	5	41	63%
		PM-18	1	1	5	5	5	5	5	5	5	5	5	5	5	57	88%
		PM-28	3	1	5	4	3	5	2	5	1	5	2	2	5	43	66%
		PM29	3	2	5	4	–	4	–	5	5	5	5	1	5	35	54%
Total WS per Case (X)			277	219	248	174	186	294	96	253	100	231	208	204	265		
Overall Level of Performance per Case (%)			87	68	78	54	58	92	30	79	31	72	65	64	83		

Step 9: Interpretation of the performance results

Once the overall level of performance was calculated, in order to provide a uniform measure across all the transport projects, the final score for each case was multiplied by 100 (to portray the result as a percentage). The maximum weighted score is the same for all performance measures in a mean zone, i.e., 260 for WS_A, 195 for WS_B, 130 for WS_C and 65 WS_D. The results provide invaluable information about the overall performance of the case studies chosen and the performance of important performance measures. A 4-point scale was then developed to interpret the results on a Likert scale (please refer to Figure 15.1). PPP transport projects that achieve an overall performance score of equal to or above 75 per cent are considered as 'excellent'.

Findings and discussions

Based on the analysis described above, the findings obtained from the case studies are given below (please refer to Table 15.3).

The Coen Tunnel has achieved an excellent level of performance score (approx. 87 per cent). This is due to the project achieving either an excellent or a good level of performance for most of the performance measures, although there are some exceptions. Some of these exceptions are risk allocation (PM-6), the time required to get to the financial close (PM-17) and the legal challenges faced during the tendering process (PM-18). Although the project is a success according to the level of performance given in Table 15.3, users and private partners have a neutral point of view in terms of financial benefits achieved by them.

The M6 Toll Road, overall, has achieved a level of performance of 68 per cent, which denotes a good level of performance according to the Likert scale given in Figure 15.1. The reasons the project may not have achieved the required level of excellence could be relating to poor specified objectives in the contract (PM-1), lack of performance targets given in the contract (PM-10), prolonged period of tender (PM-17), the legal challenges faced during the tendering process (PM-18) and lack of financial benefits for the users (PM-28).

The M80 Haag Stepps Road has an excellent level of performance (78 per cent) according to Table 15.3. This is due to the project achieving either an excellent or a good level of performance for most of the performance measures, although there are some exceptions. One of the main exceptions relates to the very low number of bidders participating during the tendering process (PM-16); this may have reduced the level of competitiveness of the bidders.

The A19 Dishforth Road has a performance score of 54 per cent. Although, according to Figure 15.1, the score means a good level of performance, it is

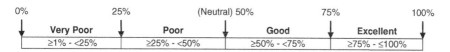

Figure 15.1 Scale for interpreting the overall performance results.

marginalises on a neutral level. Even though some high-ranked PMs (according to Table 15.2) have achieved good or excellent performance, there are some others with very poor results, which may have contributed to the lack of success of the project. Some of these poorly performed performance measures are lack of penalties for non-performance (PM-12), lack of renegotiations (PM-14) and lack of a proper monitoring process for project performance (PM-25). It should also be noted that there was a lack of information on performance of some performance measures, which may have contributed to the neutral level of performance overall.

The Via-Invest Zaventem project has a performance score of 58 per cent. According to Figure 15.1, this can be considered as a good level of performance, although at the low end of the spectrum. One of the main reasons for this result is the cost of the project (PM-20), as it has exceeded the projected budget. Poor monitoring mechanisms (PM-25) and lack of financial benefits for users (PM-29) have also contributed to the project not achieving 'excellent' performance. Similar to A19, Via-Invest also had a lack of information with regard to some performance measures.

The A-23 Beira Interior Toll Road Project has achieved a performance level of 92 per cent, which is excellent. This is due to the project achieving either an excellent or a good level of performance for most of the performance measures throughout. Notwithstanding, it must be noted that the project has gone through a renegotiation process, which may have eventually resulted in the positive results.

The Olympia Odos Motorway has a performance score of 30 per cent. Although this comes under the category of 'poor' performance according to Figure 15.1, it marginalises on 'very poor' performance as well. One of the main reasons for this negative result is due to the project not reaching completion stage. The project has had many delays (PM-19) and cost overruns (PM-20), which may have contributed to the aforementioned result. The project issues have also been exacerbated by lack of penalties for non-compliance for contract specifications (PM-22), lack of provisions for amendments of the contract (PM-13) and problems with project financing.

The Athens Ring Road, i.e. the Attica Tollway has achieved an excellent level of performance with a performance score of 79 per cent. This is due to the project achieving either an excellent or a good level of performance for most of the performance measures, although there are some exceptions. Some of these exceptions are absence of procedures for amendments, dispute resolution or termination (PM-13), lack of renegotiation (PM-14) and taking a prolonged period of time during the tender period (PM-17).

The Ionia Odos Motorway's performance is similar to Olympia Odos. It has achieved a performance score of 31 per cent. Although this comes under the category of 'poor' performance according to Figure 15.1, it marginalises on 'very poor' performance as well. This is due to the failure of many performance measures – delays, cost overruns and lack of penalties (PM-19, PM-20, and PM-22 respectively), cash-flow shortfall (PM-27), lack of monitoring (PM-25), lack of finance availability (PM-26).

The Rio-Antirio Bridge, has achieved a level of performance of 72 per cent, which means 'good' although at the high end of the spectrum given in Figure 15.1. The project has achieved good mean scores for many performance measures, with some exceptions such as lack of penalties for non-compliance (PM-22), lack of performance targets specified in the contract (PM-10) and time overruns during tender stage (PM-17).

The R-2 Toll Road has a performance score of 65 per cent according to Table 15.1. This comes under a good level of performance with a mix of good mean scores for some PMs. The reason the project may not have achieved 'excellent' standards could be delays and cost overruns (PM-19 and PM-20), cash flow shortfall (PM-27), the need for renegotiations (PM-13), and a lack of financial benefits for the private partner (PM-29). This is an interesting project to be studied. One of the main reasons for this is that, although the performance score is categorised as 'good' and many performance measures have high mean scores, the project is still in renegotiations due to financial distress.

The Eje Aeropuerto Toll Road (Airport axis), M-12 is very similar to the R-2 project discussed above, with a performance score of 64 per cent.

The M-45 Loop Road has obtained a performance score of 83 per cent (excellent) during the performance analysis. Obviously, performance was strong in many areas to achieve the above result. However, there are some exceptions such as cost overruns (PM-20), and the need for renegotiations that has eventually been covered by the grantor (PM-14). The grantor, as the sole off-taker of the project, has faced difficulties in settling all committed payments to the concessionaire. There are also some media criticisms with regard to this project due to private partners obtaining high profits from the project.

Taking all of the above, the summary of the performance level of all projects can be portrayed as shown in Figure 15.2. According to the Figure, A-23 has the highest score of performance, whereas Olympia Odos (and Ionia Odos) stands as the lowest performing of the 13 projects. Both Olympia Odos and Ionia Odos should be evaluated again once they reach project completion.

According to Figure 15.3, it is apparent that PM-8 (assigning clear roles and responsibilities) and PM-18 (legal challenges faced during the tendering process)

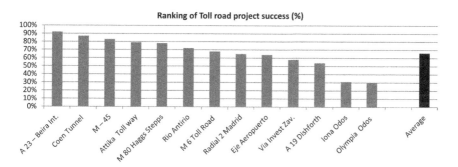

Figure 15.2 Ranking of toll road project success.

Figure 15.3 Ranking of performance measures score.

have, overall, been successfully achieved/fulfilled in most of the projects with a success score of 88 per cent. PM-9 (minimum standards for the condition of infrastructure and equipment are specified in the contract), PM-15 (guarantees are specified in the contract), and PM-21 (project is completed according to specifications) are also not far off with a percentage score of 85 per cent, and PM-7 (deliverables are clearly specified) with 82 per cent, which are all excellent. In contrast, the lowest scored performance measure across all projects is PM-5 (transfer of risks to the private sector) with a percentage score of 28 per cent. This may raise questions about the lack of risk allocations in PPP projects. Although there are many studies on risks and risk allocation, the performance results highlight that the area of 'risk' needs further investigation in PPP projects.

Considering the performance of the overall KPIs (please refer to Figure 15.4), KPI-3 (contract specifications) is the highest performing KPI in most of the projects, meaning that many PPP projects do have clear deliverables, specifications and roles and responsibilities specified in the contract. Within KPI-3, the only weakness is lack of specifications of performance targets and penalties for non-compliance in many PPP contracts. Perhaps the reason for this could be that, since PPP projects form the basis for a long-term relationship between the private and public sector, specifying penalties may be deemed to jeopardise the 'trust' factor and the coordination and collaboration between the two parties. KPI-1 (objectives) seems to be the lowest performing KPI in many of the projects due to lack of specification of SMART objectives (specific, measurable, achievable, relevant and time-bound) failure to achieve project's objectives and users' benefit.

Having applied the Delphi analysis to the 13 projects and having looked at Figures 15.3 and 15.4, the average score of performance measures and the related KPIs can be considered as a benchmark for comparing other projects as well as comparing the same projects at different intervals.

It is worth noting how the two most successful projects, namely Beira Interior and Coen Tunnel that have a success score of approximately 90 per cent, have achieved a high level of performance especially in higher weighted mean zones such as, for example, WS_A and WS_B. In contrast, less successful projects such as

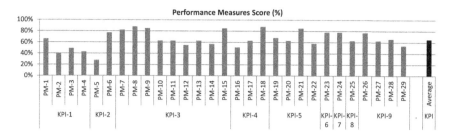

Figure 15.4 Performance measures score.

Olympia Odos and Iona Odos, which have a success score around 30 per cent, have achieved a lower level of performance in most of the mean zones. Indeed, the 12 performance measures that come under the higher weighted mean zones (WS_A, and WS_B) may have contributed to the high percentage score of success for the high performing projects as the two mean zones account for a maximum score of 200; while the remaining 17 performance measures of the lower weighting zones (WS_C, and WS_D) only account for about 120. This shows the importance of fulfilling performance measures in higher mean zones as they have a significant impact on the overall level of performance of PPP projects.

Summary and conclusions

In this research, a methodology for measuring the success of PPP projects has been developed. The methodology has been applied and tested for 13 road projects carried out in some PPP 'active' countries within the EU (i.e. UK, Spain, Portugal, Greece, Belgium and the Netherlands). The methodology adopted, firstly, developed nine KPIs defined by 29 performance measures (PMs) using the qualitative content analysis. These then have been refined, prioritised and weighted using a three-stage Delphi technique to evaluate expert consensus on the importance of KPIs and performance measures. The final weighted performance measures have then been used to evaluate the level of performance of the 13 projects. The success of the 13 projects (PPP road projects) has been measured and a ranked using an equation presented in this chapter.

The results obtained can be used for both benchmarking purposes and for *ex-post* evaluation of PPP projects. Of the 13 projects tested, there are five projects with a very high percentage of success. First is the A-23 Beiras Interior (Portugal) project, which has gone through renegotiation, after which the grantor changed the charger toll to users. Secondly, the Coen Tunnel, which is the first project procured through a competitive dialogue route in the Netherlands. The third most successful project of the 13 projects is M-45 (Spain). In this project, the initial shadow toll concession contract was modified to absorb some project cost overruns. Attica Tollway (Greece) comes forth in the success analysis, followed by M80 Haags (UK). Olympia Odos and Ionia Odos are the two projects that marginalised on a very poor level of performance due to heavy cost overruns and time overruns. The success of the other six projects of the 13 case studies can be categorised as 'good', although some come at the lower end of the success percentage spectrum (for example, the A19 in the UK), whereas some others are placed at the higher end of the spectrum (for example, Rio Antirio, Greece). For many of the (comparatively) less successful projects the financial crisis has had a significant impact, which has resulted in renegotiations.

Other than highlighting the results as above, the main purpose of the research was to present a methodology to measure the success of selected projects. The overall methodology can be presented as a performance measurement system (PMS) that has been tested on the 13 road projects in the EU. The PMS can be used on a variety of PPP case studies to identify overall successes (or failures) of projects. It can also be used to analyse how success could be evaluated from a set of KPIs and performance measures. Furthermore, the assessment can present results in terms of the performance of dominant KPIs and performance measures, which could be useful when prioritising project tasks. This approach is valid and may be used for other PPP road projects as well. The analysis can also be extended to other modes of transport within the PPP context.

References

Akintoye, A., Beck, M. and Hardcastle, C. (2003) *Public-Private Partnerships: Managing Risks and Opportunities*. Oxford: Blackwell Science

Ashley, D. B., Lurie, C. S. and Jaselskis, E. J. (1987) 'Determinants of construction project success'. *Project Management Journal*, 18 (2), pp. 69–79

Atkinson, R. (1999) 'Project management: cost, time and quality, two best guesses and a phenomenon, it's time to accept other success criteria'. *International Journal of Project Management*, 17(6), pp. 337–342

Aziz, A. (2007) 'Successful delivery of Public-Private Partnerships for infrastructure development'. *Journal of Construction Engineering and Management*, Vol. 133, No. 12, pp. 918–931

Boles, C. and Liyanage, C. (2013a) 'M6 Toll (BNRR)' in A. Roumboutsos, S. Farrell, C. L. Liyanage and R. Macário *COST Action TU1001 Public Private Partnerships in Transport: Trends & Theory P3T3, 2013 Discussion Papers Part II Case Studies*. ISBN 978-88-97781-61-5

Boles, C. and Liyanage, C. (2013b) 'M80 Haggs to Stepps' in A. Roumboutsos, S. Farrell, C. L. Liyanage and R. Macário *COST Action TU1001 Public Private Partnerships in Transport: Trends & Theory P3T3, 2013 Discussion Papers Part II Case Studies*. ISBN 978-88-97781-61-5

Boles, C. and Liyanage, C. (2013c) 'A19 Dishforth DBFO' in A. Roumboutsos, S. Farrell, C. L. Liyanage and R. Macário *COST Action TU1001 Public Private Partnerships in Transport: Trends & Theory P3T3, 2013 Discussion Papers Part II Case Studies*. ISBN 978-88-97781-61-5

Bryde, D. J. and Brown, D. (2005) 'The influence of project performance measurement system on the success of a contract for maintaining motorways and trunk roads'. *Project Management Journal*, 35(4), pp. 57–65

Chan, A. P. C. (2001) 'Framework for measuring success of construction projects'. *Report 2001-003-C-0*. Available online at: http://eprints.qut.edu.au/26531/1/2001-003-C-1_ Framework_for_Measuring_Success.pdf1

Costa, J., Couchinho, R., Ribeiro, J. and Macário, R. (2014) 'A23-Beira Interior' in A. Roumboutsos, S. Farrell and K. Verhoest *COST Action TU1001 – Public Private Partnerships in Transport: Trends & Theory: 2014 Discussion Series: Country Profiles & Case Studies*. ISBN 978-88-6922-009-8

COST TU1001 (2013a) *Public Private Partnerships in Transport: Trends and Theory P3T3 – 2013 Discussion Papers: Part I Country Profiles*. COST Action TU1001. Available online at: www.ppptransport.eu/docs/Book_part_1.pdf

COST TU1001 (2013b) *Public Private Partnerships in Transport: Trends and Theory P3T3 – 2013 Discussion Papers: Part II Case Studies*. COST Action TU1001. Available online at: www.ppptransport.eu/docs/Book_part_2.pdf

COST TU1001 (2014) *Public Private Partnerships in Transport: Trends and Theory P3T3 – 2013 Discussion Papers: Country profiles and Case Studies*. COST Action TU1001. Available online at: www.ppptransport.eu/docs/2014_Discussion_Papers.pdf

Cox, R. F., Issa, R. R. A. and Aherns, D. (2003) 'Management's perception of key performance indicators for construction'. *Journal of Construction Engineering and Management*, 129(2), pp. 142–151

Cruz, C. and Marques, R. (2011) 'Revisiting the Portuguese experience with Public-Private Partnerships'. *African Journal of Business Management*, 5 (11), pp. 4023–4032

Eisenhardt, K. M. (1989) 'Building theories from case study research'. *Academy of Management Review*, 14, pp. 532–550

Farinde, O. and Sillars, D. (2012) 'A holistic success model for the construction industry' in: A. Javerick-Will and A. Mahalingam (Eds) *Working Paper Proceedings* of the Engineering Project Organisation Conference, Rheden, The Netherlands, 10-12 July 10-12 2012. Available online at: www.epossociety.org/EPOC2012/Papers/Farinde_ Sillars.pdf

Freeman, M. and Beale, P. (1992) 'Measuring project success'. *Project Management Journal*, 23 (1), pp. 8–17

Halkias, B., Roumboutsos, A. and Pantelias, A. (2013) 'Attica Tollway' in A. Roumboutsos, S. Farrell, C. L. Liyanage and R. Macário *COST Action TU1001 Public Private Partnerships in Transport: Trends & Theory P3T3, 2013 Discussion Papers Part II Case Studies*. ISBN 978-88-97781-61-5

Harris, S. (2004) *Public Private Partnerships: Delivering Better Infrastructure Services*. USA: Inter-American Bank Sustainable Development Department

Hodge, A. and Greve, C. (2007) 'Public–Private Partnerships: an international performance review'. *Public Administration Review*, 67 (3), pp. 545–558

Khosravi, S. and Afshari, H. (2011) 'A success measurement model for construction projects'. *International Conference on Financial Management and Economics*. IPRD vol 11. Singapore: IACSIT Press

Li, B., Akintoye, A., Edwards, P. and Hardcastle, C. (2005) 'Perceptions of positive and negative factors influencing the attractiveness of PPP/PFI procurement for construction projects in the UK'. *Engineering Construction and Architectural Management*, 12 (2), pp. 125–148

Liyanage, C. and Villalba-Romero, F. (2015 accepted for publication) 'Measuring success of PPP transport projects: a cross case analysis of toll roads'. *Transport Review*.

Nikolaidis, N. and Roumboutsos, A. (2013) 'Ionia Odos Motorway' in A. Roumboutsos, S. Farrell, C. L. Liyanage and R. Macário *COST Action TU1001 Public Private*

Partnerships in Transport: Trends & Theory P3T3, 2013 Discussion Papers Part II Case Studies. ISBN 978-88-97781-61-5

Nguyen, L. D., Ogunlana, S. O. and Lan, D.T. (2004) 'A study on project success factors on large construction projects in Vietnam'. *Engineering Construction and Architectural Management*, 11(6), pp. 404–413

Njuangang, S., Liyanage, C. and Akintoye, A. (2014) *Raising the Profile of Facilities Management in Healthcare – Managing Performance of Infection Control.* Lancaster, UK: University of Central Lancashire

Papanikolas, P., Diakidou, A., Roumboutsos, A. and Pantelias, A (2014) 'Rio-Antirio Bridge' in A. Roumboutsos, S. Farrell and K. Verhoest *COST Action TU1001 – Public Private Partnerships in Transport: Trends & Theory: 2014 Discussion Series: Country Profiles & Case Studies.* ISBN 978-88-6922-009-8

Phua, F. T. T. (2004) 'Modeling the determinants of multi-firm project success: a grounded exploration of different participant perspectives'. *Construction Management and Economics*, 22 (5), pp. 451–459

Pinto, J. K. and Slevin, D. P. (1988) 'Critical success factors across the project life cycle'. *Project Management Journal*, 19 (3), pp. 67–75

Qiao, L., Wang, S., Tiong, R. and Chan, T. (2001) 'Framework for critical success factors of BOT projects in China'. *The Journal of Project Finance*, March, pp. 53–61

Rangel, T. and Galende, J. (2010) 'Innovation in Public–Private Partnerships (PPP): the Spanish case of highway concessions'. *Public Money and Management*, 30 (1)

Roumboutsos, A. and Nikolaidis N. (2013) 'Olympia Odos Motorway' in A. Roumboutsos, S. Farrell, C. L. Liyanage and R. Macário *COST Action TU1001 Public Private Partnerships in Transport: Trends & Theory P3T3, 2013 Discussion Papers Part II Case Studies.* ISBN 978-88-97781-61-5

Savindo, V., Grobler, F., Parfitt, K., Guvenis, M. and Coyle, M. (1992) 'Critical success factors for construction projects'. *Journal of Construction Engineering and Management*, 118 (1), pp. 94–111

Shaoul, J., Stafford, A. and Stapleton, P. (2007) 'Evidence and policy'. *A Journal of Research, Debate and Practice*, 3 (2), pp. 159–179

Shenhar, A. J., Levy, O. and Dvir, D. (1997) 'Mapping the dimensions of project success'. *Project Management Journal*, 28 (2), pp. 5–13

Takim, R. and Adnan, H. (2008) 'Analysis of effectiveness measures of construction project success in Malaysia'. *Asian Social Science*, 5 (7)

Takim, R., Akintoye, A. and Kelly, J. (2004) 'Analysis of measures of construction project success in Malaysia' in: F. Khosrowshahi (Ed.) 20th Annual ARCOM Conference, 1-3 September, 2004, Heriot Watt University. *Association for Researchers in Construction Management*, Vol. 2, pp. 1123–33

Taylor, J., Dossick, C. and Garvin, M. (2009) 'Conducting research with case studies' in *Proceedings of the 2009 Construction Research Congress.* Seattle, WA, ASCE, Reston, VA, 5–7 April

Toor, S. R. and Ogunlana, S. O. (2008) 'Critical COMs of success in large-scale construction projects: evidence from the construction industry'. *International Journal of Project Management*, 26 (4), pp. 420–430

van den Hurk, M. and Van Gestel, K, (2013) 'Via-Invest Zaventem' in A. Roumboutsos, S. Farrell, C. L. Liyanage and R. Macário *COST Action TU1001 Public Private Partnerships in Transport: Trends & Theory P3T3, 2013 Discussion Papers Part II Case Studies.* ISBN 978-88-97781-61-5

Villalba-Romero, F. J. and Liyanage, C. (2014a) 'Radial 2 (R-2) Toll Motorway' in A. Roumboutsos, S. Farrell and K. Verhoest *COST Action TU1001 – Public Private Partnerships in Transport: Trends & Theory: 2014 Discussion Series: Country Profiles & Case Studies*. ISBN 978-88-6922-009-8

Villalba-Romero, F. J. and Liyanage, C. (2014b) 'Eje Aeropuerto (M-12), Airport Axis Toll Motorway' in A. Roumboutsos, S. Farrell and K. Verhoest *COST Action TU1001 – Public Private Partnerships in Transport: Trends & Theory: 2014 Discussion Series: Country Profiles & Case Studies*. ISBN 978-88-6922-009-8

Villalba-Romero, F. J. and Liyanage, C. (2014c) 'M-45 Toll Motorway' in A. Roumboutsos, S. Farrell and K. Verhoest *COST Action TU1001 – Public Private Partnerships in Transport: Trends & Theory: 2014 Discussion Series: Country Profiles & Case Studies*. ISBN 978-88-6922-009-8

Voordijk, J. T. (2013) 'Coen Tunnel' in A. Roumboutsos, S. Farrell, C. L. Liyanage and R. Macário *COST Action TU1001 Public Private Partnerships in Transport: Trends & Theory P3T3, 2013 Discussion Papers Part II Case Studies*. ISBN 978-88-97781-61-5

Voss, C., Tsikriktsis, N. and Frohlich, M. (2002) 'Case research in operations management'. *International Journal of Operation and Production Management*, 22(2), pp. 195–219

Yin, R. K. (2009) *Case Study Research: Design and Methods (4th Ed). Applied Social Research Methods V.5*. London: Sage Publications Inc.

Zhang, X. (2005) 'Critical success factors for Public Private Partnerships in infrastructure development'. *Journal of Construction Engineering and Management*, January, pp. 1–14

16 Performance monitoring and assessment

Conclusions, future research and policy recommendations

Champika Liyanage

A number of CSFs appear dominant in different literature sources and within the case studies. For example, risk allocation appears to be a dominant factor in the process of early appraisal and identification of PPP projects. The approach to controlling or mitigating risk is either by incorporating effective management controls through the public agency and engagement of the private party in the project from the earliest possible stage, or by encouraging the use of KPIs to incentivise the operator/contractor. Allowing innovation to overcome negative issues that can prevail is also a good way to control and mitigate risks.

Along with risk, 'trust' appears to be another critical factor that can enable success in PPP, particularly in infrastructure projects that are of high value and that have longer term commitments. Effective management by the public sector agency is suggested as integral to nurturing the 'trust' factor.

A question of the exclusivity of CSFs and KPIs in terms of being project specific is worthy of exploration. For example, when the public contracting authority is creating a PPP scheme for road infrastructure, factors and indicators can be either employed in a uniform manner or, perhaps, respective input may be received from the private sector stakeholder during the tender stage to suit the project context. Some projects suggest that the latter is most likely to occur, especially when they are procured through the competitive dialogue route. Selecting factors unique to each project could ensure the success of that particular project. The Coen Tunnel project is a good example.

It is also important to research how the private sector stakeholders view KPIs. Does the private sector view KPIs as bringing value to a project or merely as a reporting requirement of the contract? This may reflect whether the results of KPIs have a punitive or negative performance-related payment structure.

The perception of a PPP infrastructure project from a social point of view is intrinsic to the development of the public and political environment of a PPP. Support is garnered from the political bodies while the public acceptance of the PPP model is upheld. However, if the method of payment structure utilised causes stress to this relationship then that support may become quickly exhausted. Payment for the infrastructure can have a social bearing especially when direction payment from the users is involved, e.g. toll payment. In such cases, the public perception will determine success through usage of the infrastructure.

Further research

The KPIs and performance measures that have been developed in this research study need to be integrated into an automated tool so that stakeholders in PPP transport projects can easily use this to regularly quantify the performance of their projects. This automated tool should be linked to different stakeholder objectives as well, so that the success of the project from different stakeholder viewpoints can also be assessed.

There is a need to investigate whether the CSFs, KPIs and performance measures that are developed in this research study apply to different modes of transport PPP. Also, more research is needed to ascertain what kind of variations exist (if any) in the application of the CSFs, KPIs and performance measures to different types of PPP.

The success criteria developed in this study by Liyanage, Villalba-Romero and Njuangang have only been tested for roads. In order for these success criteria to gain the prominence they deserve, they need to be tested with more road projects and other modes of transport PPP as well.

Policy recommendations

Many case studies did include set performance targets in their contracts. This may lead to lack of performance of contractors during the different stages of the project. Therefore, initiatives should be taken by the public sector to include performance targets and incentives relating to achievement of such targets within the PPP contracts. These incentives should not be used to penalise contractors who do not perform, nor as a carrot and stick approach. Incentives should be perceived as 'motivators' for bettering overall performance.

Performance measurement should be frequently carried out in different stages of a PPP project at given intervals (for example, quarterly, yearly, etc.). The performance data obtained during these stages should be used for performance improvement as well as for benchmarking purposes. This approach would lead to improved overall performance.

User benefits are seldom measured in many PPP transport projects. The public sector needs to take steps to make sure these are measured and achieved in all PPP projects. This way, the negative public perception of PPP projects can be addressed as well.

Part 4

Efficiency

17 Efficiency in transport PPP

An introduction

Aristeidis Pantelias

Introduction

Part 4 of this book focuses on topics of efficiency. Efficiency can be perceived differently depending on the context within which one considers it. In the context of this book it is related to the concepts of standardisation and contextualisation and how they affect the successful delivery of PPP projects.

While standardisation is necessary in order to improve market efficiency, reduce transaction costs and increase transparency and accountability, contextualisation is what makes PPP projects relevant to their end users and caters to their inherently individual characteristics. Striking a balance between the two is not easy, as the two exist in natural tension. In the end, however, what matters is not if or how one should become more dominant than the other but, rather, how the two can work together in a complementary way to support the successful implementation of these complex projects.

The chapters in this Part of the book examine different aspects of standardisation and contextualisation. This may not be immediately apparent as their titles might lead the reader to believe that they are dealing with seemingly unrelated topics. The connection is explained in the subsequent chapter summaries; their contents are viewed under the lens of efficiency, which is, ultimately, the underlying driver behind both standardisation and contextualisation.

Contributions

Chapter 18, by Dewulf, Garvin and Duffield, investigates the tension between standards and context for PPP projects. This is the chapter that sets the scene for the remaining two. The study begins with an overview of standardisation and contextualisation and a discussion on why they are both important to PPP projects. The authors explore how the two affect PPP delivery and implementation in practice, offering relevant insights from the countries of their own professional activity. The Netherlands, the United States of America and Australia are examined under the authors' lens, thus elevating the profile of the study to a multinational standard. The authors find their respective countries to be operating under a different balance of standards versus context, covering the entire spectrum of possible states of equilibrium. The Netherlands appears to be operating in a more standardised PPP environment in contrast to the US, where context seems to be more dominant. In Australia, PPP projects are delivered in a setting that aims to strike a balance between the two.

Chapter 19, by Suárez-Alemán, Roumboutsos and Carbonara, deals with the transport PPP market and the role of strategic investors in PPP delivery. The study considers the business models of the transport modes and how the respective value propositions are supported by the technical and other competences of the project sponsors. This chapter contributes to the discussion on efficiency by focusing on how different firms have used their capabilities and strengths in order to standardise and expand their business in the PPP market. The study seeks to identify reasons behind the evident market concentration and respective markets of operation and future growth. Construction companies appear to dominate this category following a trajectory that usually starts with road projects and ends up in various different PPP projects and modes. Port operators appear to be a separate, isolated category due to the intricacies of port operations and the specific business model and expertise required to operate them successfully. From the study it becomes apparent that strategic investors play on their strength and ability to standardise business processes and models and apply them to different sectors. This seems to be the *modus operandi* for most strategic investors, with the exception of port operators that appear to be solely focused on their core and primary business due to the inherently contextualised nature of port operations.

The third contribution to this Part (Chapter 20), by Roumboutsos, Pantelias and Sfakianakis, explores the issue of creditworthiness for transport PPP projects. Efficiency is again the underlying thread as project credit assessments serve as a standardised market signal to potential investors with respect to the ability (or inability) of a project to honour its debt obligations. While such a standardisation opens the infrastructure debt market to a wide range of potential investors, the tension with context is ever more apparent as PPP projects are not directly comparable to one another due to their inherently unique characteristics. The authors explain how changes in the project finance market have created a new trend towards the assessment of project creditworthiness and they highlight the need to supplement existing assessment methodologies with the consideration of project risks and their relation to the risk management and risk-bearing capacity of the concessionaires, among other relevant factors. In order to do so, a stepwise methodological framework is proposed that aims to balance the standardised nature of the assessment of project creditworthiness with contextual, project-specific risk considerations. The development of this framework brings forward a number of interesting observations and conclusions with potential repercussions on relevant policies and practices.

18 Multinational comparison of the tension between standards and context in PPP

*Geert Dewulf, Michael J. Garvin
and Colin Duffield*

Introduction

Since the late twentieth century, governments worldwide have begun to depend rather heavily on market mechanisms and have structured various sectors to function under free-market principles. Consequently, many Public Private Partnerships (PPPs) have been launched, where project-oriented services are provided by private enterprises via long-term contractual arrangements with the public sector. Global developments are driving the PPP marketplace towards common practices and a degree of normalisation. Alternatively, project strategies from jurisdiction to jurisdiction are frequently different, which results in distinctive project implementation approaches. In short, standardisation enhances open markets while contextualisation accounts for the variance in PPP project objectives, conditions and stakeholders.

Despite the tendency toward liberalisation and decreasing direct command and control by government, we also observe a growing number of norms to promote market stability as well as transactional legitimacy and accountability. Market rhetoric advocates that consistent or standard approaches will drive value, market confidence and stability, while lowering transaction costs. Further, uniform planning, procurement and contractual protocols enhance the transparency and accountability of PPP arrangements. Alternatively, another school of thought suggests that demands for standardised practices and accountability reduce the possibility of generating contextualised solutions for a community, reduce the potential for innovation, or distract public organisations from the constituents they seek to engage and represent (Black 2008).

The general paradox between standards and context has been a subject of debate in planning and governance practice and literature where institutions are often perceived as rigid fixtures, hindering solutions to planning problems (Dembski and Salet 2010). Rules and procedures are often restrictive and limit opportunities to find creative solutions that meet the requirements of a specific situation (Zonneveld *et al.* 2011). This is in line with 'adaptive governance' theory that stresses the importance of learning (in projects) and coproduction between stakeholders for designing solutions for today's problems; governance requires flexibility or adaptability to specific circumstances. However, rules and procedures are often implemented to enhance legitimacy. With growing liberalisation and competition, various forms of oversight are introduced that serve to control and enforce compliance with behavioural standards other than those laid down for the proper functioning of markets (Prechal and van Rijswick 2006).

This debate is related to the broader discussion about governance. Hierarchical steering models are based on the idea of uniformity and stability in society, while network models rely on variety and dynamics (de Bruijn and Ten Heuvelhof 2008). A similar distinction is made by Van Gunsteren (1994, cited in Hajer 2011). He distinguishes between two governance styles: (1) analysis and instruction and (2) variety and selection. The first refers to the central rule approach, which impedes learning potential, while the second one focuses on the analysis of the problem and tries to engage and stimulate actors to solve the problem. This is in line with Ostrom (1990) who stresses the importance of aligning organisational structures to local situations and the need to increase learning potential.

A similar debate is now prevalent in PPP. With their emergence, we observe a growing set of procedures and calls for standardised approaches. Many believe that the absence of common comprehensive procurement legislation hampers the development of PPP (Jooste *et al.* 2011). Standardised PPP arrangements 'can introduce clear lines of accountability, transparency of outcomes and performance, clarity as to the roles and responsibilities of the contracting parties, an assessment of project risks, competition for the delivery of services, and the motivation to succeed' (Stone 2006: 172). Others, however, stress the importance of aligning PPP schemes with situational characteristics (see, for example, Dewulf *et al.* 2012). The challenge for large-scale infrastructure projects generally, and PPP particularly, is balancing standardisation, which is driven by market and sociopolitical forces, and contextualisation, which is driven by end user expectations, local norms and objectives, and unique project characteristics.

In general, the literature on standardisation lacks a sustained theoretical argument to explain institutional standard arrangements (Mattli 2001) or empirical analyses of the consequences of standards in various domains (Timmermans and Epstein 2010). We hope to develop a better understanding of the emergence of standardisation and its consequences in the context of public-private arrangements. To do so, we study the formation and implementation of PPP standards in three developed jurisdictions: the Netherlands, Australia and the United States. We explore the challenge of standardisation and contextualisation by first describing the rationale to standardise PPP processes on the one hand and the need for contextualised solutions on the other. Subsequently, we describe our multi-national case study, with an emphasis on exploring how the drivers of standardisation and contextualisation have impacted environments at the national, programmatic and project levels. Finally, the results of the case studies are compared and some basic conclusions are drawn.

Standardisation and contextualisation

Drivers of standard PPP processes

In the context of the previous discussion, two major drivers generally are pushing the standardisation of PPP: market-based factors and socio-political factors. The market-based drivers are influenced by globalisation, transaction costs and market precedents, whereas the socio-political drivers are shaped by public and legislative scrutiny as well as procurement regulations.

Market drivers

As the world becomes increasingly flat, many large consulting, engineering and construction firms from across the world are quite active in the infrastructure marketplace. The history of industrial economy indicates that the need for standards emerged when production processes and sales crossed geographical borders (Chandler 1977). Currently, shortages in the labour market in both volume and specialisation are also fuelling this development. Moreover, to enhance competition, public sector clients have opened the tendering process, enabling greater involvement of foreign companies. The flow of capital made possible by the global financial markets further heightens opportunities for investors and financial intermediaries. Not surprisingly, PPPs have become a popular target – despite the recent worldwide economic crisis. Today, the infrastructure market is, for the most part, an open global one, and common statutory requirements and regulatory procedures stimulate this open market system.

Many argue (Grimsey and Lewis 2004; Yescombe 2007) that PPP projects have economies of scale. Consequently, these projects tend to be large and complex; bidding costs are typically high and certain procurement obligations, such as security requirements like letters of credit, can limit those qualified to participate. Thus, the number of available bidders is often low. In addition, the nature of PPP projects often requires the development of new or modified contracts for each project, which is time consuming and costly. Consequently, key stakeholders are pushing for standardised procurement processes and contracts to decrease transaction costs.

Socio-political drivers

Standardisation is not just the result of market pressures. Governments and courts have stimulated standardisation (Timmermans and Epstein 2010). Further, as the new public management paradigm has evolved and been liberalised, so too has the scrutiny of government. Legislative bodies, governmental auditing offices, non-governmental organisations and the public in general have focused their attention particularly on the public-private interface. This scrutiny on public-private arrangements has increased efforts to improve accountability and transparency. For instance, Buxbaum and Ortiz (2009) examine such issues as well as governmental responses in the US PPP market.

Shaoul *et al.* (2009) identify two streams of accountability: (1) upward – macro accountability to the legislature and the public as taxpayer and electorate, and (2) downward – micro accountability to the public as service users. To safeguard the public interest or taxpayers' money at the macro-level, governments have implemented various central governance rules and procedures. In Europe, for instance, PPP concessions are subject to rules and principles resulting from the European Union (EU) Treaty: the principles of equal treatment, mutual recognition, proportionality and transparency. These principles are translated in the EU Directives for the coordination of procedures for the award of public contracts. The transparency principle, for example, safeguards the clarity of the contracting public authority's steps in all phases of the procurement procedure. Similarly, contract provisions and performance standards function in a similar way at the micro-level; these requirements compel PPP contractors to deliver user services as contractually defined.

The literature focused on accountability and transparency tends to take a pessimistic view of PPP (see Froud 2003 as an example). Interestingly, a few have considered a different perspective while focusing on the transparency and accountability issue. Grimsey and Lewis (2007) recognise that long-term arrangements potentially limit government flexibility; however, they contend that a conventional delivery (i.e. unbundled separate contracts) is executed in an 'environment largely removed from the economic signals to which private entities are exposed ... and the principals involved are often insulated from the consequences of their actions and decisions' (p. 172). Certainly, infrastructure decisions have consequences across generations but, as Stone (2006) indicates, politicians and government officials making such decisions bear little personal responsibility for their consequences and so have little incentive to change their behaviour. Further, Stone suggested, as stated previously, that mature policy and standardised PPP arrangements create clear lines of accountability, transparency of outcomes, clarity of roles and responsibilities, assessment of project risks, and incentives to succeed.

Standardisation implies that practices or temporary endeavours become institutionalised. Institutions then provide rules in order to reduce uncertainty in social (economic) exchange (Dembski and Salet 2010). The role of institutions is to guide actions in projects through formal and informal codes of conduct. Besides rules, procedures and formalised behaviour (regulative mechanisms), institutional theory also distinguishes normative elements or socially internalised control mechanisms and cultural-cognitive elements or shared concepts of social reality (Scott 2008). While the principal focus here is on formal mechanisms, we recognise the importance of alignment between formal and informal elements. Additionally, legislation, while formalised through a distinct decree, takes shape gradually, within evolving patterns of social expectations (Dembski and Salet 2010).

Drivers of contextualisation

Despite their good intentions, laws and procedures often hinder project solutions or hamper flexibility or adaptability to specific situations, which is paramount in today's society. Hayek (1973) argues in his classic work that laws and legislation have a conditioning rather than an instrumental role. Legislation should safeguard the public interest and is not meant to organise specific purposeful actions. Purposive action needs flexibility and adaptability to changing conditions (van Rijswick and Salet 2012).

Shaoul *et al.* (2009) criticise general governance guidance codes since they tend to favour the upward accountability stream, despite the fact that many policy programmes and executive agencies emphasise the interests of consumers and taxpayers. Indeed, flexibility to delineate specific project requirements and service provisions is a necessity to satisfy the interests of the diverse users of infrastructure. Furthermore, motives for infrastructure programmes and projects differ by country, region and situation; therefore, approaches that fit their context are essential.

As the end users of infrastructure receive more attention, the means for delivering infrastructure needs to evolve as well. A balance between 'bottom-up' perspectives and 'top-down' policies and practices appears vital. Davies *et al.* (2010) provide a lens to examine this transition, adapted from the literature on business models. They contend that the utilisation of PPP represents an effort by clients, consultants and contractors to provide better value to infrastructure end users through the implementation of different business models. A business model refers to how a firm, endowed with given technology, capabilities and assets, successfully configures its organisational structure (Teece 2010) and transactional relationships with external stakeholders (Amit and Zott 2001). Further, it focuses on the way to deliver value for the customer and identifies both a firm's strategic choices and operational implications and profit potential, which can be analysed, tested and validated (Shafer *et al.* 2005). A business model should then be aligned to the specific circumstances of a project. Despite this perspective, PPPs with very similar models are regularly implemented despite differing policy, economic and regional contexts across countries. Contracts are often not tailored to project-specific needs but copied from other projects and contexts (Blanken 2008).

In search of a trade-off

As the prior discussion highlights, market-based and socio-political factors tend to force the PPP market toward common frameworks and processes in order to open markets, lower transaction costs and increase the transparency and legitimacy of transactions. At the same time, the importance of infrastructure users, as well as the demand by clients for some project to project flexibility, cultivates the need for contextualised arrangements. These two prevailing trends are often at odds with one another.

The adaptive governance discourse emerged as a reaction to the regulatory hierarchical approach of governance in the past. Adaptive governance focuses on bottom-up decision-making, multi-interests, informal processes and contextualisation (Brunner 2010). Governance approaches should be attuned to specific circumstances; a trade-off between standards and context exists, which is often manifested as a choice between regulation and flexibility. However, the trade-off is complex and the dominance of one dimension over another is not necessarily desirable. For instance, a strong emphasis on adaptability, flexibility and informal relationships might lead to less legal protection of interested parties and a lower level of protection of general societal interests such as socio-ecological systems (van Rijswick and Salet 2012). In addition, regulations must be structured to preserve efficiency while also protecting consumers from, for instance, opportunistic monopolists (Estache 2004). Despite the wide array of publications on the institutional drivers of PPP policies (Jooste *et al.* 2011; Mahalingam and Delhi 2012), little attention is paid to the tension between regulative institutional mechanisms and the need for contextual solutions. Hence, we focus on this tension by examining the extent to which political and market drivers (summarised in Table 18.1) are influencing context-based implementation of PPP at the national, programmatic and project levels in three different countries.

Research methodology

A multinational case study of the Netherlands, Australia and the United States explores the tension between standardisation and contextualisation. The context for each case is the institutional and market setting for PPP, while the units of analysis are the national, programmatic and project environments in each country. Within each environment, we explored how the drivers of standardisation and contextualisation are influencing policies, organisations, and organisational responses and practices. Data was collected from secondary sources such as procurement regulations, policy reports and legal/procurement documents. In addition, we interviewed personnel inside national or state PPP units (public executive organisations responsible for following governing policies and implementing PPP programmes and projects) using a semi-structured approach.

Table 18.1 Drivers for standardisation versus contextualisation

Standardisation	*Contextualisation*
upward accountability	downward accountability
norms	adapted
decrease transaction costs	value for local needs
generality	variety
transparency	flexibility

To gauge the tension between standardisation and contextualisation, we adopted a multi-faceted approach. First, we studied the congruence between policies and practices in the programmatic environment with the socio-political and market forces present in the national environment. We also assessed the extent to which regulations hinder the context specific choices. To analyse contextual characteristics, we used the institutional pillars of Scott (2008): regulative, cognitive and normative elements. Our assumption is that these institutional pillars will influence the way actors in a programmatic environment adapt standards developed at the national level. Second, organisational responses to standardisation generally and during project implementation were appraised by examining the interview results and the secondary data following guidance from the literature. Oliver (1992) distinguishes five responses to institutional pressures varying from passive acceptance to active resistance: acquiesce, compromise, avoid, defy and manipulate. Alternatively, Bromley and Powell (2012) suggest that, in lieu of varying levels of acceptance, organisations might also detach or decouple their official structure from the operational structure. Our analysis focused on the nature of the organisational responses to policies, regulations and market forces in the national environment, using these notions as a guide. Finally, with respect to contextualisation, we distinguished two 'context' levels: (1) regionally-based forces such as variance from inter-jurisdictional norms and the increased accommodation of local stakeholder interests[1]; and (2) project-specific forces such as the scale of the project, the financial constraints and the interests of stakeholders or community.

Following this general logic, each case was analysed to assess the level of standardisation and contextualisation present. Standardisation was gauged by the strength of market and socio-political forces found that were pushing the PPP environment toward normalised policies and practices. Similarly, contextualisation was evaluated by the strength of regional/local and project-based forces that were countering or balancing the drive toward normalisation and promoting outcomes that were sensitive to regional or local needs and requirements. An adjectival rating scale from low to high was used based on the evidence gathered. For instance, the literature illustrated that standardisation is a function of both market and socio-political forces, so standardisation would rate high, for example, if procurement regulations are restrictive, standard contracts are frequently employed, national institutions exist to promote common practices, and market precedence is typically followed from project to project.

Case Netherlands

The Netherlands is a member of the European Union (EU). The EU operates via supranational institutions such as the European Commission and intergovernmental agreements. Hence, the PPP landscape in Europe emerged from a variety of national PPP policies to a more standard and unified PPP policy. As a member state, the Netherlands must comply with EU policies, so its national, programmatic and project environments are influenced tremendously by the EU.

National environment

The evolution of PPP policies among European countries is, not surprisingly, varied. PPP arrangements boomed in the United Kingdom while in Austria and Sweden, for instance, PPP did not progress beyond the pilot phase. We also observe major differences in the transition pathway from pilot phase towards a mature market (Dewulf *et al.* 2012). Despite these differences, the European Union has strict European regulations regarding the procurement of (large) projects, stimulating an open market within Europe. Still, individual countries have their own jurisdictional authority. Typically, the national governments are responsible for national infrastructure projects (defence, road, water and rail projects) while provinces and municipalities are responsible for provincial and local infrastructure.

The emergence of concession concepts in most European countries can be seen as a reaction to government needs for funding. This was the case with the emergence of the well-known Private Finance Initiative (PFI) in the United Kingdom, but it took place in continental Europe as well. In addition, the European Commission has been encouraging member states to launch PPP programmes. For instance, the stimulus of PPP has been an important element of large policy programmes such as the Trans-European Transport Network (Ten-T). An important milestone in the PPP policy development at the European level was the publication of the Green Paper in 2004 focusing on the public procurement of PPP and, in particular, the selection of private partners. Many countries have developed a standardised procurement system and procedures.

In the Netherlands specifically, the public-private comparator (PPC) methodology has been used since 2005 to systematically assess all projects above 112.5 million euros (Ministerie 2005). Based on previous pilot projects, procedures and documents are standardised. Further, the Dutch government introduced the concept of listed risks as a fair mechanism to discuss potential risks during the procurement phase (Bos 2009) and in 2008 a handbook for Design-Build-Finance-Maintain (DBFM) was published by the government.

Programmatic environment

Public agencies

In most European member states, a PPP unit has been installed with clear and strict procedures enabling the emergence of PPP. Some public agencies have significant authority to initiate and implement PPP such as the Highways Agency in the United Kingdom, which implements the PFI for England's motorways on behalf of the Department for Transport and in accordance with the policies of Her Majesty's Treasury. EU legislation and intent is adapted to fit the specific national conditions. In the Netherlands, a specific PPP unit is not found; however, Rijkswaterstaat, which is part of the Ministry of Infrastructure and the Environment, is responsible for managing the main road and waterway networks as well as the main water systems. It is also responsible for implementing the nation's PPP programme and projects in these areas.

Private sector

The Dutch and, in general, the European PPP policy is driven by issues such as transparency, legitimacy and fair competition. The need for open competition is recognised by the industry. The PPP policy is broadly accepted in society and the level of trust between the private and public sectors has grown (Dewulf *et al.* 2012).

Project environment

Project planning

Planning for economic infrastructure is a clear mandate of the national governments, not of Europe. The planning for social infrastructure is often done at the local level. Like many countries in the EU, the Netherlands uses the public-sector comparator technique to compare the net present value of the cost of design, construction, maintenance and operation in a concessionaire's proposal with the traditional method. This instrument performs a crucial role in the decision-making. In the last decade, knowledge centres were established within the line departments, illustrating the shift from the focus on saving public money towards a focus on service quality.

Project procurement

The decision to procure a road project, for instance, through a design-build-finance-maintain (DBFM) contract is made by the Dutch Minister of Transport. Often the Competitive Dialogue (CD) procedure is applied because of the technical and financial complexities of such projects. The duration of an infrastructure contract is set at 30 years. After prequalification, five consortia are invited to participate in the dialogue. Certain Critical Aspects, as identified by the contracting authority based on risk management (items such as the stability of the existing infrastructure, air quality and lane availability during the construction stage), form the basis for some of the dialogue products that the candidates submit at the end of the dialogue stage. These dialogue products must meet a minimum quality level before the candidates are invited to bid. Four further Critical Aspects of an Action Scheme, plus the acceptance of Risks and Optional Requirements are part of the conversation during the Consultation stage. The Optional Requirements set by the contracting authority are additions to the project's scope, and candidates can choose whether or not to meet them. In a similar way, candidates could decide whether to accept risks, based on a pricing scheme, or leave these in the hands of the contracting agency.

An example of the CD procedure is The Second Coen Tunnel in Amsterdam. This project is large (estimated value $300 million NPV) and complex, and involves the maintenance of an existing, 40-year-old tunnel plus the construction of a second tunnel alongside the current one. The contract for the Coen Tunnel project was signed in 2008, and the maintenance of the existing tunnel was then transferred to the contractor. The construction stage for the new tunnel started in 2009. This concession project, the first procured using the CD procedure in the Netherlands, consists of widening approximately 14 kilometres of highways at the north and south entrances to the existing Coen Tunnel, and expanding the tunnel's capacity from two lanes to three in each direction, plus two further reversible lanes, enabling five lanes of traffic in one direction during peak hours. This project followed the implementation process just described, but it posed challenges for the Agency as well as the private sector. As one official noted: 'I think both parties were unfamiliar with the [CD procedure]. From the Agency's side, what was not clear was: how far can we go? What is allowed by the European Commission?'

Case Australia

The Australian PPP market is rather dynamic and the type and style of PPP projects have varied with changing market conditions. Similar to Europe, early PPP projects were driven by the need for investment in a tight fiscal environment; bankability of projects was critical. As the PPP market matured, the impetus for projects changed to a focus on value for money and numerous economic and social projects were delivered. With a country having nine separate jurisdictions coming together under a federation, it is understandable that differences exist between jurisdictions but, similarly, for reasons of continuity of deals and productivity, areas of consistency in approach have emerged due to the relatively small market within a country with a population of only some 23 million. Australia has three tiers of government, Federal – generally responsible for issues of national significance (like defence, interstate supply chain and taxation); States and Territories – responsible for day-to-day provision of services (for example, infrastructure, including hospitals, schools and major roads); and Municipalities – responsible for local issues (for example, planning compliance).

National environment

PPP projects initiated in the 1980s and 1990s were primarily based on full risk transfer agreements and the driving rationale for their use was a desire by governments to transfer risk to the private sector and to generate development without adversely affecting government budgets. Since these early projects, the Australian PPP industry has matured and the driving influence for more recent projects has been the desire for enhanced value. Tracking the sources of project funds available from government provides a lens for understanding who is responsible for aspects of PPP in Australia. General taxes and the Goods and Services Tax within Australia are collected by the federal government. The Federal government distributes many of these funds by consensus with state and territory governments to provide the base budgets for the states. Some monies are held by the Federal government for its own areas of responsibility and this includes some grants that are linked to projects of national importance. The States and Territories are responsible for organising the delivery of infrastructure. States funds come not only from their federal government allocation but also from duties and local taxes. The States and Territories are also directly responsible for any concessions granted to the private sector in a PPP arrangement.

The establishment of Infrastructure Australia in 2008 by the Federal government sought to prioritise projects, to create consistency across government for the procurement of major projects and, in part, to assist with deal flow and resource management. One of the first priorities and outcomes of Infrastructure Australia (IA) was the development of national PPP guidelines. Prior to the release of these guidelines, as endorsed by the Council of Australian Governments through the Federal Minister for Infrastructure and Transport, Australian PPP followed individual state and territory policies and procedures.

The introduction of National PPP Guidelines was done to create consistency in the general approach adopted for PPP procurement, but these guidelines do not prevent subtle approaches and strengths in different sectors and jurisdictions from emerging, as a state official observed: 'adaptations are within the framework of the guidance material'.

The standardised approach confirms that PPP will be used with a focus on value for money outcomes, and the clarity will be provided to the market by way of a detailed business assessment prior to sending requests to the market for bidding. The phases of PPP delivery have been standardised to include an expression of interest phase to the market, generally followed by short listing (to perhaps three bidders) and inviting these shortlisted bidders to respond to a request for proposal via an interactive tendering process. The preferred bidder will, in turn, enter a negotiation phase in advance of both contract and financial closure. Testing of the VfM proposition is done by comparison with the public sector comparator based on whole of life discounted costs. Within the national guidelines there are, however, a number of specific exclusions that allow individual jurisdictions to meet their specific legislative and governance requirements. These exclusions include the level of government approvals required, the timing of approvals, the method of conducting the public interest test, disclosure of information regarding the public sector comparator, specifics of the tendering process, probity, and the requirements for communication. One state official noted: 'interpretation of value is held by the state decision-makers, and there is no appetite to have federal "rules" imposed'.

Consideration of what is not agreed for inclusion in the national guidelines is as informative as the specifics that are included. Not agreed include: commercial principles for economic infrastructure projects; standardised contracts; clarity on government's responsibility for approvals such as design and planning; and specific risks associated with important matters such as soil contamination, refinancing, or industrial relations. However, a state official commented: 'contracts are near standard across the country but are checked and reviewed for each project'.

In late 2011, Baker and McKenzie (2012) undertook a survey of some 104 senior business owners, lawyers, project managers and CEOs, all of whom had had current experience of PPP. A key question asked was 'Does Australia need a more centralised approach?' (to PPP). Eighty-three per cent of private sector interviewees sought a simplified procurement process. About 70 per cent of interviewees were of the view that government should be more active in coordinating projects. A sentiment commonly represented was 'states run their own projects and the Commonwealth separately does its own things. It would be better to have a whole of Australia approach...' (a senior government official, Baker and McKenzie (2012)).

States and Territories are the responsible government for implementation of infrastructure projects and, therefore, it is at this level where legislation, if required, is formed. The requirement of the States is that the option of a project being delivered as a PPP is a serious consideration in the business case. The federal government exerts its influence as a funder. PPP projects are subject to all normal project requirements for planning, heritage, environmental and work approvals. Enabling legislation exists for projects to be designated of state significance, thus theoretically fast tracking some of these approval processes. Generally, such fast tracking is not undertaken and due process is followed to ensure full stakeholder engagement.

Project specific agreements, decisions and concessions are made by the jurisdiction responsible for the project. All three levels of government are involved in approvals and these can bring significant risk to a project.

Programmatic environment

Public agencies

Specific advocates for PPP from government are far less prevalent than specialist teams of project staff focusing on major infrastructure investments. These government agencies seek to identify the 'best' value from a range of alternative delivery mechanisms. The most recently formed group of this sort is Infrastructure New South Wales (NSW), which was established in July 2011 with the express purpose of developing a 20-year infrastructure strategy. One of the most successful governmental teams in Australia is the Partnerships Victoria group within the Department of Treasury and Finance, Victoria.

Private sector

Australia has an active PPP market and private participants strongly recognise the need to maintain a consistent flow of projects if a mature industry is to be maintained. The opportunity for governments to bring forward projects due to the cash flow arrangements within PPP is an encouragement for governments to adopt a PPP approach along with the increasing evidence of value for money savings in capital expenditure (Raisbeck *et al.* 2010). Infrastructure Partnerships Australia is the peak body representing industry and conducts itself on the basis of being a conduit for the latest information. It influences policy discussion and debate on the basis of informed research and dialogue. There is also a very strong culture within Australia for dealing fairly and transparently with the market, and the private sector reciprocates this approach.

Project environment

Project planning

Planning for both economic and social infrastructure is a clear mandate of government in Australia. Until the introduction of Infrastructure Australia, there was some criticism that not enough long-term planning of infrastructure was occurring, but this is changing at all levels of government as evidenced by the formation of Infrastructure NSW and Infrastructure Queensland.

Specific project planning is governed by the Infrastructure Australia PPP guidelines whereby an underlying philosophy is for government to be clear in what it requires and then engage the market through a competitive process to achieve a commercial outcome. An important lesson learnt by the Victorian project team was that process clarity and a clear commitment to proceed with projects in accordance with the established process increased the private sector's confidence and led to good project outcomes. A state official noted: 'the state has standardised commercial principles – agreed with industry over a period. Each new project tends to use the last project's contract as the starting point for review and confirmation that the approach is still optimal ... there is potential to modify contracts albeit only around the margins.'

Project procurement

The Linking Melbourne Authority (LMA) in Victoria provides an excellent example of the national policy in action. This agency (under various names) has delivered the Melbourne City Link toll road ($1.81 billion capital value), Eastlink toll road ($2.6 billion capital value) and the Peninsula Link (an availability-style PPP worth $849 million NPV in Feb 2010 dollars). The most recent of these road projects, the Peninsula Link, reached financial close in February 2010. This 27km freeway, linking the Eastlink toll road to Melbourne's Eastern Peninsula, applied the national PPP guidelines, and a saving against the risk adjusted public sector comparator of $9 million was claimed. The procurement process was managed by the LMA. The tendering process shortlisted three proponents from an expression of interest phase and ultimately took two bidders all the way to the final decision to award the contract to the Southern Way consortium.

In May 2011, the Victorian Auditor General (2011) released his report titled 'Management of Major Road Projects' which in part considered the outcomes of the Peninsula Link project. He confirmed that the relevant Commonwealth and state guidelines had been followed in procuring Peninsula Link. However, a lack of project assurance documentation precluded the Auditor from confirming the VfM cost differential claimed. The Auditor also recommended that, in the future, the agency ensure decision-makers were fully informed of the sensitivity of the VfM test to the discount rate chosen and that specific plans were developed to measure project outcomes.

A key to PPP in Australia is that contracts are covered by standard contract law provisions and the risk allocation is clearly presented in a draft contract that is released with the request for a tender proposal. The procurement process is overseen by detailed probity management that incorporates a probity plan to ensure fairness in the engagement process.

In summary, Australian PPPs appear still to have areas where greater standardisation may assist in reducing bidding costs. Based on industry feedback in the Baker and McKenzie (2012) survey, greater coordination from government and a centralised team of PPP experts would be of assistance. This view was confirmed by a state official: 'Australia is a small market hence there are benefits in working together to create greater depth in the market. Directions and new developments are discussed at the COAG (Council of Australian Governments) Infrastructure Working Group.'

Case United States

While the US used PPP-type arrangements prior to the Second World War, the nation's approach to procuring public works evolved to a segmented delivery and tax-based funding approach as a result of a sequence of changes in federal and subsequently state procurement laws. In the late 1980s, like other regions of the world, specific states and municipalities in the US began to experiment with PPP. Since then, the US landscape for PPP has fluctuated.

National environment

Infrastructure in the US is delivered within a complex environment where public works projects are governed by prevailing federal, state and local laws as well as the respective executive agency or jurisdictional regulations and procedures. Depending on the circumstances, the conditions associated with a project can vary dramatically. Coupled with these public laws and requirements are active private enterprises, professional societies and non-governmental organisations that influence and affect both policies and projects.

At the highest level, the Federal Acquisition Regulation (FAR) is a set of regulations issued by agencies of the federal government that govern the acquisition (or purchase) of goods and services. Beyond the FAR, conditions or requirements from federal legislation or federal regulatory bodies can influence both infrastructure policy and projects. For instance, the statutory requirements of the National Environmental Policy Act (NEPA) dictate how major projects with federal funding in the US proceed. Many view the standards of this process as overly rigid, particularly with regard to PPP, since the current process presumes a conventional project delivery. One state official observed: 'a key constraint is the environmental process – if a change in scope puts a project outside the approved environmental footprint, we would have to open the environmental reviews up again'. In addition, the Federal Highway Administration (FHWA), acting on behalf of the US Department of Transportation, oversees the national Interstate Highway System.

Unlike other countries, the US does not have a central PPP unit, and the majority of the PPP activity in the US has been confined to the transportation sector. The closest proxy that the US has is the Office of Innovative Programme Delivery, which was created in 2008 within FHWA to serve as a resource for state and local transportation agencies when implementing 'innovative strategies to deliver programmes and projects'. Currently, it is developing a set of tools to support states during PPP planning, procurement and implementation. This office has oversight of the US Department of Transportation's Transportation Infrastructure Finance and Investment Act (TIFIA) loan programme. Established in 1998, TIFIA provides loans, credit assistance and loan guarantees for surface transportation projects of national and regional significance. TIFIA loans have been the most popular tool by far; such loans have been used in multiple PPP projects to date. Besides TIFIA, tax-exempt Private Activity Bonds (PABs) have played a role in several PPP transactions. Established in 2006 as part of a federal demonstration programme, project sponsors may request authorisation to issue PABs for qualified projects.

At the federal level, the governing legislation allows exceptions to the typical project delivery process for transportation projects through the submission of variance requests known as Special Experimental Projects (SEP); currently, most PPPs requiring federal involvement must receive designation as SEP-15 projects. Recently enacted, the Moving Ahead for Progress in the 21st Century Act (MAP-21) legislation modified elements of the TIFIA programme, notably changing the amount of total project costs eligible for a TIFIA loan from 33 per cent to 49 per cent. In addition, it directed the Secretary of Transportation to develop 'standard Public Private Partnership transaction model contracts' for the 'most popular' types of PPP; an initial model contract for toll or revenue risk concessions has been created, and public comments have been received. Some states are very wary of this development. One state official observed, 'we made it clear during a recent listening session that FHWA held on standardised contracts that whatever they produce should be advisory or descriptive in nature'. Another commented, 'standardisation is almost impossible, but a template would be good'.

At the state level, each state has its own legislation governing project delivery and procurement. The majority of this legislation is focused on the transportation sector although legislation related to education facilities is also in place. For instance, Virginia's Public-Private Transportation Act (PPTA) of 1995 recognised that the 'public need may not be wholly satisfied by existing ways in which transportation facilities are acquired, constructed or improved', so it authorised private entities to 'acquire, construct, improve, maintain, and/or operate one or more transportation facilities' when doing so would 'result in the availability of such transportation facilities to the public in a more timely or less costly fashion'. Today, 33 states and one territory have legislation enabling PPP-type projects for transportation. The variance among the state legislation is substantial. In most states, the private sector is permitted to submit unsolicited proposals. In a few states, PPP are limited to pilot or demonstration projects. More indirectly, the issue of whether or not PPP are in the public's 'interest' has garnered the attention of federal, state and local legislators as well as many non-governmental organisations.

Given the diversity among the states, the 'normalising' forces within the PPP environment have come from investors, lending institutions, concessionaires, and financial, legal and technical advisors. The major players in the PPP market are somewhat limited, so frequently potential projects may have the same key organisations involved. Further, recent agreements have often looked to prior agreements for precedents with respect to risk allocation, contractual terms, etc. A state official commented, 'we generally borrow contracts from other states, and others have borrowed ours'. In short, the US PPP market is rather decentralised and standardisation occurs incrementally through diffusion of 'successful' practices.

Programmatic environment

Public agencies

At the most fundamental level, each state's Department of Transportation (DOT) manages the transportation modes under its jurisdiction, and each DOT also operates and manages its portion of the Interstate Highway System as well as all other state routes. With regard to PPP, each DOT establishes the programmatic policies and implements the PPP programme authorised by the respective legislation. PPP units do not exist currently in the US. Instead, existing divisions or special units within the Departments of Transportation are responsible for these programmes. For instance, the Texas DOT has a 'Non-traditional Projects' unit that handles PPP. In 2011, the state of Virginia established the Office of Transportation Public Private Partnerships (OTP3), which created a PPP unit that reports directly to the state's Secretary of Transportation. OTP3 also has responsibility for planning and implementing PPP across all modes of transportation within the state. Currently, this office is being reshaped into the Virginia Office of Public Private Partnerships to extend its reach beyond transportation. The authority that this unit will have is similar to the authority found in units such as Partnerships Victoria.

Private sector

Within the private sector, the most well-known advocate group for PPP is the National Council for Public Private Partnerships (NCPPP), which is a non-profit, non-partisan organisation founded in 1985. NCPPP advocates and facilitates the formation of Public Private Partnerships at the federal, state and local levels. Other organisations such as the American Road and Transportation Builder's Association (ARTBA) have dedicated divisions designed to promote and enhance PPP.

Project environment

Project planning

As mentioned previously, the statutory environmental requirements at both the federal and state level have a tremendous influence over project planning. Aside from this, the US has quite a bit of variance with regard to the structure that PPP may take. Several high profile projects were the result of unsolicited proposals. In other cases, project planning has started to evolve toward the types of approaches employed in Europe and Australia, as one state official observed, 'our agency now has a very structured decision process that includes the use of VfM analyses'. A phenomenon that is somewhat unique to the US is the pre-development agreement (PDA) for PPP. PDAs do provide certain advantages for public agencies that may not be able to define or scope a project (even with consultant support) without engaging a committed private partner. A procurement standard, however, is not in place for PDAs to maintain a level playing field and to foster accountability and transparency during its implementation.

As an example, the Capital Beltway (I-495) around Washington, DC was initially constructed in 1956 and completed in 1964. In 1998, the Virginia DOT and FHWA began an Environmental Impact Study (EIS) to examine various improvement alternatives. In 2002, FHWA approved the EIS that included several High Occupancy Vehicle lane alternatives for the Beltway. In the same year, Virginia DOT received an unsolicited conceptual proposal from Fluor Daniel to develop, finance, design and construct High Occupancy Toll (HOT) Lanes on the Capital Beltway. Although Virginia DOT advertised for competing proposals as required by its state legislation, none were received. In the spring of 2003, Virginia DOT submitted a grant application to FHWA to study HOT lanes and other 'value pricing' applications in Northern Virginia; it also held several public input meetings to solicit input regarding HOV versus HOT lane alternatives. A strong majority of the public feedback supported the HOT lanes concept. Early in 2005, the state's Commonwealth Transportation Board selected the HOT lanes plan as the preferred alternative. By 2006, FHWA gave its final approval of the HOT lanes plan.

Project procurement

States tend to maintain jurisdiction over infrastructure projects although federal requirements and approvals are necessary for projects involving federal resources or under federal jurisdiction. Standardisation in procurement processes and contract provisions is currently absent beyond the general requirements of the FAR. As early as 2000, the American Bar Association's Section of Public Contract Law promulgated its Model Procurement Code for states and local jurisdictions for this reason. However, relatively few states have adopted legislation based on the Model Procurement Code and, in those states where the Code has been adopted, it is not uncommon for the DOT to be excluded from Code requirements. Procurement processes for PPP have emerged that are similar to those in Australia or Europe; this is not surprising since many of the consultants that DOTs retain for advisory purposes have substantial experience in these global markets. Contracts are normalising to some degree as states rely on one another for precedents, while others are developing their own standards as one state official noted: 'Contracts tend to be tailored to each project, but we are developing a standard term sheet for key contractual elements that will serve as a baseline for all projects'.

For example, the Fluor Daniel team submitted a detailed proposal in 2003 for the Capital Beltway project at the request of Virginia DOT once no competing conceptual proposals were received. An advisory panel reviewed the proposal and issued its findings, recommending the project be further developed, as long as issues identified were addressed, with the goal of entering into a Public Private Partnership (PPP) contract, or comprehensive agreement, with Fluor. Meanwhile, the Australian developer Transurban joined the Fluor team in 2004, and they entered into an agreement to develop the Beltway project together. Under this structure, a concessionaire named Capital Beltway Express (CBE) was created through a 90/10 joint venture of Transurban and Fluor. The Fluor-Transurban team agreed with Virginia DOT to establish a new version of the contract, which was termed the Amended and Restated Comprehensive Agreement (ARCA).

Analysis and discussion

Cross-national comparison

Each of the cases was analysed to assess the level of standardisation and contextualisation present. Standardisation was gauged by the strength of market and socio-political forces present that were pushing the overall PPP environment toward normalised policies and practices. Similarly, contextualisation was evaluated by the strength of regional/local and project-based forces that were countering or balancing the drive toward normalisation and promoting outcomes that were sensitive to regional or local needs and requirements. Table 18.2 depicts the outcomes across the cases of the adjectival rating scheme employed.

In the three regions, we find a similar trend towards a central and comprehensive PPP archetype. However, the nature and influence of the archetype varies among the countries. In the case of the Netherlands, the forces of standardisation tend to outweigh those of contextualisation. A strong environment at the EU and national level exists to create mechanisms to keep transaction costs down, foster transparency and accountability, and to emphasise predictable/repeatable processes. Alternatively, a moderate environment is observed at regional and project levels. Clearly, adaptation to circumstantial conditions is possible and even encouraged as evidenced by the joint responsibility for PPP-related decisions between the Ministry of Finance and the line departments. Still, the market

Table 18.2 Summary

	Netherlands (NL)	Australia	USA
Standardisation			
Market forces	*High to Medium*	*Medium to High*	*Medium*
	• Emphasis on using PPP for large, complex projects.	• IA standardised phases and requirements of delivery to increase predictability and lower transaction costs.	• Strong reliance by federal and state agencies on consulting community for guidance and services.
	• Tendency to use CD procedure can drive transaction costs up.	• IA prioritisation creates project pipeline of sorts.	• Tendency to use prior agreements and contractual precedents to ameliorate transaction complexity.
		• Infrastructure Partnerships Australia (private entity) influences policy and process.	• Central PPP guidelines under development and no standards beyond FAR.
		• Emphasis on competitive awards.	
Socio-political forces	*High*	*Medium to High*	*Medium to Low*
	• Strict EU regulations.	• Establishment of Infrastructure Australia (IA) in 2008.	• Federal procurement and statutory requirements imposed when federal jurisdiction or funds involved.
	• Overarching EU and NL principles.	• Overarching national principles.	• New federal legislation requires a model contract.
	• Standardised procedures and documents (NL).	• IA published guidelines.	• Federal instruments such as TIFIA and PABs are popular but centrally administered.
	• Published DBFM handbook (NL).	• Utilisation of standard VfM practices, etc. to foster transparency and accountability.	• Establishment of FHWA's Office of Innovative Program Delivery in 2008, but with minimal authority.
	• Utilisation of standard VfM practices, etc. to foster transparency and accountability.	• Tax loss incentive based on IA approval of project.	• Limited use of VfM practices, etc. and no national standard or model.
			• Public interest debates prevalent.

(Continued)

Table 18.2 Summary (Continued)

	Netherlands (NL)	Australia	USA
Contextualisation			
Regional/local forces	Medium • Adaptation of EU requirements to NL environment. • Joint responsibility for PPP decisions between Ministry of Finance and line departments. • Social infrastructure typically handled locally. • Knowledge centres focused on service quality in PPP.	Medium to High • Strong state PPP units and line departments. • Exclusions from IA guidelines allowed to meet local requirements. • Increased emphasis across all jurisdictions on service quality.	High • States have own legislation and regulations governing PPP. • State DOTs responsible for PPP planning and implementation. • State PPP units uncommon.
Project-based forces	Medium • Has shown tendency to follow CD procedure for PPP, which theoretically should provide scoping flexibility.	Medium • Contracting authorities have capacity to tailor project specifications and outputs. • Interactive tendering procedure for PPP and mechanisms for consideration of unsolicited proposals and capital contributions.	High • Project development approaches vary widely, i.e. unsolicited proposals. • States tend to tailor project processes and contracts to circumstances.

and socio-political environment appear to impact PPP in the Netherlands more prominently. In Australia, some similarities with Europe are observed, and Australia appears to be transitioning from a PPP environment long dominated by its States to one that is moderated by its Federal government. The advent of Infrastructure Australia and its subsequent actions are notable in this regard. However, the autonomy of states remains intact as evidenced by the exclusions in the Federal guidelines and processes and the continued significant role of state PPP units. In effect, Australia appears to be searching for a point of equilibrium. In the US, however, the federal role is limited to procurement and statutory requirements that are imposed on all public works projects where there is federal funding or jurisdiction; the strongest normalising forces are the market players themselves as they transfer their influence across the states where they work. This is not to say that the federal role is insignificant; rather, at the federal level, PPP are treated as exceptions. Accordingly, the evidence suggests a continuum from strong standardisation and moderate contextualisation to moderate standardisation and strong contextualisation across the three cases.

Discussion

The findings illustrate the rationale for the different approaches adopted such as, for example, the availability of finance and tendering norms. For instance, specific situations such as economic turmoil or cultural/historically rooted regional characteristics necessitate contextual solutions. It is also clear that further standardisation of policies, institutional approaches and project documentation may indeed lead to improvements. We can debate whether standardisation will lead to more efficiency since the costs for standardisation might be extensive. Moreover, the power of standardisation depends on whether standards are really implemented. Implementation will depend on the support of the various states and other stakeholders. Standard creation is fundamentally a social act (Timmermans and Epstein 2010). Standards are built collectively and aim to obtain legitimate coordination and comparability. Standards have to be backed up by those who are responsible for the implementation. One state official commented, 'As a sovereign state, we prefer to implement PPP based on our experience and priorities'. This perspective and other evidence gathered suggest that the response by states to such initiatives would be classified by Oliver (1992) as avoidance or defiance.

Standardisation of PPP arrangements assumes similarity between various levels of government and projects. Our analysis has clearly indicated the differences between nations and states. Moreover, the project histories showed how PPP contracts have to be customised to the specific circumstances. We do, however, see a more standardised approach in Europe, and to a lesser extent in Australia, than we do in the US. This is remarkable taking into account the cultural and economic diversity in Europe and the long history of project financing in the US (Dewulf *et al.* 2012). For reasons of competition and accountability, Europe is moderating its cultural and economic specific circumstances. According to Timmermans and Epstein (2010), standardisation connotes a dull sameness, the suppression of individuality in the service of industrial uniformity. We might then be concerned that the standardisation movement in Europe will outweigh the specific geographical needs and socio-political demands.

An important requisite for successful implementation of PPP standards is the choice of the governance level responsible for the creation and realisation of standards: national (or supra-national in the case of Europe) or state level. According to Mattli (2001) the choice should depend on the scope of the problem and the relative competencies of actors and institutions. But, the author concludes, 'no level is always best' (p. 335). Indeed, (supra-)national standards will enhance competition across geographical borders, but we might question whether (supra-) national institutions possess the capabilities to understand the specific local needs of, for instance, transportation infrastructure as well as the specific market circumstances. Evidence from our cases supports this observation. Moreover, to gain the support of states and local governments, essential for successful implementation, more attention should be paid to their incentives to support and the urge to adapt these standards. As shown in the US case, some states already have a mature PPP policy and are hence less inclined to adopt national standards than states that have just started with PPP.

Standards will be perceived as legitimate on a state or project level if they fit with the values and norms (normative supports) or cultural frames (cognitive supports) of a country or state. In many interviews, it was stressed that states are 'sovereign', implying that major decisions should be made at that level. This is probably in line with the expectations of voters or constituents. Kivleniece and Quelin (2012) showed how the success of hybrid organisations such as PPP depends on the role of external constituents. Often tensions exist between public, private and social interests. Private value claims are often challenged by external constituents such as taxpayers, voters and users of infrastructure. These constituents empower public bodies directly (by voting) and indirectly (public support), enabling these government bodies to develop a sustainable PPP policy. Standardisation at the (supra-)national level might overlook specific requirements at the local level, leading to reduced ability to engage local constituents and develop the necessary public support. Since public private arrangements are very complex and success depends on a variety of local circumstances, we might then question the appropriateness of standardisation.

Conclusion and limitations

The basis of the tension between standardisation or regulation and contextualisation was explored via existing literature and debates in various fields. Further, the factors that tend to promote or diminish both within the PPP environment were depicted. On this basis, information was gathered from the Netherlands, Australia and the US to examine the circumstances in each jurisdiction along three broad dimensions – the national, programmatic and project environments. The data collected was assessed on a basic level to broadly characterise each case. The evidence suggests that the Netherlands operates in a PPP environment more influenced by market and socio-political forces, Australia appears to be searching for a balance between standards and context, and the US finds itself in a situation where regional/local and project-based forces are more significant, although recent events at the federal level might alter this circumstance. In many respects, the regions – Netherlands, Australia, and US – are arrayed on a continuum from most standard/least contextualised to least standard/most contextualised. We cannot conclude at this stage, however, whether they are properly positioned along this continuum – presuming such a conclusion is possible. Future research can explore this further.

Inter-jurisdictional analyses are quite difficult, as others have documented and criticised. In this effort, the data collected was rather general as was the method employed to assess the impacts of drivers of standardisation and contextualisation. Further, the limited use of projects as a unit of analysis hindered the project-based observations that were possible. Future work should focus on refining the data collection and analysis method while considering whether or not a more in-depth focus on a project or a set of projects would aid in assessing how the issues discussed are manifested in actual project environments. If done, this would permit greater utilisation of the business model framework as a basis of analysis as well as assessment of stakeholder engagement and input.

Note

1 While this distinction is made, our data did not look specifically at how stakeholder interests were handled or accommodated.

References

Amit, R. and Zott, C. (2001) 'Value creation in e-business'. *Strategic Management Journal*, June–July Special, 22, pp. 493–520

Baker and McKenzie (2012) *Public Private Partnerships: Evolution or Revolution? Global Business Challenges.* Available online at: www.bakermckenzie.com/files/Publication/f926f49a-d12a-4cd4-9a3a-be74e63b45ea/Presentation/PublicationAttachment/248d75c6-bc1d-48a7-ad10-63cced1b7043/bk_australia_PPPreport_mar12.pdf

Blanken, A. (2008) *Flexibility against efficiency?* PhD Thesis. Enschede: Twente University

Black, J. (2008) *Constructing and Contesting Legitimacy and Accountability in Polycentric Regulatory Regimes.* LSE Law, Society and Economy Working Papers 2/2008, London: London School of Economics and Political Science

Bos, B. B. (2009) *Inventarisatie van mogelijke verbeteringen voor Lijstrisico's bij PPS projecten van Rijkswaterstaat.* Master Thesis. Delft University

Bromley, P. and Powell, W. W. (2012) 'From smoke and mirrors to walking the talk: decoupling in the contemporary world'. *The Academy of Management Annals*, 6 (1), pp. 483–530

Bruijn, H. de and Heuvelhof, E. ten (2008) *Management in Networks, On Multi-actor Decision Making.* London: Routledge

Brunner, R. (2010) 'Adaptive governance as a reform strategy'. *Policy Science*, 43, pp. 301–341

Buxbaum, J. N. and Ortiz, I. N. (2009) *NCHRP Synthesis 391: Public Sector Decision Making for Public-Private Partnerships*. Washington, DC: Transportation Research Board

Chandler, A. D. (1977) *The Visible Hand: The Managerial Revolution in American Business Management*. Cambridge, MA: Harvard University Press

Davies, A., Frederiksen, L. and Dewulf, G. (2010) 'Business models, infrastructure and the changing public-private interface'. *Working Paper Proceedings of the Engineering Project Organisation Conference*, Lake Tahoe, November

Dembski, S. and Salet, W. (2010) 'The transformative potential of institutions: how symbolic markers can institute new social meaning in changing cities'. *Environment and Planning A*, 42, pp. 611–625

Dewulf, G., Blanken, A. and Bult-Spiering, W. D. (2012) *Strategic Issues in Public-Private Partnerships*. London: Wiley

Estache, A. (2004) *Emerging Infrastructure Policy Issues in Developing Countries: A Survey of the Recent Economic Literature*. Background paper for the October 2004 Berlin meeting of the POVNET Infrastructure Working Group. INFVP, The World Bank

Froud, J. (2003) 'The Private Finance Initiative: risk, uncertainty, and the state'. *Accounting, Organizations and Society*, 28 (5), pp. 567–589

Grimsey, D. and Lewis, M. K. (2004) *Public Private Partnerships: The Worldwide Revolution in Infrastructure Provision and Project Finance*. Cheltenham, UK: Edward Elgar

Grimsey, D. and Lewis, M. K. (2007) 'Public Private Partnerships and public procurement'. *Agenda*, 14(2), pp. 171–188

Hajer, M. (2011) *De energieke samenleving; op zoek naar een sturingsfilosofie voor een schone economie, Planbureau voor de leefomgeving*. The Hague

Hayek, F. A. von (1973) *Rules and Order. Vol. 1 of Law, Legislation and Liberty*. London: Routledge and Kegan Paul

Jooste, S. F., Levitt, R. and Scott, D. (2011) 'Beyond "one size fits all": how local conditions shape PPP-enabling field development'. *Engineering Project Organization Journal*, 1(1), pp. 11–25

Kivleniece, I. and Quelin, B. V. (2012) 'Creating and capturing value in public-private ties: a private actor's perspective'. *Academy of Management Review*, 37 (2), pp. 272–299

Mahalingam, A. and Delhi, V. S. K. (2012) 'A contested organizational field perspective of the diffusion of Public Private Partnership regimes: evidence from India'. *Engineering Project Organization Journal*, 2(3)

Mattli, W. (2001) 'The politics and economics of international standards setting: an introduction'. *Journal of European Public Policy*, 8(3), pp. 328–44

Ministerie van Werker en Waterstaat (2005) *Nota Mobiliteit*. The Hague

Oliver, C. (1992) 'The antecedents of deinstitutionalization'. *Organization Studies*, 13, pp. 563–88

Ostrom, E. (1990) *Governing the Commons; The Evolution of Institutions for Collective Action*. Cambridge: Cambridge University Press

Prechal, S. and van Rijswick, H. F. M. W. (2006) 'Supervision and supervisory authorities: A few introductory remarks'. *Utrecht Law Review*, 2 (1), pp. 1–7

Raisbeck, P., Duffield, D. and Xu, M. (2010) 'Comparative performance of PPP and traditional procurement in Australia'. *Construction Management and Economics*, 28 (4), pp. 345–359

Scott, R.W. (2008) *Institutions and Organizations: Ideas and Interests* (3rd Ed.). Thousand Oaks, CA: Sage Publications

Shafer, S. M., Smith, H. J. and Linder, J. C. (2005) 'The power of business models'. *Business Horizons*, 48, pp. 199–207

Shaoul, J., Stafford, A. and Stapleton, P. (2009) 'Financial black holes, the disclosure and transparency of privately financed roads in the UK'. *Accounting, Auditing and Accountability Journal*, 23(2), pp. 229–256

Stone, T. (2006) *PFI – is there a better way?* London: KPMG Global Infrastructure and Projects Group

Teece, D. (2010) 'Business models, business strategy and innovation'. *Long Range Planning*, 43, pp. 172–194

Timmermans, S. and Epstein, S. (2010) 'A world of standards but not a standard world: toward a sociology of standards and standardization'. *Annual Review of Sociology*. 36, pp. 69–89

van Rijswick, M. and Salet, W. (2012) 'Enabling the contextualization of legal rules in responsive strategies to climate change'. *Ecology and Society*, 17(2), p. 18

Victorian Auditor General Office (2011) *Management of Major Road Projects*. Victoria, Australia: Victorian Government Printer, May 2011

Yescombe, E. R. (2007) *Public-Private Partnerships: Principles of Policy and Finance*. Boston: Elsevier

Zonneveld, W., Korthals Altes, W., Spaans, M., Waterhout, B. and de Wolff, H. (2011) *Knelpunten gebiedsontwikkeling: de rol van Europese richtlijnen*. Delft: Ministry of Economic Affairs, OTB

19 The transport PPP market

Strategic investors

Ancor Suárez-Alemán, Athena Roumboutsos and Nunzia Carbonara

Introduction

Although in 2012 the European Public Private Partnership (PPP) market recorded its lowest volume and number of transactions for a decade, transport has remained the most active sector compared with others such as telecoms, water or energy (EIB 2013). Additionally, transport also continues to be the largest sector in value, accounting for 59 per cent of the total market. Data also shows how this figure has grown back to 75 per cent of the overall market value (EIB 2013).

The transport sector has especially taken advantage of the PPP delivery model in Europe. Three factors have been the major drivers behind this: the growing demand for transportation services (cfr. European Commission 2011); the ability to secure potential revenue cash flows through user payments (direct through, for example, tolls, or indirect through taxation); and European transport deregulation policy supporting the introduction of the private sector in domains traditionally addressed by the state, leading to a 'lesser state – New Public Management' regime (IPPR 2001).

Three principal actor groups are involved in the implementation of PPP: public authorities, representing the public sector bound to protect public interests and legitimise the use of public funds and resources; private financiers involved in PPP project finance; and private sector equity providers (strategic investors) with the competence of securing value-for-money (VfM) through their management skills and ability to undertake a share of the overall PPP risk leading to improved efficiency and, through it, to the justification of the PPP project delivery option.

Public authorities and enabling institutions supporting the preparation, award and implementation of PPP have been the object of significant research over the last decades (cfr. Grimsey and Lewis 2002). Private financiers and measures to improve the financiability of projects and increase their creditworthiness, while always in the background, became the focus of research activity following the credit crunch and the economic crisis that followed (cfr. Demirag *et al.* 2011). Strategic investors, usually holding a minority share on financial consortia (Ashton *et al.* 2012), with the exception of the port sector, have been researched to a far lesser extent, despite their importance in achieving PPP goals and growing international dominance in the global PPP market.

Based on annual reports (Public Works Financing TM 2013), 76 per cent of all PPP projects under construction or in operation are handled by 20 strategic investors. Moreover, 71 per cent of these strategic investors are of EU origin, while the top seven positions (representing 41.3 per cent of the total market) remain occupied by the same companies, implying that the leadership of this industry is solidly established.

We address this research gap through the matching of theory and practice in order to identify the key needs for each prevailing business model and, therefore, justifying the dominance of particular industrial/trade sectors in specific models. Findings are compared with aggregate market data together with the COST Action TU1001 case study base and discussed, as we seek in-depth validation of initial assumptions. Future trends are identified. This chapter ends with conclusions and suggestions for further research and starts with the overview of the PPP market to illustrate the dominance of the transport sector within this market and the relevant importance of each transport sub-sector (mode) and, therefore, the level of required resources.

Global PPP market evolution worldwide: The significance of the transport sector

One of the major limitations in the study of the PPP market is the absence of consistent information. The World Bank Infrastructure (PPI) Project Database collects data on over 5,000 infrastructure projects in the developing world and provides information on PPI trends in developing countries, covering projects in the energy, telecommunications, water and sewerage and transport sectors. Table 19.1 illustrates investments in transport projects since 1990, while Table 19.2 describes the share in transport infrastructure per mode and region. According to the PPI, in 2013 investments in transport represented approximately 38 per cent of total investments with a total budget of 33.2 billion USD (88.5 per cent for new investment and 11.5 per cent for capacity expansion).

Table 19.1 Investment in transport projects by region (%)

Year of investment	1990-1994	1995-1999	2000-2004	2005-2009	2010-2013
East Asia and Pacific (EAP)	41.59	37.84	43.56	21.70	7.15
Europe and Central Asia (ECA)	0.08	1.32	1.22	8.09	10.86
Latin America and the Caribbean (LAC)	57.64	54.06	39.06	38.27	41.20
Middle East and North Africa (MENA)	0.00	0.77	3.76	3.80	0.32
South Asia (SAR)	0.50	2.96	8.70	20.93	36.80
Sub-Saharan Africa (SSA)	0.19	3.06	3.69	7.21	3.67
Total	100	100	100	100	100

Source: World Bank PPI database.

Table 19.2 Investment by region and mode (% of total investment) from 1990 to 2013

Mode	EAP	ECA	LAC	MENA	SAR	SSA	Total
Airports	9.00	23.92	51.10	3.80	11.17	1.00	100
Railroads	27.15	6.57	50.42	0.42	9.59	5.85	100
Roads	20.60	3.89	42.44	0.00	31.80	1.27	100
Seaports	28.34	4.50	31.25	6.68	14.96	14.26	100

Source: World Bank PPI database.

Table 19.1 shows the breakdown by regions over the years, where South Asia (SAR) and Latin America and the Caribbean (LAC) are far ahead of other regions in terms of investment as well as in the number of projects. The remarkable growth of India and Brazil constitutes the main reason for this. Indeed, we may note how, in terms of volume of PPI, the market is highly concentrated from an interregional perspective. Regarding the developing world in 2013, only six countries attracted 85 per cent of PPI commitments: Brazil (11.2 billion USD), China (4.5 billion USD), Nigeria (4.4 billion USD), India, Mexico and Honduras (8.2 billion USD) (The World Bank 2014).

By mode, roads account for almost half of the projects developed between 1990 and 2013 (49.96 per cent), followed by railroads (19.94 per cent), seaports (17.80 per cent) and airports (12.31 per cent). By region, Table 19. 2 shows how most of these transport projects are located in South Asia (SAR), Latin America and the Caribbean (LAC). This is mainly attributed to Mexico, Brazil and India respectively. The leading role of LAC is also manifest, comprising half the airports and railroads projects over the period, and being the main port investor followed by East Asia and Pacific (EAP).

Paying particular attention to Europe, Figure 19.1 (a) and (b) shows the relation (in number and value) of transport PPP with respect to the total. In terms of the total number of projects, we observe the growth of the European PPP market and that of transport PPP. Figure 19.2b demonstrates the actual importance of transport PPP in terms of value.

Over the period 1990-2013, based on a combination of sources (Kappeler and Nemoz 2010; EIB 2011; EIB 2012; EIB 2013) the total number of PPP projects in Europe is estimated to be approximately 1,680, representing an investment of over 300 billion euros and, therefore, setting Europe as the key region of PPP development.

Figure 19.2 (a) and (b) shows the relative share for each mode, indicating the importance of road infrastructure both in numbers and value. Notably, in Europe, the port sector is not represented in the respective databases. This is partially due to the fact that ports, prior to the starting point of data presented, had undergone reform and were either privatised (the case of UK ports) or have followed the comprehensive or landlord port model (cfr. Cullinane and Song 2002). In this case, concessions have been granted by the landlord port authority and are not always registered in central databases. In addition, PPP in ports may be characterised as non-financial from the public sector point of view as they do not incur cost in initial investment or remuneration; on the contrary they follow concession models, which generate public income (Meersman *et al.* 2014).

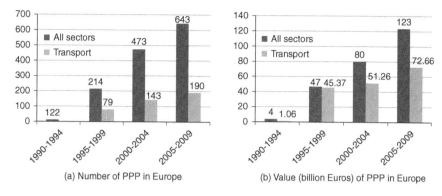

Figure 19.1 PPP projects in Europe over the last decade. The role of transport.
Source: EIB, HM Treasury, Kappeler and Nemoz 2010 (authors' compilation).

However, one additional point of interest is the average size of transport PPP. Based on figures between 1990-2009, the average value of a transport PPP project in Europe is over 400 million euros, suggesting technical, operational and financial complexity that may be addressed by larger project sponsors (strategic investors). The size of the European PPP market also suggests its importance in project sponsor competence building. Consequently, the role of these strategic investors becomes crucial in developing transport infrastructure through PPP schemes.

Theoretical foundations: PPP transport infrastructure business models and resources

A business model defines the way in which a company delivers value to customers, entices customers to pay for value, and converts those payments to profit

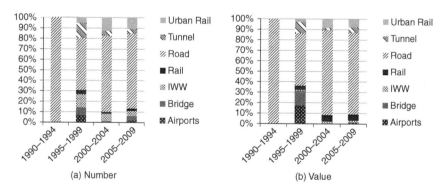

Figure 19.2 PPP projects in Europe over the last decade. The role of road transport.
Source: EIB, HM Treasury, Kappeler and Nemoz 2010 (authors' compilation).

(Teece 2010). In essence, a business model embodies nothing less than the organisational and financial 'architecture' of a business (Chesbrough and Rosenbloom 2002). Following this definition, a PPP transport infrastructure business model can be described by two main components of a business model: the PPP organisational structure (Williamson 1983; Miles *et al.* 2009) and the PPP financial structure. As for the first business model component, the PPP organisational structure is shaped by the relational structure established by the multiple actors involved in a PPP project. As a PPP usually involves the bundling of the construction and operation phases, we consider the relational structure that develops between the 'builder' and the 'operator'. Therefore, to describe the different PPP transport infrastructure business models and explain how and why these emerge, the PPP relational structure needs to be characterised and the rationale for inter-organisational relationships provided. With this aim, we combine the concepts and notions developed by strategic behaviour theory with those of the resource-based view to examine the factors that explain the behaviour of the competence-providing actors involved in a PPP transport infrastructure project. Specifically, adopting such an alternative approach, we develop a conceptual model that explains the PPP relational structure by defining the rationale of the builder to remaining in or stepping out of the PPP partnership (Special Purpose Vehicle – SPV), and identifying the resource characteristics of the two actors (builder and operator) that are the antecedents of the builder's organisational choices during the operation phase of the PPP project, such as choosing to leave the PPP consortium (stepping out of the SPV), acquiring the operator, or remaining a partner of the operator in the consortium.

Explaining PPP infrastructure resources: A conceptual model

According to strategic behaviour theory, the choice of the builder depends on the possibility of increasing his competitive advantage, measured as the additional profit during the operation phase of the PPP project (Axelrod 1984; Parkhe 1993). The resource-based view identifies the resources and capabilities controlled by a firm as sources of the competitive advantage. Thus, the choice of the builder depends on the possibility of gaining additional valuable resources (Das and Teng 2000). In other words, the builder will remain in the consortium when it can obtain tangible and intangible resources, such as, for example, competences and capabilities, possessed by the operator that are valuable and essential to increase its competitive position in the PPP market.

Both the approaches also give reasons for alliance dissolution. In particular, following the strategic behaviour theory, the builder will abandon the partnership, namely step-out from the SPV, when the costs of the coalition (coordination costs, the opportunity cost of being involved in a specific PPP project) are higher than the additional profits.

According to the resource-based view, the builder will step-out of the SPV when he finds it useless and too costly to obtain the resources possessed by the operator. In particular, the operator's resources will be perceived as useless when the builder can continue to operate in the PPP market even if he doesn't possess those complementary resources. On the other side, when the operator's resources are too costly to imitate with respect to their value, remaining in the SPV will put the builder at a competitive disadvantage.

On the basis of the different strategic goals pursued by the builder we can distinguish two main types: the profit-seeking and the resource-seeking. Drawing on the above arguments and considering the two types of builder, it is possible to define the basic alternative decision of the builder: remain in or step out of the SPV (Figure 19.3).

Once we have explained under which conditions the builder chooses to remain partner with the operator over the PPP project's operational phase, we now examine whether and how the specific resource profile of the operator can influence the two alternative choices of the builder: acquire the operator or remain a partner of the operator in the consortium. While both the partnership through the SPV consortium and the acquisition of the operator can accomplish the objective of obtaining the operator's resources, the resource-based view (RBV) defines under which conditions the partnership is favoured over the acquisition.

First, the partnership serves as a more viable option than the acquisition when not all the resources possessed by the operator are valuable to the builder. Second, since a certain degree of asset specificity is usually involved, some of the less valuable or redundant resources in an acquisition cannot be easily disposed of without taking loss (Ramanathan *et al.* 1997). Hennart and Reddy (1997) reason that when unwanted assets are mixed with needed assets, and the two are not readily separable, acquisitions inevitably result in unneeded assets. When undesirable assets are not easily separable, partnerships allow the builder to access only the desired assets while bypassing non-desired ones, thereby augmenting overall value. Thus, the distinctive advantage of staying in the consortium for the builder is to have access to precisely those resources that he needs.

The second condition that determines the choice of the builder refers to the specific resource profile of the operator, which can influence the two alternative choices: acquire the operator or remain partner of the operator in the consortium.

According to Miller and Shamsie (1996), all resources, on the basis of their inner characteristics of imperfect mobility, imperfect imitability and imperfect

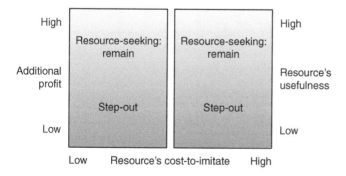

Figure 19.3 Builder's alternative decisions.

substitutability, can be classified into two broad categories: property-based resources and knowledge-based resources. Property-based resources are legal properties owned by firms, including financial capital, physical resources, human resources, etc. Owners enjoy clear property rights to these resources, or rights to use the resources, so that others cannot take them away without the owners' consent. Thus, property-based resources cannot be easily obtained because they are legally protected through property rights in such forms as patents, contracts and deeds of ownership.

The key difference between property-based resources and knowledge-based resources springs from the fact that 'the protection of knowledge barriers is not perfect' (Miller and Shamsie 1996). Whereas property-based resources have legal protection, knowledge-based resources are more vulnerable to involuntary transfers.

As a consequence, the acquisition of the operator will be a preferential choice when the builder wants to gain access to the property-based resources possessed by the operator. On the other hand, the builder will prefer to remain partner to the operator in the consortium when he wants to obtain access to additional knowledge-based resources, since these resources spill over the boundary of the partner firm (Figure 19.4).

PPP transport infrastructure business models

Transport infrastructure generates value for users and for society. In the PPP model, in order to generate and offer value, resources are combined in the exploitation of the infrastructure asset. Each mode requires a particular combination and provides value to a different 'customer segment'. In this context, a business model may describe the operation of transport infrastructure. Business models describe how resources are combined and transformed in order to generate value for customers and other stakeholders, and how rewards are realised (Magretta 2002). Business models relate to value chains (Porter 1985), value streams (Davies 2004), and value

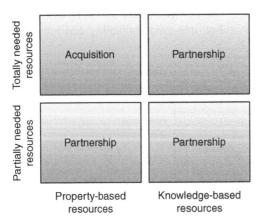

Figure 19.4 Builder's relational decisions.

constellations (Normann and Ramirez 1994) among multiple business actors. In these models, the quest is to identify the elements and relationships that describe the business. Osterwalder (2004) defines a business model as being 'the rationale of how an organization creates, delivers, and captures value' and any business model can be fully characterised in nine dimensions or building blocks, being: customer segment; value propositions; channels; customer relationships; revenue streams; key resources; key activities; key partnerships; and cost structure.

While the key value proposition is transport service in the PPP business model, financing, sharing of project risks, competences needed to achieve the required activities including managing risks and then securing an adequate revenue stream are central to its justification and, in many ways, define the type of partner with whom an effective partnership may be established. Identifying these items for each transport mode leads to the general description of the type of resources required in the respective business models, both in the construction and in the operation phase. These are also characterised as property-based versus knowledge-based and in terms of their cost-to-imitate versus their usefulness in profit generation. More specifically, profit generation is linked to the ability to manage revenue streams, while knowledge-based resources concern technical competences and capabilities to address the required activities. Therefore, the description of the prevailing business models for each transport mode places emphasis on the activities required in the 'value offer' and the ability to manage the revenue risk.

Road, bridge and tunnel PPP usually involve considerable civil engineering works and respective risks. These are best managed by experienced construction companies, and this is also the case with respect to maintenance. In addition, road PPP demand/revenue risk is not independent from the decision to build, which has always been made by the state motivated by classical welfare considerations. Once completed it is not possible to change the service offer (value proposition), rendering toll rates as a tool of limited effectiveness by which to manage demand (Fayard *et al.* 2012; Bain 2009; Mackie and Preston 1998). However, demand is not independent of quality, both from an engineering and traffic management point of view. Its contribution to 'level of service' addresses the user sense of fairness (cfr. Viegas 2001), while quality standards may be included in the awarding process (cfr. Vassalo 2007). Intelligent transport systems and their harmonisation over networks improve the service level (cfr. Tomás *et al.* 2013) and stress the capability needs in respective resources.

Dehornoy (2012), in a review of 27 rail PPP projects implemented since 1980, stressed the importance of technical complexity and required interfaces, especially as the third wave of rail PPP was initiated in the 2000s. Emphasis is also placed on the provision of rolling stock and the innovative nature of these projects. One of the major conclusions of this report was that a rail PPP does not create additional value for the customer. 'What a PPP can do is reduce the cost of a project by optimizing its design and management and reduce the amount of debt that is borrowed by public authorities'. This conclusion suggests the importance of technical capability. However, over time, there has been a shift from the provision of purely transport services to the provision of 'solutions'. For example, Brady *et al.* (2005) describe how Alstrom went from providing products (subsystems like, for example, propulsion, traction, drive, electronic information systems, rolling stock and signalling systems) in 1995 to providing transport solutions such as 'train availability' and 'total train-life management'. In addition, more and more, the rail sector is exploiting ICT solutions, such as electronic ticketing and fares, combined with other modes of transport, allowing passengers seamless travel, or e-freight solutions in support of freight. Stemming from the 'always connected' idea for mobile users and providing pure internet access for passengers, network applications have extended to a better way of managing the trains in all aspects: from comfort services to cost-saving applications like remote maintenance and software upgrades, or security related applications (van Brussel 2010). Finally, value co-creation has also been recognised as a trend. For example, Jaakkola and Alexander (2014) describe the 'Adopt a Station' scheme as a partnership between ScotRail and groups of citizens invited to 'adopt' railway stations. Therefore, apart from the technical competence to address the actual delivery of rail infrastructure, rail service provision requires the capability to exploit developments in ICT and communication and endorse an entrepreneurial approach to the business and its value proposition.

Airports in many parts of the world are no longer viewed as public utilities but rather as private enterprises aiming to maximise shareholder value and profits from a fixed facility (Adler *et al.* 2010). Governance models are becoming particularly complex and the real benefit of such arrangements is ambiguous as no conclusive evidence exists of their level of efficiency with respect to ownership (Oum *et al.* 2006). Based on their location, they may be natural locational monopolies or operate in competitive markets as a result of the deregulation of both the airlines and the airports located in overlapping catchment areas (Tretheway and Kincaid 2010; Starkie 2002). Investments in airport expansion are highly risky as they depend on airline selection and the intervention of national and international regulators (Adler and Gellman 2012), and they are vulnerable to exogenous shocks (such as terrorism, extreme weather events, strikes and airline collapses). Diversifying revenue sources to minimise the economic risk of dependence on air services is sought through development of airport property considered surplus to core aviation requirements – often in the form of business parks and retail complexes (Morrison 2009). This approach is captured in the concept of the 'airport city' (Peneda *et al.* 2011), which from a spatial perspective concerns airport-centric development (Freestone and Baker 2011). This trend is more evident in major global hub airports such as Schiphol (Amsterdam), Frankfurt, Hong Kong and Dallas Fort Worth (Kasarda 2009). The 'airport city' model places the emphasis on real estate development and is combined with the tendency to secure monopoly status in cases of concessions (Cruz and Marques 2012) to further minimise the pure air-service risk. Therefore, the balance of required competence in resources shifts to the construction sector with expertise in construction, maintenance and real estate development.

The strategic importance and profitability of ports lies in securing reliable supply chains. Fee structures are used to induce incentives for concessionaires to increase traffic (Cruz and Marques 2012) and operational efficiency is key in retaining a competitive position. In addition, what is becoming increasingly important for seaports, as well as seaport users, is not merely the efficiency of the seaport *per se*, but the efficiency of the supply chain in which the seaport and its users are involved (Panayides and Song 2008). These characteristics drive the tendency towards global terminal operators and shipping lines, especially in container terminals. Notably, the private sector is involved in over 50 per cent of container terminals worldwide (Farrell 2012). In support of the pivotal role of the ability to manage the supply chain and understand global trade and transportation is the negative experience of purely financial investors. More specifically, purely financial investors, attracted by the growth prospects of the port industry between 2002-2008, were unprepared to face the particularity of the maritime industry, notably risks related to business cycles (Rodrigue *et al.* 2011).

Finally, with respect to urban transit projects, factors influencing ridership and perceived quality on a single transit line are integration into the wider transit network, scheduling, fare structures, and public policy shaping long-term land use development. These are factors typically beyond the control of the private sector partner (Siemiatycki 2010; Siemiatycki and Friedman 2012). In addition, as most of the PPPs in urban transit concern urban rail (tram and metro), management of innovation and technical complexity is important and only private partners with respective capacities are able to address the specific risk, while metropolitan operators are able to secure integration. A combination of technical competence and urban system operation seem to be the capability requirements for the prevailing urban transit model.

Identifying transport PPP resource needs

The brief overview of the prevailing business models for each transport mode indicates differences in capability needs in order to address the value proposition and risks related to revenues of each mode. These capabilities seem to range from technical competence to market/sector expertise with overlaps but also with definite boundaries, as in the case of ports. The evolution in governance models and value proposition creates capability needs and presents opportunities for strategic investors to expand activities, as in the example of airports. Table 19.3 schematically shows the capability mix required to address each business model. Notably, in every mode the construction phase and, to a lesser extent, the operation phase require technical expertise. The intensity of this expertise varies between transport modes as does the type of expertise required. The operational phase in all cases is characterised by the ability (knowledge resources) to manage the demand risk and the ability to improve and extend the service offer both in terms of quality and range of offering. However, by studying Table 19.3 similarities and dissimilarities may be identified. The rail and urban transit mode require the same mix of construction competences, as do the road/bridge/tunnel and the airport mode. Only the ports have low construction phase requirements. In the operation phase an experienced operator, capable of managing the demand risk, is needed in airports, ports and urban transit. The introduction of added-value services

Table 19.3 Competence requirements by mode in the construction and operation phases

Competences	Construction					Operation				
	RBT	R	A	P	U	RBT	R	A	P	U
Civil eng. (builder)	High	Low	High	Low	Low	High		High	Low	
M/E systems (builder)		High			High	High				High
Traffic demand (operator)						Low	Low	High	High	High
ICT						High*	High*	High*	High*	High*
Added value business						Low	High*	High*	Low	Low

Legend: RBT: Road/Bridge/Tunnel; R: Rail; A: Airports; P: Ports; U: Urban.
*based on Business Model Evolution

requires specialised competences in rail (new trend) and airports (established trend). ICT requirements are found across all modes of transport.

Following this analysis, the next step is to identify whether acquisitions or partnerships between builders and operators prevail for each mode based on the conceptual framework described earlier. Obviously, the operation phase includes capabilities that endorse a different cost-to-imitate by the builder and the operator. These relations are illustrated in Figures 19.5 and 19.6 for the builder and operators respectively.

The study of Figures 19.5 and 19.6 allows for following conclusions to be derived from a theoretical approach:

- Road/bridge/tunnel is dominated by construction companies (civil engineering competences) in both the construction and operation phases as a relatively low cost is required by them to imitate both the operator and the added-value offering.

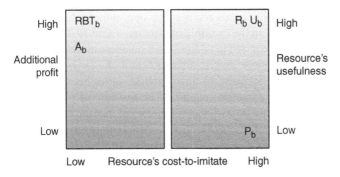

Legend: RBT: Road/Bridge/Tunnel; R: Rail; A: Airports; P: Ports; U: Urban.
Subscripts b: Builder; o: Operator.

Figure 19.5 Builder's cost-to-imitate operator's competences.

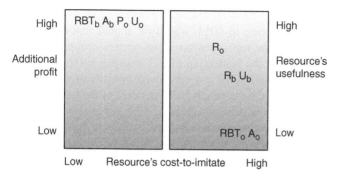

Figure 19.6 Builder's and operator's cost-to-imitate added value competences.

- Airports require a mix of competences in the operation phase. Construction companies require lesser cost to imitate added-value services (real estate). In addition, if air transport-related revenues are protected (minimum revenue guarantees or monopoly status), construction companies have an advantage.
- Ports are heavily dependent on the capabilities of the operator. Builder competences even in the construction phase are of low value allowing, in this case, the operator to dominate both PPP phases.
- Rail and urban transit will include multiple actors throughout phases as the usefulness of resources remains and the cost of imitating added-value services is similar.

Finally, while clearly distinctive competences characterise ports, rail and urban transit, a common resource base exists for both the road and airport modes.

Considering the option of acquisition or of retaining the partnership, Table 19.3 indicates that the potential for acquisition exists only between similar types of resources, i.e. between builders or between operators of the same resource. There is also potential with respect to ICT services.

Matching theory and practice

The theoretical findings of the previous section are hypotheses to be tested against market information. This is conducted on two levels: aggregate market data and case study information.

Global transport PPP strategic investors/developers

Identifying the market actors with respect to transport PPP strategic investors/developers and the key characteristics of the particular market segment are important. The Public Works Financing TM report (2013) forms the basis of the ranking in Table 19.4. These firms represent 76 per cent of all PPP projects under construction or in operation in 2013. Based on annual reports (Public Works Financing TM 2013), the top seven positions remain occupied by the same companies, implying that the leadership of this industry is solidly established. Moreover, when considering the projects under construction or operation in 2013, the top ten companies represent 52.14 per cent of the total number of projects – an increase from the previous share of 50.2 per cent – indicating a market concentration and the respective dominance of these specific firms. Additionally, by collecting data from main transportation developers included in Table 19.5, we find that 32.5 per cent define themselves as Design-Build-Finance-Operate-Maintenance (DBFOM) firms, as opposed to Design-Build-Maintenance schemes (DBM, 2.5 per cent), SPV developers (2.5 per cent) or the 10 per cent that declare themselves to be solely financial, operator or builder firms.

Combining the requirements in competences for each transport mode with the international share of each mode in the provision of PPP in the transport sector, the ranking of the world's largest transportation developers in 2013, based on the number of projects under construction or operation (Table 19.4), is not surprising. Construction companies hold the top positions, as their competences with respect to civil engineering works are key in addressing the road/bridge/tunnel business

Table 19.4 Ranked world's largest transportation developers in 2013[*]

#	Company	Share of total projects	#	Company	Share of total projects
1	ACS Group/Hotchief	7.98%	21	Camargo Correa	1.99%
2	Global Via – FCC – Bankia	6.41%	22	Bilfinger Berger	1.85%
3	Macquarie Group	6.27%	23	Andrade Gutierrez	1.85%
4	Abertis	5.84%	24	Odebrecht	1.85%
5	Vinci	5.41%	25	Reliance	1.85%
6	Hutchison Whampoa	4.84%	26	Empresas ICA	1.71%
7	Ferrovial / Cintra	4.56%	27	Strabag	1.57%
8	NWS Holdings	3.85%	28	Transurban	1.42%
9	EGIS projects	3.56%	29	Eiffage	1.42%
10	Bouygues	3.42%	30	IRB Infrastructure	1.28%
11	Sacyr	3.28%	31	Balfour Beatty	1.28%
12	IL&FS	2.56%	32	Fluor	1.28%
13	Atlantia	2.56%	33	BRISA	1.14%
14	Meridiam	2.56%	34	Impregilo	1.14%
15	Acciona	2.28%	35	Skanska	1.14%
16	John Laing	2.28%	36	Isolux Corsan	1.14%
17	Alstom	2.14%	37	Ideal	1.14%
18	Road King	2.14%	38	Itinere	0.85%
19	SNC-Lavalin	2.14%			

Source: Authors' compilation from Public Works Financing TM report (2013).
[*]Ranking base: No. of projects currently under construction or operation.

model, which represents the overwhelming majority of transport PPP awarded as described in the initiating section of this chapter.

Moreover, according to Table 19.5, 57.5 per cent of the international market actors are of EU origin. By nationality, leading the rank are four firms of Spanish origin, namely: ACS Group, Globalvia, Abertis and Ferrovial. This country represents 8.6 per cent of European Union (EU) PPP projects (12.8 per cent in value) over the decade 1995-2006 (Allard and Trabant 2011; Blanc-Brude *et al.* 2007) or 10.1 per cent in number (11.4 per cent in value) over the period 1990-2009 (Kappeler and Nemoz 2010). Notably, between 1967 and 1975, 2,042 km of toll highways were granted by the central government of Spain on the basis of toll highway concessions. Evidently, stemming from this experience, Spanish companies have gained competitive advantage in the international toll road industry in the last two decades (Carpintero 2011). A similar rationale may apply to other EU-origin transportation developers.

Competitive advantage is also achieved through the standardisation of institutions, regulations and legislation with respect to tendering and contracting, which minimises transaction costs. A study by Dudkin and Välilä (2005), based on the

Table 19.5 World's largest road developers and main activities[*]

	Initial activity	*Current activities*
ACS Group	Roads, social infrastructure and further PPP projects.	Airports, roads, social infrastructure and further Public Private Partnership projects.
Hochtief[**]	Airports.	Airports, roads.
G. Via – FCC – Bankia	Roads.	Roads, ports, airports, railways, etc.
Abertis	Roads.	Roads and airports.
Vinci	Roads.	Roads and airports.
Ferrovial / Cintra	Roads.	Roads and airports.
Bouygues	Roads.	Roads, rail, telecommunications, residential, energy, etc.
Sacyr	Roads.	Roads, rails, hydraulics, airports, ports and urbanisation projects, high-speed railway lines, metros, airports, motorways, highways, etc.
Macquarie	Roads.	Roads.
John Laing	Home construction.	Roads, railways, hospitals, schools, etc.
EGIS projects	Construction and civil nuclear engineering.	Urban development, airports, hospitals, tramways, motorways, port terminals, etc.
NWS Holdings	Logistics.	Roads, energy, water and ports projects.
OHL	Ports.	Roads, railways, hospitals, etc.
Hutchison Whampoa	Ports.	All transport infrastructures.

Source: Companies' websites.
[*]By invested capital in 2013.
[**]ACS, which already owned 30 per cent of Hochief, increased its stake to 50.16 per cent in 2011, taking over control of the company.

analysis of a sample of PPP projects in the UK, Ireland, Netherlands and Portugal, estimated that the average bidding cost in a PPP project is approximately 13 per cent of project capital value. The larger contribution to this transaction cost comes from bidders: the joint bidding cost of awarded and failed bidders is almost 9 per cent of the project capital value. Yescombe (2007) shows that, depending on project characteristics and sector, tendering costs can reach 5–10 per cent of the capital cost of a project. Therefore, internalising the transaction costs related to bidding and exploiting standardisation is a considerable incentive (Roumboutsos *et al.* 2013).

This is of particular interest as in the mid-1990s the sector was fragmented and characterised by poor productivity (cfr. Egan 1998; Latham 1994). It is also interesting to note that EGIS projects, a road operator, holds the ninth position. This fact suggests the ability of construction companies to expand their competences to include operation.

Reflecting the share of urban rail and rail (see Figures 19.1 and 19.2), Alstom is the first developer in the ranking with expertise in rolling stock. One of its competitors, Impregilo, figures in 34th position.

Based on the analysis of the PPP transport business models, it is evident that construction companies may extend their activities from roads to airports and rail, especially with respect to civil engineering works and real estate development (see airports). In fact, firms included in Table 19.4 are not only active in the transport sector but extend concession activities to other sectors, mainly energy (25 per cent) and telecommunications (17.5 per cent). This is also interesting as ICT and energy take on increasingly important roles in the value proposition of transport business models.

Table 19.5 shows the initial activity in comparison with current activities of the top transportation developers. Initiating activities from the road sector and extending to airports seems to be the norm.

With respect to developers active in the port sector, only Hutchison is found in the top list. The reason may be the relatively small cost of port infrastructure and the fact that the specific company is active in other sectors as well. Moreover, based on the analysis of transport PPP business models, concessioners tend to be entities able to attract traffic and operate competitively in the sector. Their importance, as noted in the business model analysis, is not with respect to the complexity (and investment) of the PPP. It is defined based on the level of throughput achieved (see Table 19.6) as it reflects their competence in the specific market.

As Table 19.6 points out, the maritime transport sector is highly concentrated. While the absorption process in this industry is still growing (OECD 2014), five firms currently make up almost 30 per cent of the total market. Between them, only Hutchison, as a subsidiary firm of Hutchison Whampoa Limited, is active in the development of other transport modes. Table 19.6 suggests that, with respect to ports, sector expertise and ability to control the supply chain are the basic competencies required. In this context, the port business model creates boundaries to the expansion of activities of other PPP transport infrastructure developers.

Table 19.6 Main international terminal operators' equity-based throughput in 2012

#	Operator	Million TEU	Per cent of world throughput
1	PSA International	50.9	8.2
2	Hutchison Port Holdings	44.8	7.2
3	APM Terminals	33.7	5.4
4	DP World	33.4	5.4
5	COSCO Group	17	2.7
6	Terminal Investment Limited (TIL)	13.5	2.2
7	China Shipping Terminal Development	8.6	1.4
8	Hanjin	7.8	1.3
9	Evergreen	7.5	1.2
10	Eurogate	6.5	1

Source: Drewry Maritime Research (2013).

The COST Action TU1001 case study database

PPP case studies developed under the Cost Action TU1001 framework are listed in Table 19.7, representing 40 transport PPP cases implemented in Europe over the last decades. While the list represents a convenient sample, it provides the opportunity to approximate how the top global transport PPP developers are presented in European PPP projects. While column 3 shows the different project sponsors involved in each project, column 4 points out those included among global leaders.

More specifically, according to Table 19.6, 80 per cent of the PPP projects analysed included at least one global leader as project sponsor. Additionally, 25 per cent of the projects involved two or more global leaders. Although most of the construction companies introduced in Table 19.5 are included in these PPP projects database, ACS (12.5 per cent, the current global leader), Vinci (12.5 per cent) and Ferrovial (10 per cent) are best represented.

In terms of competence in the business model requirements, the listing provides justification for the hypothesis built in previous sections. Roads, bridges and tunnels are predominately addressed by construction firms. Tram and rail projects include in the project sponsor consortium firms specialising in the provision of the required capabilities (for example, Alstrom, Bombardier-ANF, Siemens) as well as urban transit operators (for example, RATP, Transdev, Pingat Ingénrierie SNC Lavalin, Grupo Barraqueiro, Transport de l' Agglomeration Caennaise). Port projects are undertaken by firms with specific expertise (for example, EMS, COSCO, Grimaldi, Hutchison, PSA). Notably, the Port and Marina of Larnaca Development PPP project, which includes in its scope the port and marina of Larnaca as well as real estate development (and therefore includes construction companies), has not been able to secure financing over the last two years.

Conclusions

In PPP, the private sector is usually referred to in general terms. Little has been reported with respect to the strategies and development of strategic investors:

Table 19.7 PPP case studies from *COST Action TU1001* database

#	Title (Country)	Sector	Year awarded	Project Sponsors (PS)	PS among global leaders
1.	Via-Invest Zaventem (BE) (van den Hurk and van Gestel 2013).	Road	2007	CFE, CEI-De Meyer, Ways and Freytag Ing., Vinci, Smet-Tunn.	Vinci
2.	Istrian Y Toll Motorway (CR) (Grubišić Šeba 2014).	Road	1995	Bina-Istra, Istarka autocesda and Bouygues.	Bouygues
3.	Ionia Odos Motorway (GR) (Nikolaidis and Roumboutsos 2013).	Road	2006	Ferrovial, ACS and Gekterna.	ACS, Ferrovial
4.	Olympia Odos Motorway (GR) (Nikolaidis and Roumboutsos 2013).	Road	2007	Vinci, Hochtief, Ellaktor, J&P Avax, Gekterna and Athena.	Vinci, Hochtief
5.	Moreas Motorway (GR) (Dimitropoulos et al. 2014).	Road	2007	AKTOR concessions, S.A., J&P-Avax S.A., Intracom Holdings.	N
6.	Central Greece Motorway (GR) (Nikolaidis and Roumboutsos 2014).	Road	2007	ACS, Ferrovial, Gekterna.	ACS, Ferrovial
7.	Attica Tollway (GR) (Halkias et al. 2013).	Road	1996	Ellaktor, J&P AVAX and Piraeus-ATE Bank, Egis.	N/Egis[1]
8.	Bre.Be.Mi. Toll Road (IT) (Carbonara 2014).	Road	2009	Auostrade Lombardi (main sponsor, 79%, 21 firms).	N
9.	E-39 Klett-Baardshaug (NO) (Bjørberg et al. 2014).	Road	2003	Skanska Norway and John Laing.	John Laing, Skanska
10.	E18 Grimstad – Kristiansand (NO) (Odeck 2014).	Road	2006	Bilfinger Berger, Sundt AS and E. Pihl & Son AS.	Bilfinger Berger
11.	A2 Motorway (PL) (Łukasiewicz 2014).	Road	1997 (2009)	Kulczyk Holding, Meridiam, Strabag AG and KWM Invest.	Meridiam, Strabag
12.	A22 – Algarve (PT) (Costa et al. 2014).	Road	2000	Ferrovial, Cintra (main sponsors, 75%, 9 firms).	Ferrovial / Cintra, Agroman
13.	A23-Beira Interior (PT) Costa et al. 2014).	Road	1999	Scutvias (a consortium of Portuguese firms).	N
14.	C-16 Terrassa-Manresa Toll Motorway (SP) (Cabrera and Suárez-Alemán 2014).	Road	1987	Ferrovial.	Ferrovial

#	Project	Type	Year	Consortium	Current operator
15.	Radial 2 Toll Motorway (SP) (Villalba-Romero and Liyanage 2014).	Road	2000	ACS, Acciona, Aurea, Avasa.	ACS new Abertis
16.	M-45 Toll Motorway (SP) (Villalba-Romero and Liyanage 2014)	Road	1998	OHL, Sacyr, Cintra, ACS, Dragados, FCC.	Cintra, ACS, Abertis, Globalvia
17.	Airport Axis Toll Motorway (SP) (Villalba-Romero and Liyanage 2014).	Road	2002	OHL, ENA.	OHL
18.	A19 Dishforth DBFO (UK) (Liyanage and Boles 2013).	Road	1996	Sir Robert McAlpine Ltd.	N
19.	M80 Haggs to Stepps (UK) (Liyanage and Boles 2013).	Road	2009	Bilfinger Berger, John Graham and Northstone.	Bilfinger Berger
20.	M6 Toll (BNRR) (UK) (Liyanage and Boles 2013).	Road	1992	MEL, Macquarie.	Macquarie
21.	Horgos-Pozega, Toll Motorway (RS) Vajdic and Mladenovic 2013).	Road	2007	FCC and Alpine Mayreder Bau GmbH.	FCC
22.	Rio-Antirio Bridge (GR) (Papanikolas et al. 2014).	Bridge	1996	Vinci, Hellenic Tech., J&P, Athena S.A., Proodetyki S.A. and Pantechniki, S.A.	Vinci
23.	Lusoponte Bridge (PT) (Miranda Sarmento 2014).	Bridge	1994	Macquarie, Vinci, Mota/Engil, Somague Itinere, Teixeira Duarte.	Macquarie, Vinci
24.	Coen Tunnel (NL) (Voordijk 2013).	Tunnel	2008	Dura Vermeer, TBI-Bouw, Vinci concessions, Besix. Group, CFE, Arcadis, and Dredging Int.	Vinci
25.	Durrës Port East Terminal (AL) (Dedej and Shiko 2014).	Port	2013	EMS Shipping.	EMS
26.	Adriatic Gateway Container Terminal, Rijeka (CR) (Juretic and Farrell 2014).	Port	2000	ICTSI and Luka Rijeka.	N
27.	Port and Marina of Larnaca Development (CY) (Christodoulou and Efstathiades 2014).	Port & Dev.	2012	Lous Group, Bouygues, Iacovou Brothers, Petriolina, Costa Crociere, Marinamam, GCC and Amsterdam Log. Group.	Bouygues
28.	Piraeus Container Terminal (GR) (Farrell 2013).	Port	2008	COSCO	COSCO

(Continued)

Table 19.7 PPP case studies from *COST Action TU1001* database (Continued)

#	Title (Country)	Sector	Year awarded	Project Sponsors (PS)	PS among global leaders
29.	Muelle Costa Terminal, The Port of Barcelona (SP) (Cabrera et al. 2014).	Port	2011	Grimaldi	Grimaldi
30.	Barcelona Europe South Container Terminal (SP) (Suárez-Alemán and Cabrera 2014).	Port	2006	Hutchison and Grupo Mestre.	Hutchison
31.	Sines Container Terminal (PT) (Farrell 2013).	Port	1999	PSA Corp.	PSA Corp.
32.	Intern. Airport of Tirana (AL) (Dedej and Shiko 2013).	Airport	2004	Hochtief.	Hochtief
33.	Larnaca and Paphos International Airports (CY) (Christodoulou and Efstathiades 2013).	Airport	2005	Bouygues, Egis, Cyprus Trading Corp., Hellenic Mining and others (10).	Bouygues/EGIS
34.	ARN-STO Rail link (SE) (Ågren and Olander 2013).	Rail	1994	Macquarie.	Macquarie
35.	FERTAGUS Train (PT) (Rosario et al. 2013).	Rail	1999	Grupo Barraqueiro and Arriva.	N
36.	Caen TVR (FR) (Bonnet and Chomat 2013).	Tram	2000	SPIE Batignole and Bombardier-ANF.	N
37.	Metro Sul do Tejo (PT) (Macário et al. 2013).	Tram	2002	Grupo Barraqueiro, Arriva, Siemens, Ensulmeci, Sopol, Ascendi.	Siemens
38.	Reims' Tramway (FR) (Bonnet and Chomat 2013).	Tram	2006	CDC, Alstom, Transdev, Caisse d'Epargne, Bouygues, Colas, Pingat Ingénrierie SNC Lavalin.	Alstrom, Bouygues
39.	Metrolink, Manchester (UK) (Villalba-Romero and Liyanage, 2014).	Tram	1999	RATP.	RATP
40.	Port of Antwerp Deurganckdock Lock (BE) (Nieuwenhuysen and Vanelslander 2013).	Lock	2011	Jan De Nul nv, CEI, De Meyer NV, Betonac NV, Herbosch-Kiere NV, Antwerpse Bouwwerken NV.	N

Source: The authors.
¹Small share.

those who contribute equity and apply management skills and expertise in order to potentially achieve value for money and justify the PPP infrastructure delivery option. The present chapter contributes to addressing this gap by identifying the key actors in the global PPP transport market and understanding their strategies.

Stemming from the theoretical foundations of strategic behaviour and resource-based view theory, a conceptual model of the partnership architecture of the private partners involved in PPP is constructed to guide the analysis of findings with respect to the overview of the prevailing business models for each transport mode and their evolution. It was concluded that, with respect to capabilities required either to produce the 'value offer', enhance it or to manage the revenue stream, while clearly distinct competences characterise ports, rail and urban transit, a common resource base exists for both road and airport modes. Also, while construction companies dominate roads in both the construction and operation phases, airports require a mix of competences during the operation and ports are extremely dependent on the capabilities of the operator. Thus, capacities seem to range from mostly technical competence (roads, tunnels and bridges) to mostly market/sector expertise (ports), passing through specific combinations of them (airports, rail or urban transit projects).

Considering the development of the international PPP market, both in the developing world and in Europe, especially with the large share of road PPP projects, it became evident that construction companies have become the global leaders in transport development. Our empirical analysis confirmed this approach by analysing 40 transport PPP cases implemented in Europe over the last decades. In addition, the Cost Action database confirmed the predominance of global leaders also in Europe (80 per cent of total projects), which have developed expertise in PPP through the standardisation of capacity building and the internalisation of transaction costs.

PPP transport business models showed how most road developers were originally general construction companies, which focused on roads and then they moved to very different sectors, predominately airports as the latter evolved in way that required competence available to or easily acquired by the road constructors. However, while we observed that construction companies moved into other modes, ports will always be separate due to the need for the competence to control supply chains and market knowledge. Thus, in general, we observed how agent strategies depend and evolve based on their competence (and capability building) but also on transport business model evolution.

Further research should be focused on the systematic data collection process of private agents. The proper identification of success indicators in PPP by modes would also allow the implementation of a correlation analysis between these main providers and successful cases of PPP schemes. Questions such as whether the level or type of expertise – technical, sector-based or a specific mix of them – have an impact on the level of operational efficiency of the transport infrastructure remains.

Moreover, it was suggested that strategic investors also achieve competitive advantage through standardisation, especially during the tendering stage leading to market concentration. While this may be more beneficial than a fragmented market, it does raise questions with respect to market competition issues.

References

Adler, N. and Gellman, A. (2012) 'Strategies for managing risk in a changing aviation environment'. *Journal of Air Transport Management*, 21, pp. 24–35

Adler, N., Liebert, V. and Yazhemsky, E. (2010) 'Benchmarking airports from a managerial perspective'. Working Paper at the Center for Transportation Studies, Sauder School of Business, University of British Columbia

Ågren, R. and Olander, S. (2013) 'ARN-STO rail link (Arlandabanan)' in: A. Roumboutsos, S. Farrell, C. L. Liyanage and R. Macário *COST Action TU1001 Public Private Partnerships in Transport: Trends & Theory P3T3, 2013 Discussion Papers Part II Case Studies*. ISBN 978-88-97781-61-5, COST Office, Brussels. Available online at: www.ppptransport.eu

Allard, G. and Trabant, A. (2011) 'Public-Private Partnerships in Spain: lessons and opportunities'. *International Business & Economics Research Journal (IBER)* 7.2

Ashton, P., Doussard, M. and Weber, R. (2012) 'The financial engineering of infrastructure privatization'. *Journal of the American Planning Association*, 78:3, pp. 300–312

Axelrod, R. (1984) *The Evolution of Cooperation*. New York: Basic Books

Bain, R. (2009) 'Error and optimism bias in toll road traffic forecasts'. *Transportation*, 36(5), pp. 469–482

Blanc-Brude, F., Goldsmith, H. and Valila, T. (2007) *Public Private Partnerships in Europe: An Update*. Economic and Financial Report. Luxembourg: EIB

Bonnet, G. and Chomat, G. (2013a) 'The Reims Tramway' in: A. Roumboutsos, S. Farrell, C. L. Liyanage and R. Macário *COST Action TU1001 Public Private Partnerships in Transport: Trends & Theory P3T3, 2013 Discussion Papers Part II Case Studies*. ISBN 978-88-97781-61-5, COST Office, Brussels. Available online at: www.ppptransport.eu

Bonnet, G. and Chomat, G. (2013b) 'The Caen TVR' in: A. Roumboutsos, S. Farrell, C. L. Liyanage and R. Macário *COST Action TU1001 Public Private Partnerships in Transport: Trends & Theory P3T3, 2013 Discussion Papers Part II Case Studies*. ISBN 978-88-97781-61-5, COST Office, Brussels. Available online at: www.ppptransport.eu

Brady, T., Davies, A. and Gann, D. M. (2005) 'Creating value by delivering integrated solutions'. *International Journal of Project Management* 23, pp. 360–365

Brussel, W. (van) (2010) *Bringing ICT services to trains' technical and economic challenges*. Ninth Conference on Telecommunications Internet and Media Techno Economics (CTTE), Ghent, 7-9 June 2010, IEEE, DOI: 10.1109/CTTE.2010.5557705

Cabrera, M. and Suárez-Alemán, A. (2014) 'C-16 Terrassa-Manresa Toll Motorway' in: A. Roumboutsos, S. Farrell and K. Verhoest *COST Action TU1001 – Public Private Partnerships in Transport: Trends & Theory: 2014 Discussion Series: Country Profiles & Case Studies*. ISBN 978-88-6922-009-8, COST Office, Brussels. Available online at: www.ppptransport.eu

Cabrera, M., Suárez-Alemán, A. and Trujillo, L. (2014) 'Muelle Costa Terminal, the Port of Barcelona' in: A. Roumboutsos, S. Farrell and K. Verhoest *COST Action TU1001 – Public Private Partnerships in Transport: Trends & Theory: 2014 Discussion Series: Country Profiles & Case Studies*. ISBN 978-88-6922-009-8, COST Office, Brussels. Available online at www.ppptransport.eu

Carbonara, N. (2014) 'Bre.Be.Mi. Toll Road' in: A. Roumboutsos, S. Farrell and K. Verhoest *COST Action TU1001 – Public Private Partnerships in Transport: Trends & Theory: 2014 Discussion Series: Country Profiles & Case Studies*. ISBN 978-88-6922-009-8, COST Office, Brussels. Available online at: www.ppptransport.eu

Carpintero, S. (2011) 'The competitive advantages of the Spanish companies in the international toll road industry'. *Journal of Civil Engineering and Management*, 17, 4, pp. 483–493

Chesbrough, H. and Rosenbloom, R. S. (2002) 'The role of the business model in capturing value from innovation: evidence from Xerox corporation's technology'. *Industrial and Corporate Change*, 11 (3), pp. 529–555

Christodoulou, C. and Efstathiades, C. (2013) 'Larnaca and Paphos International Airports' in: A. Roumboutsos, S. Farrell, C. L. Liyanage and R. Macário *COST Action TU1001 Public Private Partnerships in Transport: Trends & Theory P3T3, 2013 Discussion Papers Part II Case Studies*. ISBN 978-88-97781-61-5, COST Office, Brussels. Available online at: www.ppptransport.eu

Christodoulou, C. and Efstathiades, C. (2014) 'Larnaca Port and Marina re-development' in: A. Roumboutsos, S. Farrell and K. Verhoest *COST Action TU1001 – Public Private Partnerships in Transport: Trends & Theory: 2014 Discussion Series: Country Profiles & Case Studies*. ISBN 978-88-6922-009-8, COST Office, Brussels. Available online at: www.ppptransport.eu

Costa, J., Couchinho, R., Ribeiro, J. and Macário, R. (2014) 'A22 – Algarve' in: A. Roumboutsos, S. Farrell and K. Verhoest *COST Action TU1001 – Public Private Partnerships in Transport: Trends & Theory: 2014 Discussion Series: Country Profiles & Case Studies*. ISBN 978-88-6922-009-8, COST Office, Brussels. Available online at www.ppptransport.eu

Costa, J., Couchinho, R., Ribeiro, J. and Macário, R. (2014) 'A23-Beira Interior' in: A. Roumboutsos, S. Farrell and K. Verhoest *COST Action TU1001 – Public Private Partnerships in Transport: Trends & Theory: 2014 Discussion Series: Country Profiles & Case Studies*. ISBN 978-88-6922-009-8, COST Office, Brussels. Available online at: www.ppptransport.eu

Cruz, O. C. and Marques, R. C. (2011) 'Contribution to the study of PPP arrangements in airport development, management and operation'. *Transport Policy*, 18, pp. 392–400

Cruz, O. C. and Marques, R. C. (2012) 'Risk-sharing in seaport terminal concessions'. *Transport Reviews*, 32(4), pp. 455–471

Cullinane, K. and Song, D. W. (2002) 'Port privatization, policy and practice'. *Transport Reviews: A Transnational Transdisciplinary Journal*, 22:1, pp. 55–75

Das, T. K. and Teng, B. S. (2000) 'A resource-based view of strategic alliances'. *Journal of Management*, 26(1), pp. 31–61

Davies, A. (2004) 'Moving base into high-value integrated solutions: a value stream approach'. *Industrial and Corporate Change* 13, pp. 727–756

Dedej, A. and Shiko, V. (2013) 'International Airport of Tirana' in: A. Roumboutsos, S. Farrell, C. L. Liyanage and R. Macário *COST Action TU1001 Public Private Partnerships in Transport: Trends & Theory P3T3, 2013 Discussion Papers Part II Case Studies*. ISBN 978-88-97781-61-5, COST Office, Brussels. Available online at: www.ppptransport.eu

Dedej, A. and Shiko, V. (2014) 'Durrës Port East Terminal' in: A. Roumboutsos, S. Farrell and K. Verhoest *COST Action TU1001 – Public Private Partnerships in Transport: Trends & Theory: 2014 Discussion Series: Country Profiles & Case Studies*. ISBN 978-88-6922-009-8, COST Office, Brussels. Available online at: www.ppptransport.eu

Dehornoy, J. (2012) 'PPP in the rail sector – a review of 27 projects, SNCF French National Railways'. MPRA Paper No. 38415, April. Available online at: http://mpra. ub.uni-muenchen.de/38415

Demirag, I., Khadaroo, I., Stapleton, P. and Stevenson, C. (2011) 'Risks and the financing of PPP: perspectives from the financiers'. *The British Accounting Review*, 43, pp. 294–310

Dimitropoulos, I., Diakidou, A. and Roumboutsos, A (2014) 'Moreas Motorway' in: A. Roumboutsos, S. Farrell and K. Verhoest *COST Action TU1001 – Public Private Partnerships in Transport: Trends & Theory: 2014 Discussion Series: Country Profiles & Case Studies*. ISBN 978-88-6922-009-8, COST Office, Brussels. Available online at: www.ppptransport.eu

Drewry Maritime Research (2013) *Global Container Terminal Operators Annual Review and Forecast*. London, UK: Drewry Independent Maritime Advisors

Dudkin, G. and Välilä, T. (2005) *Transaction Costs in Public-Private Partnerships: A First Look at the Evidence. Economic and Financial Reports*. Luxembourg: EIB

Egan, J. (1998) *Rethinking Construction*. London, UK: Department of Trade and Industry

EIB (2010) *Review of the European PPP market in 2010*. European PPP Expertise Centre, Luxembourg: European Investment Bank publications

EIB (2011) *Review of the European PPP market in 2011*. European PPP Expertise Centre, Luxembourg: European Investment Bank Publications

EIB (2012) *Review of the European PPP market in 2012*. European PPP Expertise Centre, Luxembourg: European Investment Bank Publications

EIB (2013) Review of the European PPP market in 2013. European PPP Expertise Centre, Luxembourg: European Investment Bank Publications

European Commission (2011) *The White Paper COM (2011)*. Brussels: European Union

Farrell, S. (2012) 'The ownership and management structure of container terminal concessions'. *Maritime Policy Management*, 39 (1)

Farrell, S. (2013) 'Piraeus Container Terminal' in: A. Roumboutsos, S. Farrell, C. L. Liyanage and R. Macário *COST Action TU1001 Public Private Partnerships in Transport: Trends & Theory P3T3, 2013 Discussion Papers Part II Case Studies*. ISBN 978-88-97781-61-5, COST Office, Brussels. Available online at: www.ppptransport.eu

Farrell, S. (2013) 'Sines Container Terminal' in: A. Roumboutsos, S. Farrell, C. L. Liyanage and R. Macário *COST Action TU1001 Public Private Partnerships in Transport: Trends & Theory P3T3, 2013 Discussion Papers Part II Case Studies*. ISBN 978-88-97781-61-5, COST Office, Brussels. Available online at: www.ppptransport.eu

Fayard, A., Meunier, D. and Quinet, E. (2012) 'Motorway provision and management in France: analyses and policy issues'. *Networks and Spatial Economics* 12: pp. 299–319. DOI 10.1007/s11067-009-9122

Freestone, R. and Baker, D. (2011) 'Spatial planning models of airport-driven urban development'. *Journal of Planning Literature* 26, pp. 263–279

Grimsey, D. and Lewis, M. K. (2002) 'Evaluating the risks of Public Private Partnerships for infrastructure projects'. *International Journal of Project Management*, 20 (2), pp. 107–118

Grubiši Šeba, M. (2014) 'The Istrian Y Toll Motorway' in: A. Roumboutsos, S. Farrell and K. Verhoest *COST Action TU1001 – Public Private Partnerships in Transport: Trends & Theory: 2014 Discussion Series: Country Profiles & Case Studies*. ISBN 978-88-6922-009-8, COST Office, Brussels. Available online at: www.ppptransport.eu

Halkias, B., Roumboutsos, A. and Pantelias, A. (2013) 'Attica Tollway' in: A. Roumboutsos, S. Farrell, C. L. Liyanage and R. Macário *COST Action TU1001 Public*

Private Partnerships in Transport: Trends & Theory P3T3, 2013 Discussion Papers Part II Case Studies. ISBN 978-88-97781-61-5, COST Office, Brussels. Available online at: www.ppptransport.eu

Hennart, J. F. and Reddy, S. (1997) 'The choice between mergers/acquisitions and joint ventures: the case of Japanese investors in the United States'. *Strategic Management Journal*, 18(1), pp. 1–12

HM Treasury (2012) *UK Private Finance Initiative Projects: Summary data as at March 2012.* Infrastructure Statistics UK. Available online at: www.gov.uk/government/statistics/pfi-projects-data

Institute of Public Policy Research (IPPR) (2001) *Building Better Partnerships: The Final Report of the Commission on Public Private Partnerships.* London: Institute of Public Policy Research

Jaakkola, E. and Alexander, M. (2014) 'The role of customer engagement behavior in value co-creation: a service system perspective'. *Journal of Service Research*, 17(3) pp. 247–261

Juretic, S. and Farrell, S. (2014) 'Adriatic Gateway Container Terminal, Rijeka' in: A. Roumboutsos, S. Farrell and K. Verhoest *COST Action TU1001 – Public Private Partnerships in Transport: Trends & Theory: 2014 Discussion Series: Country Profiles & Case Studies.* ISBN 978-88-6922-009-8, COST Office, Brussels. Available online at: www.ppptransport.eu

Kappeler, A. and Nemoz, M. (2010) 'Public-Private Partnerships in Europe: before and during the recent financial crisis'. *Economic and Financial Report* 2010/04. Available online at: www.eib.org/epec/resources/efr_epec_ppp_report1.pdf

Kasarda, J. (2009) 'Airport cities'. *Urban Land*, April, pp. 56–60

Latham, M. (1994) *Constructing the Team.* London, UK: HM Stationery Office

Liyanage, C. and Boles, C. (2013a) 'A19 Dishforth DBFO' in: A. Roumboutsos, S. Farrell, C. L. Liyanage and R. Macário *COST Action TU1001 Public Private Partnerships in Transport: Trends & Theory P3T3, 2013 Discussion Papers Part II Case Studies.* ISBN 978-88-97781-61-5, COST Office, Brussels. Available online at: www.ppptransport.eu

Liyanage, C. and Boles, C. (2013b) 'M80 Haggs to Stepps' in: A. Roumboutsos, S. Farrell, C. L. Liyanage and R. Macário *COST Action TU1001 Public Private Partnerships in Transport: Trends & Theory P3T3, 2013 Discussion Papers Part II Case Studies.* ISBN 978-88-97781-61-5, COST Office, Brussels. Available online at: www.ppptransport.eu

Liyanage, C. and Boles, C. (2013c) 'M6 Toll (BNRR)' in: A. Roumboutsos, S. Farrell, C. L. Liyanage and R. Macário *COST Action TU1001 Public Private Partnerships in Transport: Trends & Theory P3T3, 2013 Discussion Papers Part II Case Studies.* ISBN 978-88-97781-61-5, COST Office, Brussels. Available online at: www.ppptransport.eu

Łukasiewicz, A. (2014) 'A2 Motorway' in: A. Roumboutsos, S. Farrell and K. Verhoest *COST Action TU1001 – Public Private Partnerships in Transport: Trends & Theory: 2014 Discussion Series: Country Profiles & Case Studies.* ISBN 978-88-6922-009-8, COST Office, Brussels. Available online at: www.ppptransport.eu

Macário, R., Ribeiro, J. and Couchinho, R. (2013a) 'Metro Sul do Tejo' in: A. Roumboutsos, S. Farrell, C. L. Liyanage and R. Macário *COST Action TU1001 Public Private Partnerships in Transport: Trends & Theory P3T3, 2013 Discussion Papers Part II Case Studies.* ISBN 978-88-97781-61-5, COST Office, Brussels. Available online at: www.ppptransport.eu

Macário, R., Ribeiro, J. and Couchinho, R. (2013b) 'FERTAGUS Train' in: A. Roumboutsos, S. Farrell, C. L. Liyanage and R. Macário *COST Action TU1001 Public*

Private Partnerships in Transport: Trends & Theory P3T3, 2013 Discussion Papers Part II Case Studies. ISBN 978-88-97781-61-5, COST Office, Brussels. Available online at: www.ppptransport.eu

Magretta, J. (2002) 'Why business models matter'. *Harvard Business Review* 80(5), pp. 86–92

Mackie, P. and Preston, J. (1998) 'Twenty-one sources of error and bias in transport project appraisal'. *Transport Policy*, 5(1), pp. 1–7

Meersman, H., Van de Voorde, E. and Vanelslander, T. (2014) 'Future port infrastructure finance: lessons and recommendations' in: H. Meersman, E. Van de Voorde and T. Vanelslander (Eds) *Port Infrastructure Finance* (pp. 229–237). Abingdon: Routledge

Miles, R., Miles, G., Snow, C., Blomquist, K. and Rocha, H. (2009) 'Business models, organizational forms and managerial values'. Working paper, UC Berkeley, Haas School of Business

Miller, D. and Shamsie, J. (1996) 'The resource-based view of the firm in two environments: the Hollywood film studios from 1936 to 1965'. *Academy of Management Journal*, 39(3), pp. 519–543

Miranda Sarmento, J. (2014) 'Lusoponte Bridge' in: A. Roumboutsos, S. Farrell and K. Verhoest *COST Action TU1001 – Public Private Partnerships in Transport: Trends & Theory: 2014 Discussion Series: Country Profiles & Case Studies*. ISBN 978-88-6922-009-8, COST Office, Brussels. Available online at: www.ppptransport.eu

Morrison, W. G. (2009) 'Real estate, factory outlets and bricks: a note on non-aeronautical activities at commercial airports'. *Journal of Air Transport Management* 15, pp. 112–115

Nieuwenhuysen, C. (van) and Vanelslander, T. (2013) 'Port of Antwerp Deurganckdock Lock' in: A. Roumboutsos, S. Farrell, C. L. Liyanage and R. Macário *COST Action TU1001 Public Private Partnerships in Transport: Trends & Theory P3T3, 2013 Discussion Papers Part II Case Studies*. ISBN 978-88-97781-61-5, COST Office, Brussels. Available online at: www.ppptransport.eu

Nikolaidis, N. and Roumboutsos, A. (2013a) 'Olympia Odos Motorway' in: A. Roumboutsos, S. Farrell, C. L. Liyanage and R. Macário *COST Action TU1001 Public Private Partnerships in Transport: Trends & Theory P3T3, 2013 Discussion Papers Part II Case Studies*. ISBN 978-88-97781-61-5, COST Office, Brussels. Available online at: www.ppptransport.eu

Nikolaidis, N. and Roumboutsos, A. (2013b) 'Ionia Odos Motorway' in: A. Roumboutsos, S. Farrell, C. L. Liyanage and R. Macário *COST Action TU1001 Public Private Partnerships in Transport: Trends & Theory P3T3, 2013 Discussion Papers Part II Case Studies*. ISBN 978-88-97781-61-5, COST Office, Brussels. Available online at: www.ppptransport.eu

Nikolaidis, N. and Roumboutsos, A. (2014) 'Central Greece Motorway' in: A. Roumboutsos, S. Farrell and K. Verhoest *COST Action TU1001 – Public Private Partnerships in Transport: Trends & Theory: 2014 Discussion Series: Country Profiles & Case Studies*. ISBN 978-88-6922-009-8, COST Office, Brussels. Available online at: www.ppptransport.eu

Normann, R. and Ramirez, R. (1994) *Designing Interactive Strategy: from Value Chain to Value Constellation*. Chichester: John Wiley and Sons

Odeck, J. (2014) 'E18 Grimstad – Kristiansand' in: A. Roumboutsos, S. Farrell and K. Verhoest *COST Action TU1001 – Public Private Partnerships in Transport: Trends & Theory: 2014 Discussion Series: Country Profiles & Case Studies* ISBN 978-88-6922-009-8, COST Office, Brussels. Available online at: www.ppptransport.eu

OECD (2014) *The Competitiveness of Global Port Cities*. Edited by Olaf Merk. OECD Publishing. DOI:10.1787/9789264205277-en

Osterwalder, A. (2004) 'The business model ontology: a proposition in a design science approach'. *Thesis pour l'obtention du grade de Docteur en Informatique de Gestion.* École des Hautes Études Commerciales de l'Université de Lausanne

Oum, T., Adler, N. and Yu, C. (2006) 'Privatization, corporatization, ownership forms and their effects on the performance of the world's major airports'. *Journal of Air Transport Management*, 12(3), pp. 109–121

Panayides, P. M. and Song D.-W. (2008) 'Evaluating the integration of seaport container terminals in supply chains'. *International Journal of Physical Distribution & Logistics Management*, 38 (7), pp. 562–584

Papanikolas, P., Diakidou, A., Roumboutsos, A. and Pantelias, A. (2014) 'Rio-Antirio Bridge' in: A. Roumboutsos, S. Farrell and K. Verhoest *COST Action TU1001 – Public Private Partnerships in Transport: Trends & Theory: 2014 Discussion Series: Country Profiles & Case Studies*. ISBN 978-88-6922-009-8, COST Office, Brussels. Available online at: www.ppptransport.eu

Parkhe, A. (1993) 'Strategic alliance structuring: a game theoretic and transaction cost examination of interfirm cooperation'. *Academy of Management Journal*, 36, pp. 794–829

Peneda, M. J. A., Reis, V. D. and Macário, M. R. (2011) 'Critical factors for development of airport cities'. *Journal of the Transportation Research Board* 2214, pp. 1–9

Porter, M. E. (1985) 'How information gives you competitive advantage'. *Harvard Business Review* 63(4): pp. 149–160

Public Works Financing (2013) *International Major Projects Report*, October. Available online at: www.pwfinance.net

Ramanathan, K., Seth, A. and Thomas, H. (1997) 'Explaining joint ventures: alternative theoretical perspectives' in: P. W. Beamish and J. P. Killing (Eds) *Cooperative Strategies: Vol. 1. North American Perspectives* (pp. 51–85). San Francisco, CA: New Lexington Press

Rodrigue, J-P., Notteboom, T. and Pallis, A. A. (2011) 'The financialisation of the port and terminal industry: revisiting risk and embeddedness'. *Maritime Policy & Management: the flagship journal of international shipping and port research*, 38:2, pp. 191–213

Roumboutsos, A., Ågren, R. and Suárez Alemán, A. (2013) 'PPP supply market: building expertise or pure concentration?' Conference: Global challenges in PPP: cross-sectoral and cross-disciplinary solutions? Antwerp, November 6-7, 2013

Sicmiatyck, M. (2010) 'Delivering transportation infrastructure through Public-Private Partnerships: planning concerns'. *Journal of the American Planning Association*, 76, pp. 43–58

Siemiatycki, M. and Friedman, J. (2012) 'The trade-offs of transferring demand risk on urban transit Public Private Partnerships'. *Public Works Management & Policy* 17(3) pp. 283–302

Starkie, D. (2002) 'Airport regulation and competition'. *Journal of Air Transport Management* 8 (1), pp. 63–72

Suárez-Alemán, A. and Cabrera, M. (2014) 'Barcelona Europe South Container Terminal' in: A. Roumboutsos, S. Farrell and K. Verhoest *COST Action TU1001 – Public Private Partnerships in Transport: Trends & Theory: 2014 Discussion Series: Country Profiles & Case Studies*. ISBN 978-88-6922-009-8, COST Office, Brussels. Available online at: www.ppptransport.eu

Teece, D. J. (2010) 'Business models, business strategy and innovation'. *Long Range Planning*, 43, pp. 172–194

Tomás, V. R., Castells, M. P., Samper, J. J. and Soriano, F. R. (2013) 'Intelligent transport systems harmonisation assessment: use case of some Spanish intelligent transport systems services, IET'. *Intelligent Transport Systems*, 7 (3), pp. 361–370

Tretheway, M. W. and Kincaid, I. (2010) 'Competition between airports: occurrence and strategy' in: P. Forsyth, D. Gillen, J. Muller and H.-M. Neimeier (Eds) *Airport Competition: The European Experience*. Aldershot: Ashgate Publishing Ltd

Vajdic, N. and Mladenovic, G. (2013) 'Horgos-Pozega, Toll Motorway Concession' in: A. Roumboutsos, S. Farrell, C. L. Liyanage and R. Macário *COST Action TU1001 Public Private Partnerships in Transport: Trends & Theory P3T3, 2013 Discussion Papers Part II Case Studies*. ISBN 978-88-97781-61-5, COST Office, Brussels. Available online at: www.ppptransport.eu

van den Hurk, M. and Van Gestel, K. (2013a) 'Brabo 1, Flanders' in: A. Roumboutsos, S. Farrell, C. L. Liyanage and R. Macário *COST Action TU1001 Public Private Partnerships in Transport: Trends & Theory P3T3, 2013 Discussion Papers Part II Case Studies*. ISBN 978-88-97781-61-5, COST Office, Brussels. Available online at: www.ppptransport.eu

van den Hurk, M. and Van Gestel, K. (2013b) 'Via-Invest Zaventem' in: A. Roumboutsos, S. Farrell, C. L. Liyanage and R. Macário *COST Action TU1001 Public Private Partnerships in Transport: Trends & Theory P3T3, 2013 Discussion Papers Part II Case Studies*. ISBN 978-88-97781-61-5, COST Office, Brussels. Available online at: www.ppptransport.eu

Vassallo, J. (2007) 'Implementation of Quality Criteria in Tendering and Regulating Infrastructure Management Contracts'. *Journal of Construction Management and Engineering* 133(8), pp. 553–561

Viegas, J. M. (2001) 'Making urban road pricing acceptable and effective: searching for quality and equity in urban mobility'. *Transport Policy*, 8, pp. 289–294

Villalba-Romero, F. J. and Liyanage, C. (2014) 'Radial 2 (R-2) Toll Motorway' in: A. Roumboutsos, S. Farrell and K. Verhoest *COST Action TU1001 – Public Private Partnerships in Transport: Trends & Theory: 2014 Discussion Series: Country Profiles & Case Studies*. ISBN 978-88-6922-009-8, COST Office, Brussels. Available online at: www.ppptransport.eu

Villalba-Romero, F. J. and Liyanage, C. (2014) 'M-45 Toll Motorway' in: A. Roumboutsos, S. Farrell and K. Verhoest *COST Action TU1001 – Public Private Partnerships in Transport: Trends & Theory: 2014 Discussion Series: Country Profiles & Case Studies*. ISBN 978-88-6922-009-8, COST Office, Brussels. Available online at: www.ppptransport.eu

Villalba-Romero, F. J. and Liyanage, C. (2014a) 'Eje Aeropuerto (M-12), Airport Axis Toll Motorway' in: A. Roumboutsos, S. Farrell and K. Verhoest *COST Action TU1001 – Public Private Partnerships in Transport: Trends & Theory: 2014 Discussion Series: Country Profiles & Case Studies*. ISBN 978-88-6922-009-8, COST Office, Brussels. Available online at: www.ppptransport.eu

Villalba-Romero, F. J. and Liyanage, C. (2014b) 'Metrolink Light Rail Transport, Manchester' in: A. Roumboutsos, S. Farrell and K. Verhoest *COST Action TU1001 – Public Private Partnerships in Transport: Trends & Theory: 2014 Discussion Series: Country Profiles & Case Studies*. ISBN 978-88-6922-009-8, COST Office, Brussels. Available online at: www.ppptransport.eu

Voordijk, J., T. (2013) 'Coen Tunnel' in: A. Roumboutsos, S. Farrell, C. L. Liyanage and R. Macário *COST Action TU1001 Public Private Partnerships in Transport: Trends &*

Theory P3T3, 2013 Discussion Papers Part II Case Studies. ISBN 978-88-97781-61-5, COST Office, Brussels. Available online at: www.ppptransport.eu

Williamson, O. E. (1983) 'Organizational innovation: the transaction-cost approach' in: J. Ronen (Ed.) *Entrepreneurship*. Lexington, MA: Lexington Books

Yescombe, E. R. (2007) *Project finance [Wybrane elementy finansowania struktural-nego]*. Kraków: Oficyna, a Wolters Kluwer business (p. 63)

20 A methodological framework for the credit assessment of transport infrastructure projects

Athena Roumboutsos, Aristeidis Pantelias and Emmanouil Sfakianakis

Introduction

The need to bridge the infrastructure gap and yet not to place additional burden on already indebted and over-stretched public budgets, has favoured the so-called innovative procurement methods involving the private sector. These take on various forms with respect to private sector involvement and remuneration schemes and are grouped under the general term Public Private Partnerships (PPPs). In general, and in contrast to traditional public funding of infrastructure projects where each project phase (design, construction, operation and maintenance) is undertaken separately and funding is provided by the state, the PPP model envisages infrastructure delivery in a more integrated manner. More specifically, a private party may assume the responsibility for the design, build, finance, operation and maintenance of an infrastructure asset, providing the intended public service over a long concession period. During the period in question, any direct and/or indirect revenues generated by the project are used to repay lenders and generate returns for investors.

While the principal reason for endorsing PPP is securing finance (Aziz 2007), increased efficiency is also targeted through numerous other features such as: equitable risk allocation, design and construction practices leading to optimal operation and maintenance (life cycle management considerations), and private sector efficiencies and skills in the provision of a public service to offset the cost of private finance and secure public sector Value for Money (VfM) (Bing *et al.* 2005). The ability of certain assets to generate direct revenues has favoured some sectors over others, transport being one of them. Wider economic growth coupled with increased traffic demand and the gradual acceptance of the 'user pays' principle have favoured the creation of remuneration schemes where revenues are directly collected by the private party (for example, tolled facilities), in addition to unitary government payment schemes (for example, availability payments or shadow tolls). The choice of the model obviously rests on a number of considerations, one of which is the ubiquitous issue of allocating traffic risk (i.e. revenue risk) on the private or the public side of the deal.

Project finance has been a convenient vehicle in addressing PPP finance as this financing technique is based on lending against the future cash flows of a project that is legally and economically self-contained. Although the underlying financing principles are the same, PPP projects have certain characteristics that set them apart from other general industry projects that also use project financing, and these will be discussed in the following sections. Until recently, the key lenders for such projects were commercial banks (mostly relational) supported by government guarantees and, in some cases, multilateral institutions. The financial and economic crisis has had a profound impact on the worldwide PPP financing scene by limiting the availability of, on the one hand, commercial bank loans and, on the other, government guarantees. The tightening grip of international banking conventions (Basel II and III) together with the sovereign debt crisis that followed the financial crisis have further ascertained that the old model of PPP financing needed to be reconsidered. In response to these international changes, PPP promoters have turned to international capital markets as other project and corporate ventures have done in the past. In order for PPP projects to be able to raise funds in the capital markets, they need to be assessed in terms of their credit quality. Credit ratings, in this context, become an important indicator of their financial attractiveness and their ability to secure finance, as they provide an independent and objective measure of credit quality.

Furthermore, the renewed interest of project promoters in capital market financing has revitalised the discussion of whether or not infrastructure represents a financial asset in its own right. A number of assumed financial characteristics that have been attributed to infrastructure projects (i.e. predictable and stable cashflows, inflation protection, attractive returns, low correlation to economic cycles and other asset classes, etc.) would presumably justify investments by institutional investors such as pension funds or insurance companies (cfr. Inderst 2010). Very importantly, a mere 3 per cent asset allocation shift into infrastructure by such institutional investors worldwide would result in some EUR 500 billion pouring into such projects (Inderst 2010). The current narrative seems to imply that investing in infrastructure would be low risk. However, existing evidence is limited and controversial, while in the specific case of transport infrastructure the consideration of risk for such investments is also mode-dependent. It is possible that infrastructure risks feature a comparatively low correlation with the general business cycle, which may explain their attractiveness to various investors (Inderst 2010). But the absolute size of the downside risks is substantial and bites into the expected cash flows of projects, thus reducing their credit potential.

Currently, Credit Rating Agencies (CRAs) rely on project-rating models that, in many ways, revert to the credibility of the respective project promoter (sponsor) or the public authority (government) that acts as a guarantor for it (Roumboutsos *et al.* 2013). This may have positive or negative ramifications on the project's ability to raise (re)financing and to (re)negotiate terms of contract, which need to be based on the objective assessment of the creditworthiness of the project itself.

Adding to the complexity of any PPP arrangement is the fact that transport PPPs bear additional complexity, which is due to asset specificity (Evenhuis and Vickerman 2010) and the way it reflects on revenue risk. The financial and economic crisis has further aggravated this problem as, faced with which, the private sector shows itself to be inherently risk-averse. It is not surprising that, in 2013, over 90 per cent of the PPP transactions closed were authority-pay PPP (for example, availability payments, shadow tolls, etc.) (EPEC 2014). Such schemes add additional burden to governments' budgets and limit the scope of PPP but they offer the advantage of being usually used as a mechanism of reducing revenue risk for private investors. On the negative side, they also limit the VfM of a PPP and they obscure further the creditworthiness of a project as, under such arrangements, it tends to reflect the creditworthiness of the respective public authority (or government), a creditworthiness which may be totally irrelevant to and independent of the PPP project itself.

Understanding the general characteristics and the specificities of transport PPP, as well as the risk allocation and mitigation measures adopted in a specific arrangement and their evolution over the life-cycle of the project, are fundamental in assessing the creditworthiness of a PPP project. In this chapter, following the thorough presentation of the underlining issues of creditworthiness, project credit assessments and transport PPP, risks are analysed and key elements are illustrated. A methodological framework for the objective assessment of creditworthiness is then presented and discussed. Conclusions and further research close the chapter.

Financing PPP Projects

PPP projects are usually financed through project finance, which is based on lending against the future cash flows of a project that is legally and economically self-contained. Project finance structures have the following major attributes. First, the project is governed by an independent company, the SPV (Special Purpose Vehicle or Special Purpose Company or Project Company), which lies at the heart of all its financial and contractual obligations. Project sponsors are required to be part of this new legal entity which is, however, legally (and fiscally) independent of the sponsors' corporate status. Secondly, project (and investment) risks are allocated to the various contractual parties during project structuring based on the parties' ability to manage and bear them. The SPV has very limited capacity to bear risks and usually only retains residual risks that cannot be allocated elsewhere or insured against. Naturally, some of the risks are allocated to and born by the contracting authority with which the SPV signs the project agreement. Thirdly, risks usually vary over the life cycle of a project. This characteristic justifies eventual changes in the financial structure of the project during its life cycle in order to achieve savings and/or benefits from the different pricing of risk. During the construction phase, projects are usually financed with sponsor equity (many times complemented with other types of quasi-equity financing) and bank loans or other forms of debt (such as bonds). Once the project becomes operational, sponsor equity is usually 're-cycled' (i.e. bought by operators or other equity investors), while initial debt arrangements may be substituted by different ones (for example, commercial bank debt may be refinanced by long-term bonds), if this is considered beneficial for the lenders and/or the project. Last, project finance transactions are usually highly leveraged, meaning that the overall financing is composed predominantly of debt and less of equity. The exact debt to equity ratio is determined based on a number of considerations and reflects the riskiness of the project as perceived by its lenders. Less risky projects may be able to achieve higher leverage while riskier ones will inevitably need larger equity cushions for lenders to feel comfortable.

Comparing PPP projects with other industry projects one needs to appreciate a few differences that set them apart. A fundamental difference between the two is that PPP projects are meant to deliver services that are usually considered to be of public responsibility. The 'public good' character implies that the public-sector contracting authority will, on the one hand, safeguard the project and, on the other, provide subsidies or other forms of financial aid (such as guarantees) while, possibly, bearing more risks than in a typical project finance transaction in order for the project to be implemented and infrastructure programmes to progress. A second difference can be found in the level of risks that PPP SPVs are required to bear. Although, in most cases, the various risks are 'passed-through' to other project participants through back-to-back contracts or are insured against, certain risks may eventually rest with the SPV depending on the nature of the transaction. In most cases these are residual risks that cannot be insured against but can be absorbed by the sponsors' equity. However, in the case of user-remunerated PPP models (for example, toll roads), demand risk, if so allocated, may rest with the SPV despite the fact that in many cases it can be partially mitigated by minimum revenue (or demand) guarantees. In addition, many risks may be voluntarily retained by the SPV, such as innovation risks, in an effort to increase efficiency (Roumboutsos and Saussier 2014). Another difference can be observed in the level of gearing of PPP projects. Because PPP projects correspond to assets of public use and carry the implicit assumption that the public sector will always guarantee their life-long viability, such transactions have on average been considered less risky than usual project finance ones, thus resulting in higher gearing ratios. This perception was mostly founded on the consideration that, for PPP projects, the remuneration model was based on government unitary payments (such as availability payments) under the implicit assumption that counterparty (sovereign) risk was minimal or practically non-existent. The recent sovereign debt crisis, coupled with a few notable failures of PPP projects structured on user-based remuneration models, has changed this initial perception of risk and has made it clear that not all PPP projects may be protected against credit risk.

Another consequence of the perceived vested interest of the public sector in PPP projects is that it has allowed traditionally risk-averse lenders to participate in PPP financing and stay involved in such projects longer than would be originally expected. Commercial banks (relational or not) have been the primary lenders to PPP projects, many of them providing loan tenures that went deep into their operational life. The financial crisis signalled a change in such attitudes, not least because of the change it brought to the banks' own lending model (more focus on balance sheet consolidation, preference for high 'velocity of capital', shorter tenures, early re-financing incentives, etc.). At the same time, international banking conventions (Basel II and III) have imposed further disincentives for long-term lending in 'risky' assets, thus limiting further the capability and appetite of such banks to support PPP financing. As PPP projects are in many cases still at the top of the priority lists of governments, other financing solutions have been sought involving, at an initial stage, the participation of multilateral agencies (development banks and Export Credit Agencies) and, at a second stage, the exploration of the appetite of international capital markets. Whereas multilateral agencies rely on their own due diligence in order to decide whether to participate or not in a PPP project, capital markets have long relied on specific metrics of credit quality in order to make their financing decisions. This has inevitably created the need for measuring the creditworthiness of PPP projects.

Creditworthiness and the shift towards project credit assessments

The concept of creditworthiness refers to whether a party that enters into a financial contract can meet its contractual obligations or not. In particular, creditworthiness refers to the ability of a borrower to repay its debt or to the ability of an issuer who issues a financial instrument to meet its repayment financial obligations within the timeframe foreseen in the contract. The assessment of creditworthiness is a dynamic and forward-looking exercise. Throughout an economic cycle, the economic agents' creditworthiness varies and fluctuates. Therefore, even though such assessment could use historical financial information from economic agents, the objective should be to indicate their financial behaviour and evaluate how intrinsic and external factors could influence credit trust.

With reference to the methods to evaluate creditworthiness, what is usually implemented is a combination of distinct qualitative and quantitative features of either the entity or the instrument that is in the scope. The sources of quantitative and qualitative information could be either public and external or private and internal. For example, with reference to quantitative information, there are particular economic, financial and statistical metrics that can be utilised. On top of that, an imperative element of the creditworthiness assessment is the integration of qualitative information, drawn from data and derived after the quantitative inputs. This typically relates to business/product structures, corporate strategies and behaviours and other external qualitative factors.

Creditworthiness is directly linked with the probability of default by the obligor. In essence, obligors who have a lower probability to default on their financial obligations can be considered more creditworthy and vice versa. Therefore, the probability of default is an indication and can serve as a measure of creditworthiness. The probability of default could depend on the ability or the intention of the obligor to meet his/her financial obligations. Default itself can take many forms depending on the financial instrument in reference, its structure, the issuer, the related parties and the contractual clauses.

Institutions, organisations and scholars have developed distinct definitions of default, which depend on the purpose of use and context of this measure. There are common elements though, which can be identified in all these definitions. In general terms, default indicates delays in or omission of contractual financial obligations; it can also be linked to other events (i.e. distressed exchanges, bankruptcy, liquidation, etc.) occurring either individually or in combinations. Creditworthiness concerns the assessment of the likelihood of default on obligations or delayed payment of debt. In the context of PPP, project credit assessments effectively serve as an objective indicator of the likelihood of default of a project, an indicator on which capital markets can rely in order to make their financing decisions.

In the transport sector, financing PPP projects favoured a new financial market. The main driving forces included the international economic growth rates in the 1990s, the funding gap of the public sector and the demand for maintenance, upgrading and expansion of ageing transport infrastructure able to support new travel patterns and to endorse the demand for smarter technologies. PPP market actors include: investment funds (such as infrastructure funds or other equity/debt funds); strategic investors (comprising contractors/operators such as ACS, Vinci, Cosco, etc., as well as other industrial firms); institutional investors (such as pension funds, insurance companies and sovereign wealth finds) and other intermediaries. The contribution of all these investors to PPP financing has fluctuated over the years for a number of reasons, but predominantly because, in many cases, they had been crowded out of the market by cheap commercial bank credit. The lack of the necessary sophistication has been another reason. Notably, with the exception of strategic investors who usually have specific and extensive project expertise, other investors lack the ability to manage PPP project risks and rely mostly on structured finance arrangements and financial engineering in order to mitigate their financial risks. With the change of the underlying model of PPP finance, as previously explained, and the new flow towards capital market financing, the need to measure project creditworthiness has been back in the market more strongly than ever before.

Project credit assessments and transport PPP risks

Credit Rating Agencies have been swift to meet the market need for measuring the credit quality of projects. To do so they have developed relevant methodologies. The challenge in implementing such methodologies is to adequately represent the individual project risk status, given that they may be linked to other outstanding methodologies, such as corporate or structured finance credit rating methodologies (Roumboutsos *et al.* 2013). This is important as project ratings have an effect on the ability of projects to raise initial debt or issue new debt in case of future refinancing needs while, at the same time, they influence their ability to effectively negotiate contractual terms with lenders and investors.

As mentioned in Roumboutsos *et al.* (2013) there are two important difficulties in achieving reliable PPP project credit ratings: the first has to do with the fact that SPVs are independent entities with no past and inexistent (or limited) recourse to their sponsors' parent companies. The second is that infrastructure assets have certain attributes that make them dissimilar to commercial investments. The implication coming from these two observations is that PPP projects cannot be reliably evaluated based on their comparison with similar investments (i.e. other projects). In this sense relative credit assessments do not seem apt to capture a realistic credit profile of such projects, pointing to the need for absolute assessments of credit risk. CRAs have had a relatively good track record with respect to relative risk ratings, but not so much with respect to absolute risk ones (Cantor and Packer 1994; White 2010). At the same time, due to the proprietary nature of their models, CRAs follow different methodologies when it comes to project ratings. Most of these methodologies allow for expert judgement and ratings are typically issued based on the deliberations of relevant rating committees consisting of experts who nevertheless may not be relevant to the project under consideration (Roumboutsos *et al.* 2013). Last but not least, project ratings can be solicited by interested sponsors and are not issued automatically for all projects that reach the point of going to the market to seek financing. This fact limits the overall number of outstanding ratings on the one hand and, on the other, makes it hard to statistically compare ratings of projects with similar characteristics so as to verify their validity or draw more generalised conclusions. At the same time, it would be expected for credit ratings for PPP projects to be directly connected to project risks and their evolution over the life-cycle of their underlying contractual agreement, as they form the basis of PPP structuring and are crucial to their overall viability. Such a risk-based approach to PPP creditworthiness would require an in-depth knowledge of the particularities and specific conditions of each individual project, rather than just a measure of the creditworthiness of its sponsors, whether private or public.

Scholars and practitioners have produced numerous listings of project risks (cfr. Grimsey and Lewis 2004). However, as Kwak *et al.* (2009) stated, there is no list of risks that is applicable to all PPP projects and there is not one risk classification approach universally accepted as the best. The risks of a PPP project are affected by several factors such as the type and scale of the project, the country in which the project is located, and the model of PPP implemented, to name but a few of cardinal importance. Individual project risks vary over time and therefore any appropriate representation would also need to take into account their time dimension, i.e. the entire asset life cycle for the duration of the project agreement.

The reference to the project agreement is of fundamental importance as risks in PPP projects are managed contractually. As per the 'traditional' risk management approach (cf. Loosemore *et al.* 2006), risks are initially identified and analysed with a view to estimating their likelihood and impact. Subsequently, they are allocated 'to the party best able to manage them at the minimum cost'. Depending on the outcome of this allocation, risks usually end up being absorbed or mitigated by the various project participants or insured against. The success of the aforementioned process is based on how equitable and appropriate the risk allocation ends up being, as well as on the identification of appropriate mitigation and insurance measures. All these relationships are meticulously documented in lengthy contracts that bind all project participants together for the duration of the project or until a mutually agreed exit date allows them to disengage from it.

The evaluation of the creditworthiness of a PPP project is directly related to the financial performance of the SPV that delivers it. This performance is measured in terms of the expected operational cash-flows of the project. In the end what matters is that revenues need to be greater than costs during the project's operational phase in order for debt to be serviced and expected returns to be generated for its investors. The risk of failing to reach either of these fundamental financial targets has also been defined in the literature as the project's 'investment risk' (cfr. Pantelias and Zhang 2010).

The measurement of creditworthiness corresponds only to the debt repayment side of investment risk as creditors are not interested in the upside potential of a project but just in the servicing of debt. Nevertheless, creditworthiness would be expected to be related to the difference between the actual versus the expected operational project cash-flows as these would determine the potential of cash available for debt repayment. Operational project cash-flows are affected by a large number of parameters that correspond to various engineering (macro- and micro-), economic and financial project characteristics. The inherent variation of these parameters is what translates them into risks, which are attributed to the various project characteristics, phases and details of the contractual agreement. These risks are then, in turn, translated into costs under a certain level of expectation, which ultimately influence the balance between the overall revenues and costs of the project.

Furthermore, risks that influence project revenues and costs are usually interrelated, as they are many times influenced by the same underlying parameters. The correlation between them makes the evaluation of the overall riskiness of a project even harder for a number of reasons:

- projects are unique in nature and cannot be easily compared with one another with respect to their individual risks;
- information on project risks may be difficult to capture due to commercial sensitivity issues or lack of appropriate documentation;
- the quantification of the correlation between risks remains elusive in most cases;
- the risks and their underlying parameters, as well as their correlation, may be changing during the life-cycle of the project.

Mapping the system of individual project risks, their relations and interdependencies, is core to understanding the overall potential impact of a risk eventuation. The realisation of a particular risk – oftentimes initially assumed independent – may influence/trigger other risks (possibly allocated to other parties), which may, in turn, influence both costs and revenues. Figure 20.1(a) and (b), for example, illustrate such interdependencies, for the specific case of construction cost overrun and reduced construction performance, respectively. The potential of construction risks (construction phase) to influence revenues (operation phase) and cash-flow schedule is apparent. However, this does not necessarily mean that

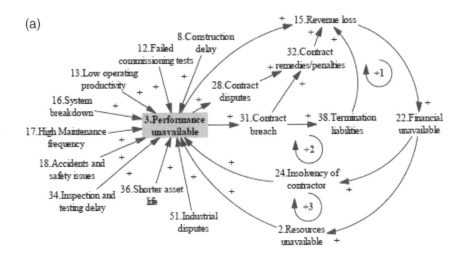

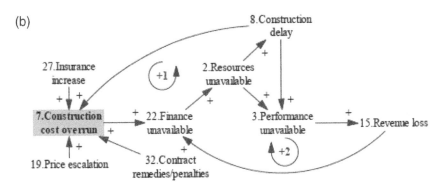

Figure 20.1 General illustration of a dynamic system of PPP project risks with respect to performance (20.1a) and cost overrun (20.1b).

Source: Jang, S. G. 2011

revenues will be influenced. The system of project risks is dynamic and should be studied in combination with the ability of the party to which they have been allocated to manage and contain them. Managerial mitigation strategies and contingency plans may limit or totally contain the potential impact. Managerial monitoring of the dynamic system of risks is crucial in preventing risk triggers and preparing for unforeseen risks and, therefore, safeguarding the project from downside impacts while exploiting potential opportunities. These managerial activities are usually not considered in the purely financial assessment of credit-worthiness. They are, however, related to the managerial capacities of the parties directly involved in the management of the project, and are important in the VfM assessment, the cornerstone of the PPP rhetoric. They should, therefore, also be considered as part of assessing the potential creditworthiness of the project. In most projects (including those in the transport sector), the parties' ability to manage risks is rather focused on the containing risks, which influence costs and the respective side of the cash-flow equation.

Revenues in a transport project are, in most cases, related to the demand risk. This, in turn, is directly related to the accuracy of demand forecasts, which are partly dependent on the respective models and techniques (i.e. factors and assumptions influencing their accuracy) and on a possible 'optimism bias' on the side of policy decision-makers (Flyvbjerg *et al.* 2005). However, apart from these well-known and well-documented concepts, there is a dual managerial aspect to the assessment of demand risk: first, the party to which it has been assigned may be able to manage it; and, second, various contractual 'securities' may be provided in order to mitigate or eliminate this risk. In the first case, demand risk may be managed by the party to which it has been assigned depending on the underlying PPP business model. In many projects the SPV may have the ability to influence demand for the asset's core services, such as the ones offered in the case of port terminal operators. In other cases the core infrastructure service may be 'bundled' with other commercial activities, which aim to balance the influence of the 'core' demand risk within the revenue risk, such as in the case of airport infrastructure. Therefore, demand and revenue risk should always be considered with respect to the business model applied for the particular PPP project (i.e. whether the project merely aims to provide a service or it is expected to generate new business as well) (Roumboutsos and Pantelias 2015). In the second case, the treatment of demand risk within transport PPP project agreements often consists of specific contractual arrangements conceived as security. Such arrangements include exclusivity rights, measures enhancing network effects and others. For example, the Lusoponte concession (Portugal) included the Vasco da Gama bridge (greenfield project) and the 25 de Abril bridge (brownfield) and, hence, the concessionaire had full control over the Tagus River crossing (Miranda Sarmento 2014).

However, in many transport PPP cases, part (or the totality) of revenue risk, may be assumed by the public sector either directly (for example, availability fee remuneration) or indirectly (for example, government guarantees, subsidies, etc.). This is a valid approach if the public party is the most able to manage it, otherwise the misallocation of the demand risk may limit private sector incentives.

Clearly, the capacity to cope with cost overruns/delays and revenue risk largely defines the creditworthiness of a PPP project. In this context the approach that considers the creditworthiness of the government (sovereign) as a proxy for the creditworthiness of the project itself seems valid, under the assumption that the creditworthiness of the SPV and the project sponsors is safeguarded through structured finance arrangements and that the demand/revenue risk is ultimately borne by the public sector. However, there is one key consideration that may elude the aforementioned approach but which is quite fundamental to PPP project structuring: the process of risk allocation in PPP projects is (or at least should be) primarily based on the ability of parties to manage risks. Consequently, prior to assessing the capacity of a project to cope with risks that may eventually impact cost and revenue, one must assess its capacity to manage these risks.

This observation circumscribes the fundamental difference between a PPP project and other credit-rated instruments (or projects) in what could be a novel approach for the objective assessment of project creditworthiness. The first should be based on the assessment of the project's risk management capacity while the second on the assessment of the obligor's potential to meet obligations based on his/her financial background and other collaterals.

Methodological framework

While currently there are mature and precise techniques to measure risks, it remains unclear how to integrate different risk types to obtain the overall project risk (Li *et al.* 2012). A number of methods have been employed, ranging from simple summation (assumes no correlation of risks) to more complex mathematical models, with the banking industry mostly using the variance-covariance approach (McNeil *et al.* 2005). However, the inter-relation between risks is far from independent or linear. On the contrary, as described earlier, risks, when eventuating, trigger a dynamic system and finally impact cost, or revenue or both (Jang 2011).

Risk is usually quantified in relation to the expected value of its impact and probability of occurrence. In many cases it also includes a term reflecting the vulnerability of the system. This term describes how 'open' the system is to a certain risk. In addition, risks are assessed with respect to an agent's attitude towards risk. Risk-averse parties will assume less risk than risk-prone ones. Risk averseness (or proneness) concerns behaviour that may change over time, as do the policies adopted based on strategic objectives. Furthermore, attitude towards risk is not (or should not be) independent of the agent's total risk portfolio as it is generated by the number and types of undertakings included in it. Most importantly, good risk management practices call for a risk, which has been identified and assessed, to be properly allocated and then addressed/mitigated. Next, the risk should be ultimately reassessed with respect to any residual consequences that cannot be further mitigated (or insured against) and that may need to be absorbed in case of its realisation (or if mitigation measures and/or contingency plans fail). In this context, it is important to assess first, the appropriateness of risk allocation and then, the level of managerial flexibility that influences its mitigation and, finally, the ability to absorb/bear risk within a portfolio.

This approach forms the basis of the proposed methodological framework, which incorporates the special characteristics of transport PPP previously identified, i.e., the dynamic correlation of risks and the vulnerability of such projects to demand/revenue risk. The overview of the framework is illustrated in Figure 20.2. The framework defines six levels (steps) of assessment:

Level 1. Assessment of risk allocation with respect to risk management capacity.
     After a risk has been identified and its probability of occurrence and expected impact have been determined, this step assesses whether:

i. The risk was contractually assigned to the party most able to manage it. More specifically, it means assessing whether the specific risk is within the control of the party to which it has been assigned. Often, due to the political decision-making process, many risks are inappropriately allocated from the outset (cfr. Roumboutsos and Pantelias 2015).

ii. The project agreement (or any other legally binding procedure or document) provides managerial flexibility to the party to which the risk was assigned. Real options, contingency plans, etc. should all be considered in this assessment.

Level 2. Assessment of risk allocation with respect to risk-bearing capacity. This concerns assessing whether:

i. The risk was assigned to the party most capable of bearing the cost of it in case it eventuates. This is independent of the general ability of a party to manage this risk and, in many ways, may be contractually defined. For example, innovation carries risks, which are associated with construction or operation risk depending on its implementation. Bearing the cost of innovation failure may be assigned contractually to any party.

ii. Risk mitigation instruments (such as minimum revenue guarantees) are put in place in the case where risk is not assigned to the party most able to cope with it.

Level 3. Mapping of the dynamic system of project risks. Mapping the dynamic and interrelated system of components of the PPP arrangement for all the risks that have been assessed, with emphasis placed on the correlation of costs and revenues over time, is the focus of this step. More specifically, at this level:

i. The recurring importance of some risks may be identified. For example, in Figure 20.1a, the risk of unavailable resources received a triple impact multiplier.

ii. The potential of the adopted mitigation measures, real options and other securities considered at Level 2 is assessed for the system of risks, together with their overall ability to safeguard the investment.

Level 4. Assessment of PPP Business Model vulnerability. The provision of traffic infrastructure may be accompanied by (or bundled with) other services and/or commercial activities, which may generate revenues. At this level the combined value proposition is assessed, especially with respect to the different customers to whom it is targeted. While demand may be protected through exclusivity rights, and network effects may be contractually (or not) harnessed in support of the core infrastructure service, other services may also be included, contributing to revenues. The robustness of the business model with respect to revenue risk relies on the bundling of offered services (value proposition) with different sources or triggers of respective demand risk. Additionally, the ability of the project SPV to influence demand for core services is assessed together with its impact on expected revenue streams.

In the absence of the above, the PPP arrangement may be found to be vulnerable to the residual risks of Levels 2 and 3.

Level 5. Assessment of counterparty total risk exposure. This concerns the total risk exposure of key project implementation counterparties (for example, sub-contractors, operator(s), and the public sector but also the SPV to the point that this has been contractually foreseen) in consideration of their respective risk portfolios. Over the life-cycle of a PPP project many fluctuations of cash-flow levels may be expected. The ability of each party to address short or medium term negative cash-flows is also dependent on their respective risk portfolios as generated by their respective undertakings. This assessment, however, does not affect the SPV and its sponsors as their total risk exposure is limited to their committed project equity due to the ring-fencing of the project through its inherent PPP (project) financing structure. Notably, if a new risk is small and/or uncorrelated with the risks of the party's existing portfolio, the party's overall exposure should remain small as the risk is diversified. If a new risk is large and/or highly correlated with the risks of the existing portfolio, the overall exposure may increase. For example, demand for a toll road may be correlated with the strength of the local economy and therefore with the value of the government's portfolio of assets and liabilities (its tax revenue tending to rise and its spending on social welfare tending to fall when the economy is strong). For the same reasons, demand risk may be strongly correlated with customers' portfolios. It may be less correlated, however, with the risk portfolio of an international firm (private counterparty) (Irwin 2007).

In practical terms, with respect to the government, this level assesses whether government liabilities generated from the PPP project are registered in the public forecasts, according to the applicable accounting standards (such as Eurostat or other International Public Sector Accounting Standards – IPSAS). Experience shows that under Eurostat's criteria many PPP assets and related liabilities are recorded off the governments' balance sheets (Funke *et al.* 2013).

Notably, Level 5 is not necessarily restricted to the creditworthiness of the government (sovereign), as the residual risks that need to be absorbed may be particularly small, or may not significantly impact the government's overall risk exposure, or may even improve the balance within the risk portfolio.

Level 6. PPP credit assessment. This concerns the determination of PPP creditworthiness based on the combination of the assessments for all counterparties in Level 5, but also on the outputs from the previous levels of assessment. At this final level the various risk exposures (and/or counter-acting mitigation measures and arrangements) of all project counterparties are considered with respect to their influence on the ability of the project to service its debt obligations. As a side note, and with respect to project sponsors and the SPV, their total risk exposure assessment is reflected by the gearing ratio of the project. Lower gearing ratios denote higher equity buffers for creditors and thus higher project creditworthiness.

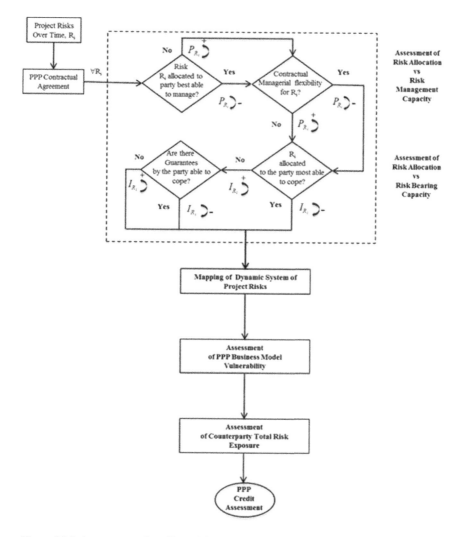

Figure 20.2 Assessment of creditworthiness methodological framework.

Notably, the proposed methodological framework has at its heart at all levels the ability to manage rather than just absorb risk. In many ways the final assessment of the creditworthiness of such projects depends on the success of risk allocation and the foreseen risk mitigation measures. If risk allocation and mitigation are successfully planned, then the project may be robust enough to sustain deviations from the expected occurrence of its various risks, especially in light of the difficulty in estimating them with precision. The emphasis on mitigation and managerial flexibility is assessed throughout. For example, at Level 4, the business model is assessed with respect to its resilience to deviations caused by risks impacting cost and/or revenues. Assessing the balance of the risk portfolio of key project implementation counterparties (Level 5) can also be considered as an evaluation of potential mitigation measures identified at the previous levels.

Evidently, the implementation of the above methodological framework is hampered by a number of shortcomings:

- information on project risks and other contractual information may be difficult to obtain due to confidentiality and other commercially sensitive issues;
- mapping of risk correlations requires deep knowledge and understanding of the projects' structure and implementation strategy;
- the overall risk exposure of the project counterparties may not be accessible (not only on the basis of the particular project).

At the same time, the vulnerability of a framework that focuses on government (sovereign) creditworthiness must also be highlighted. Lack of detailed information on risk allocation and mitigation, in combination with the legal and fiscal autonomy of the SPV that disconnects it from its sponsors' parent companies, leave governments as the only major counterparty to be assessed with respect to project creditworthiness.

With respect to project sponsors it is true that strong strategic industrial investors in PPP have prevailed despite adverse market conditions and occasional failures of individual projects in their portfolios. Their corporate status can play a role in the positive assessment of project creditworthiness as, despite their disassociation (fully or in part) from the SPV's financial performance, their own strong balance sheets serve many times as an implicit guarantee for a project that goes to the market to obtain financing. In contrast with the above is the fact that small and medium-sized companies, on account of their relatively weaker financial background, are not able to compete with their larger counterparts unless they obtain sufficient monetary backup from financiers (Cheng *et al.* 2007). On the same account, financiers are usually reluctant to support alternative schemes including alternative project sponsors; such lack of support can impede the commencement of a project despite the fact that the latter was designed following a business model approach (an example is the Larnaca Port and Marina development project in Cyprus (Christodoulou and Efstathiades 2014)). In an attempt to overcome this issue, the Flemish and Dutch PPP procurement system sets up separate tenders for the technical and financial part of the PPP project (cf. van den Hurk and Verhoest 2013; Dewulf and Castano 2013). However, in this case, while overcoming initial transaction costs, governments end up making themselves directly responsible for project creditworthiness and, in essence, cancel the incentives of risk management.

Finally, securing finance for transport PPP depends also on the mode under consideration. Ports are a characteristic example where financing is not guaranteed by the government but is the sole responsibility of the project sponsor. Notably, global terminal operators and shipping lines govern this market and are responsible for building, sustaining and expanding the respective service and business. Their dominant position stems from their knowledge of the risks involved, their understanding of global trade and transportation and, ultimately, their ability to manage related risks. In the period 2002-2008, globalisation and its associated global trade growth incited an intense phase of capital accumulation in the port industry. Institutional investors have entered this market despite the fact that project performance was solely attributable to the managerial capabilities of the concessioners. The growth prospects and capital requirements to finance port terminal projects attracted the attention of large financial firms and an array of new actors (such as sovereign and pension funds) took various ownership stakes and created a bubble. Ever since, the financial sector is rediscovering, rather reluctantly, the risks that are part of the maritime industry, notably those related to business cycles (Rodrigue *et al.* 2011).

The above example demonstrates the importance of the ability to manage risks *vis-à-vis* the assumed attractiveness (and creditworthiness) of the investment. It also highlights the importance of the underlying PPP business model and its vulnerability or resilience. Another pertinent example is to be found in a PPP arrangement addressing the construction and operation of a tramway: within an urban transit system it is vulnerable to demand and competition risk while, if operated as part of the entire urban transit system, it provides managerial flexibility and leads to successful applications (crf. The Reims tramway (Bonnet and Chomat 2013)).

Conclusions

The need to seek PPP financing from capital markets introduces the need for objective project credit assessments. Financial intermediation theory considers credit ratings as a means by which to reduce information asymmetry about *ex-ante* economic value and the likelihood of financial distress (Millon and Thakor 1985). As infrastructure programmes contemplate the need to tap into new risk-averse pools of funds, such as institutional investors, community bonds and other low risk-seeking investors, to secure low cost finance, credit ratings may increasingly be considered to acquire the status of a public good (Duan and van Laere 2012).

The proposed methodological framework for assessing PPP creditworthiness is based predominantly on the dual assessment of the management of risks over the project's life-cycle and of the underlying PPP business model, on top of other factors. This is in line with the generally accepted notion of risk management being the cornerstone of PPP infrastructure procurement and delivery and constituting one of its main justifications in terms of value-for-money.

In the proposed approach, PPP creditworthiness is not determined by the creditworthiness of the contracting public authority, nor is it capped by it. Its step-wise structure provides a rational approach for project credit assessment regardless of the availability of accessible information. Most importantly, following the proposed methodology, a PPP project may have a credit assessment more favourable than that of the project's public counterparty.

The framework may also be used to guide decision-makers in setting up a PPP business model, so as to enhance its overall creditworthiness with measures other than the provision of government guarantees. The latter may, on the one hand, impede managerial measures and innovation and, on the other, further burden the government's exposure to risk with an overall negative additional impact on sovereign creditworthiness (Irwin 2007).

Last but not least, the proposed approach brings forward a number of issues that need to be addressed on a policy, managerial and technical level. Such issues are:

- Balancing risks and rewards for all project participants. Financial engineering has facilitated the development of sophisticated techniques for investors to reorganise debt, maintain interest rate flexibility and restructure dividend payout and debt repayment schedules. However, Ashton *et al.* (2012) show in their analysis that 'while these techniques significantly increase returns to investors, they pose risks to the public sector because they increase the investor's indebtedness, require higher annual revenues to cover costs, and potentially encumber the public sector with responsibilities to creditors and counterparties should purchasers default on the concession agreement'. Consequently, while governments, due to financial engineering on the SPV side, are often driven to bearing the lion's share of project risks, they do not share in equal measure the benefits of such structured finance solutions, as the latter are in many cases too complicated or sophisticated for their existing in-house expertise and are therefore often ignored or forgone.
- The need for the creation of wider PPP business models. In projects where revenue risk is solely reflecting traffic demand risk, the creation of a system of additional transport-related, commercial and/or other services may balance the overall cash-flow risk. At the same time, managerial and business flexibility may provide means to contain the traffic demand risk and its fluctuations over the life-cycle of the project.
- The need to develop sophisticated tailor-made risk management approaches. Such approaches should be sought within PPP projects with a level of sophistication that goes beyond the requirement to comply with simple monitoring procedures and protocols. The introduction of techniques and models supporting managerial flexibility can also be of great importance to the success of such projects and should be further explored by relevant parties.

Acknowledgements

This research was generated through COST Action TU1001.

References

Ashton, P., Doussard, M. and Weber, R. (2012) 'The financial engineering of infrastructure privatization'. *Journal of the American Planning Association*, 78:3, pp. 300–312

Aziz, A. M. A. (2007) Successful delivery of Public-Private Partnerships for infrastructure development'. *Journal of Construction Engineering and Management*, 133(12), pp. 918–931

Bing, L., Akintoye, A., Edwards, P. J. and Hardcastle, C. (2005) 'The allocation of risk in PPP/PFI construction projects in the UK'. *International Journal of Project Management*, 23, pp. 25–35

Bonnet, G. and Chomat, G. (2013) 'The Reims' Tramway' in: A. Roumboutsos, S. Farrell, C. L. Liyanage and R. Macário (Eds) *COST Action TU1001 – Public Private Partnerships in Transport: Trends & Theory P3T3, 2013 Discussion Papers Part II Case Studies*. ISBN 978-88-97781-61-5, COST Office, Brussels. Available online at: www.ppptransport.eu

Cantor, R. and Packer, F. (1994) 'The credit rating industry'. *Federal Reserve of New York Quarterly Review* 19, pp. 1–26

Cheng, E. W. L., Chiang, Y. H. and Tang, B. S. (2007) 'Alternative approach to credit scoring by DEA: Evaluating borrowers with respect to PFI projects'. *Building and Environment*, 42, pp. 1752–1760

Christodoulou, C. and Efstathiades, C. (2014) 'Larnaca Port and Marina Re-development' in: A. Roumboutsos, S. Farrell and K. Verhoest (Eds) *COST Action TU1001 – Public Private Partnerships in Transport: Trends & Theory: 2014 Discussion Series: Country Profiles & Case Studies*. ISBN 978-88-6922-009-8, COST Office, Brussels. Available online at: www.ppptransport.eu

Dewulf, G. and Castano, J. M. (2013) 'The Netherlands' in: K. Verhoest, N. Carbonara, V. Lember, O. H. Petersen, W. Scherrer and M. van den Hurk (Eds) *COST Action TU1001 – Public Private Partnerships in Transport: Trends & Theory P3T3, 2013 Discussion Papers Part I Country Profiles*. ISBN: 978-88-97781-60-8, COST Office, Brussels. Available online at: www.ppptransport.eu

Duan, J-C. and van Laere, E. (2012) 'A public good approach to credit ratings – from concept to reality'. *Journal of Banking & Finance*, 36, pp. 3239–3247

EPEC (2014) *Market Update: Review of the European PPP Market in 2013*. Luxembourg: European PPP Expertise Centre (EPEC at the EIB)

Eurostat (2012) *Manual on government deficit and debt: implementation of ESA 95, 2012 edition* (pp. 241, 267–68). Luxembourg: European Commission

Evenhuis, E. and Vickerman, R. (2010) 'Transport pricing and Public-Private Partnerships in theory: issues and suggestions'. *Research in Transportation Economics*, 30, pp. 6–14

Flyvbjerg, B., Skamris, M., Holm, M. and Buhl, S. L. (2005) 'How (in)accurate are demand forecasts in public works projects? The case of transportation'. *Journal of the American Planning Association*, Vol. 71, No. 2, pp. 131–146

Funke, K., Irwin, T. and Rial, I. (2013) *Budgeting and Reporting for Public-Private Partnerships*. Washington DC, USA: Fiscal Affairs Department, International Monetary Fund. Available online at: www.internationaltransportforum.org/jtrc/DiscussionPapers/jtrcpapers.html

Grimsey, D. and Lewis, M. K. (2004) *Public Private Partnerships*. Cheltenham, UK: Edward Elgar

Hurk, M. (van den) and Verhoest, K. (2013) 'Flanders, Belgium' in: K. Verhoest, N. Carbonara, V. Lember, O. H. Petersen, W. Scherrer and M. van den Hurk (Eds) *COST Action TU1001 – Public Private Partnerships in Transport: Trends & Theory P3T3, 2013 Discussion Papers Part I Country Profiles*. ISBN: 978-88-97781-60-8, COST Office, Brussels. Available online at: www.ppptransport.eu

Inderst, G. (2010) 'Infrastructure as an asset class'. *EIB Papers*, ISSN 0257-7755, Vol. 15, Iss. 1, pp. 70–105

Irwin, T. (2007) *Government Guarantees: Allocating and Valuing Risks in Privately Financed Infrastructure Projects*. Washington DC: World Bank, ISBN-10: 0-8213-6859-1 (electronic)

Jang, S. G. (2011) 'A concessionaire selection decision model development and application for the PPP project procurement'. Southampton, UK: University of Southampton, PhD Thesis

Kwak, Y. H., Chih, Y. and Ibbs, W. (2009) 'Towards a comprehensive understanding of Public Private Partnerships for infrastructure development'. *California Management Review*, Vol. 51, No.2, pp. 51–78

Li, J., Feng, J., Li, M. and Xu, W. (2012) 'Risk integration mechanisms and approaches in the banking industry'. *International Journal of Information Technology and Decision Making*, 11 (6), pp. 1183–1213

Loosemore, M., Raftery, J., Reilly, C. and Higgon, D. (2006) *Risk Management in Projects*. London, UK: Taylor & Francis

McNeil, A., Frey, R. and Embrechts, P. (2005) *Quantitative Risk Management: Concepts, Techniques, and Tools*. New Jersey, USA: Princeton University Press

Millon, M. and Thakor, A. (1985) 'Moral hazard and information sharing: a model of financial information gathering agencies'. *Journal of Finance*, 40, pp. 1403–1422

Miranda Sarmento, J. (2014) 'Lusoponte Bridge' in: A. Roumboutsos, S. Farrell and K. Verhoest (Eds) *COST Action TU1001 – Public Private Partnerships in Transport: Trends & Theory: 2014 Discussion Series: Country Profiles & Case Studies*. ISBN 978-88-6922-009-8, COST Office, Brussels. Available online at: www.ppptransport.eu

Pantelias, A. and Zhang, Z. (2010) 'Methodological framework for the evaluation of financial viability of Public-Private Partnerships: investment risk approach'. *Journal of Infrastructure Systems*, 16(4), pp. 241–250

Rodrigue, J.-P., Notteboom, T. and Pallis, A. A. (2011) 'The financialization of the port and terminal industry: revisiting risk and embeddedness'. *Maritime Policy & Management: The Flagship Journal of International Shipping and Port Research*, 38:2, pp. 191–213

Roumboutsos, A. and Pantelias, A. (2015, forthcoming) 'Allocating revenue risk in transport infrastructure PPP projects: how it matters'. *Transport Reviews*, DOI: 10.1080/01441647.2014.988306

Roumboutsos, A. and Saussier, St. (2014) 'Public-Private Partnerships and investments in innovation: the influence of the contractual arrangement'. *Construction Management and Economics*, 32:4, pp. 349–361

Roumboutsos, A., Sfakianakis, E. and Pantelias, A. (2013) 'Transport infrastructure project credit rating methodology and current practices'. Global Challenges in PPP: Cross-sectorial and Cross-disciplinary Solutions? Conference, Antwerp, November 6-7

White, L. J. (2010) 'Markets: the credit rating agencies'. *Journal of Economic Perspectives*, 24(2), pp. 211–226

21 Efficiency in transport PPP

Conclusions, future research and policy recommendations

Aristeidis Pantelias and
Athena Roumboutsos

Overview

Part 4 begins with a study on standards versus context from the perspective of PPP delivery in an international setting. PPP strategic investors and mode-specific business models are subsequently discussed within the transport PPP market, offering insight on the way these investors tend to standardise their business development based on their strengths and expertise. Interestingly, strategic investors appear to be evolving (contextualising) their business development as their competence grows on the one hand, and their transport mode-specific business models evolve over time, on the other. Lastly, the assessment of project creditworthiness is investigated and new parameters are offered for consideration in an effort to add a degree of contextualisation to a process that is, by nature, largely standardised in order to serve its intended purpose.

In all contributions it is apparent that standardisation and contextualisation are in tension but, at the same time, they are both important in achieving successful project results and overall efficiency. As mentioned in the introduction to this Part, efficiency can ultimately be achieved by combining the two and harvesting their complementarities. Each project, country and PPP market may need to strike a different balance between them in order to achieve the best results. This should not be considered a problem but, rather, as additional proof that standardisation should only go as far as the need to consider contextual issues makes the balance between them efficient.

Chapters 19 and 20 suggest that over-standardisation may lead to suboptimal results. Roumboutsos, Pantelias and Sfakianakis base their arguments as well as their model on the fact that 'standard' treatment of PPP creditworthiness may penalise good projects and mislead investors, while simultaneously reducing the effectiveness of contractual flexibility (another form of contextualisation that improves efficiency). Suarez-Aleman, Roumboutsos and Carbonara suggest that project sponsor competence has been built on standardisation leading to market concentration. The impact on competitiveness has not been discussed.

A final point concerns the issue of transparency. Dewulf, Garvin and Duffield consider it a driver for standardisation. At the same time, contextualisation of creditworthiness cannot be achieved without transparency, as noted by

Roumboutsos, Pantelias and Sfakianakis. Transparency is also required in project sponsor partnerships (within SPVs) in order to achieve an effective complementarity of sponsor competences and, thereafter, effective and efficient value services (Suarez-Aleman, Roumboutsos and Carbonara).

Future research

The arguments above lead to the formulation of a basic hypothesis: standardisation is the first step in achieving successful contextualisation, in the same way that one first sets the boundaries of a system and then formulates the relations within.

Notably, contextualisation requires a certain level of competence and expertise. Flexibility can only be successful if the variants of flexibility are well known. Contextualisation also supports innovation, which is yet another efficiency driver.

Standardisation, however, seems to be the prudent way forward when expertise and respective competences are poor, especially with respect to reducing transaction costs. However, the situation becomes suboptimal in cases of asymmetry in competence and expertise between the interacting parties. In this case, rents may be achieved by the more competent party. These may lead to further asymmetries and hamper the use of other efficiency instruments such as innovation and entrepreneurial skills, especially as these introduce additional risk and uncertainty.

Identifying the impact and influence of standardisation and contextualisation on overall PPP project efficiency is yet to be researched and related to the performance of PPP projects in transport as well as other sectors. Given its importance it is, hopefully, only a matter of time until it gets the attention it deserves and it should feature prominently in forthcoming PPP research agendas.

Policy recommendations

Identifying the balance between standardisation and contextualisation is crucial in order to achieve overall PPP efficiency. Policy- and decision-makers should decide where to strike the balance in each case depending on the existing competences and expertise of the entire spectrum of actors involved in the PPP project setting: the public sector (contracting authorities), project sponsors, and financial markets. Additionally, it is important that this balance is achieved for the entire duration of a PPP project and is not confined to specific project stages. Standardisation, as introduced by Dewulf, Garvin and Duffield, is usually applied to the early (initiating) stages of the PPP procurement process. It would also be extremely helpful and beneficial if it were to be applied (together with the necessary level of contextualisation) to later stages of the project, such as contract implementation. Last but not least, transparency and availability of information is of paramount importance in achieving this balance and subsequently attaining increased efficiency.

Although formulating successful policy recommendations will always be an art as much as a science, positive input towards striking a balance between standardisation and contextualisation could also come from the promotion and adoption of other efficiency instruments such as innovation, contractual flexibility, the use of innovative financing instruments and alternative mitigation strategies, among others.

Appendix: COST Action TU1001

Case study database on PPP in transport

Athena Roumboutsos and
Champika Liyanage

Introduction

The growing economic importance of the Public Private Partnership (PPP) model for project delivery has triggered research interest with respect to private involvement in project delivery and the financing of public infrastructure and social projects. Case research has proven to be a powerful research method, particularly in the development of new theory, in environments characterised by the growing frequency and magnitude of changes. This is the case of PPP in transport, where it is important to support knowledge transfer between transport subsectors and across countries where PPPs are applied. A case protocol suitable to describe PPP in transportation is presented.

The use of the Public Private Partnership (PPP) model for project delivery, especially for infrastructure projects, has increased over the past decades. Within the remit of PPP, research has been, in principal, focused on the understanding of relationships and their cause-and-effect phenomena, as well as on theory building and theory testing (Tang *et al.* 2010).

In case research, the central notion is to use case studies as the basis to develop theory inductively. The theory is emergent in the sense that it is situated in and developed by recognising patterns of relationships among constructs within and across cases and their underlying logical arguments. According to Eisenhardt and Graebner (2007), a major reason for the popularity and relevance of theory building from case studies is that it is one of the best (if not the best) bridges from rich qualitative evidence to mainstream deductive research. The challenge herein is developing theoretical constructs that are derived from and could be tested through case research, completing a circle of inductive theory building from cases and deductive theory testing by using cases to test theory.

While case studies have been used as one of the main research methods, it remains difficult to build on reported cases and test constructs as cases are described and analysed by focusing on specific aspects with particular institutional settings and contexts. In addition, few PPP contractual agreements have completed their full contract cycle and, therefore, an *ex-post* analysis and assessment is not possible while their final outcome is unknown and they are embedded in the realm of incomplete contracts. The creation of a set of cases to compare and upon which to test theory requires a systematic protocol that may describe all features of the PPP arrangement and take into account the specificities of the asset delivered. This creates difficulties when considering projects in transportation, not only because of the multiplicity of contractual arrangements but also due to the individual characteristics of the various subsectors.

Hence, while case studies have been the basis for research in PPP, generalising findings, transferring knowledge to other contexts and retaining up-to-date information so as to avoid cases becoming obsolete and, therefore, maintaining the credibility of results, form the key challenges of this research approach.

This has been a central challenge of research undertaken within the context of COST Action TU1001 on 'Public Private Partnerships in Transport: Trends and Theory' in order to identify clusters of similar approaches and their underlining reasons of development, and to test the theory developed. These challenges are further discussed in the following section. In transport PPP, it is important to identify the suitability for knowledge transfer between transport subsectors and across countries where PPPs are applied. This effort led to the development of a case protocol suitable to describe PPP in transportation. The proposed case 'protocol' is presented in the third section. Its key characteristic is the ability to compare seemingly different cases across different sectors, different regions and different countries. In the fourth section, related issues and measures required to secure objectivity and continuous updating are discussed. This appendix concludes with a discussion on the validity and applicability of the database over time and potential extensions to other sectors where PPPs are implemented.

Addressing the case study challenges in transport PPP

Choice of research approach

The choice of a research approach is a fundamental part of the research process. The main aim of choosing a research approach is to establish the best possible way of answering the research questions (Blaikie 2000). The research problem of COST Action TU1001 is particularly concerned with developing a theoretical basis for PPP in the transport sector, thus it is largely qualitative in nature and the research needs in-depth understanding of the concept and nature of PPP and associated complexities attached to it. In addition, the concept under scrutiny (i.e. PPP) is context dependent (i.e. influenced by elements such as stakeholders, politics, risks, society, market conditions, culture, legal and institutional framework, etc.). Therefore, the research is interdisciplinary as it interlinks the disciplines of social science, finance and economics, management, construction, law and many others, creating further complexities if issues are studied in isolation from particular analysis viewpoints.

There are a large number of strategies of inquiry available for qualitative research (Creswell 2007). Among these, the strategies concerning phenomenology, grounded theory, ethnography, case study and narrative research represent the most commonly used approaches. Furthermore, these strategies all have well-established systematic procedures for inquiry with rigorous methods for data collection and analysis (Creswell 2007). Considering the strategies available for qualitative research, the main strategy adopted for COST Action TU1001 is the case study approach. However, it is used in combination with some aspects relating to grounded theory analysis.

According to Yin (2009), case studies are the preferred research strategy when, 'a "how" or "why" question is being asked about a contemporary set of events, over which the investigator has little or no control'. Case research may be on a single case (see Flyvbjerg 2006 for an interesting reference to Galileo, p. 225) or multiple cases. In this sense each case serves as a distinct experiment that stands on its own as an analytic unit. Like a series of related laboratory experiments, multiple cases are discrete experiments that serve as replications, contrasts and extensions to the emerging theory (Yin 2009). Taylor *et al.* (2009) suggest that case study research should attempt to achieve depth by including multiple polar cases and multiple analytically similar cases. What is achieved through this approach is the element of verification or testing of theory as it shifts from deductive to inductive or the need to apply replication logic (Eisenhardt 1989).

Hence, case studies have the characteristic of being specific (with boundaries) rather than general. Stake (2000) views a case to be an 'integrated system' with an identity, purpose and working parts. Yin (2009) states that case studies are suitable for occasions where the phenomenon being studied cannot be clearly separated from its context. The issue then raised is how findings may be transferred to other contextual environments and institutional settings, and under which prevailing conditions.

Challenges of the P3T3 case studies

Scholars, over the years, have identified the challenges facing case research, especially as research relying on rich qualitative data is becoming more common and, thus, care is needed in drawing conclusions able to be generalised from a limited set of cases and in ensuring rigorous research.

Yin (2009) has described in detail the aspects relating to case research design. Voss *et al.* (2002) provide a roadmap for designing, developing and conducting case-based research. The present work therefore draws on that of Yin (2009) and Voss *et al.* (2002). According to the latter, it is important to identify when to use case research. They propose a template as a guide for the case research method. In Table A.1, their proposal is extended to include and represent the particular needs of transport PPP. More specifically, for (transport) PPP decision-making models and the construct of Value for Money, are issues to be identified in case studies and tested; the identification of critical success factors (CSFs) and potential Key Performance Indicators (KPIs) may be retrieved through case comparative studies; the impact of institutions and market drivers are also factors to be studied. In addition, their varied application in different countries and the potential of experience transferability across the various modes of transport infrastructure and service, as well as countries, is an important determinant. Therefore, 'transferability' of results is added to the initial list proposed by Voss *et al.* (2002). Table A.1 explains the research design of this particular research by matching the research purpose of COST Action TU1001 with the methodology.

The next important challenge is developing the design of case studies (Yin 2009) or otherwise the research framework, constructs and questions (Voss *et al.* 2002) for case research. This challenge includes the study questions, its propositions, its unit(s) of analysis, the logic linking the data and, finally, the analysis criteria to interpret the findings. This ultimately leads to developing a theory with respect to the subject under study or identifying the basic 'factor' connecting the various actors and elements of the study. Herein Eisenhardt's (1989) work is also considered, as he has brought together much of the previous work on building theory from case research, taking into consideration the work of Glaser and Strauss (1967) on grounded theory.

In PPP there is substantial institutional, archival and popular literature and debate concerning the political, social and economic acceptance of the scheme. The latter has been generally focused in varying forms around the issue of Value for Money (VfM), loosely defined as the optimum combination of life cycle costs and quality to meet user requirements (Grimsey and Lewis 2005; Akintoye *et al.* 2003; Debande 2002). However, at its heart it remains a risk-sharing problem between two (or more) risk-averse agents. In PPP this has been the 'factor'. This 'factor' is identified in both research (cfr. Tang *et al.* 2010) and basic policy documents (cfr. EC 2004; EIB 2005). Furthermore, it is also important to consider the specificities of transport PPP with respect to risk (Roumboutsos *et al.* 2012). These specific factors with respect to transport PPP have been considered.

Moreover, case research needs to be based on construct, internal and external validity and be reliable. These issues are addressed in the structured protocol of the case studies as presented in the next section. Notably, extra rigour is placed on this item, as cases are collected from within different environmental contexts. Comparability of cases is challenged both on the subject (various modal applications of PPP) as well as cultural perception and the institutional level of the actual application and its investigators.

Finally, a key difference between quantitative and qualitative research approaches lies with different reasoning behind sampling approaches (Patton 1990). While quantitative research tends to favour larger, randomly selected samples, qualitative research mostly focuses upon smaller, purposefully selected samples (Patton 1990; Miller and Alvarado 2005). The main focus of random sampling in quantitative research is to achieve generalisation to a larger population. Conversely, the main focus of purposeful sampling is to gain in-depth understanding from a fewer number of information rich cases. Patton (1990) has identified 16 different techniques of carrying out purposeful sampling. These include: extreme or deviant case;

Table A.1 Matching research purpose with methodology

Purpose	Research question	Research structure	Transport PPP P3T3 research requirements
Exploration Uncover areas for research and theory development.	Is there something interesting enough to justify research?	In-depth case studies. Unfocused, longitudinal field study.	Potential similarities and differences between country and modal applications of PPP. Changes over time and with respect to external events (e.g. economic crisis).
Theory building Identify/describe key variables. Identify linkages between variables. Identify 'why' these relationships exist.	What are the key variables? What are the patterns or linkages between variables? Why should these relationships exist?	Few focused case studies. In-depth field studies. Multi-site case studies. Best-in-class case studies.	Factors leading to successful PPP in transport (CSF).
Theory testing Test the theories developed in the previous stages. Predict future outcomes.	Are the theories we have generated able to survive the test of empirical data? Did we get the behaviour that was predicted by the theory or did we observe another unanticipated behaviour?	Experiment. Quasi-experiment. Multiple case studies. Large-scale sample of population.	Decision models and PPP arrangements tested against empirical cases and findings.
Theory extension/refinement To better structure the theories in light of the observed results.	How generalisable is the theory? Where does the theory apply?	Experiment. Quasi-experiment. Case studies. Large-scale sample of population.	Testing theories developed across transport subsectors.
Transferability To identify the extent to which theories may be applied to other sectors and/or subject areas.	Under which conditions do theories apply in other sectors or subjects?	Experiment. Quasi-experiment. Multiple case studies. Large-scale sample of population.	Input from other PPP sector applications and output from transport PPP to other sectors. The same applies for countries and/or regions.

Source: Authors' compilation based on Voss *et al.* 2002.

intensity; maximum variation; homogeneous; typical case; stratified purposeful; critical case; snowball or chain; criterion; theory-based or operation construct; opportunistic; random purposeful; political importance; convenience; combination of mixed and purposeful sampling.

COST Action TU1001 includes more than 100 researchers from 29 countries, primarily from the EU. This has been the determining factor in the selection of the sampling method, which is, in principal, convenience sampling within a general snowball/chain approach through which interesting cases are collected. Notably the researcher, a member from the Special Purpose Vehicle (SPV) or sponsor and a member from the public sector, prepare each case jointly in order to secure objectivity. The number of the researchers involved suggests that even though the sampling method is that of convenience, the end result is a randomly purposeful sample.

The approach to data collection, i.e. through a form of triangulation since all interested parties are involved in the preparation of the case study, allows for future interest to be generated in continuing to have all views represented in updated versions. This point will be discussed further later in the appendix.

P3T3 transport PPP: A case study protocol

One of the key challenges, as may be identified from Table A.1 above, is the different level of analysis and data coding needed to understand all issues investigated. 'The devil is in the detail' is an expression commonly used to describe the importance of in-depth description of cases. Moreover, numerical data are required to verify theoretical developments.

Focusing on risk as the key factor of PPP, Roumboutsos (2010) presented a contextual framework based on the transport PPP context for risk analysis in order to compare and identify the potential of knowledge transfer between the road and port transport subsectors. This contextual framework, by describing a set of 'what', 'why', 'who', 'whom', 'which-way', 'where', 'when' and the 'whole', compromises the proposed 'contextual Ws Risk Analysis Framework' (Figure A.1) and forms the basis of the proposed Case Study Protocol.

The framework provides the 'story telling' basis for the case study as it considers all key aspects of the PPP arrangement:

Who: the initiator;
Why: the reason this model of public project delivery was selected;
What: the scope of project;
Whom: the required qualities of the private entity(ies);
Which-way: the tendering process and the structure of the contractual arrangement;
Where: the project's location, describing both the locality and the institutional setting;
When: the timing of the contractual implementation and the project timeline and, finally,

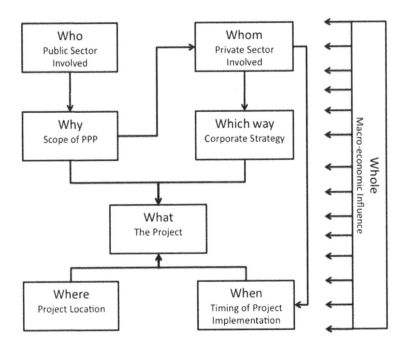

Figure A.1 Contextual Ws Risk Analysis Framework.
Source: Roumboutsos 2010.

Whole: the macroeconomic impact on the project. This is of significant importance
for projects in the transport sector where demand is derived from other activities correlated to macroeconomic local, regional, national and global figures.
'Who-for': is also added to the above contextual framework describing the users.

These elements form the overall 'story line' for all cases, and these are also seen
as subjects requiring 'normalisation'. The protocol reverts to fuzzy logic and the
concepts of graduation and granulation. In fuzzy logic, everything is, or is
allowed to be, granulated, with a granule being a clump of attribute-values drawn
together by indistinguishability, similarity, proximity or functionality. Graduated
granulation, or equivalently fuzzy granulation, is a unique feature of fuzzy logic.
Graduated granulation is inspired by the way in which humans deal with
complexity and imprecision (Zadeh 2008).

In the following section, the 'granule' of PPP cases is identified along with the
respective 'attribute-values'. The Ws Contextual Framework, described previously, represents the granulated environment within the fuzzy logic approach in
this comparison methodology. The granular value of each W is expressed through
a set of linguistic variables. Each linguistic variable has been chosen to reflect the
source of impact on the W granular value.

More specifically, one of the most notable characteristics in the 'What' granule (i.e. the transport project) is describing its function as, predominantly, a node or a link within the transport network. The other very dominant characteristic, especially with respect to the PPP arrangement, is the level of its 'temporary' monopoly: how exclusive its use is (Evenhuis and Vickerman 2010). In addition, transport infrastructure forms part of a network and its 'value' is characterised by the level of integration. Integration may take on various (and hopefully all) forms: physical, operational, information, regulatory. This attribute is included in the 'What' granule. The advantage and value-added characteristic of PPP is considered to be bundling of construction and operation. It is, however, important to view other aspects in bundling creating additional value such as non-transport related activities included in the project (for example, commercial activities included in airport development projects). For completeness, vertical bundling is also included in this 'granule' registering possible downstream bundling that may be connected to downstream innovations (for example, electrification of the road sector).

'Who' describes the initiating public authority. The predominant characteristic variable is proposed to be the level of government in terms of decision and regulating ability, describing a locally driven or a nationally driven initiation of the project. It is also important to identify and compare with the level of central government involvement.

With the 'Why' characteristic, the search is initiated for the underlying motivation for proceeding with a PPP; a way of financing the investment or delivering a service. In addition, in the EU, many transport PPP projects are related to the TEN-T. This attribute is also registered.

While the narrative concerns the description of the project sponsors, financiers, Special Purpose Vehicle description, the (With) 'Whom' granule 'normalises' the private entity. More specifically, the private entity, depending on project needs and objectives, which in many cases also depend on the transport subsector, may have multiple objectives, especially with respect to the nature of the downstream market. Handling the downstream market may be service-based, i.e. the private entity is only required to operate the service/asset, etc. or business development, when the private entity is required to strive in a competitive environment. An example is the difference in the competitive nature of motorway downstream markets and the downstream markets of railways or ports, which are oligopolistic and more subject to rapid changes, and where actors have strategic power and use it.

The attributes related to 'Who-for' concern the type of users, ranging from industrial to private, and the number of users the infrastructure or service addresses.

The 'Which-way' refers to the key characteristics of the tendering process and the contractual agreement. With respect to the tendering process, there are a variety of procedures that may be followed. Their key 'factor' is the level of 'openness' that is registered and followed by the number of bidders per stage and total tendering duration. The description of the contractual agreement concerns the description of the level of involvement of the public and private sector in the project, the remuneration scheme and the existence of guarantees and renegotiation clauses. The remuneration scheme is scaled with respect to the level of securities offered. 'Which-way' includes the principal factor of PPP: risk allocation (Roumboutsos *et al.* 2012). The linguistic variable values for risks reflect the gradients of risk-sharing from solely the private sector assuming the specific risk to solely the public sector taking over. In an 'open-ended' fashion, the protocol also includes key performance indicators (KPIs) included in the contract.

Location – 'Where' – is principally described in this analysis by an urban–regional variable. The granule also includes the attribute of the impact the transport project has on the transport market.

When – time – refers to the maturity of the investment, reflected in the level of need for the project.

Finally, the 'Whole' expresses the vulnerability of the investment/project to macro-economic and social influence. Here, the relation between forecasted and actual demand is an important element.

The identified linguistic variables are presented by 'W' in Table A.2. Verhoest *et al.* (2013) provide further information with respect to 'Where' and the 'Whole', while Roumboutsos and Liyanage (2013) provide information on the other granules.

Based on the above-mentioned project characteristics (further elaborated in Table A.2 below), a number of hypotheses can be formulated and tested; providing all cases in the specific protocol allows comparisons with respect to particular 'granules' or cases as a whole. By focusing on the specificities of the transport sector, projects across transport subsectors may be compared. The protocol also allows for testing logic within a particular case.

The 'granules' and their attributes (variables) of Table A.2 are provided on qualitative scales. In order to avoid and reduce bias (even though these ratings should normally be discussed between three parts – researcher, private entity, public authority) each attribute is accompanied by a respective narrative justifying choice of rating.

Finally, each case study is situated within a specific contextual/institutional setting formulated by rules and codes related to both the transport sub-sector and the country or region in which it is implemented. For reasons of economy, as many cases are implemented within the same institutions, and respective needs of comparability/transferability, this information forms a separate information set linked, however, to each case study.

On an institutional level, the 'granules' included are (Verhoest *et al.* 2013 and cfr. Roumboutsos and Liyanage 2013; EBRD 2012; WB 2012; EIB 2011; OECD 2010 and IMF 2004):

- economic-financial context (stability of macro-economic conditions; level of public debt and budgetary equilibrium; access to capital and credit markets; existence of sound capital markets; effects of financial and budgetary crisis on PPP in the country under review; level of investment needs);

Table A.2 Linguistic variables of granular value of the Ws Contextual Framework

Linguistic variable	Variable range					
Granule: 'What' – the project						
Node – link	Within a node	Pure node	Like a node	Like a link	Pure link	Within a link
Level of exclusivity	Competitive environment	Not exclusive	Quite not exclusive	Somewhat exclusive	Rather exclusive	Exclusive
Level of integration	No integration	Physical integration	Operational integration	Information integration	Authority/regulatory integration	Other
Level of bundling (horizontal)	Description coded in the process					
Level of bundling (vertical)	Description coded in the process					
Granule: 'Who' – the public initiator						
Level of direct government involvement	No government involvement	Limited government involvement	Some government involvement	Government involvement	Significant government involvement	Direct government involvement
Nationally-locally driven	Nationally driven	Mostly nationally driven	More nationally driven	More locally driven	Mostly locally driven	Locally driven
Granule: 'Why' – the scope of PPP						
Finance – service-based approach	Solely service-based approach	Mostly service-based approach	More service-based approach	More finance-based approach	Mostly finance-based approach	Solely finance-based approach
Project included in TEN-T	No	Yes	Priority project	Core project	Periphery project	
Granule: 'Whom' – private party						
Business developer	Business servicer	Mostly business servicer	More business servicer	More business developer	Mostly business developer	Business developer

(Continued)

Table A.2 Linguistic variables of granular value of the Ws Contextual Framework (Continued)

Linguistic variable	Variable range					
Granule: 'Who-for'						
Type of users	Only industrial	Principally for industrial users and some private users	Equal use by industrial and private users		Principally for private users and some industrial users	Only private users
Number of users	Identifiable	Small number	Large number			Public use
Granule: 'Which-way'						
Tendering procedure						
Process	Open call	2 stage procedure	Competitive dialogue	Restricted call	Negotiations	Other
No of bidders						
Duration	1st stage	2nd stage	...	...	...	Final stage
Contract structure						
Private provision	Design	Construction	Operation	Maintenance	Financing	Ownership
Public provision	Design	Construction	Operation	Maintenance	Financing	Ownership
(Re) payment scheme	Availability fees and subsidy	Availability fees	Shadow tolls and subsidy	Shadow tolls/no subsidy	User fees and subsidy	User fees no subsidy
Payment recipient	Public	Private			Both	
Guarantees	Yes	No			Description coded in the process	
Renegotiation clauses	Yes	No			Description coded in the process	
Risk allocation						
Design and construction risks	Totally private	Mostly private	Rather private	Rather public	Mostly public	Totally public
Maintenance risk	Totally private	Mostly private	Rather private	Rather public	Mostly public	Totally public

	Totally private	Mostly private	Rather private	Rather public	Mostly public	Totally public
Risk of exploitation	Totally private	Mostly private	Rather private	Rather public	Mostly public	Totally public
Commercial/revenue risk	Totally private	Mostly private	Rather private	Rather public	Mostly public	Totally public
Financial risk	Totally private	Mostly private	Rather private	Rather public	Mostly public	Totally public
Regulatory risk	Totally private	Mostly private	Rather private	Rather public	Mostly public	Totally public
Force majeure	Totally private	Mostly private	Rather private	Rather public	Mostly public	Totally public
Environmental risk	Totally private	Mostly private	Rather private	Rather public	Mostly public	Totally public
Social risk	Totally private	Mostly private	Rather private	Rather public	Mostly public	Totally public

Granule: 'Where' – project location and institutional framework country-specific information

Urban – inter-urban – regional	Urban	Outer urban	Mostly inter-urban	Inter-urban	Mostly regional	Regional
Project significance on transport market	Not significant at all	Of little significance	Significant	Very significant	Of extreme significance	

Granule: 'When' – project (investment) timing

Severity of project need	Not very needed	Needed to a point	Rather needed	Needed	Great need	Very severe need

Granule: 'Whole' and institutional framework country-specific information

Impact/influence of macro-environment	No exposure / influence	Very little exposure	Exposure	Some exposure	Significant exposure	Extreme exposure

- political commitment to PPP (PPP-policy framework (in general and in the transport sector specifically); previous and current PPP-experience; political stability; change in PPP policies because of the financial budgetary crises);
- legal and regulatory framework for PPP (existence of a specific PPP or concession law (in general or in transport); scope and boundaries of specific PPP law; elements provided in the legal framework (including the public procurement law);
- institutional setting – PPP-supporting institutions (acting public institutions – PPP support units; procedures for project appraisal and prioritisation – role of main actors in project stages; standardised processes and documents).

It is important to note that the objective is to collect and parameterise case studies so as to provide the ability for researchers to analyse, identify patterns and deduct theories, test theories and, finally, to identify mechanisms with potential for transferring findings to other contextual settings. In this aspect, the endeavour concerns a data collection exercise.

In conclusion, by following the proposed protocol – project granules and attributes; contextual granules; randomly purposeful sampling; triangulation of data collection (research, private sector, public sector independent input and desk research) – the validity and credibility of the collected case studies may be demonstrated (Gibbert *et al.* 2008), as they feature:

- reliability (the study can be repeated, with the same results);
- internal validity (a causal relationship, whereby certain conditions are shown to lead to other conditions, as distinguished by spurious relationships);
- construct validity (defined operational measures for the concepts being studied);
- external validity (potential for study's findings to be generalised).

Data organisation

Both Yin (2009) and Stake (2000) recognise the importance of effectively organising data. The advantage of using a database to accomplish this task is that raw data are available for independent inspection. Using a database improves the reliability of the case study as it enables the researcher to track and organise data sources including notes, key documents, tabular materials, narratives, photographs, and audio files, which can be stored in a database for easy retrieval at a later date. In the particular case of the COST Action TU1001 case collection, this is of particular importance, as the study object (the PPP contractual arrangement and its implementation) is exposed to continuous change over time.

There are various commercial databases available with respect to storage of case-study type data (for example, CAQDAS, NVivo, etc.). These, normally, provide search capabilities. These are all important when developing a case study database (Wickham and Woods 2005). The advantages and disadvantages of such databases have been reported in the literature (Richards and Richards 1994; 1998), one of the greatest drawbacks being the distancing of the researcher from the data. However, as the objective of case study data collection is the analysis rather than the raw data, small emphasis has been given to 'storage' by researchers. In a study by Gibbert and Ruigrok (2008) concerning case study research in ten leading journals for the period 1995-2000, less than a third (51 articles over 159) made a reference to data storage. This is to be expected as case research rarely includes a large number of cases to be analysed. It is usually confined to time and location addressing very specific research questions. The value rests with the analysis, as no alternative use of the data collected is foreseen.

Case studies collected under COST Action TU1001 have a number of particularities that are related to the research object and the research objectives:

- They are collected to serve multiple research objectives as shown in Table A.3. These correspond to both theories to be deducted and theories to be tested.
- They are vulnerable to change, as PPP contracts are incomplete in nature.
- The supply side of the market (i.e. both PPP sponsors and financiers) is extremely dynamic.
- They concern megaprojects with multi-stakeholder impacts and influences.
- Data is collected from multiple sources and, finally, the immediate providers of case data may change, as frequent changes in personnel both in the private and, mostly, in the public sector have been commonly witnessed.

These characteristics set particular requirements. Case data needs to be organised but also data needs to be accessed by a large number of interested parties and continuously updated in order to secure validity. Validity, in a multi-stakeholder environment, also concerns the consideration of multiple inputs from sources with diverged interests. It requires both a narrative and a quantitative part.

Storing the COST Action TU1001 case studies in a Wiki environment presents a number of advantages and responds to most requirements:

- information is accessible by an unlimited number of users;
- information may be updated at any time by an unlimited number of interested parties;
- references and justification documents may be uploaded;
- it allows for both narrative and quantitative data.

Key concerns of its operation involve:

- the willingness to allow voluntary data updates, especially as many consider PPP case information as privileged or confidential, and
- the accuracy of the information uploaded.

The latter emphasises the need for an administrator facility, which would allow for information to be validated before it is available on site. The first challenge needs to be addressed through appropriate marketing and dissemination activities, so as to create motivation. The positive anticipated outcome of this endeavour is

Table A.3 Comparison of strategies of inquiry for qualitative research

	Narrative	Phenomenology	Ethnography	Grounded theory	Case study
Focus	Exploring the life of an individual.	Understanding the essence of the experience.	Describing a culture-sharing group.	Developing theory grounded in data.	In depth description and analysis of one or more cases.
Unit of analysis	One or more individuals.	Several individuals sharing an experience.	Group sharing a culture.	A process, action or interaction involving many individuals.	An event, programme or activity.
Discipline background	Anthropology, literature, history, psychology, sociology.	Philosophy, psychology and education.	Anthropology, sociology.	Sociology.	Psychology, law, political science, medicine.
Type of problem best suited to be addressed	To tell stories of individual's life experiences.	To describe the interpretation of a shared experience.	To describe/ interpret the shared patterns of a culture.	To develop theory grounded in the views of the participants.	To provide an in-depth understanding of a case or cases.

Source: Creswell 2007

a PPP database that is readily available and accessible, self-updated and accurate. It would also secure the quality of case studies as it promotes:

- transferability (McCutcheon and Meredith 1993; Halldorsson and Aastrup 2003), as the extent to which studies may be applied to other contexts may be continuously asserted by its users;
- truth-value (Guba and Lincoln 1989), as input from various stakeholders on a specific protocol should merge towards objectiveness;
- traceability (Halldorsson and Aastrup 2003) as documentation and data sources may be uploaded and referenced on site.

Conclusions and further research

Usage of PPP procurement methods, especially for infrastructure projects, has increased over the past decades. The purpose of using such arrangements enables governments to produce infrastructure with capacity for the growth of the wider economy without impacting upon the public account. Due to the large and complex nature of the PPP delivery and the project itself, it becomes difficult to gather data from a range of infrastructure projects and study them against a common basis. However, as part of the COST TU1001 project on PPP, there was a need to scrutinise the different arrangements that different projects have used in procuring infrastructure projects using PPP. Case research has been identified as the best method for fulfilling the aforementioned need, as it not only allows in-depth exploration but forms the basis for building and/or testing theory, theory extension, theory refinement and transferability.

Within case research methodology, a case study protocol for transport PPP has been presented in this Appendix. This protocol has been used to collect information on cases within the context of COST Action TU1001. They have been set up to answer the 'why', 'what', and 'which-way' issues of Public Private Partnerships in transport. They also highlight the need to continue observing cases as they evolve over their contract life cycle, influenced by external events such as the economic crisis and internal events such as changes in ownership.

An active Wiki database is proposed to address issues of continuity, quality and timeliness. Its effectiveness remains to be tested. However, this novel approach opens new horizons with respect to the study of PPP in general, as it may be extended to include cases from other infrastructure sectors and case study research, and it provides the potential to allow for further analysis and inter-temporal analysis of data collected.

References

Akintoye, A., Beck, M. and Hardcastle, C. (2003) *Public-Private Partnerships: Managing Risks and Opportunities*. Blackwell Science, Oxford

Blaikie, N. (2000) *Designing Social Research: The Logic of Anticipation*. Cambridge: Polity Press

Creswell, J. W. (2007) *Research Design: Qualitative, Quantitative, and Mixed Methods Approaches* (2nd Ed.). Thousand Oaks, CA: Sage

Debande, O. (2002) 'Private financing of transport infrastructure: an assessment of the UK experience'. *Journal of Transport Economics and Policy*, 36(3), pp. 355–387

Eisenhardt, K. M. (1989) 'Building theories from case study research'. *Academy of Management Review*, 14, pp. 532–550

Eisenhardt, K. M. and Graebner, M. E. (2007) 'Theory building from cases: opportunities and challenges'. *Academy of Management Journal*, 50(1), pp. 25–32

European Commission (2004) *COM 327 final: Green Paper on Public-Private Partnerships and Community Law on Public Contracts and Concessions*. Brussels: EC

European Investment Bank (2005) *Evaluation of PPP Projects Financed by the EIB*. Luxembourg: EIB Publications

European Investment Bank (2011) *Study on PPP Legal & Financial Frameworks in the Mediterranean Partner Countries. Volume 3: Best Practices and Lessons Learned: Selected Experiences from Other Countries*. Luxembourg: EIB Publications

European Bank for Reconstruction and Development (2012) *Concession/PPP Laws Assessment*. London: EBRD

Evenhuis, E. and Vickerman, R. (2010) 'Transport pricing and Public-Private Partnerships in theory: issues and suggestions'. *Research in Transportation Economics*, 30, pp. 6–14

Flyvbjerg, B. (2006) 'Five misunderstandings about case-study research'. *Qualitative Inquiry*, 12 (2), pp. 219–245

Gibbert, M., Ruigrok, W. and Wicki, B. (2008) 'What passes as a rigorous case study'. *Strategic Management Journal*, 29 (13), pp. 1465–1474

Gibbert, M. and Ruigrok, W. (2008) 'The "What" and "How" of case study rigor: three strategies based on published work'. *Organizational Research Methods*, 13(4) pp. 710–737

Glaser, B. G. and Strauss, A. L. (1967) *The Discovery of Grounded Theory: Strategies for Qualitative Research*. Chicago: Aldine Publishing Company

Grimsey, D. and Lewis, M. K. (2005) 'Are Public Private Partnerships value for money? Evaluating alternative approaches and comparing academic and practitioner views'. *Accounting Forum*, 29, pp. 345–378

Guba, E. and Lincoln, Y. S. (1989) *Fourth Generation Evaluation*. Newbury Park, CA.: Sage

Halldorsson, A. and Aastrup, J. (2003) 'Quality criteria for qualitative inquiries in logistics'. *European Journal of Operational Research*, 144(2), pp. 321–32

International Monetary Fund (2004) *Public-Private Partnerships*. Washington, DC: IMF

Lewis, M. W. (1998) 'Iterative triangulation: a theory development process using existing case studies'. *Journal of Operations Management*. 16, pp. 455–69

McCutcheon, D. and Meredith, J. (1993) 'Conducting case study research in operations management'. *Journal of Operations Management*, 11(3), pp. 239–56

Miller, F. A. and Alvarado, K. (2005) 'Incorporating documents into qualitative nursing research'. *Journal of Nursing Scholarship*, 37 (4), pp. 348–353

Organisation for Economic Cooperation and Development (2010) *Dedicated Public-Private Partnership Units. A Survey of Institutional and Governance Structures*. Paris: OECD

Patton, M. Q. (1990) *Qualitative Evaluation and Research Methods*. USA: Sage Publications Inc.

Richards, L. and Richards, T. (1994) 'From filing cabinet to computer' in: A. Bryman and R. G. Burgess (Eds) *Analysing Qualitative Data* (pp. 146–172). London: Routledge

Richards, T. J. and Richards, L. (1998) 'Using computers in qualitative research' in: N. K. Denzin and Y. S. Lincoln (Eds) *Collecting and Interpreting Qualitative Materials* (pp. 445–462). London: Sage

Roumboutsos, A. (2010) 'A Ws Contextual Risk Analysis Framework: mapping knowledge transfer potential between road and port Public Private Partnerships'. *CIB World Congress*, The Lowry, Salford Quays, UK, May

Roumboutsos, A., Pellegrino, R., Vanelslander, T. and Macario, R. (2012) 'Risks and risk allocation in transport PPP projects: a literature review' in: A. Roumboutsos and N. Carbonara (Eds) *COST Action TU1001, Public Private Partnerships: Trends & Theory, 2011 Discussion Papers*. ISBN 978-88-97781-04-2, COST Office, Brussels

Roumboutsos, A. and Liyanage, C. (2013) 'Public Private Partnerships in transport: case study structure' in: R. Roumboutsos, S. Farrell, C. L. Liyanage and R. Macário (Eds) *COST Action TU1001 – 2013 Discussion Papers: Part II Case Studies*. ISBN: 978-88-97781-61-5, COST Office, Brussels

Stake, R. E. (2000) 'Case studies' in: N. K. Denzin and Y. S. Lincoln (Eds) *Handbook of Qualitative Research* (2nd Ed., pp. 134–164). Thousand Oaks, CA: Sage Publications, Inc.

Tang, L. Y., Shen, Q. and Cheng E. W. L. (2010) 'A review of studies on Public–Private Partnership projects in the construction industry'. *International Journal of Project Management*, 28 (7), pp. 683–694

Taylor, J., Dossick, C. and Garvin, M. (2009) 'Conducting research with case studies' in: *Proceedings of the 2009 Construction Research Congress*. Seattle, WA, ASCE, Reston, VA, 5–7 April

Verhoest, K., Carbonara, N., Lember, V., Petersen, O.H., Scherrer, W. and van den Hurk, M. (2013) 'Introduction: national context for PPP – policy, regulation and supporting institutions' in: K. Verhoest, N. Carbonara, V. Lember, O. H. Petersen, W. Scherrer and M. van den Hurk (Eds) *COST Action TU1001 – 2013 Discussion Papers: Part I Country Profiles*. ISBN: 978-88-97781-60-8, COST Office, Brussels

Voss, C., Tsikriktsis, N. and Frohlich, M. (2002) 'Case research in operations management'. *International Journal of Operations & Production Management*, 22 (2), pp. 195–219

Wickham, M. and Woods, M. (2005) 'Reflecting on the strategic use of CAQDAS to manage and report on the qualitative research process'. *The Qualitative Report*, 10(4), pp. 687–702

World Bank Institute and Public-Private Infrastructure Advisory Facility (2012) *Public-Private Partnerships. Reference Guide*. Version 1.0. Washington, DC: The World Bank

Yin, R. K. (2009) *Case Study Research: Design and Methods (4th Ed.): Applied Social Research Methods V.5*. London: Sage Publications Inc.

Zadeh, L. A. (2008) 'Is there a need for fuzzy logic?' *Information Sciences*, 178, pp. 2751–2779

Index

Printed and bound by CPI Group (UK) Ltd, Croydon, CR0 4YY
01/05/2025
01858432-0007